DEDICATIONS

Just to get started on the right foot, I turn my Spotlight on my maternal Grampa – I always called him Grampa – who I knew as **Dominic Figer**, born Domenico Ficarra in Pace del Mele, Provincia di Messina, Sicilia, Italia on February 15, 1885.

I learned, sometimes the hard way, that he was among the wisest men on earth. He influenced the foundational philosophies that have guided me all these years. Grampa was the All Time *Numero Uno* American Patriot! He taught me to respect the Flag as I would the Cross.

He encouraged me to be an excellent student. He constantly emphasized and encouraged me to "Be Number One!" in whatever I chose as my life's endeavor and in every other important instance. And he taught me that the Golden Rule is 100% True and in effect 100% of the time.

Most of all, as is true for several of my cousins, he made me feel like I was His Number One.

To My Grampa Dominic, I Dedicate This Book.

High School years have proved to be profoundly pivotal in the lives of millions of people. Me, too. In tenth grade I was blessed to meet **Edward Saleem Ferris**, the Mayfield High School Teacher and Coach who would positively impact the lives of countless Mayfield students, nobody more than me. He elevated my image of who I am. He lifted and clarified my vision of greater objectives that lay before me. And among my fondest memories, he declared and demonstrated that I was one of his all-time favorites.

To My Coach, Ed Ferris, I Dedicate This Book.

Cosmo Sardo reluctantly hired me (it took 12 years for me to find out it was initially "reluctantly") when I was 22 years old and his next youngest employee was 44. Cosmo and his sister/receptionist, **Maria,** recognized my God-given talent way before my understanding and favored me with more than my share of clients. Constantly.

Cosmo's operational policies were viewed as eccentric by most of the other employees, me too through employee infection, until I left his employ and clearly saw that Cosmo's rules were Stepping Stones to Success. I adopted his policies as my own.

One day in mid 1972, I arranged to have lunch with my father, **Paul**, who started working at Cosmo's shortly before me and continued uninterrupted through my ownership of the salon. As I said hello to Cosmo that day, I added that I'd like to talk to him privately sometime.

"Sure, call me anytime," he said pleasantly.

Moments later, while dad was getting us a table at **Schwab's Pharmacy** around the corner, I went to the back of the drugstore to the payphones and called Cosmo. That evening he and I met privately for dinner at the fabulous **Saratoga Restaurant** on Sunset Boulevard. We toasted each other with our after dinner Tuaca, sealing the agreement for my becoming the second (so who knew then that it was also the 'final'?) owner of Cosmo's Hairstyling Salon.

That dinner was easily one of the most exciting of my life, thanx in great part to dear friend **Rudy Waxman**, who coached me on the fine points of this negotiation and much more. I revere Cosmo Sardo by granting him Godfather Status. Rudy was a uniquely special friend and mentor who all these years later remains in a class by himself.

To My Dad Paul, I Dedicate This Book.
To My Boss Cosmo Sardo, I Dedicate This Book.
To My Dear Zia Maria, I Dedicate This Book.
To My Dear Friend and Mentor Rudy Waxman, I Dedicate This Book.

✫

John Marc "Johnny" Gentri is proof-positive that I am truly Blessed. We had Magic from that first handshake. He and I have a mental/spiritual hookup that can best be explained in metaphysical terms, though the statement might make Johnny blush, as he was a sincere, practicing Catholic. No pair of brothers has ever been more connected than Johnny and me. He made sure my writing career had a Hollywood baptism.

To M'Bro Johnny Gentri, I Dedicate This Book.

CONFESSIONS...

of a

HOLLYWOOD HAIRSTYLIST

By
Little Joe Micale

CONFESSIONS...
of a
HOLLYWOOD HAIRSTYLIST

By
Little Joe Micale

FIRST EDITION
Copyright © 2010 by Buona Fortuna Publishers

Cover Creation & Book Design by Renny Severance and Little Joe Micale

Published and printed in the United States of America.
ISBN: 1450536557

✫

I received a promotional flyer from one of the weekly newspapers serving the beach cities just southwest of Los Angeles. They were starting a Personals Column with all services free.

I wasn't interested.

Maybe a week later, I was reaching for my dictionary to look up a word (Spelling? Meaning?) starting with the letter S, when I wondered if I could write a personals ad wherein all 40 words started with the letter S and delivered a message.

Silly! Fergettit!

But I couldn't.

I made a list of 75 words and found 125 more in that same dictionary. 40 jumped from the list onto another piece of paper. Mission accomplished. Cool!

I crumpled the paper and scored two points. On second thought I retrieved it, put it in an envelope and sent it off with a request to "find her!"

I got several calls. One was from a 22 year old gal who said that she and two friends read the ads weekly and wondered why nobody used imagination. "Then you come along and blow the lid off!" She said the three wished me a happy life. Sniff.

Another caller said she was my Soul Mate. "What are you doing tonight?" sez her. "It's Saturday; I have plans," sez I. "Break 'em," sez she. "I'll call y'back," sez me.

Some plans. It was going to be another night at my haunt, the **Casa Vega Restaurant** and bar in Studio City. Alone. So I called back.

Beautiful beginning, hey what? But there was no middle; ergo, the end. Clunk!

Then **Ginny** called, left a message. "If you already found someone, my best to you both. If not, I'm a Sorta Short Spaghetti-Sipping Sicilian too, so…"

We played phone tag. Finally on Tuesday, we talked. I found that she was of Executive Mind, Accomplished and Self-Sufficient. Lotsa fun and fulla laughs, too. We arranged to talk the next evening.

On Wednesday I told her about a movie script I was writing. The story had everything to do with Angels. In a couple of scenes there was Sicilian dialogue between two characters. She asked me to read that part to her. She gave me better Sicilian phrases to replace my baby-talk. She even spelled it. OMG!

On Thursday, more phone smiles, so we made plans for Friday. "Some people make a date for coffee or a drink," I said, "But with you, I think we are going to be friends forever, so how 'bout we have dinner together. There's a new restaurant in Santa Monica called **Ristorante Positano**. They're not Sicilian but they cook from scratch and it's delicious with a dynamite atmosphere."

For reasons neither of us can recall, we arranged for me to pick her up from her office building on Avenue of the Stars in Century City at 5:30 pm on March 10, 1995.

The parking attendant had me wait "over there." I got out, leaned against the fender and saw Ginny walking my way. As she closed the gap I said, "Oh my God, you're gorgeous!"

Not to be outdone, she kissed me smack on the lips!

Dinner was great. Conversation rivaled the phone calls. She says I said Badda-Boom along the way. We went to **Dear John's** in Culver City for a nightcap with **John DeNicola**, my bartender friend and client. He saw we had something special, he told me later.

On Sunday, March 19, we drove to San Diego to visit with my **Uncle Dom & Aunt Mary**. Homemade Rigatoni w/the works for brunch, oh boy!

As Ginny and Aunt Mary cleared the table and disappeared into the kitchen, Uncle Dom held up his right hand with thumb and index finger touching and said, "I really like this one!"

"Good," I said, "Cuz I'm gonna marry her."

He got excited, said we should have the wedding in his Chula Vista restaurant, **The Poor Gourmet**. (The business was named in honor of my paternal grandparents, who were both born in Sicily.)

"Mary!" Uncle Dom exclaimed as he burst into the kitchen. "The kids are going to be married in our restaurant!" Aunt Mary rubbed her forearm and said, "Uhoo, I got goose-bumps!"

On Sunday, November 12, 1995, more than 80 guests came from Los Angeles and elsewhere dressed in Roaring Twenties garb and witnessed a mob-flavored wedding between a Flapper and a Don. The neighborhood thought it was a movie set. Or a Time Warp. We wrote our own vows to be sure we are on the same page(s). Forever! (*Per sempre* in Sicilian)

As a punctuating gesture, Ginny gave me a gift of gold, custom-made cufflinks adorned with Angels. I gave her a gold wristwatch engraved on back with the words, "Oh My God, You're Gorgeous!"

A short time into our life together I learned that she can make a Sauce "Mama Style." Yes, a Delicious Rating right up there with *my* Mama. With all that, know that I recognized Ginny as my wife with my original "...you're gorgeous" declaration.

Ginny has typed every word I've written since, including everything in this book... except this dedication to her.

Hey, gotta have something in the SURPRISE category, right?

To My Mom Patricia Ann (Pearl to the family), I Dedicate This Book.
To My Uncle Dom and Aunt Mary, I Dedicate This Book.
To My Wife and Sweetheart Ginny (aka Georgina),
I Dedicate This Book.

ACKNOWLEDGEMENTS

Milt Rosen, my late dear friend and Writing Guru, encouraged me to write my first book, called *Someday*. Though as yet unpublished, its time is nigh. Much of who I am as a writer I attribute to Milt.

When I met **Scott Martel**, he was the editor of **The Islander Newspaper** on **Sanibel Island, Florida**. I asked Scott if I might write an article on the young people who worked as Police Assistants on Sanibel. He agreed to publish the piece under my byline if it was acceptable and pay me a stipend of $25. Sometime after that article was published, I wrote a profile on a local artist named **Barney Ballard**.

All the above occurred in 2001, memory tells me. The two articles were my first contributions to a newspaper. I had no idea that my writing had just taken a major directional change and in final analysis, a major career move.

Thank you, Scott Martel, now an ordained minister working as a Missionary with orphaned children in Africa.

I extend a huge **THANK YOU** and I bow with Extreme Gratitude to my first newspaper publisher, **Ms Tonya Squibb** and the Executive Editor, **Mr. Renny Severance**, for all their help and encouragement.

In the latter part of 1999, I established **Beverly Hills Hair Design** on Sanibel Island. Tonya's office, the executive offices of the newspaper, was located three doors away. We developed a casual, friendly relationship.

I was introduced to Renny in August of 2002. He, along with Tonya, consented to having me write a series of columns for **The Islander Newspaper** and other selected publications of **The Breeze Group of Newspapers**. (More details will be found in the body of this book.)

The columns were based on my experience as Hairstylist to the Stars in Hollywood/Beverly Hills and were called **DATELINE: The Hollywood File**.

Recently, Renny also helped awaken me to the fact that Self Publishing had evolved into a viable method of publishing commercially-worthy books. Many times he alerted me to new sources of information on this fast-growing industry. When I decided to write this book, Renny volunteered to be my Editor.

While we are professional colleagues, Renny and I have become dear friends. Our wives, Ginny and Ronni, are often included in our recreational plans. It's a wonderful arrangement!

Tonya and I have remained great friends with every indication leading me to believe we are together in this thing called Life forever!

For the past couple of years, Renny and I have been enthusiastic golf partners. What more could a man ask?

I conclude by repeating a big **THANK YOU RENNY**, if only to prove that sometimes – like right now – human words are totally inadequate.

With Extreme Gratitude I also thank **The News-Press**, a **Gannett Newspaper** and **Ms. Carol Hudler**, Publisher; **Tom Hayden**, Cape Coral Editor, and **Brian Hubbard**, Assistant Cape Coral Editor, for the opportunity to write two columns for the publication.

One column was called *Cape Profiles*, featuring stories of persons living and/or working in **Cape Coral, Florida**. The other column was called *Little Joe's Hollywood* and featured stories of my experience as Hairstylist to the Stars in **Hollywood** and **Beverly Hills, California**.

The readers of The News-Press elected me *Best Columnist of Southwest Florida, 2007* runner-up. I am eternally Grateful and Humbled by this magnificent recognition.

I most sincerely thank The News-Press and all people concerned for the honor of writing columns for the publication.

I saved this one for last as any fool knows that she ain't last. I thank my **Dear Wife Ginny** for all her Understanding, Assistance and mostly, her Love.

Ginny types every word I write at the blinding speed of 140 wpm. (I peck out about tree…) She has built-in Spell-check and is an awesome Proofreader, two talents that are invaluable… yeah, I mean *priceless.*

Ginny types for me as I prefer to write longhand, especially since learning for a fact that the best creative work is accomplished with a pen rather than a keyboard. You could look it up.

Ginny is my Partner every which-way imaginable. We work together, home and away. Many of our Goals, Dreams and Desires are identical while some are diverse, making all quite compatible. She is a major Opera *Afficionado,* if you will... or won't. I prefer football.

I once asked if she liked John Elway, the Denver Broncos' great who was the Granada Hills High School QB when my kids were in the area grade school. She asked if he was a Baritone or Tenor. WTH. See what I mean?

When we recited our Wedding Vows on November 12, 1995, we thanked our deceased Grandparents for putting us together, though, best as we know; they did not meet on this realm. *I Most Sincerely Thank Them Here Again.*

TABLE OF CONTENTS

STARDUST SECTION

The following people who appear in this section had been, with a few exceptions, on Little Joe's "Hollywood To-Do List" when his newspaper column was brought to a halt by the "downturn in publishing economics."

Nick Adams
Jack Albertson
Alan Alda
Richard Anderson
Roon Arledge &
    Chet Forte
Buddy Arnold
Frank Avianca
Richard "Dick"
Bakalyan
Gene Barry
Robert D. Bash, Esq.
Paul Benedict
Richard "Dick"
Benedict
Harve Bennett
Jack Berle
Milton Berle
Edward Binns
Robert Blake
Pat Boone
Marlon Brando
Fanny "Baby Snooks"
    Brice
Lloyd Bridges
Joe E. Brown
Lenny Bruce
Lonnie Burr
Pat Buttram
Michael Callan
Corrine Calvet
Rudy Campos
Dr. Ed Cantor

Jody Carmeli
Jack Carney
Scott Carpenter
Jim Carrey
Charlie Chaplin, Jr.
Dick Clark
Mickey Cohen
Dennis Cole
Nat "King" Cole &
    Natalie Cole
Gary Collins
Nick Colosanto
Tim Conway
Ben Cooper
Jacques-Yves Cousteau
Robert Cummings
Mike Curb &
    Jimmy Webb
Tony Curtis
Patsy D'Amore
James Darrin
Gray Davis
Roger Davis &
    Jaclyn Smith
John Dean
Freddie de Cordova
Frank De Felitta
Raymond De Felitta
Angie Dickenson
Troy Donahue
Joey Dorando &
    Art Aragon
Harry Drucker

Angelo Dundee
Clint Eastwood & Jo
Hymes
Vince Edwards &
    Linda Foster
Mama Cass Elliot
Nanette Fabray
Peter Falk
Grampa Dominic Figer
Mike Garcia
Alan Garfield
Judy Garland &
    Sid Luft
Errol Garner
John Marc Gentri
Betty Grable &
    Harry James
Art Graham
Gary Graham
Coleen Gray
Harry Guardino &
    Eddie Guardino
Huntz Hall
Mickey Hargitay &
    Zoltan Hargitay &
    Mariska Hargitay
Pat Harrington, Jr.
Mariette Hartley
Paul Harvey
Peter Haskell
Matt Helreich
Michael Herron
Charlton Heston

Mo Howard
Howard Hughes
James Hutton &
Timothy Hutton
Norman Jewison
Arte Johnson
Victor Jory
Alex Karras
Casey Kasem
& Jean Kasem
Scott Kaufer
Josh King
Burt Lancaster
Don Lane
Paul Leavitt
Francis Lederer
Ruta Lee
Jack Lemmon
Tommy Leonetti
Buddy Lester &
   Jerry Lester
Greg Lewis
Joe E. Lewis
Jerry Lewis
Louie Lomax
Eddie Maghetto
Lee Majors
Karl Malden
Jane Mansfield
Rocky Marciano &
   Andy Granatelli
Dean Martin
James McArthur
Gardner McKay
Sergio Mendez
Robert Middleton
Mark Miller
Rick Monday
Marilyn Monroe
Terry Moore

Vic Morrow
George Murdock
Stu Nahan
David Nelson
Earl Nightingale
Frank Novak
Warren Oates
Carroll O'Connor
Donald O'Connor
Jess Oppenheimer
Freddie Otash
Jerry Paris
Ed Peck
George Peppard
Paul Petersen
Charlie Picerni
Paul Picerni
Bobby Pickett
Michael J. Pollard
Poncie Ponce
Stephanie Powers
Vincent Price
Joe Pyne
George Raft
Alan Reed
Barron Richard
Rennick
Debbie Reynolds
Bobby Rhea &
   Gene Kelly
Tony Robbins
Ronnie Robertson
Edward G. Robinson, Jr.
Buddy Rogers
Wayne Rogers
Caesar Romero
Mickey Rooney
Milt Rosen
Joe E. Ross
Jacques Roux

Lauro Salas
Larry Sands
Joe Santos
Telly Savalas &
   George Savalas
Leon Schwab
Johnny Seven
Frank Sinatra
Red Skelton
Sidney Skolsky
Slash
Jack Soo
Connie Stevens
James Stewart
Jerry Stiller &
   Anne Meara
Larry Storch &
   Norma Storch
Barbra Streisand
Vic Taback
Mel Torme &
   Tracy Torme
Rip Torn
Regis Toomey
Ritchie Valens
Dean Valentine
Dick Van Dyke
Val de Vargas
Robert Wagner
Ray Walston
Burt Ward
Rudy Waxman
Jesse White
Billy D. Williams
Tom Williams
Treat Williams
Jonathan Winters
Robert Wright &
   George Forrest
Burt Young

CONFESSIONS...
of a
HOLLYWOOD HAIRSTYLIST

I Confess! I never intended to cut hair for a living. I never even considered the idea of being a Barber or a Beautician. What about a Hairstylist, you say? HA! The term, the function, didn't exist when I was a teenager.

Hey, I only started cutting hair for some guys in my dorm in the earliest days of my freshman year at Ohio University. Those first few haircuts happened as the result of a bad joke... till I realized that I made seven bucks the first time out. That's $7.00! Wow, I was smiling alright, but back in the day, that was big money and an amount like that was never a joke.

A couple of short years later, after moving to Hollywood so my dad could chase his dream of being a movie actor, I was among the most surprised people on earth to find that, after a few stutter-steps, I became part of the first wave of Hollywood Hairstylists with Movie and TV Celebrities among my clients.

Wow again, as Plan A for my new life in California was to attend UCLA and pursue a career in writing. Haircutting was only supposed to be a steppingstone to getting my degree.

I Confess! I am like so many millions of people who started on one Life-path and transitioned, uh, make that Zigzagged, to another. My initial experience with writing started when I wrote my first scripts that my classmates brought to life in the fourth grade. Then in high school, my English teacher was the first "authority figure" who said that I (Who, y'mean ME?) should write for a living. Yeah, sure, I thought. Heck, ever since I was 13, I *knew* I was going to be driving a big red cement truck and earn "really big bucks," so what about that? I should write for a living, huh? Gimmie a break. As you can see, I had no idea these early forays into the World of the Written Word were a peek-a-boo into my future.

But true to the old saying, Life is Funny. More proof? Check out the varied experiences with Hair and Hollywood found in my columns that appear in this book. The whole process of living the events and then writing about them in newspaper columns was a labor of love that was extremely fun and exciting, another Zig. I got into haircutting in the Hollywood area due to a nasty comment, including more Zags. I found, starting from my very first day with Cosmo, that among my clients were so many of Hollywood's Celebrities. And the writing blossomed, too, surprise-surprise, mucho-thanx to my quasi twin-brother and partner, **Johnny Gentri**.

The columns selected for this book mainly focus on Hollywood Celebrities like *Dirty Harry's* alter ego, **Clint Eastwood**; Hollywood writer **Sydney Skolsky;** Movie Icon & Sex Goddess **Jayne Mansfield**; dear friend **Telly** *"Kojak"* **Savalas**; *Cheers* Bartender **Nick *"Coach"* Colosanto**; *Kung Fu's* **Philip Ahn**; *Top 40 Countdown King* and forever friend **Casey Kasem**; Screen Beauties **Connie Stevens, Stephanie Powers, Debbie Reynolds** and **Judy Garland**; Comic Icon **Red Skelton**; the Comedy Team of **Jerry Stiller** and **Anne Meara**; **Tony Curtis** and **Larry Storch,** who with his wife **Norma…** oh, you'll see. Also, you will meet a non-reclusive, forget-his-reputation, **Howard Hughes!** And everyone will certainly enjoy, I'm sure, an intimate look at the life of Character Actor **Paul J. Micale**, my father, who is best remembered as **Father Carmine** in the *Rocky* series of movies that starred **Sylvester Stallone, Talia Shire** and **Bert Young**. Then comes the **"Stardust"** section, containing sketches of more than **300 Celebrities**. Does Stardust contain glimpses of future columns? Hey, bottom line, Life is unpredictable, but wouldn't that be something?

I also threw in a few columns on my early experiences that cover events that helped shape the rest of my story.

September 11, 2001. The mere thought of the date often gets my emotions liquefied. Every American can remember where they were and how they felt when they heard the news and saw it all unfold. Thousands (millions?) of stories have been told and written, covering most every angle.

One year later, I was asked to write a column for my local newspaper that memorialized **Mickey Rothenberg**, a dear friend and client who perished on **American Flight 93**. That column started a new direction in my writing life. Except in the wispiest of daydreams, I never thought I would ever write a series of newspaper columns. I continually thank Mick for the nudge.

The message is clear. Life can take some extreme, positive turns. Of course, negative stuff happens, too. Today, tomorrow – nobody knows what they will bring. That's why I find Life to be so exciting.

I Confess! When I started writing columns about my experiences as Hairstylist to the Stars in Hollywood, I knew I had an endless supply of stories about celebrities that only I could tell. See, all the stories happened to and around me. I could easily write thousands more, including stories on today's Hollywood.

Before writing that first column, I realized that I would be exposing myself, my philosophies, my inner thoughts and my perspective. Not a problem, since I have nothing to hide. Thus far in life I've made good decisions and some real stinkers, by the bunches each. Sometimes, especially after a sour decision, there is a real hesitation; and always, finally, I remind myself to move forward, or to at least move.

My self-confidence, self-esteem and self-image are above the norm only because way too many people erroneously underrate themselves. Why? We all know that a baseball player who has a .300 batting average also FAILS seven out of 10 times at bat and is paid MANY MILLIONS per year... or six figures per game! He's a winner, folks, so take a lesson: Transpose THAT! Join the millions of us who have an attitude that says...

I Love Life and Can Hardly Wait For the Next Event, Coming Any Moment Now.

And be aware, I find that no event is truly minor; but some can seem to be and might, for many years, remain mislabeled. Would I change anything in the past if I could? Sure. But I know that my best influence is right now, right here.

One other fact, please. Several of my columns were published before the thought occurred to me that the combined stories could be misconstrued an autobiography of sorts. Not quite true, but while friends and the public were being entertained, I was revisiting some valuable Life Lessons and again focusing on people and relationships I consider invaluable.

By now you should be getting a good idea of why I have so often declared to be the luckiest guy alive. You will see in these pages that it's not an exaggeration. The only flaw in the statement is the overall concept of Luck. See, I don't believe in luck, even though I realize that many people do, so I sometimes use the term as a communication tool.

I'm a Cause-'n-Effect guy. I mean, just because the Cause is unknown does not mean there is none. I think some people jump to the conclusion of calling that unknown quantity "luck." Not me. As I see it, there is always a Cause. Sure, there are a bunch of Causes that remain unknown for a while; maybe years. Or forever. We'll see. As far as I'm concerned, the Fat Lady isn't even warming up. This same philosophy leads to my understanding that there are no such things as Coincidences or Accidents, but right here I want to emphasize that I am not attempting to sway anyone's thinking. Everyone is free to come to their own conclusions; I'm just declaring my own.

The bottom line is that ever since I stopped believing in luck, I've had BUNCHES of it.

One more thing, just for further clarification: I'm a **Lou Tice/Zig Ziglar/Jim Rohn** type of guy. My Grampa Dominic provided the basics, proving once and for all that I'm profoundly blessed. No capish? You will.

When I finally went to hair school at **Mohler's Barber College** in downtown Los Angeles, one of my instructors suggested that I apply for a job in Hollywood with **Cosmo Sardo**, owner of a "hair *saloon*," he called it, "…right around the corner from **Schwab's Pharmacy**, the place where all the Hollywood celebrities hang out."

I must Confess that the thought of working in such a place was intriguing, to say the least, so I passed the info to my dad. I knew that Schwab's was reportedly the place where **Lana Turner** was discovered sipping on a Chocolate Soda. **Marilyn Monroe** was supposed to be a regular; too, along with **Clark Gable** and **Everybody** who ever graced the Big Silver Screen.

Wow, I thought, right around the corner could be a very exciting place to work, indeed!

I'm going to begin with the first story I wrote for a newspaper about my Hollywood experience at Cosmo's, though it is not the column that kicked off my entrée into the world of writing an ongoing series of newspaper columns. I'm saving that very first column for later. Don't worry; I'll announce *numero uno* with trumpets blaring.

Please keep in mind that these columns were originally written a week or two apart. They are sometimes initially repetitive so both loyal and casual readers would have a good chance of getting the whole picture.

Now let me introduce you to Cosmo Sardo, my first Boss, the man I revere as though he were my uncle – or Godfather - and the owner of the salon "…40 paces around the corner…."

✯✯✯

Chapter 1.
Hollywood Spotlight on Cosmo Sardo

"Known The World Over" was the registered slogan of **Cosmo Sardo's Barber - Hairstyling Salon and Art Gallery**. The ten-private-haircutting-booth salon was located at the beginning of the world-famous Sunset Strip at 1452 N. Crescent Heights Boulevard. That was just about 40 paces around the crescent-shaped corner from 8000 Sunset Boulevard, the address of **Schwab's Pharmacy**, the famous Hollywood Hangout.

The salon reflected the name of the owner, Cosmo Sardo, a six foot tall, slender, dignified-looking man who earned a reputation for being "eccentric," even by Hollywood standards. He was born in Boston, Massachusetts, on March 7, 1909. As a young man, Cosmo moved to Hollywood to pursue his life-long dream of acting in the movies. No wonder he and my dad got along so well.

In the movie industry in the early 1940s, Cosmo became a specialist known as a "Dress-Extra," a foreground-actor who maintained an extensive (yes, and expensive) professional wardrobe. He used a bedroom in his home as a haberdashery to hold all the outfits (he had 75 tuxedos of various type and apparent vintage) he wore in the hundreds of movie and TV shows he appeared in over the course of his approximately 50 year career. Sure, you saw him. Early on, he was the corpse in the movie *D.O.A.* starring **Edmond O'Brian.** Remember now? Nice suit.

Cosmo was also noted among directors and actors as a "business" guy. In a movie or TV show, say the Star and a Main Character are in a scene together. A third actor would often be necessary to do "business," often without lines. That "business" earned extra pay for the actor. That was Cosmo's other specialty.

Digressing just a bit, a perfect example of the above scenario was witnessed again just a short while ago. One evening, my wife Ginny and I were surfing the channels, looking for "something interesting." I came upon a *Columbo* episode from the 1970s. As I tuned in, **Peter Falk**, as the Rumpled One, was in a fine restaurant in a booth, conversing with the Guest Star. (The restaurant was probably the famous **Smoke House Restaurant**, also a personal favorite, located across the street from **Warner Brothers Studios** and used in countless movies and TV shows.) A waiter entered the shot and the Guest Star ordered a drink.

The waiter was Cosmo Sardo. I let out a yell. "Hey, that's my old boss Cosmo!"

In the next scene, Cosmo went to the bar get the Guest Star's drink. The bartender said something as he handed the drink to Cosmo. Cosmo then served the drink.

In the above Columbo episode, Cosmo never said a word, but he directly shared a scene with the Stars. That's "business," calling for extra pay for Cosmo. And by the way, the bartender was portrayed by my father, actor **Paul J. Micale**. Y'think I let out a yell for Cosmo, I scared our two German Shepherds, Bella and Vita, with the yell for my dad.

(I find the thrill of seeing Cosmo and my dad making what amounts to a surprise visit via TV just about impossible to explain, as both are no longer alive. Such occurrences are positively emotional and super-special.)

Cosmo, desirous of eating regularly in his early Hollywood experience, bought the hair salon (where he had been employed) from two attorneys who decided they had made a bad investment. That was sometime in 1939, I think. Three times I asked Cosmo the actual date. Result? Three different answers. That's another of the hodgepodge Hollywood birth-date stories. With any luck, we'll never know for sure.

While high-ranking business executives from all walks of life had standing appointments at Cosmo's, the place was more noted for catering to a seemingly infinite group of Hollywood's most popular and brightest Stars. Cosmo's had more than a four-decade-long history of being, according to Cosmo, "the most popular and famous hair salon in the Hollywood/Beverly Hills area." Small wonder.

Though the fact was not public knowledge, not even to regular (the well-heeled but non-entertainment types) patrons of Cosmo's salon, almost all producers, directors and casting directors who patronized the place came in on the cuff. Yep, Cosmo's. So naturally, reciprocity bloomed, garnering Cosmo more work than he otherwise would have enjoyed. Some might have called it unethical. Some certainly called it good business. See, in Hollywood, there was always the story behind the story. Still true, too. Imagine the book I could write.

The "cuffed" hair service was performed by various staff stylists, but especially by Cosmo's cousin, **Nunzio "Johnny" Tringali**, born in

Agusta, Sicily. More importantly, Nunzio was noted as Hollywood's *Numero Uno Tonsorial Artiste*, or more commonly in American jargon, the Top Dog, the guy who cut the hair of the likes of **Clark Gable, Robert Taylor, Errol Flynn, John Wayne, Sandy Koufax** (how'd HE get in there?) **Cary Grant, Wayne Rogers** and more, but gotta stop. Nunzio never dropped names and abhorred when others did in his behalf, so please, don't ask for more. Today, Nunzio is 93 and still works three days a week, even though someone else has to drive him to work. I just called and wished him a Happy New Year for you. He sends his love. (Nunzio lived to be 97.)

Oh, the "Art Gallery" thing in the name. On various walls hung 2 by 4 foot oil paintings of mostly nude *Playboy* Centerfold types with a two-inch price tag lodged in the lower right hand corner of the overly-ornate frames. While the tag was small, to make them squint, Cosmo said, the price was akin to the cost of four Rolls Royce tires, with rims. Over a twenty year period, I only remember one sale, but how 'bout we save that story for a future column.

I had been thrilled when Cosmo consented to hire me, if only on a part-time basis.

"I've never had anyone as young as you work here, you're the only apprentice ever and I'm pleased that you're also attending beauty school. Can't learn too much, y'know," Cosmo said as he greeted me that first morning.

Absolutely nobody, myself especially, would have dreamed that several years into the future, I would buy Cosmo out, bring in a bevy of female clients along with female hair-cutters joining the existing staff and ride out the final years of "Hollywood's Most Famous and Fabulous Hair Salon, Ever!" (According to His Eminence, Don Cosmo Sardo.)

Oops, did it again. Windy me, outta space before I'm out of story. Don't move away. The fun is just beginning.

Chapter 2.
Cosmo's Hairstyling Salon – Day One

Newspapers limit the number of words per overall column. I must Confess that at first, confining the stories to a fixed number of words caused me some consternation. Before long, I found that my stories flowed more smoothly, but on those occasions when I would be cutting out too much meat, I'd write a two-parter. Happened right from the get-go.

Join me that first day as Cosmo lays down the law and also meet **Robert Cummings, Donald O'Connor, Sydney Skolsky** *and a* **Tall Guy with Wild Hair***. Talk about spinning my head!*

In the column from last week it was pointed out that **Cosmo's Hairstying Salon** was located about 40 paces around the corner from **Schwab's Pharmacy**, the famous Hollywood Hangout. Cosmo, known as being eccentric, consented to hire me part-time for three basic reasons, given that I was only 22 years old and the next youngest staff member was double my age at 44. The three reasons, in no special order are; A) As a favor to my father who was already working there; B) He was encouraged by my "pleasant and enthusiastically persistent ways while using several approaches to ask for a job," Cosmo said years later, and; C) He felt he had a true "Acid Test," tailor-made for me, that would settle the matter of my worthiness for employment very quickly.

Nepotism found a home in Hollywood well before my time and since. Take **Kirk Douglas** and **Michael**, for example. **Henry** and **Jane Fonda**. **Donald** and **Keifer Sutherland.** Ah, but the rule only applies when the offspring has the talent AND can take the heat of the shadow of the accomplished parent. Where are the **Crosby** boys or the many **Mickey Rooneys**? Can you visualize **Edward G. Robinson, Jr.**? Or **Charlie Chaplin, Jr.**? It is my privilege to say both were friends, people I truly liked. Sad to report, both personified the Ultimate of Unhappy; suicides. See what I mean? Conclusions can offer a treacherous jump. Gotta see the whole picture.

That first morning Cosmo filled me in on some of his ironclad pet rules.

"People who patronize us are always referred to as 'clients,' never 'customers' like in other haircutting establishments."

I can still visualize Cosmo saying it, his index finger drilling an invisible hole into the air above his right ear. "Clients are people who warrant and receive professional service in a professional atmosphere," Cosmo pontificated in his oft-observed laborious manner, "...whereas customers are people who go somewhere else, take a number, like in a bakery, yuck!, and have their hair transferred from their head to the floor. We give our clients an appointment, not a number."

Whenever the story is related verbally, I do a caricature portrayal of Cosmo's demeanor and mannerisms, with listeners usually getting a good chuckle, but back then, I did a great job of not busting a gut laughing. That Cosmo was the epitome of Somethin' Else. Believe it.

As Cosmo was ranting, I saw a familiar figure over his shoulder, entering from the door to the parking lot behind our row of stores.

"'S'cuse me, Cosmo," I interrupted, peering around Cosmo's shoulder. "That man coming in the back door looks like **Robert Cummings**."

"Of course he's Bob; been a client here for years," Cosmo said as he walked toward Nunzio's booth to intercept Cummings. Nunzio slapped his chair with his chair-cloth as he rather nonchalantly greeted Cummings with a dry, "Hello, Bob." As Cosmo introduced us and the words "Nice to meet you" had hardly escaped my lips, Cosmo squeezed my elbow and lead me toward the front desk.

"We never crowd our clients, it's not professional," Cosmo said quietly while shifting so that his back was to Cummings. "Besides, he in particular hates to have anyone try to converse with him while he is getting his haircut."

Was Cosmo exaggerating? What's the difference; he was The Boss.

Cosmo further told me to watch Nunzio as he worked, for he was the unchallenged "...best ever. Don't let watching be obvious. Watch through mirrors."

Later, as Cummings was getting brushed 'n tidied by one of the two porters, Nunzio's next client walked up behind Cummings and said hello with a slap on Bob's back. As Cummings turned around in surprise, the little guy did a quick soft-shoe and ended by extending his right hand, palm up. Turned out to be **Donald O'Connor**.

"Holy smoke," I said softly to myself, "...and it's only 10 a.m."

Sometime later, my Acid Test came waddling through the front door. **Sidney Skolsky**, the famous writer for *Photoplay Magazine*, the Number One entertainment publication at the time, was going to be sitting in my chair to get a shave! Cosmo warned me that Sidney had baby-tender skin and a barbed-wire-tough beard and only he could shave Sidney without irritating him.

Cosmo further said that if I could please Sidney, I'd have my first regular client. He never said I had to please him or be out on my ear, but that was the plan that I learned about several years later.

Sidney literally plopped into my chair. "Lookit, kid," he started, "I got this really tough beard 'n my skin is tender as a baby's butt, and ever-one who shaves me irritates the @O&%$ outta me, 'specially Cosmo, so whatever y'do, I don't wanna walk outta here red as a beet, get it?"

He was red as a beet.

If they taught me anything in barber school it was to use extra-hot towels and a freshly honed razor on a person with a tough beard. Sidney said, "The hotter, the better." Hey, they steamed for a reason.

After taking the first couple of strokes with my extra-sharp razor, Sidney looked up at me and said, "Nice touch." He then closed his eyes and went to sleep, snoring softly.

When I finished, Sidney got up and stroked his face with his hands and the back of his fingers. I had to turn away and chuckle as he stuck his tongue out like a German Shepherd and licked his face looking for stubble. Pleased with the result, Sidney turned to **Sam Keston**, a Cockney Englishman who worked in the chair next to mine. "I don't get it, Sam. This kid just gave me the shave of my life."

"Of course he treated you right," Sam answered. "He's the best in the world. Why else would we hire a kid?"

What a surprise! Sam and I had just been introduced that morning and had not had an opportunity to say another word to each other.

Turning to me, Sidney asked if I would like to have a cup of coffee with him.

I said "Sure" and it was off to Schwab's, Sidney taking my arm about 20 paces into the journey. I thought nothing of the arm since Sidney was in his senior years. As I was to find out sometime later, Sidney did not require stability. If he liked someone, he made physical contact, it was just that simple. And at that moment, I was the only one who didn't know.

(Later I would learn that the actors who frequented Schwab's constantly studied people and certainly, they had studied Sidney's habits and idiosyncrasies for years.)

As Sidney and I walked into Schwab's, it seemed like everyone gave Sidney a big hello. People sitting in the booths beckoned to him to join them and to "bring your friend." One young, tall, slender actor with hair all askew came running up, his arms flaying as he was obviously angry about something, talking so fast I don't remember exactly what he was saying except that he ended with "So what do you make of that?"

Sidney, calm and cool, flicked him off with his hand as he said "We'll talk about it later. Say hello to Little Joe here. Next time you need a haircut, go see him, he's the best in the world. Joe, say hello to **Clint Eastwood**."

The next morning Eastwood walked into Cosmo's, went up to the front desk and said, loud enough for everyone to hear, "I want a haircut with Little Joe. I hear he's the best in the world."

The entire staff looked like they were comparing wrinkled brows. Cosmo was smiling ear to ear. I was floored, even embarrassed before these masters of the Hollywood haircutting world.

"You're starting beautifully," Cosmo whispered to me later.

And I'm outta space again....

✯✯✯

Starting beautifully, indeed. Within a very short time I was counting many Hollywood Celebrities among my clients. **Gardner McKay**, *Star of the TV series, Adventures in Paradise, was one as was* **Nick Adams**, *Star of The Rebel,* **Poncie Ponce**, *Star of Hawaiian Eye,* **Philip Ahn**, *who so often played a bad Jap in the movies that the studio had to provide round-the-clock protection and teen throb,* **Troy Donahue**, *just to name a few.*

Long before my first year was out, I realized that my profession had found me, rather than the other way around. Not so bad, I figured, as I felt I could pursue a career as a freelance writer from behind the chair just as easily as from teaching high school English and maybe, I'd be better off working for Cosmo as the income would be definitely greater. The perspective from years later strongly indicates that I had chosen a great way to go.

Chapter 3.
Little Paulie's Big Dream
(Part 1 of 2)

*I Confess that to tell my own experiences accurately, I gotta tell about my father, actor **Paul J. Micale**, for our story lines are as inseparable as, well, Father and Son.*

Yep, no way to tell it all in one gulp. Dad's story is a true testament to those who forge ahead, chasing their Dream to a positive conclusion in spite of almost everyone around them saying the likes of, "Yer too old" and "What makes you think yer good enough" and 'Ferget it cuz you ain't got no chance a'tall."

I promise to tell more of dad's experiences as we go along, but I'm sure you'll get a kick outta what amounts to his Bio.

Getting into the movies is no bite of cannoli. The story of one of Hollywood's brightest stars tells it all. **Marilyn Monroe** got thrown out of every major studio and several high-profile agents' offices before she was finally "discovered;" and later, she couldn't find Norma Jean in all that platinum and finery. Looked and looked 'til she was 36 years old, then came to rest just beyond a diabolical door. Sad, yes, but the story's theme is as old as the hills, it's being played out today and by all indications it will play through eternity.

When people, especially very young people, get bitten by the Movie Bug, they focus on the middle part of Marilyn's experience rather than the beginning or the end. "The negative won't happen to me," they say. "After all, that doesn't happen to everyone." And you know what? They're right. Positive expectations bring positive results; negative expectations are the pavement on the road to Hell.

Ever hear of **Paul Micale**? If he were in the night sky, he wouldn't be in the Big Dipper, but he'd be visible. He serves here as a thematic example worthy of close scrutiny. Paul was born in Cleveland's Little Italy on January 2, 1916. His parents had emigrated from Sicily a year or so before, coming to America to pursue their dreams of ample work, a decent home and a good neighborhood in which to raise their children. Really unique, huh?

Growing up "down the hill," as the area has been referred to for more than a century, Paul was one of those millions who was fascinated by the movies he saw at his local movie house. He especially liked going downtown to the fabulous **Hippodrome Theater** or the elegant **RKO Palace**, but any movie, anywhere, was always his newest favorite. Here, jump into my TimeMachine. I'll set the date for a particular moment in 1926. Watch closely, now.

"More than anything else, I want to be a movie actor," young ten-year-old Paulie told his mother for the umteenth time.

"My dear, sweet-a son, your dreams are soooo big," she exclaimed in frustration, throwing her arms to the sky. "D'you know where Hollywood is?" she asked.

"Yeah, it's where they make movies!" Paul said excitedly.

"It's a million miles away!" his mother responded in a louder tone.

"We could take the train!" Paul shouted back.

Some years later, Paul's mother, the benevolent matriarch of her family who came to be called Nonna once grandchildren arrived, finally consented to his pursuing an acting career in Hollywood. As the story goes, she invited *everybody* to his Eighteenth Birthday and Hoo-Ray for Hollywood Going Away Party. The whole neighborhood showed up, drank two barrels of made-it-in-the-basement wine, ate themselves silly and bid *ni viriemu,* Sicilian for *arrivederci*, to each other around midnight as Paul had a ticket on the 8 a.m. train the following morning. Move over, **Clark Gable**.

Paul didn't sleep much that night, too many visions of co-starring with the likes of **Helen Hayes, Lynn Fontanne, Katharine Hepburn**.... Heck, even a mouse named **Mickey** had his star take off like a rocket, splashing upon the Silver Screen that year.

Nonna scurried around the house that morning calling to Paul that it was time to leave, only to finally find him sitting in the family's grocery truck, ready to go, and even his tie was knotted properly. The not-so-old Model A chugga-chugged along the road headed for the train station downtown, located in the new skyscraper appropriately named **The Terminal Tower**. Not more than a block away, Grampa, known throughout the neighborhood by this time as "Mister Joe the Grocer," pulled to the curb in front of a not very tall gray building.

"Come with me," Nonna said to Paul. "No, leave your suitcase in the truck," she added.

'Maybe she's gonna buy me a new suit,' Paul thought as he looked at his watch and fretted.

It was a smock, not a suit. Turns out Nonna didn't sleep much that night, either. "Running off to Hollywood is foolish," she told the shocked young Paul. "Better you should learn a trade. One day you'll thank me for bringing you here to barber school." Nonna lived to be 89 years old. It is uncertain if Paul ever *properly* thanked her, but it's a documented fact that Paul adored his mother and father.

It is important to know that Nonna provided Paul with several years of expensive violin lessons and acting classes at a time when most kids were fortunate to eat properly once in a while. In her considered opinion, going so far away to a place that had a dark side to its reputation was inviting too much trouble for someone as young and inexperienced as Paul. The timing of her decision was disconcerting to Paul, certainly, but who's to say, she was probably right, for her legacy to her family - including generations yet to come - is a long life graced with a canopy of success.

As **Paul Harvey** has said so well for so many years, "In a moment, you'll know the r-r-rest of the story." Just let me adjust the dial on my TimeMachine and we'll flash ahead in years.

There. It's May, 1959. Paul has been married for 22 years to his soul-mate, Patricia Ann, whom he most always calls Honey, letting the rest of the world call her Pat. They have two children. JoAnn, the youngest, is just completing her sophomore year in high school; and Joe, named for his grocer grampa per centuries-old Sicilian tradition, has just returned home after completing his sophomore year at Ohio University. The family is just sitting down to dinner.

Normally at dinner they would bring each other up-to-date on the latest news, but tonight, Joe and JoAnn sense that their parents have something important to say, so there is a period of silence. Finally, the bomb drops as Paul says, "Your mother and I have some exciting news. We're moving to Hollywood."

Had he said they were moving to the dark side of the moon, that would have been flabbergasting. There is no word, or group of words, to depict how his news shocked his son and daughter, especially since, they said later, they recognized that the statement was factual. And final.

A few weeks before, Paul had the leading role in a play titled *Wayside* at the **Cleveland Playhouse**, one of the most respected legitimate theaters in the entire Midwest. **Columbia Pictures** bought the story for a movie, the Columbia executive saying that if Paul lived in Hollywood, he would be given the lead role in the movie.

"But I've never been in a movie, not even as a walk-on," Paul said to the exec. "Why would you give me the lead?"

"Because you're an excellent actor, you brought that role to life and you're portraying a one-armed man," the exec replied, "and stars are reluctant to play people who have limbs missing."

Either the exec had a very misanthropic point of view, or thespian perspective has changed considerably. In any event, Paul told the exec that he and his family were scheduled to move to Hollywood "in about two months."

"Great!" the exec said. "When you get out there, I'll put you in other productions, too. I'll help you get a good start with your movie career."

That night Paul went home, took Pat by the hand and said, "Honey, what would you think of moving to Hollywood?"

Oops, I'm out of space. I'll finish this for you next week. *Ni viriemu!*

Chapter 4.
"Hey Ma, Lookit Me!"

(Part 2 of 2)

Following is the wrap-up telling how Dad-the-Actor made it into the movies. Yes, you certainly knew him, so this will be fun.

I Confess! To say that **Jimmy Durante** was an entertainer is as great an understatement as saying that **Rembrandt** was a painter. The world loved to make fun of Durante's large, banana-like nose, but Jimmy did a better job of it, adding his famous 'take' on the audience for a punctuating gesture

Durante was noted for an array of bits and zingers that were an integral part of his trademark routine. His performance would usually contain an instance where some foil would get a laugh at Jimmy's expense. Durante, with a sudden expression of exasperation on his face, would stand with feet apart, look directly at the audience and then raise his arms rather stiffly, bringing them down with a dual slap on his thighs as he proclaimed, "Ever-buddy's tryin' ta get inta d'act!" If he said it a million times, it got a laugh a million times, because the way he delivered it, the line was a *scream*. And, it was true.

Those who live in the Hollywood/Beverly Hills area will tell you that most of the eleven million people in the greater Los Angeles area have some degree of desire to be in the movies. If someone adds, "Everybody but me," check to see if it's said while smiling.

On the other hand, thousands of people each year go to Hollywood openly declaring that they want to be a movie actor. Eh, make that movie STAR, though most won't use the S word except to select, close friends, or to strangers who they think will never be seen again and maybe, only when drunk or otherwise highly affected.

All that brings us back to our case-in-point, Paul Micale. As stated earlier, Paul wanted to be a movie actor from childhood, a fact he repeated to his mother *ad nauseam*. Paul thought he was taking the train to Hollywood the day after his 18th birthday, but instead, his mother and dad put him in the family grocery truck and took him to barber school. Can anyone possibly imagine Paul's disappointment? Not likely, according to Paul.

For the next several years, Paul made his living as a barber, satisfying his urge to be a performer by expanding the band he started as a teenager and, as might be imagined, honing his acting skills by joining various little theater groups in and around his birth city of Cleveland, Ohio.

In the late spring of 1959, Paul had the lead role in a play, titled *Wayside,* that was making its world premier at the Cleveland Playhouse. Columbia Pictures bought the rights to the story, the Columbia exec giving Paul a virtual guarantee that the lead in the movie would be his if only Paul lived in Hollywood. When Paul "lied" to the exec, saying that the move to Hollywood was imminent, the exec further stated that he would help Paul get roles in other films, too.

Paul and his wife, Pat, decided that Paul would drive fabled Route 66 to Hollywood that Labor Day weekend with Pat staying behind until the house sold, then bring the kids and join him.

When Paul arrived in Hollywood he took a room at the actor-friendly **Mark Twain Hotel** on Wilcox Avenue in the heart of Hollywood. There he befriended other serious movie wannabes like himself. He soon got more than just a taste of Hollywood's Catch 22 Axiom: "To get a movie role (even a 'bit' part), first you need an agent; to get an agent, first you need a movie role." Everyone who experienced the process represented that it was nerve-wracking, to say the least. Durante called the whole mess "da pits."

"Make the rounds of the studios," Paul was advised by his new friends. "Try to get inside, go to the commissary and just talk to anybody who will talk to you." Not very sophisticated or scientific, everybody agreed, but the methodology had been known to work, but don't ask "For who?" because no name could be culled from memory.

Anyhow, about the fifth time Paul went to **Paramount Studios**, the security cop at the gate came out of his shack and shook his head as Paul approached. Putting his hands on hips and cocking his head, the cop said, "Hey Cleveland, you got an appointment this time?"

"No," Paul replied, hoping he was effectively hiding the frustration he felt and wishing he could think of something clever enough to say that would gain his entry into the studio.

Shaking his head again, the cop turned and pointed down the street beyond the famous arched entrance. "See the third and fourth sound-stages on the right?" the cop said a bit gruffly. "If you ever get a chance to get on this lot, turn right between them and go to the third building on the left. On the corner of the building you'll see a plain brown door. It opens to an inside stairway that leads to the second floor. At the top, go down the hallway to the second door on your left. The producer who has that office is from Cleveland." Having said that, the cop walked about five paces away and folded his arms across his chest as he intently gazed skyward, his back to Paul.

"It took more than a moment for me to realize what was happening," Paul told his family some time later, "but when I caught on, I softly said 'Thanks;' softly because of the lump that suddenly stuck in my throat."

Paul told himself to "Be calm; don't run…" to the street between the third and fourth sound stages where he turned right. He tried to get himself to walk more nonchalantly, even though he felt like he would never reach the third building on his left. Upon arriving, there was that plain brown door, just as the cop said, and inside, a rather dingy wooden stairway creaked as he made his way up. When he went down the hallway and reached the second door on his left, he entered, expecting a reception area. Instead, it was the private office of a very surprised young lady.

"She was in her early twenties, pretty, and dressed so nicely I wondered if she was an actress, but I soon realized that she was the secretary, and the producer's office was the door marked 'Private' behind her," Paul related. "I was shocked; totally embarrassed, shoulda knocked."

When she uttered, "May I help you?" Paul reached into his briefcase and took out a resume he had carefully typed and handed it to her, mumbling something that is forever lost in the woodwork of time. As she quickly scanned through the resume she smiled slightly, the smile broadening as she went further down the page. There were no movie or TV credits; only various stage plays and the name of the characters Paul had portrayed in each. About the moment she was asking "How did you get in here?" the 'Private' door opened and a man in a brown suit emerged.

"This man's a stage actor," she said, gesturing to Paul, her smile very broad now. "From Cleveland," she added, obviously fighting an urge to laugh out loud. The producer snatched the paper from her and browsed over the resume with a slight wrinkle on his brow. "I don't know how he got in here," the secretary volunteered.

"I see you've performed in several plays with the **Chagrin Valley Little Theater**," the producer said. "My good friend Charlie Smith is with that company. He stars; directs. Ever work with him?"

A different kind of lump was in Paul's throat now, for remembering names was always a challenge. "I'm not sure," Paul said. "Um, what does he look like?"

"Oh," the producer said, "I also see that you've done some work with the **Cleveland Playhouse**. Certainly you know Robert Alders. Everybody knows Bob."

Paul was ready to cry. "Robert... Bob," he said quietly. "I... I don't recognize that name either... me and my lousy memory for names, but I always know my lines."

"Now wait a minute," the producer said. "You've got to know Estelle Walters. She's been around forever," he said, throwing one arm in a huge circle.

"Sir," a dumbfounded Paul said, "Maybe I'll remember later and kick myself, but right now... um... I... um... don't recognize any of those people." At that moment, Paul realized that the secretary had turned her head and was doing a lousy job of stifling her snickers.

"Come into my office," the producer said as he turned and headed for the 'Private' door. Inside, he handed a script to Paul. "Turn to page 34," he said. "You read 'John;' I'll read 'Sam'. John is a forest ranger. He's at his command post in a forest, and he's radioing smoke on the horizon to Ranger HQ. Get it?"

The dialogue for both parts was short and succinct rather than the type of meaty stuff actors would rather portray to showcase their thespian abilities. After a few lines, Paul turned the page. The next line belonged to the producer, but instead of reading the line, he looked at Paul, put his hand on his chin, and asked, "Can you be here at 6:30 tomorrow morning?"

"I'll be here with bells on," Paul replied.

Later, referring to a hurriedly scribbled note he made upon leaving the producer's office, Paul asked Pat if she remembered the three people the producer had mentioned, as Pat's memory for names was extremely good.

"Never heard of them," Pat replied.

Paul went on to enjoy a successful career that covered more than 30 years, appearing in TV shows such as *Bonanza, The Untouchables, Gomer Pyle, Laverne & Shirley, Streets of San Francisco, Barnaby Jones, Kojak, the Rockford Files, Columbo, To Rome With Love,* and more.

Of his many movies, his favorites were *Pocket Full of Miracles, Love Bug Rides Again, Lady Sings The Blues, Captain Newman, M.D., Miracle on Ice,* and certainly not least, he appeared as **Father Carmine** in *Rocky II, III* and *V.* It was truly a wonderful dream-come-true ride.

Oh yes, the play Columbia bought? They never made the movie. Nobody did. And the exec? Paul never saw him after that night in Cleveland. The man was transferred to Columbia's New York office before Paul arrived in Hollywood that September. While he had no influence on any particular role that Paul was awarded, who is to say what might have been had he not provided Paul's pivotal inspiration to move to Hollywood.

Paul and Pat spent their last days at the **Motion Picture and Television Home** in Woodland Hills, California. To qualify for residency, an actor must attain a certain level of income for each of 20 years, as one and one half percent of those earnings go to the benefit of the home. Paul was proud to have 27 qualified years.

Sydney Skolsky, the famous writer for the then top-selling entertainment publication, **Photoplay Magazine**, told me that "… your dad is the happiest actor in Hollywood… thinks he moved to Heaven!"

A warm exaggeration from a close friend? Don't believe it. I know for a fact that Paul would not call a moment of it "Da pits."

✻✻✻

Chapter 5.
Barber School – Day One

*My mother, sister and I flew Continental Airlines in their then-new Boeing 707 into LAX and joined my father in Hollywood on December 21, 1959. We spent the first few nights at the **Mark Twain Hotel** in Hollywood before moving to an apartment in Van Nuys on Woodman Avenue owned by dad's life-long buddy, Nick Leo. While beyond the imagination of some, every moment of my life in Southern California was absolutely exciting. And people ask "DO" I miss it and "WHY?" HA! When you finish this book, I trust that most questions will be answered. If not, contact me. I don't bite.*

*Hey, I wanna take you to **Mohler's Barber School** where my first haircut was enough to make the teacher shout, stomp 'n scream. I constantly hadda tell my instructors to forget the hair on the floor, check out the hair on the head. Grrrr!*

"**O**h boy! Finally, after more than two years of giving haircuts while at Ohio University, I'm finally going to learn something technical about giving a good haircut!"

The thought was going through my mind, over and over, ever since signing up for barber school. About a month before, I had been to see a movie at the **Victory Drive-in Theater** in Van Nuys with a pretty red-headed girl named Sherri. She was as sweet as… wait a minute; that's another story.

As I was on the way to the snack-bar to get us Cokes and popcorn, an idea struck like a thunder bolt. And I mean a complete idea with i's dotted and t's crossed.

"Why not go to barber school days, work nights at this drive-in, then finish my education at **UCLA** a year hence?

Wow, what a Boss idea! When I finished college, I could throw the license in a garbage-can and become a high school English and business teacher as I pursued my main goal of being a professional writer. I could even coach wrestling and football!"

I made an immediate commitment to the whole plan.

The first day in **Mohler's Barber College**, we new students made up the work-for-free Freshmen Section, the group of chairs in an alcove at the back right-hand corner of the school and effectively separated from the rest of the students.

Mohler's was located at the corner of 3rd and Main Street in downtown Los Angeles, an area that was frequented by homeless bums and winos. Now, right here, please understand that those two names were acceptably descriptive then, not the derogatory, politically incorrect designations of today.

My first "patron" – as we were instructed to call them - wanted a haircut, not a shave like seemingly 99% of the free-bee services given in our section. SOP was to drape him, then call an instructor. I called, but he motioned me to begin as he was coaching another freshman who just opened his barber's straight razor and was about to take (and give?) his first stroke.

I picked up a small, narrow strip of hair on my patron's crown. Snip! Taking additional small strips, measured with the previous cut, I moved forward toward his forehead. A few cuts into the job, the head instructor, **Mr. Guy Otesen**, ran toward me from my left, arms flailing and shouting. Startled, I looked to my right to see if there was a fire, but a few feet beyond me was the back brick-wall of the building.

"You started at the crown!" he shouted as he ran right up to me.

Ah-HA! There must be a certain place to start. "Where should I have started?"

"You didn't read the book!"

He's right. I was sure he didn't mean *Mandingo*, but I wondered what book he meant. "What book?"

Oh, he looks exasperated. Hmm, did I say something wrong?

"*The Official Barber School Textbook*, on PAGE THREE, says that a man's haircut is always started at the LEFT SIDEBURN!"

Now that's dumb. Why start there? "Left sideburn? What the... Why there, of all places? And who wrote the dumb book, anyhow? Musta been some ninny who doesn't know a thing about giving a haircut."

"I DID!"

Mr. Otesen's eyes were blazing as he called for everyone's attention.

"Here's a student who started the patron's haircut at the CROWN. If ANYONE starts anywhere except the LEFT SIDEBURN, you will FLUNK the state exam and be back here for SIX MORE MONTHS!

You will be charged half a full tuition, which means one hundred fifty bucks! Got that?"

Later, when I was finished with my first school haircut, my patron, a big burley man, was most complimentary.

"Hey Shorty, you give a good haircut."

He apologized for not having any money for a tip. (They told us tips were rare and that a quarter was a big tip.)

Believe it or not, I lived through that day, though a whole bunch more happened. Anyhow, a few days later, my first patron returned.

"Hey Shorty, first time in my life I got compliments on my hair. I'll see you again."

With that, he offered me a dollar! I started to refuse so he stuffed the dollar in my shirt pocket, turned and walked out, his right hand running through his hair.

Mr. Otesen walked up to me and spoke in a voice loud enough for everyone to hear, his normal habit.

"Never refuse a tip. Let people say 'thank you' their way. Makes 'em feel good."

"I thought you were mad at me."

"I'll get mad at you many times before you graduate. That's when you should listen best."

I'd have to write a book to tell all that happened in the "wine country" that was also known as downtown Los Angeles. I promise another chapter soon.

★★★

Like I said earlier, I was very excited to be going to barber college that first day. In the two years I had given haircuts while attending **Ohio University,** *nobody taught me any technique. Yes, my father was a barber, but he was in Cleveland and I was 225 miles away.*

That first day in barber school was truly eventful. There was no "911 Call" for emergencies, so people would call the Fire Department for emergency help. The school called TREE TIMES that day. Yeah, tree. I'll 'splain later.

The first time, one of the new students who had never used (seen or held?) a barber's straight razor cut a patron's cheek to the bone! Blood everywhere! Then deja vu all over again! The third time, a patron lifted his pant leg to ask the new student's advice for a "sore" on his leg. The sore, about a three-inch elliptical circle, was literally crawling with maggots. The poor kid puked all over the place.

Some years after completing barber school, I learned that in the hair profession, there is a rule that says; "Those who can, do; and those who can't; teach." That may sound a little harsh at first, but there's more than an ounce of truth, I find.

See, anyone who can build a decent following of clients/customers will earn around two or three times a teacher's pay. I know, I just ticked off a bunch of teachers, but hey, I didn't make the rule; I only learned it. The same rule applies in some other professions, too. Now I guess I just ticked off a bunch more teachers.

*When I moved to Florida in 1999, I applied for a job as a teacher in a local barber school as I didn't want to build a following from scratch. The school owner offered me $7 an hour. When I protested and said I owned **Beverly Hills Hair Design** in Beverly Hills, California; he offered me $7.50. See what I mean?*

My original plan in 1960 in Los Angeles was to get a barber license so I could work legally while finishing my education at UCLA. I intended to major in English and make business my minor. Upon graduation from UCLA, I planned to teach English and business classes in high school while pursuing a career as a freelance writer. Great plan, I thought. Still do.

*The plan/life-altering factor was **Cosmo Sardo**. He hired me. My first regular client turned out to be **Sidney Skolsky**, the famous and powerful Hollywood Icon who sent me Movie Stars and TV Stars as clients, helping to make me among the first of those known as a Hairstylist to the Stars rather than a Barber to the Stars.*

*The difference between barber and hairstylist can't be called big, it's HUGE. Ask any true hairstylist like **Sam Russo** or **Eddie Carroll** or **Eddie Maghetto** or **Bobby Russo** or **Edie Crispell** or **Joe Torrenueva** or **Jay Sebring** or **Felice** or **Bernie Roberts** or **Gary Marks** or **Ben Garcia** or **Ralph Trejo** or **Don Sitanni** or **Phil Fayne** or **Ann Brown** or **Gene Shacove** or go to 'Vegas and ask **Michael French**.*

*Wow! That's some group! I know, some are no longer alive but all are dear friends and colleagues. And true **hairstylists**, not barber-stylists.*

*Notice I did not list **Nunzio Tringali**, who I dearly love and respect. Nunzio was a Barber to the Stars, and THE VERY BEST, I might add,* *whose results were on a par with the very best hairstylists. As good as Nunzio was, he – like the overwhelming majority of barbers – could not make the transition to Hairstylist. But then, Nunzio didn't have to, he was that good.*

Most barbers think that the difference between a barber's haircut and a hairstylist's haircut is that the hairstylist shampoos the hair first then finishes with a hand-held hair dryer. The statement is not an over-simplification, as there is no relation WHATSOEVER to the truth.

A true Hairstylist and a true Barber give totally different haircuts, the difference in technique understood by the hairstylist while being a total mystery to most barbers. But like Cosmo said years ago, most men seem to prefer a barber's haircut and though the truth may hurt some people's feelings, most executive-minded men prefer a hairstyle.

Please understand, I am not trying to make barbers angry at me as I consider them to be brothers, but there is a tremendous difference between a barber and a hairstylist and the difference is a hell of a lot greater than a shampoo and the price of the haircut. The difference is much akin to the comparison of a Boeing 737 Jetliner to a Piper Cub. I'd need to write a book to explain it clearly, but enough for right now, folks.

Chapter 6.
Hollywood Spotlight on Milt Rosen

I Confess! This is a perfect time to meet another Uncle Miltie, this one loved by all. I'm tooting the horn of the Hollywood writing icon/ mench who - I'm so privileged to say - was my writing Guru.

Does the name **Arthur Godfrey** ring a bell? How about **George Gobel**? No, this is not a trick to expose your age. Remember *The Joey Bishop Show?* Okay, okay, enough already! Are shows like *The Brady Bunch* or *Baa Baa Blacksheep* or *The Carol Burnett Show* a more comfortable or better group of choices to bring to the fore?

This seemingly nostalgic quiz is to spotlight one of Hollywood's favorite, most highly respected and accomplished writers, **Milt Rosen**. Milt wrote all the mentioned shows, and oh so many more. To paraphrase an old friend of Milt's, you ain't heard nothin' yet! You could look up **Al Jolson**. Sure, dig him up, whatever.

I recently talked to good friend, **Judy Rosen**, Milt's "child bride" in 1960; his widow. My wife Ginny and I wouldn't think of going to Los Angeles without a visit with Judy. I asked Judy if I could borrow some of the many scripts Milt wrote for *The Dean Martin Celebrity Roasts*, or maybe *The Danny Thomas Show*. She'd already donated them to various museums and libraries, including some from *The Bob Newhart Show*, and more. Great material can certainly be found all through those scripts, as true comedy is timelessly locked into the now.

Milt Rosen represents so many other great writers who seem to remain mysteriously unfamiliar to the public in general in spite of the fact that their names are emblazoned all over their work. To help this effort, Judy was asked to send a copy of Milt's bio material.

"Oh, God," she replied. (Reminds me; he wrote for **George Burns**, and also for **George & Gracie**, not to mention **Bob Hope, Milton Berle, the Smothers Brothers, Victor Borge**...) "Nobody has asked for a bio on Milt for at least 30 years!" Judy exclaimed. "I don't even know if such a thing exists, but I'll scrounge around and get back to you."

Maybe a week later, four typewritten pages arrived in the mail, obviously compiled more than a couple of years ago. Frankly, I was not aware of most of his credits as Milt only referred to a past activity when it helped exemplify a particular point he was making. He didn't have to drop names; rather, the best known Hollywood bigwigs bragged on working with him!

Milt wrote for dozens more of the most popular TV shows that have not been mentioned here, so I'll end the list by saying that Milt was the head writer for *Baretta*, starring the now besmirched actor, **Robert Blake**. (I consider Bobby a personal friend though our involvement was limited over the years and I'm truly saddened by his legal troubles. I know him as a great guy.)

Milt wrote for dozens of the most popular TV shows, including several of the *Academy Awards* shows of the past two decades, or stepping back a bit again, there were episodes of *Bewitched, Flying Nun, Chips*.... He wrote quite a few movies, too. Ever see *Do Not Disturb*? How about *Sunshine*? *Paris Holiday* reportedly did a hefty number at the box office, but they would never tell me what it was. Then there is my personal favorite that I never saw in it's entirety called *The 30 Foot Bride of Candy Rock*. Hey, don't laugh, I wrote all the dialogue for *The Incredible Two-Headed Transplant*, that obviously forgettable epic that set the all-time record as the most money-making second feature in drive-in movie theater history produced by **American International Pictures**, so there. I'd push for a re-release but ghost writers don't get residuals.

Tellya what I'm gonna do. I'm going to lift some verbiage from Milt's Celebration of Life program that was shared by family and friends at Milt's internment on August 15, 2000. The tribute is from the pen and heart of **Ray Hoese**, who, like I, can proudly proclaim for a lifetime to be one of Milt's favorite protégés. You could ask Judy.

"In 1924, when Milt was 2, his family was chased from Poland by anti-Semitic forces. Milt returned the favor (after growing up in the Bronx) as a Chief Navigator in the US Air Force, leading his squadron of B-17's in 25 sorties over France and Germany. Serving in England and France, his fluency in French was established, as well as his love of Europe.

Milt is a graduate of C.C.N.Y. as well as the prestigious writing program at the University of Iowa. He later moved to Los Angeles where his skill and talent were quickly recognized and put to work. His creativity knew no bounds. Starting in the early days of television, he never looked back, creating an incredible body of work. As a result, Milt's influence can be found in every facet and corner of media, from the biggest names in movies, (**Arnold Schwarzenegger** would insist upon getting in his two cents worth of praise if he were here, I'm sure - JM) television and radio, to the music industry, books, magazines, comics and even the Internet. He wrote for hundreds of different television shows and specials, countless movie polishes, authored 14 published books, ghost authored at least that many more as well as dozens of short stories. Just three short weeks ago (before his death from cancer - JM) he was still working on four different projects.

Some knew him for his comic genius; some knew him as a brilliant writer of mystery and fiction; some knew him as the ever-wise, ever-patient father, and loving husband. He was known for his writing classes from USC and UCLA, to the Valley's Every Woman's Village. Most participants became students for life - calling Milt for advice and help throughout their careers and lives. This includes top network executives and some of the most successful people in show business. Milt's extended family included just about everyone who ever spent more than five minutes with him - doctors, waiters, billionaires, jockeys, musicians, politicians, printers, lawyers, plumbers, gamblers, Indian Chiefs, neighborhood kids, barbers and thoroughbred horses - as well as more comedians, actors, writers and directors than you could ever list. The word "friend" just doesn't come close to what Milt was and is to so many people. Look up "Mensch" in God's dictionary. You'll see that boyish grin Milt is famous for...."

Milt and I had only seven years together. I say "only" with the deepest sense of gratitude I can possibly muster, for no words in any language can adequately express how privileged I am for the fact that he made sure I knew that he enjoyed sharing so many of his soul's insights with me. Part of what I'm doing now is keeping a promise to share the benefits previously received. And as a final thought, I'll take quality over quantity any day.

Chapter 7.
Hollywood Spotlight on John Marc Gentri

They say that anyone who has one truly good friend in life is rich. By that criteria, I'm Confessing to being a Jillionaire. See, I've got brothers named Joseph, Eddie, Danny, Forrest, Nonnie, Sam and Clay. Now meet Johnny, my twin.

It was a case of love at first sight, pure and simple. Well, it was certainly pure. Simple needs a bit of an explanation. I'm building up to describing the moment I first met **John Marc Gentri**.

Our first meeting occurred while I was giving him a haircut. We had a marvelous, highly personal and deeply intimate conversation. The subjects we discussed, especially the frankness, were preceded by a bond of friendship that occurred unobserved, seemingly mystically or perhaps as though on another level of existence that is not explainable by my five common human senses any better than as described here.

That initial meeting was one of a very few incidents I've ever experienced where two men are introduced, they exchange some seemingly insignificant words, and a friendship almost instantly evolves, bringing into being a relationship that is best described as Brotherhood. That was the case of Johnny and me, pure and simple. Now you Capish?

In that first conversation I learned that Johnny earned his BS degree in Communications at New York's Fordham University and completed his graduate work in Southern California at Loyola U., that picturesque haven near the Pacific Ocean. Johnny even taught there, but only for a short while.

During his Hollywood career - the only career he ever wanted - he from time to time wore the hat of producer, director, actor, stand-up comic, entertainer and certainly not least, writer. As is common in Hollywood, Johnny often wore more than one hat at a time, though he "...never pumped gas...."

I also learned that John was the father of five (5!) kids (at the time there was 10 year old Maria; John - 9; Pina - 8; Lisa - 6; and not quite a baby anymore, Christopher - 5) and that their mother, Catherine, was no longer alive. Before too many sad feelings could settle in, Johnny said he had recently married a lovely lady named Joanie. (They would have two children together, Joseph and David. I learned a short time later that Joanie was, just a few years before, runner-up to Miss Montana.) Since this story is many years old, I can say that my initial feelings are absolutely confirmed as our friendship/kinship has proved to be a wonderful example of eternal love, even surviving death.

Continuing to focus on our initial conversation, Johnny related that he was not committed to any particular aspect of the entertainment field, though he did say that he got his biggest thrills from his writing and then acting out his own material. He also said that his greatest concern was to "…provide appropriately…" for his family. Seems like the old Feast 'n Famine routine had intruded too much into the life of the Gentri household.

He inquired about my dreams and goals, thinking they were all related to the hair business, for he had come to me that day because he was referred for a haircut by one of my favorite clients and Johnny's fellow actor, **Vic Morrow**. I remember surprising John, and especially myself, by admitting to him that cutting hair was originally only intended to provide a financial stepping-stone through college.

I went on to relate that my high school English teacher and college English prof had both strongly urged me to become a professional writer. I also mentioned that my college Dean of Men confirmed through special testing that my interest in the literary/entertainment world was "off the charts," whereas my attraction to the conservative business world with subjects like accounting and economics was notably lacking. I capped my comments by stating that I indeed intended to write professionally.

When Johnny asked if I'd ever attempted to write for movies or TV, I replied that I had no idea how to implement Step One. He piqued my curiosity when he promised to get back to me on that. Of course, I'd heard THAT one before.

A few days later he called and invited me to his home for a writing session. That was when I met Joanie and the kids for the first time. As is not often the case, my love for Joanie was also instant and as though she were my sister. Even the kids were all so familiar. Spooky, bordering on deja vu, but in a very pleasant, non-threatening way; a true enigma at the time.

Johnny and I settled into his writing nook, consisting of a small desk in a corner of the dining room. He said he was working on an assignment to write 20 questions and answers for *Hollywood Squares*.

"Y'mean all those questions 'n answers are written, that they're not spontaneous?" I asked, totally surprised.

"Everything on TV is written. No exceptions," he stated. "Sponsors don't like surprises."

Johnny sat down at the typewriter and with his two index fingers, he staccato-blurted out "Fade in:" in the upper left-hand corner of a blank piece of paper. I was soon to learn that he always typed, like a blur, with those two fingers.

"Okay. Gimmie a good question for the show," he said with fingers poised above the keyboard. Like magic, I gave him a good question. We both laughed. And like magic, he spoke and rat-a-tat-tatted the answer on the paper. We laughed some more.

"Okay. Your turn for a good question," I said. He spoke and rat-a-tat-tatted the question on paper. We laughed again. As I spoke the answer, he did the rat thing on the keyboard. More laughter.

Joanie peaked her smiling face into the room from the kitchen. "Sounds like I got two more kids in here!" she said pleasantly, enthusiastically. That little scene was to repeat itself countless times over the ensuing years.

Yep, that's how it started, how it developed our oft repeated pattern of working together.

Squares liked our work and asked for twenty more. What a pip!

One of my hair clients was **Paul Leavitt,** also a good, personal friend, who introduced me to deep sea fishing in the Pacific Ocean. Paul had been with me from my first year working for Cosmo's and was the producer of the TV show, *Tarzan.*

"If I write a script for *Tarzan*, would you read it?"

"You're a writer? Since when?" Paul said with eyes bugging out of his head.

"Since fourth grade. Do you mind if I write with a partner?"

"Write with King Kong if you want. A writer!"

Two weeks later I handed Paul our script. Later in the day, he called. He thought it was an elaborate joke that his assistant, Jerry, and I had cooked up. Tarzan already had a very similar story, produced and in the can, and even the guest star's character name was identical. Paul confided to me that *Tarzan* was folding, "Or you guys would have the next assignment."

A short time later, Johnny was hired to produce and write a TV show called *Boutique*, a TV talk show that focused on the fashion industry. We wrote the pilot script together. It was the first show to call itself a "TV Magazine." Johnny hired me as his co-writer. That caused me to quit my regular job with Sam Russo so I could work at the CBS offices on La Brea Avenue, right next door to **Pink's Hotdogs**. I also arranged to work at a place called Archie's where I could cut hair part-time.

Before the first show was produced, our intended star, **Pat Harrington**, opted out to be the new host of a popular national game show, so Johnny took over as Star of *Boutique* with a lady Co-Star named **Susan Brown**. Between producing and starring, there was hardly any time left to write, so I became the guy at the typewriter. While Johnny used two fingers to type, I used all of mine, if ever so slowly. T – H – E… Hey, I'd a taken off my shoes if….

I wrote the first 58 shows. Several shows are worthy of mention, so I'll save all that for another day.

There's bunches more to tell about m'bro, Johnny Gentri, and our writing experiences together. Oodles more.

I'll get back to you on that.

Chapter 8.
A Hollywood Hero

I Confess! EVERYBODY has a story to tell. I heard the following tale long ago. This event happened years before I heard about it when a truly dark day was... aw, shucks, I don't wanna give it away. This is EASILY one of my all-time favorite stories wherein I played no role except to pass it on to you. And by the way, I could start every column off by saying, "And now Ladies 'n Gentlemen, one of my favorite stories..." or words to that effect. In any case, Enjoy!

Another of the many names for Hollywood is Storyland Heaven. The town is the world's magnet for dreamers who are attracted by their hope of becoming part of a greater story. And y'know what? For some, the relatively few, their dream comes true; they become part of an unimagined particular, for what they realize is usually not quite what they had in mind, but it most definitely is a dream that could only come true in Hollywood.

Say hello to Ritchie. He's 13 years old as his story unfolds. His dad died a while back, rather mysteriously, leaving an omnipresent cloud on Ritchie's consciousness.

Ritchie's Mom had to get a job. Given that Mom hadn't worked since before Ritchie was born, she found herself highly unqualified for everything. The best job she could get hardly paid the bills.

Ritchie started selling papers on Hollywood Boulevard. He was usually able to sell his load so he could contribute his meager take to his Mom. Ritchie would patrol the famous boulevard where, over time, the intersection of Highland and Hollywood became the center of his "route."

Not too far off that corner was **Patsy D'Amore's Villa Capri,** the famous, fabulous and popular nightspot that was frequented by Hollywood Royalty. Perhaps its most prominent celebrity patron was **Frank Sinatra**. Rumor was that Sinatra owned "a piece a the joint," as one wag put it. (Recently, **Filomena D'Amore**, Patsy's daughter, confirmed to me that Patsy and Frank were indeed partners.)

In more than a year of hawking papers, Ritchie had never even seen Sinatra. Maybe the Sinatra story was more Hollywood Bull, Ritchie thought. That's the way it goes in Hollywood, oftentimes. Kinda like the story of **Marilyn Monroe** sipping a chocolate soda at **Schwab's.** Nobody Ritchie knew ever saw Marilyn Monroe in Schwab's, let alone drinking a chocolate soda.

Whatever, this evening Frank and Marilyn were not part of Ritchie's thoughts. Tonight his mind was troubled far more than usual. Ritchie's Mom had lost her job. She'd get another one right away, she had assured Ritchie, but right now they were $10 short of paying the rent, due tonight, and flat out of money for food. Some graham crackers and a mostly spent jar of peanut butter were the bounty Ritchie saw in the cupboard this morning. And wouldn't you know it, Ritchie still had a fist-full of papers t'night, with the clock on the corner showing 7:34 p.m., a half hour past his "head for home" time.

The unsold papers represented most of Ritchie's take. Money already collected was for buying his load of papers tomorrow. If these didn't sell, what would he and Mom eat tonight, Ritchie wondered. If they dared use the money in his pocket, he would have no ability to buy papers tomorrow. As it was, he'd probably cut school again, get a head start on tomorrow evening, but he'd only pick up an hour, not a big enough edge at all, but....

People were scarce tonight, Ritchie noted. Then he realized he felt that peculiar heaviness in the middle of his chest. Shifting focus to his forehead, Ritchie became conscious of his frown. That, his Mom had helped him understand, was his body letting him and the whole world know that he was worried. "Gotta sell those papers, but first take a breath; unwrinkle...."

Ritchie found himself heading west toward Highland Boulevard. A couple stopped him, bought a paper. Waited for change. No tip. That's the way it goes, sometimes.

He crossed Highland, turned north, but suddenly the thought occurred to him that he was on the wrong side of the street if he wanted to head home to Burbank. A man stopped him, took a paper; gave him a quarter. "Keep it," he said.

"Thanks, Mister," Ritchie said, and under his breath, "You should only know how much I mean it."

A bit further up, a black limo pulled to the curb, let out three men. Ritchie started walking toward them.

"Hey kid. Kinda late to be selling papers, ain't it?" the man in the hat said.

"Little bit, maybe, " Ritchie heard himself answer.

"How many y'got left?"

"Six...eight...um…" Ritchie said, wondering if the twilight was playing tricks with his focus.

"Gimmie 'em. I'm meeting a bunch of people inside who love t'read."

"I was sure I was dreaming," Ritchie reported later. "I don't have that kind of luck."

"Keep the change," the man said, slapping a bill into Ritchie's hand.

With a quick glance at the bill he saw a five and locking in on the man's blue eyes, Ritchie stammered, "Gee, thanks Mister Sinatra."

"Oh Ritchie!" his Mom exclaimed as he related the story to her. "But, you sure it was Frank Sinatra?"

"Musta been, Ma," Ritchie said with plenty of sparkle in his eyes. "Who else would give me a fifty dollar bill?"

I'll bet I have at least a million dreamy Hollywood stories. Be really tough to top this one, though.

If the above story didn't wet your hanky, check yer pulse. After the column appeared in the newspaper, people wanted to know more of the adult Ritchie. He became the youngest ever Senior VP of a high ranking Fortune 500 company, then he broke away and established his own business. Y'knew it hadda be something like that, right?

Chapter 9.
Schwab's Pharmacy; Hollywood's Hangout

Right now let's take another trip in my fabulous TimeMachine and visit **Schwab's Pharmacy** *where we meet Gorgeous Jane, Dirty Harry, The Sucker-Slurper, Vic d'Cook and Nick d'Coach.*

For Movie Buffs who followed the happenings in and about Hollywood from the 1930s through the early 80s, one of the places that attracted a major degree of attention was **Schwab's Pharmacy**. Actually, there were three locations that operated simultaneously under the name of **Schwab's** during the '50s and '60s. The pharmacy of primary interest for experienced movie 'n TV buffs was located at 8000 Sunset Blvd., at the corner of Crescent Heights Blvd., the official beginning of the famous Sunset Strip.

Cosmo's Hairstyling Salon, where I started my hair career and twelve years later became the owner, was just about 40 paces around the corner at 1454 N. Crescent Heights Boulevard.

Nightclubs including **Gazzari's, Whisky-a-Go-Go** and **Sneaky Pete's** were just a few blocks West. (Note: Across Sunset Blvd. and heading North, Crescent Heights becomes Laurel Canyon Blvd., the main artery through the Santa Monica Mountain Range that leads into the city of Sherman Oaks in the San Fernando Valley.)

Schwab's was not like any other drugstore, anywhere, then or now. On any given day there could be any number of Hollywood's most recognizable stars and starlets milling around, shopping or grabbing a bite to eat. Producers, directors, grips, gophers, really an amalgam of industry people would be sitting around, some eating, some sipping coffee, tea or soda. Actually, most were just really hanging out, seeing and being seen, often scrounging around - yesterday's words for "networking" - looking for their next movie or TV gig.

Sidney Skolsky, the famous columnist for *Photoplay*, the number one entertainment magazine at the time, wrote his by-line under the heading, *From a Stool in Schwab's*. Apropos of Hollywood, there seem to be more stories about Sidney than the squared number of the many columns he wrote. Reportedly, if Sidney said something positive about an actor or actress in his column, that person got calls for work. Conversely, if his commentary was on the negative side; well, Podunk, Idaho was said to offer a more receptive clime.

Clint Eastwood was a fixture in the early sixties long before he gave life to Dirty Harry. He was the first Hollywood notable Sidney introduced me to. **Telly Savalas** was a fixture almost daily, even carrying over into the seventies when *Kojak* ruled TV Land. **Vic Taybak** (star of the TV show, *Alice*) sat in the same booth each visit like he owned it. **Nick Colasanto** (his last role was "Coach," the original bartender of *Cheers* fame) walked around the place like a Buck General at the Officers Club.

One day, arriving for lunch, Sidney Skolsky beckoned me to his table. I didn't notice the blond sitting across from him until he said, "Joey, say hello to **Jane Mansfield**." I checked my pulse. Sure, it was racing. Good buddies **Alan Garfield, Greg Lewis**; um, better stop here, or use this to start a book. Maybe we can do more another time.

Hey, care to take a virtual tour? Just squint and focus, it's a hoot unless too much energy is used. That's it, just walk through the front door....

A pathway is created by an eight foot long enclosed glass display case forming the right-hand border. To the left are wire display racks of greeting cards, postcards and various items. Even a six-sided cylindrical rack displaying authentic Hollywood sunglasses. If you've forgotten yours, grab a pair. Never let it be said that you went to Schwab's without shades. You'd kill all chance of getting discovered, unless they were looking for background extras for *Grand Old Oprey*.

Turning right at the end of the glass case, an adjoining display case continues for perhaps 20 feet with a cash register at midpoint. Across from the end of the case to the left is the bottom L of a soda fountain bar with about 25 stools. Until 1965 they were round and back-less. Remodeling brought overstuffed seats with backs. Really nice. Just try to find a readily available stool any time of day. The good news? They turned over faster than might be expected. Waitresses need their tips, y'know, and all the girls could boast many years on the job. Oh yes, that's the very same counter where Lana Turner was discovered, "sipping on a chocolate soda," or so the story goes. True? Who cares, it still gives the buffs goose-bumps.

Coming up past the cashier's counter is the wide arched entry to the dining room. Standing in the entry awaiting booths we find a group of maybe 20 to 40 people, time of day notwithstanding. The wait, surprisingly, is not unbearable. Don't stare, now, and for the love-a-Mike, don't yelp. It's what's-his-name all right, his name'll come in a minute.

Glancing over the lunch menu we see a feature called simply, Chinese Dinner, including fried rice or steamed, it says. The word is that this dish in particular beats the heck out of Benihana's, Hung Chow's or any other restaurant serving food of the Orient.

The taste of the fresh and generous helping of meat-loaf with sliced mushrooms in brown gravy exceeds the memory of grandma's. Yes, that's crazy. But True!

Burgers? Better than your own back yard, most say. And maybe bigger. Unbelievable? Yep, but a new believer often acts as though the experience was just this side of ecstasy.

When **Leon Schwab**, the managing partner of the four Schwab brothers who owned and operated the famous drugstore was asked the secret of the delicious food, he credited the more than 30 year reign of Tony, the cook, eh, chef.

Stories abound that Leon Schwab had an unwritten policy that no actor (or for that matter, no serious entertainment industry person) would ever leave Schwab's premises hungry, even if the tab had to be carried over an extended period of time.

"As a matter of fact," Leon related on condition that the subject not be approached again, "in all the years of helping people, we never lost a dime. Even those who went back home sent us a check; some, many years later, and some others, for a lot more than they owed."

He couldn't help but say it like a proud uncle.

Schwab's is gone now, bulldozed as a small crowd of people cried. Me, too. In it's place is an ominous looking structure about four stories high. The new building was supposed to be 27 stories, but really, the tale is not worth the ink.

Where is the new Hollywood Hangout? No such animal. Gazzari's, Sneaky Pete's, Sidney, Leon and the fabulous Schwab's, famous for a half century, all had their run. I'm so privileged to have caught so much of the ride.

✷✷✷

Chapter 10.
Star Search

That was fun, so why get off now? The above column and the next were not written in sequence, but they fit together nicely. Coming up are Bits 'n Pieces along the terrain known as The Sunset Strip in Forever Fabulous Hollywood. Again, meet **Telly Savalas**, *learn more about my dear friend and also a guy who could really tickle the ivories, plus cameos by some all-time favorite friends.*

People all over the country talk about all the fun that can be experienced on an Easter Egg Hunt. In certain sections of the mid-west, stories abound regarding the taking of initiates on a Snipe Hunt. But maybe the biggest fantasy hunt of them all is going to Hollywood on a Star Hunt.

"Oh there's What's-Her-Name," or "Isn't that Who's-It over there," is often heard spoken rather breathlessly by star-seeking men and women alike. Some are visitors to the city, while others are long term residents. Those who have a case of Star Fever usually have it chronically; and for such condition, there is no cure.

Way back about the time I went to work for Cosmo, I was driving down Hollywood Boulevard one day when a traffic light turned red, so I stopped. Crossing left to right in the crosswalk in front of me was **Joe E. Brown**. I'm aware that I stared, not sure if he was a look-alike or the real item. Gave me that flat-hand fan-wave and the big open mouth. Yep, it was him, all right. Still makes me laugh thirty-something years later.

Telly Savalas and my dad were two not-so-young hopefuls who became friends shortly after each arrived in Hollywood. Telly's mom was Sicilian, his dad Greek. Sicily was heavily influenced by Greek culture going back thousands of years and was an official part of Greece for one 300 year stretch, hence the many bonds and similarities between the two peoples, continuing on to descendants here in America. Our families celebrated holidays, even casual weekends, together. Then Telly became *Kojak*. What a thrill for all of us, just like a cousin hit it big.

One day I was approaching Schwab's at lunch-time and Telly was walking toward me from Schwab's parking lot. I stuck out my hand with a "Hi Telly," only to have him slap my hand away and give me a bear hug. "What's the matter," he said in mock anger with his patented grin in place. "I don't see you for a couple of months and you get formal on me?" That was Telly; as his star got bigger and brighter, his friendly, down-to-earth persona became more obvious.

By the way, in case you don't know. On the set one day, a friend attempted a practical joke by putting a sucker in Telly's jacket pocket, hoping to break his concentration and pull a "Gotcha" on him. Telly went with the flow and *Kojak* had a distinctive trademark.

One of the businesses between Cosmo's and Schwab's was a bar called **Sherry's**. A horseshoe shaped bar, seating maybe 25 people, dominated the place. A few tables and a baby-grand piano-bar, seating maybe 10 people, occupied the balance of the rectangular room.

One evening after work, co-worker **Sam Keston** asked me to have "a bit of a taste" with him. Sam, a Cockney who lived in the East End of London most of his life, was at the time seventy-something. He was also the man who taught me the intricacies of the Sicilian Razor Cut. (Another story; another time.) Sam also taught me to drink Haig & Haig Scotch, neat.

Shortly after Sam and I took stools at the main bar, a black man about my height but definitely older and stockier than me entered. He wore a pleasant expression as he sat on the stool next to me. The man seemed so friendly that the thought crossed my mind that perhaps we had met, but as we casually greeted each other, I realized he was a stranger. Without knowing what we were drinking, he ordered a Haig & Haig, neat, with the comment, one of Sam's pet axioms, that silly people put ice in good scotch and thereby blow 12 years of aged perfection. Neither Sam nor I said a word, but Sam had a smile from ear to ear.

After a couple of sips, the stranger got up and walked over to the piano and seemed to stare at the keyboard.

"Play it if you wish," said my friend and client **Linda**, the beautiful bartender with long, flowing blonde hair who sent me business like she was getting a commission.

He sat and started to play, moaning softly occasionally, mesmerizing the small group of people in the place, for he was obviously an accomplished pianist. When he finished, the small crowd applauded exuberantly, me especially.

As he returned to his stool, I said, "Hey, you play just like **Errol Garner**!" Yep, that's who he was, as everybody knew but me. At least I gave 'em all a good laugh.

Schwab's, Cosmo's (called Little Joe's the last seven years of its existence), Sherry's; all gone now for many years. We visited LA this past summer. Bumped into **Mel Gibson** at a place called the Hamburger Hamlet on South Beverly Drive. See, the stars still shine their magic in Hollywood. And nobody asked, "Who dat?"

I Confess that I am not presenting these columns in the exact order written and I am not placing them in chronological order, either. I started out in the 'as-written' order, then I saw fit to shuffle them a bit for your added enjoyment.

Come on a ride down fabled Hollywood Boulevard, circa 1959, and then be transported to 1968 where you will find yourself at an extravagant Hollywood First Night Premiere.

While Hollywood Boulevard has experienced some cosmetic relief lately, I doubt it could ever live up to the glitzy expectations of movie buffs who make their first trek to GlamourPuss, USA. And just to be extra-clear and accurate, I Confess that I Love Hollywood!... and I'll take it without changing a thing.

Wear yer shades, Dude.

Chapter 11.
"I'm a Bagel on a Plate Full of Onion Rolls!"

I clearly remember the day after my mother, sister and I flew to Los Angeles to join my father to start our new life in Tinseltown. That morning, Dad took us on our first drive east to west along Hollywood Boulevard.

I wanted to cry.

Hollywood Boulevard looked like the main street in a town called Slumville. The pedestrians looked raggedy; homeless. Young people were dressed like it was Halloween. Seemingly every female was caked with makeup, but none achieved glamorous, at least not in my book. I was ready to check with Continental for the next flight back. Well, that's pushing it, but "shocked" is also an understatement.

On the plus side, I marveled at all the famous movie theaters in such close proximity. I recall **The Vine Street Theater** and just about a block to the west was **The Pacific**. I especially gawked at **The Egyptian**, looking a bit the worse for wear in stark daylight.

A block west and across the street was the **El Capitan**, made even more famous as the set for the extremely popular 50s TV show, *This Is Your Life* starring **Ralph Edwards.**

Then proceeding another short block on the north side was the most famous of all, **Grauman's Chinese Theater**, (now the **Mann Chinese Theater**) where Stars of the highest magnitude (like **Marilyn Monroe, Clark Gable, Errol Flynn** and OH SO MANY MORE) placed their hands and/or feet in wet cement to be forever memorialized.

I feared my family arrived in Hollywood a bit late, as the site was not the Glitter Gulch I had envisioned; but alas, I figured wrong. The rather rickety boulevard still had plenty of punch and sting, continuing on to this day.

The first time I went to **Grauman's Chinese** was to see *West Side Story* during its premier week. I saw the movie again at a neighborhood theater, but seeing it at Grauman's was completely different, a far more dramatic and exciting experience. The audience at Grauman's was more "into it," applauding everything, just like a stage show, including opening and closing credits.

I didn't get to **The Egyptian** until several years later, but that time was an event for the ages. Among my hair clients was adult-life-long good buddy Alan Zimmelman. Alan, in his twenties, was probably the youngest general manager of a retirement home in history. AZ and I still enjoy sharing time and smiles, but 3,000 miles and a three-hour time difference makes getting together a challenge.

Another client whose friendship I thoroughly enjoyed was an "older" buddy, **Cameron Meiklejohn**. Cam was the long-time manager of the Egyptian Theater. Early in 1968, Cam hit the magic "forced to retire age of 65." It all had something to do with his insurability according to laws of the time, but excellent, dedicated professionals were even then near impossible to replace. After a brief retirement, the theater brought him back, putting the hop back in his step, as I recall him saying.

Cam was preparing for a major movie event, he excitedly related as I finished his haircut that day. He was given an open-end budget and asked to pull out all the stops to orchestrate an extravagant movie premier "like in the good 'ole days, 'n really make eyes pop."

I couldn't help but get excited with him. "That'll be something to see, I'm sure. Will it be on TV?" I asked as Cam was paying his bill.

"I'll go you one better. How would you like to come as an invited guest?"

As I was thanking Cam, saying I'd love to, AZ was my next appointment. Introductions took place. My exciting invitation expanded to four people.

"And I'll make sure all four of you are on the VIP List. You'll all be treated like Hollywood Stars!" Cam said with his ear-to-ear smile.

On Thursday evening, September 19, research assures me, AZ and I with two lovely ladies pulled up to the Egyptian Theater as searchlights painted Hollywood's sky.

Our car was taken by an attendant as fans screamed for our autographs, a few unaffected enough to wonder who the heck we were as we strolled into the theater on the VIP Red Carpet.

Inside, bright-n-snappy-uniformed ushers were standing like Oscars every 10 feet down all the aisles. Our tickets and we were passed from one to another until we reached our seats just a few rows, front 'n center, from the screen.

The place was abuzz as the cast and stars of the movie were reportedly in the audience. Seemed like everybody seated around us were recognizable VIPs. We acted like we belonged there, smiling and waving to all.

Finally, the house lights dimmed, the overture blared and the screen lit up. It was time to see what I still consider to be the single greatest performance ever on the Silver Screen, **Barbra Streisand's** *Funny Girl*. She did it all and established her star in Hollywood's section of Heaven forever!

What a movie! What a night! Every time I think about it I get pumped all over again. Next visit to New York, I wanna go visit Henry Street for Lox, Bagel 'n Cream-Cheeze. And oh man, that street better be there, too.

And the whole bowl of pastafazool was only possible on tainted but forever fabled Hollywood Boulevard.

The title of the above column is a self-effacing, tongue-in-cheek quote from Barbra in response to all the beautiful people in the cast, especially co-star **Omar Sharif**. *In all movies before and since, Streisand's performance in Funny Girl is arguably the best display of diverse talent by a Star, EVER. She can dance, sing, deliver a joke, be the straight-man, act and oh man, she can have you laughing then WHAM!, yer cryin' like a baby.*

Wow Barbara, you sure got it! You done Fanny proud, too, very proud, I'm sure.

I gotta Confess, I really love that Barbra and yes, I also love **Fanny Brice**, *who graced my living room on the radio as* **Baby Snooks** *when I was just a kid.*

Chapter 12.
Sam Keston; Better than an Oxford Education

Blimey, y'couldn't be there but this is the next best faschtookena thing! To say that Sam Keston is easily in the upper echelon of my favorite people – lifetime – is an understatement, as will be seen here. Samula appears in several columns throughout, but here he is definitely in the Spotlight... and at Center Stage.

Sam Keston is in the "Upper One Percent" of all people I ever met. He worked in the booth next to me during the first years of my professional life at **Cosmo's**. Sam was a Cockney from the East End of London and had an accent so thick that at times I thought he was speaking another language. Turned out that sometimes he was, for he would often mix Yiddish with English. *Oy vey!*

Sam helped increase my vocabulary, teaching me the proper use of many neat words, like *gonif, shlep, shicksa, goyum, shagutz, mashugena, goye shekop* and maybe best of all, how to blame everything on *Moishe Pippic*. Spelling, he didn't teach.

Sam's wonderful sense of humor led him to be always ready with quip or even a joke for many of life's situations. He'd say, "That reminds me, there was a bloke who..." and break into what I discovered to be a stock story with a nifty punch-line. I often found myself laughing more at the way he told a tale than at the content. Kinda like **Buddy Hackett**, come to think of it.

A few doors north of Cosmo's was a bar called **Sherry's**, where Sam tutored me in the fine art of sipping scotch. I still "bloody it up" with ice instead of sipping it "neat" per Sam's instructions, but every time I lift a glass, (I'm not a big drinker - never was) I automatically think of and salute my landsman, Sam Keston. *Lock Heim!* (Spelling? Sure, fix it.)

When Cosmo hired me, I was twenty-two. Sam was either in his late sixties or early seventies, I never actually asked. Whatever his age, Sam's infectious sense of humor and lively disposition caused people to like him, me especially.

Cosmo's salon was truly the forerunner for giving distinctive men's haircuts. Scissors and comb were the tools of choice with the electric clipper used mainly to cut the neckline taper. Even before going to Cosmo's, I preferred to use my scissors to create a convex finish at a man's neckline rather than the concave, typical-barber-type taper. I thought my look was more natural; softer. I also preferred to forego the shave around the ears which I felt added to the softer, more natural look.

One day back then I was giving a haircut to a man whose hair had deep waves. If wavy hair is cut on the upturn, the hair will tend to flip forward. Sometimes, cutting the waves on the downturn will cause the hair to be either too short or too long.

Sam saw me struggling as he watched through the large mirror on the wall opposite our three-sided haircutting booths. He came around the partition and asked if he could "show me a thing or two." I had no idea what he had in mind, but said "Sure."

After wetting the man's hair, Sam started using his straight razor and comb to cut the hair! I almost shouted in surprise, wondering if Sam had gone completely *mashugena*. I had to tell myself that Sam would not be shaving my client's head, but for those first few terrifying moments, I thought I might not stay conscious.

To my utter relief, Sam seemed to be removing very little hair. After several strokes, the hair was lying neatly (magically, I thought) into place with waves undulating smoothly.

The man left happy. He even gave both of us a nice tip.

"What did you just do? At first I thought you were shaving his head and we were going to be in for a fight!"

Sam laughed as he explained technique I could not see by watching without an explanation. I was thoroughly fascinated.

"So, I guess you call that an English Razor Cut?"

"Actually, it's a Sicilian Razor Cut. Y'see, years ago some bloke came to London from Sicily, worked with us several years. He taught me, now I've taught you; so we've gone full circle."

Sometime later, working on a new client with wavy hair very similar to **Caesar Romero's**, I gave him a full Sicilian Razor Cut. When I finished, the man walked to the front of the salon to pay. Everyone stopped to look. At just the right moment, Sam spoke up loud and clear.

"Now you've gone and done it, you've beat the master!"

That was Sam, never one to miss a quip, but I've never had a better compliment and never will, I'm sure. No bloke can ever top Sam Keston in my mind, one of the most influential people I've ever been blessed to know.

Good *yuntif*, folks!

I Confess; I really miss Sam and honestly, I could never get my fill if we were given another hundred years together.

Just below is the short version of a column I never got around to writing. I love sneak previews, don't you? This one's fer you, Bud!

✦✦✦

One afternoon sometime in 1962, I believe, there was a commotion at the front desk of Cosmo's. I asked Sam Keston about the ruckus.

*"Aha! That hooligan **Mickey Cohen** just came in again with a couple-a-blokes," Sam said with more than a bit of annoyance in his voice and a scrunched nose.*

As I had just finished a haircut, I started to walk my client up to the front, not my usual habit. Sam reached out and gently grabbed my arm. "Don't mix with that kind. They won't be right with you. You could get hurt when it's not your time." I thanked Sam, told him I'm just going to collect my tip, another non-habit.

Up at the front desk, Cosmo introduced me to Mickey Cohen, the reputed gangster who, to my surprise, was only an inch or so taller than me. He was pleasant with a slight smile on his face. Like other men with rogue reputations I had met, he didn't look menacing, nor did he look like a killer; but then, I had known The Old Man back home and he looked like anybody's grandfather, not the type who would have a man killed for a perceived act, or omission, amounting to disrespect.

Somebody mentioned Cleveland. "Is somebody from Cleveland?" I asked no one in particular.

"I'm from Cleveland," said one the two men with Cohen, who Cosmo identified as "Ritchie."

"What part of Cleveland?" I asked as we shook hands.

"Collinwood." His answer surprised me.

"I grew up in Collinwood. I knew two brothers starting from Brett Elementary School, Tony and Michael, with your last name."

"Sounds like my nephews," Ritchie said with a slight smile.

"Might you know my uncle? Everybody calls him Unka Louie"

Ritchie turned to the other associate. "Hey Santino, this kid is Unka Louie's nephew."

Santino was also from Cleveland, from Little Italy.

After some small talk, I prepared Ritchie for a haircut while Santino stayed with Cohen as 'the Boss' was getting his hair cut in Nunzio's chair at the front of the shop. As I started the haircut, Sam Keston went next door to Sherry's for a drink.

Later, Cohen and Santino were very complimentary, saying that Ritchie's wavy hair looked so good, so natural and that it didn't look like a fresh haircut. Cohen told Santino to let me cut his hair, that he and Ritchie would wait for him at Schwab's. As I started Santino's haircut, Sam went back to Sherry's for another drink. That was the first of the many haircuts I would give to Ritchie and Santino.

Maybe a year later, I was on my first trip to Cleveland since moving to California. It was around the 15th of August. I took my wife to Little Italy for the Feast of the Assumption where they blocked off the streets, even Mayfield Road, and the whole town celebrated like in the Old Country. I bumped into several people I otherwise might not have seen. I was shocked that most everyone seemed to know that I was giving haircuts to Hollywood celebrities "...out on the coast."

Walking down the middle of Mayfield Road, I heard someone shout, "Hey Joey." God only knows how many guys in Little Italy are named Joe, but I turned to the direction of the voice mainly for the heck of it and only slightly curious.

Up on a balcony was my friend Santino who was indeed calling out to me! It was a pleasant double surprise.

Santino invited us to join him for dinner the following Thursday night, the one night we had an open date. The next day, I got a call from Unka Louie.

I told Unka Louie my visit was going great, that I was seeing a lot more relatives and friends than anticipated. I asked if we were still on for the family dinner that evening as I was afraid he was calling to cancel.

"I'm not sure yet, but you gotta do something for me. Cancel your date with Santino on Thursday and don't make another one. I can't explain right now."

I never in my life refused to do something my Uncle asked of me, (often without knowing 'why') though I had a real hassle coming up with a story for Santino that was not pure BS. Finally, a solution occurred to me that seemed to fit best. I changed my return flight to Thursday afternoon, saying Cosmo phoned and said he had a gang of people who wanted to get in for a haircut that weekend.

Get this. After talking to Santino, I called Cosmo and asked him to book me for Friday and Saturday, as I was coming home early. I was shocked when Cosmo told me he already had the two days almost sold out and was going to call me! Wow, the way the cards fall sometime, huh? So the story I gave Santino was not so much BS after all.

Maybe a year later my Uncle came out to California on business. We had a wonderful dinner together, where he again apologized for missing the family dinner in Cleveland. I asked him about the incident with Santino and asked him if he and Santino were friends.

"I've known Santino all my life, Ritchie too, but friendship's got nothing to do with it. At the time, there was a contract out on 'Tino and I didn't want you there when the roof caved in."

So how about that, Sam Keston was absolutely right on! Thank you, Sam, for your efforts to protect me. And of course, thanx t'my Unka Louie.

On a final note, Ritchie and Santino did not live long lives. In maybe another year, both were dead. I fondly remember them as two great guys who were always very good to me.

Everything you can possibly imagine can be found in abundance in the Hollywood I lived in and love.

★★★

Chapter 13.
A Tale Of Two Puppies

This next story will stick to yer ribs, especially if you're a Puppy Person, like Ginny 'n me. Hey, Dogs are people too, y'know.

For many of us there has been a person, or perhaps a few people, who seem to be on our life's periphery rather than occupying a more important role. By circumstances not always clear or easily definable, we rarely focused very much attention on these people. Sometimes we remember their names, sometimes not. Our main memory of them might center around a certain place or incident. The one fact that underlines the referenced situation properly is its indelible place in our memory.

One of the rules of life is that we cannot go back in time and change anything. On that theme, each of us could easily write a book, I'm sure, but usually the next best option for me is to share the memory. The story I'm about to relate took place during my first year or so while working at Cosmo's Hairstyling Salon, which marks the official beginning of my Hollywood – and adult - experience.

Cosmo's was one of a dozen businesses located in a crescent-shaped, one-story building. The stucco structure followed the curve of Crescent Heights Boulevard up to its North-to-East tip, blending into Sunset Boulevard, where in a separate building, **Schwab's Pharmacy** enjoyed its 50-year reign.

The northern-most business in the twelve-unit building was the bar called Sherry's, mentioned previously. Cosmo's was located in the middle of the building with **Zeidler and Zeidler**, a famous men's clothier, next door on the immediate south.

Two businesses north of Cosmo's was a small dress shop. The owner, apparently a sole proprietor, was a short and stout middle-aged lady with a thick European accent. Clearest recall is of a vivacious person who talked rather loudly and laughed with the staccato-likeness of a machine gun.

One morning during my first year working at Cosmo's, she and I happened to pull in and park next to each other. She got out of her car with her ever-present Shitzu pal and gave me a sunshine-bright smile while bidding me good-day. I smiled back a greeting, but my breath caught in my throat as I discovered the tattooed numbers on her forearm.

First looking down at her arm and then back up to me, her smile as bright as ever, she said "I wouldn't have them removed if they gave me my weight in gold, and that's a lot of gold." She laughed as though somebody else told the joke.

I'd like to think I had an appropriate response, but truth is, I couldn't have, for I don't believe I could come up with one now, though 30-some years have passed. She pleasantly went on to say that she was "just a girl" when she was taken, that "they battered my body, but not my spirit, damn them, and I originally lived to spite them, to spit in their eye!" She said it with gusto, her smile fading momentarily, and not very loud at all.

"But you know what, dah-link?" she continued, smile again intact, as she turned to catch up to her barking Shitzu who was at her shop door, dancing impatiently while wanting to enter.

"It's better to spend energy on love," she rather flipped over her shoulder. "Hate is a weapon of the devil."

Small wonder I remember the incident like it happened yesterday. And in a moment, as **Paul Harvey** might say, you'll know the r-r-rest of the story.

Three businesses south of Cosmo's on the other side of Zeidler's was an old-fashioned beauty parlor. No, it wasn't called Pin Curl Heaven, but the name would have been appropriate. And the smell of those perms, Whew!

The owner, Philip, was probably more flamboyant than most people can imagine. He had an English accent thicker than Sam Keston's, my Cockney friend who I worked beside at Cosmo's.

Philip's dog was what some people called a rag-tag poodle-mix, decidedly off-white, weighed maybe 18-20 pounds, and so help me, seemed to be cross-eyed. The dog accompanied Philip everywhere but inside Schwab's or other stores in our block, except for the dress shop. As a matter of fact, I often saw the poodle go along the back sidewalk alone to visit the Shitzu in the dress shop.

The first time I noticed the dog's visit, I mentioned it to Keston, who informed me that the two canines had "carried on like that for years."

One morning, Keston took me out the back door to tell me a joke. Peripherally, he and I saw the dress shop owner park and start to unlock the door to her store. About the time we were laughing at Keston's punch line, the poodle exited the beauty parlor and trotted up to her. He put his front paws on her upper leg, buried his head between his paws and gave out a low, continuous howl.

The lady started to cry, her left hand patting the poodle's head and her right hand attempting to stifle her sobs. Presently, Philip came looking for the dog and saw the scene at the dress shop door. He paused, looked our way and swallowed hard, then hurriedly completed the short journey to his howling poodle and the distraught lady.

"Can you believe it!" she kept saying loudly over and over through her sobs. "Can you believe it! Last night I lost my dah-link and this one knows he lost his girlfriend. But how? Can you believe it!"

When I returned to buy Cosmo's some 12 years after he gave me my first job, the dress shop and the beauty parlor had been replaced by other businesses. If I ever knew what happened to the lady or Philip, the information is lost in the mist of Time, but now you know why the keyhole's worth of their story is vividly and forever in my memory.

I Confess! I went to a pre-school dubbed Busy Bees, available only to kids who lived in the E. 200 Street Projects on the East Side of Cleveland. One afternoon we put on a show where I did a song 'n dance routine where the limerick – I think it was a limerick – ended with the line – I'm sure of the line – "...and if you want me to amuse you I will stand upon my head!" Applause, fade-out.

Then in kindergarten at Roosevelt Elementary School, we put on a play for the whole grade school called Little Black Sambo. In the story, I gotta give my shirt to the Tiger. The audience ROARED! Even the Tiger was laughing. I had that smelly makeup on my face, my arms and my hands, but somebody forgot my body. I finally had to tell the Tiger to give me the next line so the show could go on. I could hardly wait 'til I had to give up my pants, as there was no makeup below my waist, either.

I thought I was funny enough to join **Jimmy Durante***. Or* **Baby Snooks***.*

Chapter 14.
"Dat's Why D'Lady Wuzza Champ!"

(Part 1 of 2)

Come with me now and visit William H. Brett Elementary School in Collinwood, also on the east side of Cleveland, the school I started attending in the Second Grade. Meet Mrs. Tanno, my Grade 4A teacher. She was like another aunt, maybe even closer. Whatever I am, she was a Forman of the Foundation, for she was the teacher the whole gang loved and learned a thing or two from, including how to swing fer the fences.

The recent patriotic holidays of Memorial Day and Independence Day have caused many of my thoughts to focus on various individuals who were members of the Greatest Generation. All grown-ups of my childhood were in that very special group, lucky me.

I even like their music, that melodious stuff called Swing. Let a **Glenn Miller** recording hit the air and I perk up. Maybe even tap to the beat. Same thing with the **Dorseys. Benny Goodman. The Andrews Sisters. Satchmo. Duke. The Count**.

A hallmark of the Greatest Generation is that they lived – make that 'survived' - through the most bitter part of the Great Depression, that period of economic Hell brought on by the Crash of 1929. All the hardships those people endured and the self-sacrifice they practiced due to lack of all but the most bare essentials carried over as a positive pattern of behavior that fortified them through the miseries and heartache of World War II.

Even after the War, when people "loosened up," they seemed to do so with a collective mind-set of frugality, exhibiting a conservative approach to their actions. Many still wouldn't acquire big ticket items like a house or a car until they had cash in hand.

My teachers in grade school were mostly women. By junior high and certainly in senior high school, men and women shared the function and professional title of Teacher rather equally. Here, let me adjust this spotlight just so. Watch this.

About 10 years ago while on a visit to my birth 'n youth city of Cleveland, my life-long good buddy, **Eddie Maroli**, now deceased, told me that "a bunch of the guys" had formed a club called **Collinwood Memories, Junior**. (Yes, a bunch of "other" guys - from many years before, including my Dad and Uncle

Sam - had formed a club called **Collinwood Memories**.)

Our original club roster contained something over 200 names. I was amazed to discover that I could put a face, albeit a young one, on at least 150, as we had all attended Wm. H. Brett Grade School and Collinwood Junior High together.

Recent research has revealed that a whole bunch of us (All? Can that be?!?) share a favorite grade school teacher named **Filomina Vaccarello Tanno**, otherwise known to us simply as Mrs. Tanno. Our collective affection was most prominently displayed by the occasional, very unintentional (and definitely unique – didn't happen for another teacher) slip-of-the-tongue incident where someone called her "Ma." Such outbursts always created a ton of embarrassment for the perpetrator and 10 tons of laughter for the rest of the class, with maybe a silent and prayerful, "thank-goodness-it's-not-me-this-time!" from the likes of me, when it wasn't.

"She was a good model for us Italian kids" remembers her student and our classmate **Paul DeSantis**. (Paul recently retired as a high school teacher from the Cleveland Schools System, having been named **Teacher of the Year** in 1991 and is currently teaching some classes at Baldwin Wallace College near Little Italy on Cleveland's east side.) Paul on second thought noted that "Mrs. Tanno inspired all her students… for she was a warm and caring person."

Paul's and my memory seems to suggest that Mrs. Tanno was actually somebody's aunt, though who that might be is apparently stored in a senior memory cell.

Brian DeLissio said he will always remember that Mrs. Tanno encouraged him to stay with her after school so she could tutor him (unpaid) with his English studies.

"She promoted understanding, not the boring write-it-100-times method of others," Brian relates. "I sincerely believe," Brian told me, "that without her extra help, I would never have gone on to Collinwood High, probably would have quit and worked construction or something."

Or something, indeed. Instead, Brian could brag, if he was a different type, that he even attended Fenn College, a division of Cleveland State, and enjoyed a wonderful career with Baily Meter as a senior designer.

Mrs. Tanno was short, stout to roly-poly and wore thick, dark-rimmed glasses. She was "tough but a nice person who everybody liked," to quote Eddie again. "She really jumped on us Italian kids, had a shorter fuse with us, but it was for our own good, and we knew it even then." Eddie earned a degree in engineering at Ohio State.

Eddie and I reminisced about the fact that she was always in control, except for that one time when we were all cutting up and pushed her too far. In frustration, she threw her glasses across the room, sideways, and broke them against a wall. In the instant silence and shock that act created, Mrs. Tanno broke down and cried. I felt so bad I wanted to punch somebody until I realized that I was one of the major cut-ups.

She left the room and moments later, another teacher came in to find us accusing each other of making Mrs. Tanno cry. The other teacher – Mrs. Freeman? – told us that Mrs. Tanno's daughter was in a hospital having an operation in a far-off city. She asked us to be extra considerate when Mrs. Tanno returned to the class. Mrs. Freeman appointed one of the girls to lead a discussion on ways we might improve our behavior.

There wasn't much discussion as I recall, but then, maybe there was no real need. When Mrs. Tanno returned, she behaved like nothing extraordinary had happened. Y'coulda called it Angel Class for the rest of the day.

"Mrs. Tanno was one of our older teachers," Eddie went on to say. "When Pat and I were married shortly after graduating from Collinwood, we sent her an invitation. She was unable to come but sent congratulations. I believe she was retired by then."

Mrs. Tanno taught us a principle important to the playing of drums, baseball and golf. She demonstrated that to play a drum loudly, the drummer increased the arch of his swing rather than the strength he expended.

Using me as her demonstrator, she corrected my baseball swing. When she had me take my stance and the imaginary ball was pitched, I cocked my bat backwards before taking my cut. She said my technique might work in grade school, but as competition became more keen, I'd best take a stance with my bat already cocked back so my initial movement was forward.

I thought of her words every time up to bat from that time forward. I became a prolific homerun hitter and to this day I can put it over the fence and out of the park with regularity, if only in my dreams.

The same principle, a proper backswing, holds true for hitting a golf ball for distance, she said. I wish she had also taught me how to keep my head down. And maintain my grip. And hit out of a sand-trap. And how to putt. And....

Mrs. Tanno told us a story that fourth grade year that influenced my life far more profoundly than the dynamics of a swing. I promise to share the invaluable concept with you in this very space.... next week, as I just ran out of page.

✼✼✼

Chapter 15.
"D'Lady Wuzza Champ, Part Due!"

(Part 2 of 2)

*So what made y'think I could tell all about Mrs. Tanno in one shot?
The message I got from Part 2 was that y'gotta look at every possibility,
like looking through every facet in a diamond, get all anticipated answers
and be ready for all queries. Talk about a wrap-up; this one could stay
with you FOREVER!... just like it has for me.*

Life is full of surprises, thank goodness. Some surprises are right out
there in the open, looking like a normal, every-day occurrence to the
point of not seeming to be worthy of being categorized as a surprise
at all. Perspective on certain of life's events can change dramatically with
the passing of time, transferring the "Oh, that was nice," to a realization like
"Oh my God, that was wonderful! Thank you so much!"

Lately I've been talking to a bunch of guys who I have known since
grade school. We get together periodically as a result of forming a club
called Collinwood Memories, Junior, though interestingly, many of us
reside hundreds or even thousands of miles apart.

It's a blast to keep in touch with people who were first met in childhood,
even if most of the contact today is by phone or email. I've been asking for
thoughts of our fourth-grade teacher, Filomina Vaccarello Tanno, better known
to us simply as Mrs. Tanno.

"Mrs. Tanno! What in the world makes you ask about her?" was the
reaction I got from **Fritz Quagliata**, who these days owns **Alfredo's
At The Inn**, an elite Italian restaurant located in the Holiday Inn of
Mayfield Heights, Ohio.

"She useta give me money at Christmastime so I could bring her *Torrone*
from my parents' neighborhood grocery store that was located on Kipling
Avenue by Whitcomb Rd.," Fritz related as his recall was obviously in high
gear. "She was a nice lady. I really liked her."

I didn't call Fritz's two brothers, John and Carl, but Fritz's personal
declaration of Mrs. Tanno as his "favorite teacher" had blown me away again.

Buddy Sivillo returned my call. Like the others, he declared that Mrs.
Tanno was his grade-school favorite, surprise, surprise.

"I remember the time," he said without further prompting, "when **Michael
Christopher** had been cutting up and Mrs. Tanno picked up a yard stick and

started going for him. Her classroom had those rectangular-shaped tables, remember, 'n we sat around them rather than like the individual desks in other rooms, so Michael started scooting around tables to avoid her. It got to be so funny we started laughing, 'n there was Mrs. Tanno, all five feet and 250 pounds of her, moving like a cat. She was telling the class to be quiet while on the other hand telling Michael to stop, saying that she would not hit him if he stood still. He said, 'I don't believe you!' and he kept putting another table between them. Different kids in the class were coaching, some yelling at Michael to stop and some saying t'keep on going. After quite a while, musta been 15 minutes at least, Mrs. Tanno conned Michael t'stop, and when he did, she gave him a **Whack!** with the yard stick. Boy, was Michael upset! He even said a bad word."

I'm now convinced that if I talk to 20 more people, I'd just get similar versions of what has already been reported, so I might as well cut to the chase. See, there was a lesson she imparted to us, a story with a concept that has had an ongoing major influence on my life, one that I've always wanted to share with the universe, but there was never a proper vehicle.

Mrs. Tanno said that the story had actually happened to someone she knew, a fact that fascinated me. She started by saying she was going to call him Johnnie (I figured that he was either her son or her son-in-law) and that he had worked for the New York Central Railroad for 11 years. A big promotion was in the offing and Johnnie felt he had an excellent chance of being awarded the new position. Johnnie was a conscientious worker, his job reviews were good to excellent, he was always on time to work, oftentimes working through lunch or staying extra late to finish a project. In other words, he was a good company man from anyone's point of view. His major competition for the promotion seemed to be a guy named Bill whose work profile was much like Johnnie's except that Bill had only been with the company for eight years. Johnnie felt certain he was a shoo-in for the better paying job.

On the day of the announcement of the promotion, Johnnie arrived at work extra early to check the company bulletin board. Much to his chagrin, Bill had won the promotion.

More accurately, Johnnie was devastated.

He went to his job to put in his day's work, but after about an hour he just couldn't shake his ill feelings, so he made a very important decision. He decided to confront his boss to find out why he was suffering from this seeming injustice.

Johnnie was welcomed into his boss's office with a warm smile and a firm handshake. Johnnie politely got to the point and told his boss of his disappointment at being passed over.

The boss listened sympathetically and told Johnnie that he was aware of Johnnie's positive attributes and happy that Johnnie had come to see him, for the boss considered Johnnie to be a valued employee with a bright future with the company.

"Before I answer your question directly, and I promise that I will in a bit, I need you to do something very important for me," the boss said. "I want you to go down into the yard and tell me how many cars are here presently and how many cars will be coming into our yard in the next 24 hour period."

Johnnie said "Yes sir," turned on his heel and hurried out the door. He went down the steps into the yard where he obtained the information he was asked to retrieve, moving at just less than warp speed. When he returned to his boss's office, he reported.

"We currently have 175 cars in the yard and within the next 24 hours, 225 are scheduled in."

The boss looked at some figures he had written on a run sheet. "Johnnie, that's one of the most important factors I like about you. Your numbers are absolutely accurate. Now, I need a breakdown. How many box cars are in that total; how many flat cars and how many tankers?

It was back down the stairs, the information compiled and back up where he said, "There are 75 box cars, 45 flat cars and 50 tankers presently."

As before, his boss was very pleased with the accuracy of Johnnie's report.

"One more thing," the boss said. "I need a numerical breakdown on the type of cars coming in. Would you get that for me, please?"

Johnny was gone in a flash, returning in short time. Again, his accuracy and promptness were complimented by the boss.

"Now I want you to have a seat on my couch," the boss said. "I'm going to call Bill in here and I want you to simply observe what happens without comment."

When Bill entered the boss's office, Johnnie politely stood up and congratulated him on his promotion. The atmosphere was very cordial as it should be among mature people.

The boss then turned to Bill and said, "I want you to go down into the yard and tell me how many cars are here presently and how many cars will be coming into our yard in the next 24 hour period." With that, Bill excused himself and hurried out the door.

After a reasonable amount of time had passed, pretty much the same time Johnnie had taken, Bill returned.

"There are 175 cars in the yard and within the next 24 hours, 225 are scheduled in," Bill reported.

The boss looked at the figures on his run sheet.

"Bill, thank you very much," the boss said. "Those are the same numbers that are forecast here. Now, I need a breakdown as to…"

Before the boss could say anything more, Bill said, "Of course, there are 75 box cars, 45 flat cars and 50 tankers presently. You might also want to know that of the 225 cars coming in, 100 are box cars, 50 are flat cars and 75 are tankers. No cars are leaving during the 24 hour timeframe. Do you need any other information, boss?"

After Bill had left the room, the boss turned to a very shocked, dumfounded and embarrassed Johnnie.

"You're a good man and a valued employee, Johnnie," the boss said with sincerity. "I'm sure that when the next promotion comes along, you will be so proficient at your job that I will have no choice but to award you the position."

While Mrs. Tanno was telling the story, she had us mesmerized. I remember the exclamation "Wow!" bursting forth from me. And wow it was, for that story has been a conscious guide for me countless times through the years.

A good teacher does not have to come out of the Greatest Generation or be of a certain age, nationality or race of people to have an ever-lasting effect on the lives of her students. The teacher certainly doesn't have to be a woman, either.

By the same token, a person need not be a teacher, or have any other identifying title, to have a life-long impact on the lives of other people. Part of our privilege (our responsibility?) with each other is to share useful knowledge that can have monumental impact, for such information can penetrate time and obliterate distance.

To those who reach out to help, and especially to Mrs. Filomina Vaccarello Tanno, wherever she may be, we extend our Eternal, Heartfelt Appreciation.

For many of us, such an important valediction has more profound impact if we say it in the language of the Old Country:

Noi vi ameremo eternamente!

★★★

Chapter 16.
Who is a Writer
("I Thought He Was on First!")

(Part 1 of 2)

Okay, before you catch your breath or unfasten your seatbelt, Grade 4B had a major impact too, as the true start of a career can come extremely early in life... though it may not be recognized as such until many years later.

I thought about combining the next two columns into one, but then I also thought that it might be more interesting to see them in their original form. So here goes....

After all these years, I'm breaking my vow of silence. Lately, people have asked me when and how I knew I was a writer.

Got about an hour? Then here's the short version.

Let me slingshot you back a ways. Make that Grade 4B at William. H. Brett Elementary School in Collinwood. It all started thanks to our teacher, Mrs. Clark; bless her soul. (Mrs. Tanno was our teacher in 4A, as you know.)

That first Friday, Mrs. Clark announced that the last hour of every Friday henceforth would be known as "Club Hour." The class could do any activity that was pre-planned and approved by her and a democratic vote of the class. She then asked for activity ideas for the following Friday.

A couple of hands went up. Mine was high with enthusiasm, as an idea had just pooped into my head. Or should the word be "from?"

"I'd like to put on a play." I said excitedly, even surprising myself, as numerous ideas were going off in my head at a rate that rivaled fireworks on the Fourth of July.

"Good for you!" she exclaimed. "Just the sort of idea I'm looking for, but what shall we do for a script?"

"I could write one and bring it to you on Monday," I said, already starting to see visions of a script somehow appearing on the screen in my head.

"Hmm, by Monday. Sure! How many people will you need?"

"Eight," I heard myself answer with no idea why that particular number.

"And how many rehearsals will you need?"

"Um, three, uh, four. Maybe during Geography," I said, not really expecting an affirmative response, just trolling for an opportunistic laugh.

Nobody even snickered.

"Geography, indeed! Make it a half hour after school on Tuesday and Thursday and you've got a deal," she said as she coughed into her hankie. Was that a smile in her eye? "Class, all in favor of Joe's play raise your hands."

Several kids raised their hands, some enthusiastically. Frowns were noted, especially from my good buddy, Eddie Maroli, who even turned his back with arms crossed.

"Good! Idea approved! Pick your people."

At least two said "not me." Okay, so make it six. There was also a whispered-but-audible "baloney" from dear ole Eddie. Three raised their hands with anxious, wide-eyed "Pick me" expressions.

I made some picks and ended with, "And of course, Eddie."

"I don't wanna!" Eddie bellowed, throwing daggers. Eddie's face was beet red.

"Anyone who doesn't participate gets a week's detention," Mrs. Clark stated dryly.

"Okay by me," Eddie said.

"Fine," Mrs. Clark said flatly. "A week it is. And you're still in the play."

Later, out in the back school yard, I got an earful. No, I don't remember a fight.

When I sat down that afternoon at home to write the play, I "saw" several pages of script in my mind. I gave myself the opening line, putting the character name, "Corny" (short for Corny the Corny Cop) in the left margin of the lined notebook paper, then the dialogue in the body of the page, writing margin to margin.

For direction, I put the word "Action" in the left margin and the words in the body of the page. I was surprised, some years later, when I saw a real script, as character names appeared in the middle of the page with dialogue restricted to the middle four inches of the page. "What a waste of paper," I thought.

The play was a smash hit, but too corny to recap here. After the bell, Mrs. Clark asked me if I thought I could write another play.

"Sure," I said rather matter-of-factly. "I can bring you one a week forever."

"Good! Pick out different kids. You can act in the play, too, if you want."

"Wait a minute," I said. "You gonna want me to do the *whole class*?"

"Didn't I just hear you say that you could do 'A script a week, forever?'"

"Yeah, but I just don't ever want to use Dagmar."

"And I especially want Dagmar to participate…"

Dagmar was the class Brain. Straight A's. Perfect attendance. Hair always combed and dresses neatly starched. But, except for her best girlfriend, Becky, say "hello" to Dagmar and she'd be stuck for an answer and look like a deer caught in headlights.

"That's a tough assignment, Mrs. Clark"

"I'm so happy you see it my way," she said, smiling pleasantly.

Guess we'll have to wait until next week, too, as I just ran out of page.

Chapter 17.
And Now, the REST of the Story!
(Hats Off to Paul Harvey)

(Part 2 of 2)

So, what's there to say 'cept; Here's part two....

Last week I was telling of my earliest experiences with writing while in Mrs. Clark's Grade 4B class at William H. Brett Elementary School in Collinwood. She designated the last period on Friday as Club Hour. I wrote a play and selected classmates as actors. After our performance, Mrs. Clark asked if I could write another, eventually including Dagmar, the class brain who could not answer the greeting, "Hello." Oy vey!

We fast-forward to the fourth week of Club Hour. Two kids volunteered to be in this cast for their second appearance as there were only 30 students in Mrs. Clark's class. I had not exactly saved Dagmar for the last performance; I was just postponing the inevitable, like going to the dentist or to be vaccinated.

What do you do with a Dagmar? For all her brains, she was a social ghost. In rehearsal, she couldn't remember her lines. When she spoke, she couldn't be heard. At one point she tinkled, as we called it, creating droplets on the wood floor before bolting from the room. Her girlfriend Becky stomped the spots before chasing after her into the girls' lavatory. When the two girls came out, their demeanor rather stoic, Becky said they were ready to continue the rehearsal. Even years later some debate continued as to whether she actually wet her pants, or what.

Finally it was Friday. 3:30 p.m. The bewitching Club Hour. I had been frantically scribbling away since lunch, working on a truly inspirational idea. (Some Angel must have been blowing in my ear as the idea was probably my most profound until I decided to graduate from high school.)

I gave a clipboard to Dagmar with instructions to stand on a chalk mark that positioned her with her back against the chalkboard in the front left hand corner of the classroom. Dagmar was told to hold the clipboard with both hands so that nobody could see her face, which actually was somewhat following a request she had made earlier in the week.

All Dagmar's lines, some new, were neatly printed on the paper clipped to the face of the clipboard and numbered 1 through 10. She was to watch me for her cues. I would hold up fingers corresponding to the number of the line she was to say. She was told to say her lines as loudly as she could while talking into the paper so she wouldn't have to make eye contact with anyone in the audience. Dagmar agreed to the new arrangement, for it relieved her greatly.

Showtime. Da trumpets go "Da, da-da, da-da!"

A few lines into the play it was Dagmar's turn. Just as she said the last word of her first line, applause and hysterical laughter rang out. She looked like that deer again, but she quickly ducked back behind the clipboard, holding it tight to her forehead.

Her next line, same story. Was there a bit of a smile this time?

The applause and the laughter were louder and longer-lasting with each of Dagmar's lines. All were punch lines, as you might have guessed. After the final line of the play - Dagmar's, of course - the cast formed their take-a-bow line and each, with a hand extended, palm up, beckoned Dagmar to come forward and join in.

With a smile from ear to ear, she joined the line in the middle and exclaimed, loud enough for all to clearly hear, "Hey, this is fun!"

It was only then that someone pointed out to Dagmar that the back of the clipboard facing the audience had a sign on it that read, "After I speak, **APPLAUD**." Even Dagmar liked the joke, laughing with all the rest.

On her very next birthday, she had a party that, for the first time, included several classmates. All girls, but what the heck.

And me? I'd like to tell you that I grew up to be Steven Speilberg, but I'm not even Jewish.

Chapter 18.
"Ladies and Gentlemen;
Straight From the Bar..."

(Part 1 of 2)

Didja ever notice that the word 'inspiration' seems to have a connection to the word spirit? Remember how I started, telling about Luck and Cause 'n Affect? To this day, I can only make a bad guess at the Cause, but I've been aware of and admired **Frank Sinatra** *– like* **Paul Harvey** *– seemingly forever.*

Put on your favorite up-beat Snots album and give the ditty a Ring-a-Ding-Ding. Enjoy **Joe E.** *and* **The Sands**, *too. POST TIME!*

Sundays are very special in our household. We awaken when rested instead of 6 a.m. We have a cup of coffee while casually - rather than hurriedly - reading the Sunday newspaper. We outline the events of the day, which usually means taking care of family objectives. Most always in the mid afternoon, we listen to a program called *Sounds of Sinatra* on radio.

This past Sunday at 3:30 p.m. we were driving to Lowe's to get a do-dad necessary to a project when **Sid Mark** opened his Sinatra Show with a recording of one of Frank's concerts commemorating the inimitable entertainer's 60th year in Show-Biz. Many of the biggest names in Entertainment chimed in with a few bars of one of a variety of Sinatra's most memorable hit songs.

"When are you going to do the column on Sinatra?" Ginny asked at the precise moment I was thinking that maybe I should do my next column on Sinatra. We laughed, as we usually do, at having the same thought at the same moment. Later, I sat down to write.

As my thoughts took their own heading, I drifted back to another time. **Sam Russo** is a most special friend, a hair-stylist extraordinaire and Godfather to my daughter, Trina. Sam and I go back to the beginning of everything; yep, pretty much including adulthood. He has been married to Theresa for 29 years now, but he wasn't then.

Sam and I have worked together on and off for half of our careers in four different hair salons. The last one we owned together with Theresa. The first one was Sam's, succinctly named **Russo - Distinctive Haircutting**, located on Santa Monica Blvd.

at LaCienega Blvd. **Ralph Trejo**, about 25 years our senior and one of the world's most wonderful human beings, was with us and for a year or so, Sam's cousin, **Bobby Russo**, was also there. **Phil Fayne** joined us when Bobby opened his own salon on Little Santa Monica Blvd., a salon I would work in several years down-road, but at the time, who knew? Russo's was the place I went to and joined Sam when I first left Cosmo's.

I went to work with Sam because, philosophically, we were, and still are, twins. We made Russo's the first 100% hairstyling salon in the world; no barber-type cuts, no beautician-type work. (Over the years, similar statements have been made in print, on TV and radio, without challenge.) Geometric style-cuts with blower styling, color and hair straightening were our forte. The salon's clients were primarily male, many of them celebrities. I had a goodly number of female clients comprising maybe 20% of my following at that time.

One of Sam's clients was a noted interior decorator who was awarded the remodeling project for **The Sands Hotel and Casino** in Las Vegas. Sam doesn't remember his name either, so with all due respect, I'll refer to him as Tony. He came in every two weeks, always thrilling those who were present by telling behind-the-scenes tid-bits on his work.

Then came the big news. **Frank Sinatra** was to headline the Grand Reopening with **Joe E. Lewis** (entertainer, comic, former singer; subject of the movie, *The Joker is Wild*) as the lead act. Grand Reopening? The Sands never closed! At the time, it was a knee-slapper. Tickets? Forget money. $500 bought nothing, na-da, squat. The price to get in was JUICE. Who d'ya know, baby?

Sam and I asked Tony if he could get us four tickets. He said, "Only if you kill my mother-in-law." Not sure if he was kidding, I told him that I'd do it but the sight of blood made me puke. I don't ever remember anyone laughing so much at one of my jokes. Maybe he thought I was serious, but I'll never know for sure.

Amazingly, Tony not only got us tickets, he got us comp'd! With adjoining suites, no less. Each suite had the huge basket of fruit with our favorite booze as the centerpiece. He arranged dinner at **The House of Lords** in **The Sahara Hotel & Casino**, the primo eatery then, with swank that rivals today's best. The prime rib they served us was - I know you think I'm exaggerating - overflowing the platter. And delicious!

Back at the Sands, every one of the 4000 people who lined up for the show was a VIP. We had been told to go to the front of the line as we were "Friends of Sinatra." I remember seeing several major stars in the VIP line, many giving us snake-eyes. When we gave our names at the desk, the maitre'd escorted us immediately and personally, seating us two tables from the stage. In those days, everyone ordered four drinks, all served at once. By today's equivalent, I put the tab at $50 per drink, sans tip. Sure was nice, not having to pay. Sam, always Mr. Class, slipped the maitre'd a hefty 'thank you.'

C'mon, take another virtual tour with me as you picture or imagine this set-up. The house lights dimmed. The stage curtain seemed to be aglow. The Sinatra Orchestra, from offstage, blared out the Academy Award-winning theme song, *All The Way*, from the movie, *The Joker is Wild*.

Just then a spotlight lit up stage left, and the one-and-only **Joe E. Lewis** appeared! A water-tumbler filled with booze was in one hand as he dragged a high barstool in the other. The audience rose and went totally nuts for maybe five minutes while he toasted everyone, over and over.

The guy couldn't lose. He got laughs with every comment. He pulled his signature shtick, raising his glass to the audience as he shouted, "Post Time!" And the audience, as one, would raise 4,000 glasses and shout back, "Post Time!" Everyone would take a drink and laugh like hell. Why? Beats me now. Then, it was really funny.

Halfway through his act and several Post Times later, I don't know how anybody could be sober, certainly not Joe E. He got a refill from someone in the audience, almost falling off the stage. Was it all an act? The question never occurred to me until now, so don't know.

Then appearing to me as unplanned, **Frank Sinatra** walked out from stage left with a drink in one hand and dragging a companion barstool in the other. The house went nuts all over again. Joe E. met Frank half way and they embraced, bringing the people to their feet. There wasn't a dry eye in the house and even now, I'm stopping to dab. Go turn on your favorite Sinatra album. I just did.

The two of them, Forever Frank and Sentimental Slob Joe E., sat on their stools and kibitzed to the utter joy of 4,000 eaves-dropping zealots. It was won'erful!

Suddenly Joe E. stood up, said, "I gotta go. These people wanna hear you sing," and gave Frank another big hug and waved 'g'by' to a standing, roaring and very appreciative bunch of diehard devotees.

The Sinatra Orchestra lit up the room with its mellow-brassy sound as the curtain rose and the orchestra was floated from Backstage to Front and Center. For the next 2 ½ hours, would you believe, Sinatra thrilled and mesmerized the gang of us with seemingly every song for which he is noted and loved. I'm sure it's an unnecessary use of ink to say that this was the *Numero-Uno* concert of my life.

Ohm'gosh, look at the time, it's MONDAY! Didn't mean to make this a two-parter, but gotta go. And I never got to the best part! Next week, promise!

Chapter 19.
"Presenting The Man, Mister Frank Sinatra!"
(Part 2 of 2)

I Confess! I sipped my scotch straight up and the girls still haven't washed. And I'll bet 40 Million people claim to have been among the crowd of four thousand, too.

Memory jogging is not necessary this time. While I'm writing this story on paper for the first time, I've replayed the incident in my mind countless times over the years. I'm really enjoying telling how my relatively life-long good-buddy **Sam Russo** and I got comp'd at the **Sands**. **Frank Sinatra** and **Joe E. Lewis** put on a show that will always be considered vintage Ring-a-Ding-Ding.

Continuing the story from last week, when Sam and I arrived with our wives for Show-time after dinner at **The Sahara** that evening, I didn't notice the maitre'd had given Sam a note as we were seated. After Sinatra's final curtain call, Sam said the note was from Tony, Sam's interior decorator client who had arranged our fabulous on-the-house holiday.

Tony wanted us to meet him in the lounge immediately following the show, again telling us to go to the front of the line or we would never get in. Yep, more snake-eyes. I still remember a harsh, rude female voice loudly proclaiming, "Who the #$%O! do these #$%O+@&! people think they are?" Or words to that affect. Anyhow, right up to the reception desk we nudged, bumped and 'scused us.

When we gave our names, the host sent for Tony and asked us to step aside and wait. A moment later Tony came from inside the lounge.

"How'd you guys like to meet Sinatra?" he asked, all smiles, knowing his question was ridiculous and a complete shock. "Frank's in the best mood I've ever seen since I know him."

Tony went on to caution that we would probably be in for a simple hello with a handshake, to just follow Sinatra's lead. Tony asked us to be patient, that he'd come get us when "things are right."

Talk about four excited people! Nobody wanted to go to the john for fear of missing "the moment." There were only two times in all the years in Hollywood when I was most anxious while waiting to meet a legendary star. This was one, the other being the first time I met **Red Skelton**. Yep, another column; another day.

Tony was back almost immediately. He was nervous, even expressed surprise, said Sinatra wanted to see us NOW.

He lead us through the unbelievably crowded lounge to a booth along the far wall. Seated at a small square table just a bit larger than the small round cocktail tables throughout most of the room was **The Man, Mister Frank Sinatra**. Seated next to Sinatra on his right was a man who I at first mistakenly thought was **Akim Tamiroff**. At the closest table off to the right sat two big guys, bulges in their armpits. Behind us and to our left sat two more, really ugly. I felt very safe.

Somehow, I was the person next to Tony, so I was introduced first. "Frank, this is Little Joe," I remember Tony saying.

For the life of me, Sinatra's first words to me are lost in the thrill of that exciting moment, but for sure he was warm, friendly and his handshake firm. He looked each of us in the eye when speaking and he most politely kissed the girls' hands.

Sinatra looked to the man on his right and said, "Don't my friends get to sit down?" That I remember distinctly. The man snapped his fingers. Twice. Four chairs came floating through the air and were placed at the table.

As we sat, Sinatra surprised me by asking, "What are you drinking?" I said, "Scotch, neat." He said, "Bring him Haig 'n Haig."

As he moved on, the girls were both a bit tongue-tied, so Sinatra recommended a different drink for each, saying they'd love it. Sam said, "A scotch, like Joe."

Sinatra kept the patter going like we were old friends that he hadn't seen in a while. He told Sam and me he was aware that we each had clients who were dear friends of his and he even named a couple. He told us he drove by our place "almost every day." Of course, we invited him to drop by for a cup of coffee. He said thanks, he'd do that and patted the back of his head, adding that he was happy with the guy who was cutting his hair.

We replied that **Eddie Carroll** was a close friend - still is - and that Eddie and a few select others would occasionally come by our place for a haircutting jam session, and usually a drink or two. "I know," Sinatra said. "Eddie says he'd like to hire you guys," he kidded.

I sat there savoring the moment, slowly sipping my drink when a waiter approached, bent down and whispered in Sinatra's ear. Looking up, shrugging his shoulders with palms up and open, The

Man used a lot of apologetic words. "Some people who've been chasing me around the country..." to talk some business had arrived early, so would we please not think him ill-mannered, and please, stay, enjoy. "You're my guests tonight."

Turning to 'Akim,' he said, "Get my friends a table." 'Akim' had a look of horror in his eyes that he did a lousy job of hiding. "Put the table right there," Sinatra said as he pointed to a spot just behind our chairs. "That way I can still see these lovely ladies."

I know the whole experience sounds like it was magic, like out of Hollywood's script mill, but I swear this table came floating hand to hand, and somehow the waiters fit it into a spot that didn't exist, along with a fresh tablecloth, lighted candle and ashtray.

We thanked Sinatra, everyone talking at once, him too, and he kissed the girls' hands again. As Sam and I shook hands with him, he said, "Now don't be bashful. Order anything you want. You're on me tonight."

The four of us sat there reveling in the events of that past 10 to 15 minutes, recapping for each other the words and unspoken thoughts that just marked our lives forever. The girls joked - at least I think they were joking - that they would never wash their hands again.

Talking things over, we agreed it would be too nervy to order even another drink, so we got up to leave. We discussed saying goodnight to Sinatra, but he was engrossed in conversation, so we decided to not disturb him. Sinatra saw us, stood, waved and blew kisses.

I don't recall much of the rest of that trip, or even if we flew to Vegas or drove. I'm not sure which of the gambling memories occurred on that trip. But I am absolutely certain that I will always cherish the time we sat in the lounge of the fabulous Sands Hotel and enjoyed some very friendly conversation and a drink with the extraordinary entertainer I've admired all my life, The Man, Mister Frank Sinatra.

Chapter 20.
Quo Vadis, Bobby Jackson?

Did you ever go looking for someone from years ago, even trolling Google, Yahoo and other choo-choos, only to come up empty? Frustrating, hey what? Boyhood pals create life-long bonds, even if years go by with no contact. Here you get a glimpse of life in the Fabulous Fifties. In some respects, the adjective "fabulous" didn't apply. But just like Roses grow best out of poop, friendships can take root pretty much anywhere. See what y'think.

He's in most of my grade school memories. We both went on to Collinwood, to this day a reputed rough 'n tumble seven-through-twelfth-grade high school on Cleveland's east side. In the middle of the eighth grade, my family moved to the much more benign suburb of Mayfield Heights. Right there is the beginning of the mystery surrounding Bobby Jackson.

Back at Brett Elementary School, Bobby was a natural athlete who could do it all. He liked to fight, I think, as he wouldn't back down from older, supposedly tougher guys. We never went at it, thank God.

Whenever I got to choose up sides, my first pick was always Bobby, much to the chagrin of best-bud Eddie Maroli. (Eddie turned out to be the unofficial neighborhood historian, but that's another story.) I knew I could always take Eddie with my fifth or sixth pick, but number one belonged to Bobby.

One day I was playing center and Bobby was the left fielder. We were aligned outfield-to-outfield with another ballgame. Actually, the two left fielders were almost side by side, though each team was in the other's foul territory.

The batter hit a high fly toward left and definitely wide. Bobby ran to catch it. I chased over to assist, the ball landing just behind the other leftfielder, startling him.

Normally, a ball comes into your game, you just throw it back. Normally. This day, the other centerfielder told his guy to throw it beyond their right-field area.

Words flew from us to them. Words flew from them to us. It got nasty. They threatened us. We threatened them. It got really nasty.

"Hey, why're you siding with a n_____?" their centerfielder sprayed at me.

"You dumb @#$%, don't you call Bobby Jackson a n_____!" I sprayed back.

Guys were closing in from both teams. Some were yakking, some gesturing, and some threatening.

Bobby ducked a punch and whacked the attacker in the mouth. The next few moments are a blur, but I come to focus on Bobby 'n me, standing back-t'back, taking on four guys, Italians like me, from the other team. At the scariest moment, for me at least, the gym teacher blew her whistle. Everybody tried to melt into the non-combatants.

After some scolding, the teacher forced us to shake hands, then walked away. When she was just about out of earshot, the other centerfielder glared at me and whispered.

"We won't forget this, you n_____-lover!"

I only said two words, but the teacher heard. She ran back with a vengeance, directing her comments to me and finishing by glaring at Bobby and saying "...and you too!"

Now Bobby said a bad word.

We both ended up in the principal's office. Good 'ole Miss Zites. More blah-blah-blah, but this time Bobby and I kept our mouths shut. No sense pulling detention for more than a week.

In that whole episode, Bobby was the only black kid involved, though at that time, "negro kid" was the polite term. Call any of them "black" and World War III was on.

I was not so surprised to find I was an outcast from my buddies. Not Eddie, but he had to be careful or he would have caught a whack or two. To my utter surprise, Bobby was outcast from the other black guys.

"They said," Bobby told me, "that black 'n white don't go back-t'back, no matter what. When stuff happens, we regroup by color. Youse guys use the same rule."

While it is a no-no now, thank God, that's the way it was in the neighborhood where I grew up. The population was maybe 10% black and 99% of the time we got along great – well, "peacefully" or "okay" might be more accurate than "great," but the real tricky part was complying with the many all-but-written rules regarding the one percent. I wonder what's what now that the neighborhood is 90% black and just about zero Italians, 'cept some old folks.

After a while, Bobby and I became a little tired of the inflexibility of our respective "friends." We figured "The heck with them," or words to that affect and became truly close friends.

"I'm taking you home for lunch today," I said one day.

"Home?" His eyes were saucers but his impish grin was intact. "What's for dessert, fighting everybody on your street?"

"The rule says if you're with me, you're safe."

"I'll go on one condition. You come home with me next Tuesday."

"Why next Tuesday?"

"Won't be nobody home."

We both got a good laugh on that one.

The first time was really fun, so we exchanged lunches again. And again.

Several years later, five Mayfield friends and I decided to go to one of Collinwood's Friday Night dances where a famous local band, **The Gigolos**, was the big attraction. A wind-driven winter storm was raging as we drove north on 152nd Street and approached the overpass of the New York Central Railroad Yard. On the other side of the overpass – as though separated by an invisible wall across the road - was the black section.

Driving down the overpass, we hit ice and lost traction. We slid and whacked a new car parked outside the beer-joint that was the main neighborhood hangout.

Our grill was caved in with the radiator crunched into the fan. Wouldn't start. We huffed 'n puffed. No good. The night was freezing cold and the snow started coming heavily again.

"Hey, what you doin'?" said one of the men who came from the beer-joint.

All six of us tried to explain. Who owned the new car, we asked. I suddenly realized that their group was twenty-something people. All male.

"Don't you white boys know better than t'come t'this neighborhood unescorted?!?"

They were moving in. One guy flicked a stiletto. A really big guy spoke.

"Hey you, the little guy. You name-a Little Joe?"

That surprised everyone, nobody more than me.

"See that street?" I said, pointing. "You turn left, go two blocks, turn right, and fifth house on the right is Bobby Jackson's house. Bobby here t'night?"

"I 'member Bobby useta carry him here, sometimes."

"Lemmie see that radiator," another big guy said.

A couple minutes later our car started. They waved us good-by, everybody smiling on both sides. Oh yeah, the car we hit? It had been somebody's ride from the West Side. No problem.

We lost Eddie a couple years ago or there might be no mystery at all.

I have no idea where Bobby Jackson is today. "You name-a Little Joe" rings in my heart forever. I have asked everyone, looked all over the internet, so do me a favor if you can and tell Bobby to give me a call.

I don't know about playing a game of baseball, but having a bite to eat at my house is long overdue.

Chapter 21.
"And Hold The Anchovies, Please!"

Of the many ways an actor might get a gig, this one on my pop is a Pip. "Can you chrow one in the air 'n catch it?" Eh, pass the Pepperocini, please, and gimmie soma those scacciate olives.

I love telling stories about Dad. I had a beautiful relationship with both my parents, not to be confused with absolutely perfect, but the last 30-something years were close to bumpless.

As has been said many times before, Hollywood has no front door, no "way in." If there are a million people who ever acted in a movie or TV show, there are a million stories telling how they got their first - or fortieth, for that matter - acting job.

Serious people can find countless schools or acting groups or workshops to join where they will hopefully enhance their acting skills. They might even gain all manner of insight into useful functions, such as how to ride a horse, fish for trout or swing on a trapeze.

Generally, whenever an actor is asked if he can do a certain function, like say maybe, ride a surfboard, 99 out of 100 will say "Sure!" even if they don't know Step One. Circumstances permitting, they will tout every friend, acquaintance or even a perfect stranger to find a way to learn enough about the function to perform it well enough for the role.

Adam 12 was a popular TV cop show produced by the **Jack Webb** people at **Universal Studios** during the 70s. The star was **Martin Milner**. In one of the episodes, **Tom Williams**, the show's executive producer, had cast my dad, **Paul Micale**, as an owner of a pizzeria who was robbed while making a delivery. That show went smoothly, no re-takes on Paul's scenes, so when a future script called for action in a pizzeria, Tom called on Paul once more.

When Paul went to audition for the role, his lines memorized for the customary read-through, Tom waved him off saying he knew Paul's acting ability. What Tom wanted to know was if Paul could twirl pizza dough in the air, catch it and throw again.

"When I was a kid," Paul said, "my dad had a grocery store and my mother converted a defunct barber shop next door into a pizzeria. Guess who had to make the pizzas after school? I'll bet I can still do it in my sleep."

Tom turned to the director, gave him a "See, I told you" and asked Paul to be on the set at 6:30 the next morning.

Driving west down Burbank Boulevard on his way home that afternoon, Paul saw a pizzeria named **Two Guys From Sicily** and impulsively pulled into the parking lot. The owner, a short, slender, maybe forty-ish man named Tony, was alone. Paul introduced himself, telling Tony of his involvement with *Adam 12*.

"Hey, that's my favorite show!" Tony said. "You wanna t'chrow some pizza dough? It'll come back to you like riding a bicycle."

"Uhm," Paul said sheepishly. "My mother had a pizzeria all right, but only when I was a really little kid. I've never made a pizza in my life, but I'll pay you to teach me."

"I see," Tony grinned, unable to contain a few chuckles for a moment. "No problem. Good thing you came by on a slow day."

Tony went on to meticulously explain every step of the pizza making process, even demonstrating and explaining how to make pizza dough from scratch, with all the whys and wherefores.

The two of them started throwing the pizza dough in the air, "landing everywhere but in my hands at first" Paul related later. Some kids came by and stopped to watch through the large plate-glass window. They thought it was a great show. No, they didn't want anything, they didn't have any money, they just wanted to watch. Paul said they didn't need money and asked Tony to put a couple of pizzas in the oven. More kids came. More pizzas went into the oven.

Tony's brother and the two men's wives came to work, the brother getting into the act. As the dinner crowd started arriving, the brother and the two wives took care of the business so Paul and Tony could continue with "school." Six hours passed in a flash.

Grateful, and spent, Paul said "Enough," a bit to Tony's chagrin. "How much do I owe you?"

"What-a-ya, kidding?" was Tony's reply. "I should pay you! I haven't had so much fun since I was a kid in Sicily." Paul was adamant, wanted to pay for the lessons, the pizzas for the kids, the whole wonderful, enjoyable experience.

"Come on," Tony protested. You're *famiglia* now, like a cousin." As they jostled, Tony was adamant bordering on indignant at the thought of taking money. He won the day.

Next day on the set, Boom! Smooth as glass. One take. Maybe you saw the episode, but hey, that was a long time ago and the scene was no big deal in the scheme of the show.

A couple evenings later Paul, his wife, us kids and the entire families of Nick and Joe Leo (life-long friends of Paul) and their kids, some 15 people, invaded the little pizzeria in the heart of the city of Burbank. Paul brought Tony autographed pictures from the *Adam 12* cast. No bull, Tony fought tears. And lost. But then, a feast was on!

Everyone was under strict orders to eat all they wanted, really run up the bill. End of the night, I'm sure you guessed, Tony wouldn't take any money, again. Two new cousins almost came to blows. The Leo brothers saved the day as they cajoled the two men's wives into accepting a big tip.

Every adjective, every positive and negative, is used over and over to describe Hollywood. There are literally millions of stories. This was one of Paul's favorites. Mine, too, mainly because it shows that, in the Hollywood I lived in and love, there are lots of perfect strangers.

Chapter 22.
Found In Cape Coral... Rosie The Riveter!

During and after World War II, **Rosie the Riveter** *became almost as famous an American icon as the* **Statue of Liberty**. *Rosie represented the women who took jobs that contributed to the war effort, especially those girls and women who went to work in America's factories and did "a man's job," like setting rivets in aircraft, ships and tanks or fulfilling any of a million other job-descriptions.*

Rosie the Riveter was modeled after a real woman, **Rose Will Monroe,** *who was born in Pulaski County, Kentucky in 1920 and moved to Michigan during WW II. She worked as a riveter at the Willow Run Aircraft Factory in Ypsilanti, Michigan, building B-29 and B-24 bombers for the U.S. Army Air Forces.*

Now it is my distinct Privilege and Honor to introduce another Rosie, **Mrs. Lucy DiGiacomo,** *born March 10, 1919. Ginny and I were thrilled to be among the 70 or so people to surprise Lucy on her 90th birthday.*

I confess, this Rosie wasn't really hard for me to find, for her daughter, Denise, married Ginny's cousin Joey.

Decembér is a major holiday month throughout the USA and in many countries of the world. There was one December, however, when America was rudely awakened early one morning. Thousands died rather instantly. But as one of the leaders of the attacking nation so prophetically noted, a sleeping giant had been awakened.

All aspects of life changed rather abruptly in America on Sunday, December 7, 1941. Everybody, literally every man, woman and child felt the electrifying, terrible affect of the horrors of that day. Twenty one year old Lucy Valenti and her best girlfriend Funzi, given name Carmela, were enjoying a movie that fateful Sunday evening at the Marlboro Theater in Brooklyn. The film sputtered; stopped. The house lights became bright. A man's voice spoke over the theater loudspeaker.

Hawaii had been viciously attacked, bombed by the Japanese. Heavy damage reported. Lots of smoke 'n fire. Go home, stay tuned to your radio. God Bless America!

Frightened, crying, the young women hurried home to Mama and Papa Valenti. Maybe they would all be safe. Maybe not, but they'd be together.

At that time America had been deep in the throes of the Great Depression. The implements of war were in desperate short supply, like most everything else. With our young men, the backbone of our work force destined for military service, how would such enormous needs be fulfilled?

The task fell to the women of the era. By the tens of thousands, women and teenaged girls all over the country put aside whatever plans and dreams they possessed to overtly join the war effort while keeping the home fires burning. They traded their skirts and dresses for slacks and coveralls, wrapped their hair in turbans and babushkas, rolled up their sleeves and entered the factories to build planes, ships, tanks – hence the Rosie the Riveter handle – and yes, fulfilling every need, even sewing the uniforms.

Mama Vincenza had taught Lucy to sew when "just a little girl; maybe 7, maybe 8. I believe I was about 18 years old when I got a job at the sewing factory with Mama a few years before the war started," remembers Lucy, now 90 years young. Lucy and her mom traveled on two trains and two buses each way every day to and from their home in the Bronx to the sewing factory in Hoboken.

"It wasn't all bad," Lucy emphasized. "The snow, yuck, but we had fun, too. Like there were these two girls who lived next door, or was it down the street, from Dolly Sinatra, and when Frank was in town, oh boy, what excitement!"

Once the war started, the factories were no longer sewing ladies' suits, jackets or corsets. The needs of the U.S. Army became paramount. Lucy sewed those heavy, prickly-material overcoats worn by GIs in Europe, the coats that made her uncomfortable and warm as she draped them over her lap while putting the stitches in place.

Know what else she and her girlfriends put in each one? A note. A note in the pocket of each coat that said things like, "Come Home Safe" and "You're In Our Prayers" and "Thanks, Buddy. Come By For Coffee Sometime."

In 1947 Lucy married Emil DiGiacomo, who spent his career working at the Navy Yard. Daughter Denise was born some years later. Emil was lost to cancer at the young age of 42, when Denise was just 10 years old.

In December, 1980, Denise received a phone call from her brother-in-law who had moved to Cape Coral. "I'm in a tee-shirt and shorts," he shouted, "...and I have a job for your husband!"

After spending several years caring for her parents, "Papa passed in 1977 at age 91," Lucy was retired and living comfortably in her own home. "I really didn't think I wanted to leave New York," Lucy remembers. "Funzi, sometimes with her sister Tessie, we were still enjoying movies together," she laughs, "...but I couldn't bear the thought of living so far away from my daughter."

Since arriving in 'the Cape' in 1981, Lucy DiGiacomo has been living with daughter Denise. Mainly by telephone, Lucy maintains her life-long friendship with Funzi.

"As close as my mom and I have always been," Denise said in amazement, "I never heard this complete story until now. I didn't know Mom worked on those Army coats. And those notes, can you imagine!"

Mother and daughter truly enjoy their closeness. They agree that life is more enjoyable in Cape Coral. "Love the weather! I'm really happy to live in this beautiful city," Lucy repeatedly said.

Macular Degeneration slowly took Lucy's eyesight several years ago, but friends and neighbors agree that it didn't put a dent in her spirit, for she is as vivacious, loving and lovable as ever. After all, Lucy, along with all the other Rosies, is a bonafide member of the Tom Brokaw dubbed Greatest Generation. America is eternally grateful.

Chapter 23.
Hollywood Spotlight on Larry 'n Bernie
(Part 1 of 2)

*I Confess! Here's another one that grabs me. Y'loved **Larry Storch** in F Troup and y'loved **Tony Curtis** in many flicks, but did y'know...*

The exact year is stored in a rather cloudy sector of my memory, but I'm certain it was **Don Ameche** (nee *Amici*, 1908 - 1993) who invented the telephone; and thank goodness, too. Otherwise I could never have received that exciting call from **Norma Storch** a couple of months ago.

"Is Sanibel anywhere close to Clearwater?"

Told the cities are about two hours apart, her level of enthusiasm clicked up three notches. She and her famous comic husband, **Larry Storch**, were going to be in Clearwater for a whole week as Larry was co-starring with **Tony Curtis** in the stage musical, *Some Like It Hot.*

"Any chance you and Ginny can come up and spend some time with us? You missed out on "Annie" and Reba, so I don't want you to miss this one."

Checking our schedule, we asked if January 1st would be okay. Norma echoed our thought that the first day of the new year would be prophetically appropriate. Besides, for the past 30 years I've always enjoyed spending bonus time with Norma and Larry.

"And don't forget your scissors," Norma added. "The way my hair has been cut lately, my curls have all disappeared."

Our friendship started because they came to me for haircuts but it continues out of pure love-coated friendship. Interesting, isn't it, the various ways we meet the most important people in our lives. I've been privileged to meet some of the greatest people on earth because of my hairstyling business, and I am not referring to famous people only; not by a long shot. The statement was true in the Hollywood/Beverly Hills area and that truth most certainly continues here on Sanibel. No rap intended in any way, shape or form, but after a bit more than three years of extreme scrutiny, Sanibel is precisely the primo location in more than a 100 mile radius, just as Beverly Hills was for all those years.

After talking to Norma that day, I sat there quietly for a moment, my thoughts drifting back in time. March 5, 1973, rose from the mist, as that Monday is indeed one of my most positive Red Letter Days. That is the date that I officially assumed ownership of **Cosmo's Hairstyling Salon**, the place referred to in previous columns that was located just around the corner from **Schwab's Pharmacy**, the famous Hollywood Hangout for movie industry people.

A long-time client at Cosmo's was **Dr. Eddie Cantor**, an ENT who is no relation to the famous comic by the same name. Dr. Cantor referred **Tim Conway** to me; Tim in turn referred writer-producer-director **Larry Sands**; Larry referred astronaut **Scott Carpenter**, then **Norma and Larry Storch**. Whew! I could do five columns on this one paragraph!

The Ruth Eckerd Auditorium in Clearwater is a beautiful facility. Amazingly to me, it seats just over 2,000 people and is designed without center or mid-aisles, just those on the parameter. I'm aware of similar multi-plex designs, but they seat only 100 or so people.

Some Like It Hot was fabulous, four stars in my book and I promise you, rose-colored glasses were not in play. Ten of the dancers have performed as **Rockettes**. Sugar, the Marilyn Monroe-originated character, was given new life by **Jodi Carmeli**, who previously played Maureen and Mrs. Cohen on Broadway in *Rent*. If she becomes a household name some day, I get an Attaboy, given the way I've been "Doin' it for Sug-ggaarrr...."

Tony Curtis was vintage **Bernie Schwartz**. You could feel the pulse of the audience quicken, not just on his entrance, but anytime he took the stage. Sing? Dance? He was surrounded by consummate pros, so with understandable tongue-in-cheek facial expressions, he drew the audience in and all went with the flow. It was obvious he was loving it; and very importantly, so did we.

Larry Storch was born for the stage, always perfectly cast to make sure the audience takes its place as part of the show. Larry's performance was reminiscent of his constant-show-stopping run with *Oklahoma!*

Many wise stars over the years, like Sinatra and Dionne Warwick, often beseeched Larry to go out and tenderize an audience like very few others ever could.

Tony Curtis and Larry Storch go back quite a ways; in fact, all the way to the **Proteus**. No, it didn't appear on Broadway; that would have caused quite a stir. The Proteus was a battle-worn sub-tender that was originally commissioned in 1941 as a Fulton class vessel and re-commissioned a sub tender in 1944.

We're focusing on the year 1943, when 20 year old Larry, an already seasoned nightclub comic and celebrity mimic, was sought as an advisor and confidant by a 17 year old swab named Bernie Schwartz.

"I wanna be in show biz when this is over," Bernie confided to Larry.

"Hey kid," Larry advised, "With your looks, go for modeling. That way you'll probably eat better."

After "it" was over, Bernie read in the papers that Larry was appearing at the **Copa** in New York with **Frank Sinatra**. Arriving at the Copa at rehearsal time, a security guard told Bernie to wait in the bar, that rehearsal was private.

As Bernie nervously sat waiting, he wondered if Larry would even remember him. A couple of excruciatingly long hours later, Bernie determined that this was a very important moment in his life. Bernie came to the conclusion that if he had enough - what, charisma? - that allowed Larry to so much as remember him, then Hollywood, here I come. But, God forbid, if Larry didn't even recognize him....

When Larry finally emerged from the door leading to the stage, the security guard approached, but Larry ran past him to the bar, arms outstretched, and gave Bernie the bear-hug of his life. Literally. And all heads turned as he shouted "Bernie Schwartz, my good friend!" The rest, in case you've been living on Mars, is history.

Doggoneit, done it again. Outta space. See you next time, Charlotte, et al, 'n I'll tell you the inside skinny on the making of the movie, *Some Like It Hot*" Stay tuned, 'cuz it's a pip.

Chapter 24.
Larry 'n Bernie – 60 Years Later
(Part 2 of 2)

*I Confess! Here's another one that grabs me. Y'loved **Larry Storch** in F Troup and y'loved **Tony Curtis** in many flicks, but did y'know…*

Now let me see, where did I leave off? Oh yeah, when last we were together I was telling you about two Hollywood guys who are good buddies dating back to WW II, **Larry Storch** and **Tony Curtis**. They are currently touring the country with the "new" stage musical, *Some Like It Hot.*

I'd like to say, up front, that Larry Storch and his ever lovely red-head wife, Norma, have been close personal friends for most of my adult life. I'm honored to report that they are real, down-to-earth people who live and laugh and love like so many millions of others in this fabulous country of ours, and their primary mission in life is to bring joy to those they touch. It's part of the bond we share; and that our vocabularies contain the word "retire" so that we might more politely refer to assorted mutual friends.

When Ginny and I arrived at the **Ruth Eckerd Auditorium** to see the play last New Year's Day, **Norma Storch** was waiting for us at the entrance. For the only time in 30 years, Norma and I had not seen each other in a bit more than three years, whereas three months was a long interval previously. Surprisingly to all, the event was the first time Ginny and Norma had actually met, though they had talked on the Ameche several times.

The stage show, as I previously gushed, was great. When the three of us went backstage after three curtain calls, Larry's dressing room was busy with cast members laughing and winding down after another high energy performance. Before anyone could say Enrico Caruso, Larry and Ginny were rattling off in pure Italian, Larry's favorite language after English.

"Let's go find Tony," Larry suggested. "Maybe take a picture, so bring your camera."

Up close and personal, Tony Curtis looks really good. Sure he shows some age at a healthy 77 and for the record, he is definitely friendly and gracious. I mentioned to him that my dad often talked of the fun he had with Tony and Larry when all three worked in the movie, *Captain Newman, M.D.* years ago.

"Sure, you mean **Paul Micale**," Curtis replied. "Didn't we lose him about three years ago?"

It really blew me away that he would remember, for my dad's role wasn't that big a deal, a fact I mentioned later that evening over dinner with the Storches.

"Oh yes it was," Larry said. "He played an Italian prisoner of war and he learned to dance the Horah very quickly."

Of course he's correct. In Hollywood, true professionals rightfully contend that there are no "bit" parts, only short glimpses of a character's life.

There is something I should have told Tony Curtis about his hair when I met him. As a professional hairstylist, I have always considered his hair to be the preeminent model for the ideally groomed man. I must have created at least a thousand-and-one clones over the years, beginning with me.

Oh, remember the camera? So did we. Maybe next time we'll even remember to take some pictures, but for right now, let's shift gears and focus on the making of the classic movie, *Some Like It Hot.*

According to one story from back in '58-ish, Producer **David O. Selznick** told Director **Billy Wilder**, "You want machine guns and dead bodies and drag gags all in the same picture? Forget it, Billy. You'll never make it work."

So much for predictions, even for one of Hollywood's most successful and respected moguls.

Just three short years ago and some 41 years later, the **American Film Institute** named *Some Like It Hot* the Number One Comedy, the funniest American movie ever made! AFI reports that they get almost no static on the choice.

To say that the late-great Billy Wilder was one heck-of-a director is as monumental an understatement as saying that the late-great Jimmy Durante was one heck-of-an entertainer. (Hey! Why does that sound so sim… sim… uh, familiar?)

Wilder's master-plan for casting the 1959 movie, *Some Like It Hot* was ingenious. He figured he'd have the nuts bolted with a stroke of the pen, for he was determined to sign **Frank Sinatra** to play Jerry/Geraldine opposite already-signed Tony Curtis's Joe /Josephine. Problem was, ole Blue Eyes was hip, figured "push it when yer holdin," so he had his agent ask for *three times the money* allotted for the role.

Wilder threw a fit, to understate another fact. Ah, but Tony Curtis was also hip, went to Wilder with a stroke of brilliance.

"I can get Larry Storch for you. He's my landsman. He'll win an Academy."

But Wilder had his heart set on Sinatra. So what happened? After a swift kick in the pants from the higher-ups, he reluctantly signed the kid named **Jack Lemmon**. Given the way it all shook out, Lemmon was a coup, for though he didn't win the Oscar, he was most certainly and deservedly nominated; and even more importantly for good-buddy Jack, nobody would ever refer to him again as "The Kid."

Tony should have been nominated, too. Get a copy of the film and see it again if you think I'm blowing smoke. **Cary Grant** LOVED the movie. Saw it 27 times. In 1959 alone.

There is no way to mention *Some Like It Hot* without underscoring the scintillating job **Marilyn Monroe** did in that movie. Some of Marilyn's greatest film takes, ever, are indelible, inseparable parts of that film. No actress on earth, or anywhere else for that matter, could have taken her place without the movie losing a ton of charm, glamour and sensual appeal. Heck, without Marilyn, I'll wager a gallon of Shell gas, the movie might have dropped all the way to 47th , or even worse, on AFI's list.

But! Listen up, now. Remember the scene when she opened a dresser drawer? 82 takes. Or was it 87? I left my notes in the glove compartment or somewhere, I'm not sure.

And then there was the scene on the boat where Marilyn was trying to titillate the libido of Jerry/Geraldine/phony millionaire/Tony Curtis? Well, during shooting with all the takes, re-takes, up-takes, down-takes, all those characters finally got through it okay, but Tony Curtis took advantage of one "take five" so he could go change his pants. He and Marilyn had been off-stage lovers in 1949 and '50, and for all the criticisms of Marilyn, nobody ever said she was not truly sensuous.

Bottom line is Billy Wilder. He knew what could be and he was going to get it no matter what; no matter how many takes, tears or tantrums. The man knew when to pull what trigger. Sure he was deserving of the Oscar, but **William Wyler** and *Ben Hur* copped a lot of tin that night and no one in their right mind can fault the choice. It was Ace vs. Ace.

Interestingly, some years later Wilder pulled Larry Storch aside and confided that, no knock on the affable Lemmon, had Wilder been more familiar with Storch's abilities and talents in '59, he might have gladly selected Storch to play Jerry/et al. Though Tony Curtis admired and respected Lemmon's performance, Tony had a few choice words when he heard of Wilder's comments to Storch. I think the words were, um, "Son of a Gun." Where are my notes when I need them, anyway?

All these years later and after appearing in nine movies and one stage musical together, Tony Curtis, still handsome at 77, and Larry Storch, an amazingly energetic 80, are good buddies having a ton of fun; together.

And the show? Well, a little birdie flew by me the other day, advising that I not be surprised if the play opens on Broadway before a year is out. Actually, I'd be surprised if it didn't, for it's an irrefutable fact that the ever-growing millions of movie buffs love the story, the antics and the people connected with *Some Like It Hot.*

Chapter 25.
Another Day in School, Minus the Ho-Hum

*I Confess! I wrote this next column to blow the lid off some of the idiotic principles that were taught at **Mohler's Barber College** years ago. "Give at least four haircuts an hour or go drive a truck!" They said that to me so many times that I'm almost surprised I never developed weak kidneys.*

Mohler's Barber College was mostly a shocking disappointment for me, as I indicated previously. After all, this was Hollywood, so where was all the glitter?

"Our primary objective here is to teach the basics of a haircut, a shave and facial treatment so that each student can pass the State Board exam. You will learn the art of those functions out in the field, where it takes a talented person at least four years to develop proficiency."

So proclaimed Mr. Guy Otesen, the head instructor, over 'n over, 'til I graduated. His statement has stayed with me verbatim all these years.

I mentioned that I had cut hair, sans license, for two years while attending Ohio University and that I was the only college student who shaved with a barber's straight razor. With all that, my barber school instructors were overly tough on me, I thought.

Per school policy, I'd finish a haircut, then call an instructor to check my work.

"Not enough hair on the floor," was a common – ad nauseam - first comment.

"Check the hair on his head," I said softly, I thought. "We're gonna sweep 'n dump the hair on the floor inta the garbage!"

I wasn't insubordinate, but close, they said.

"You're way too slow. Did you ever think about driving a truck (or being a plumber)?" Those two were thrown at me until the day I graduated.

They also drummed; "To make it in this business, you will need to do four (4) haircuts an hour and six (6) during rush hour."

"Rush hour" was defined as "any time two (2) or more people are in the waiting area."

I could barely manage to give two good-quality haircuts in an hour. Fact is, I heard my instructors say "drive a truck" so many times that I'm almost surprised I never did.

I was somewhat surprised to build a decent following while in barber school, just like I did at O.U. I will always remember one man, George, who told me that years previously, he had owned a small chain of stores somewhere in the Midwest that sold expensive furniture. The story was verified one day when his estranged wife showed up with a private detective while I was cutting his hair. He had been missing several years, she confirmed.

George and his wife had a rather calm discussion right then and there, but he chose to stay "on the street." George was always clean, though he lived in a "flop-house," – a dingy hotel that would charge by the night or by the week – and he worked as a dishwasher in a "greasy spoon hole-in-the-wall restaurant," he told me more than once.

"Just got tired of the rat race back home," George added, "and people living off my 20 hours a day, seven days a week, for more than 20 years. Nuts to 'em!"

Sure I cleaned that up a little bit. Had to. This IS a family newspaper, after all.

Another person who I still think of fondly is **Lauro Salas**, the former World Light Weight Champion boxer from Mexico. Lauro had scar tissue where eyebrows used to be. Not much of a nose, either. But Lauro Salas was a kind-hearted, decent human being and he was always very complimentary of my work.

There came a time when my instructors decided to force me into being "a four-haircuts-an-hour barber." No more "finger-cuts" – today called geometric angle cuts – they said. It was to be very little scissors work and mainly clipper-over-comb, bottom to top, wham-bam, thank-you-Sam and NEXT!

I was ready to quit.

That day, Lauro Salas came in and sat down. I gave him the skinny as I picked up my clipper. He had a frown on his face until I whispered that the instructor's cigarette break-time was coming up soon, so I'd fake it until they left. When the coast was clear, I put the clipper aside and switched to my scissor 'n comb and started my finger-cutting technique. Suddenly they were back, glaring at me.

"The way you like to give them-there finger-cuts, you should go to work for **Cosmo Sardo**," an instructor named Joe said. He went on to say that Cosmo owned the "hair saloon" around the corner from **Schwab's Pharmacy** where "all them-there actors hang out and them-there actors love them-there finger-cuts." Exaggerating? Not me. Joe also said that Cosmo was an actor.

My ears shot up at his comments. The day before, my dad was fired from his hair cutting job. He had left work early, as he received a phone-call from his agent who had arranged an unexpected acting interview. When Dad walked out, several people were in the waiting room. Somebody beefed. The boss said, "If you leave now, don't come back." Dad was really upset at dinner when he told us the story.

I could hardly wait to tell Dad about some actor with a Sicilian name who owned the hair salon near Schwab's. "Is Schwab's for real?" I asked my dad at dinner that night. "I thought Schwab's was Hollywood BS. A barber shop next door could be a big deal."

Next day, Cosmo hired him on the spot. Dad worked there, for Cosmo and then for me, for the next 20 years.

Good 'ole George and my friend Lauro Salas are two of the biggest reasons I have pleasant memories of barber school. 'Specially, I fondly remember the instructor named Joe.

Chapter 26.
I Wish I May, Wish I Might...

(Part 1 of 3)

*I Confess. I love this guy coming up! Oh boy, here we go. Hey, whata ya do when an Icon beckons? Ya scoot, that's what, but watch out for that crowd! Great Caesar's ghost! And thanx t'you, **Frank Novak**.* **Molto Grazie!**

Some people have an acute case of "celebrityitis," meaning they go bonkers whenever they find themselves in the presence of someone who is famous. Some friends might describe me as the emotional type. That said, I have never suffered from celebrityitis. Well, never is a big word. There was one time, a singular circumstance, that could qualify.

One of my earliest clients when I was an apprentice working at Cosmo's was a man named **Frank Novak**. Great guy; highly talented. For those who remember *The Red Skelton Show*, the opening usually featured an elaborate production number punctuated with a grand entrance by Skelton. He would be decked out in an outlandish costume that fit the theme of the production number. Once he was a goose, fully feathered with white tights and a big yellow beak.

Skelton's personal costume designer was Frank Novak.

When Frank and I had an opportunity to get acquainted enough to hang the label of friend on each other, I confided to him that **Red Skelton** was more than just a favorite celebrity to me.

Frank volunteered that Red was, off camera, a warm, sincerely friendly and deeply caring human being. Frank's information confirmed what I thought I gleaned from listening to Red on radio and watching him on TV during the previous several years of my young life. Remember, in those days most broadcasts were live as opposed to recorded, so a performance was more revealing. "Imperfections" were part of the deal, often adding to the entertainment value while exposing more of an actor's personality, wit and creativity.

Red Skelton had a young son, **Richard**. Red was a loving father who focused upon his son to the extent that part of his act featured a character he referred to as "Junior – The Mean Widdle Kid," a take-off on Richard. Stories on Junior were often woven into Red's monologue and often, the character appeared in skits. It was a warm, perhaps zany or mischievous type of fun in spite of the word "mean" in the character's title.

In real life and some years before I moved to Hollywood, Richard was diagnosed with a drastic disease: leukemia. I remember that Red took his son everywhere seeking a cure; to Europe, to Rome, where Red and his son were granted a private audience with the Pope. I was deeply affected by this situation.

Then one day a small item in the newspaper announced that young Richard Skelton had passed away. Even today the memory still has a deep, hurtful, sad edge, the kind usually felt for close family members. Time passed and I moved to Hollywood.

The next couple of visits with Frank had a warm, even more friendly overtone. He would tell me about upcoming costumes and show themes, but we didn't touch on Red's haircut.

Then came the day I now call Red Tuesday. It was 5:03 p.m. My boss, Cosmo, beckoned me to the front desk.

"Frank Novak's on the phone. They want you to go cut Red Skelton's hair! They want you RIGHT NOW," he said, his eyes bulging.

I was floored.

"They want you to go right now," he repeated. Cosmo was obviously excited as were my Dad, Nunzio, Sam Keston, the whole staff. My five o'clock appointment, who had been patiently waiting for me to finish my previous client, volunteered that he would come back tomorrow, to "...go do Skelton and be sure to tell me EVERYTHING!"

It was all so exciting, this major happening occurring only a few weeks after Cosmo had made me a full-time, permanent member of the staff with my own booth.

As I was packing my tools, I saw that my hands were shaking. That was a first! Cosmo approached to ask if I knew how to get to CBS. He also let me know that CBS Security had called back to tell me to go to the entrance gate on Fairfax Avenue, that the guard would direct me from there.

I put the top down. I had just bought the car, a white '59 Cad with a red leather interior and come to think of it, a good subject for a future column. I don't think that model ever lost its luster, certainly not in the fall of '62.

When I pulled up to the gate, the guard waved and smiled. "You must be Little Joe, Mister Skelton's hairstylist," he said.

Talk about a rush.

"See that crowd of people waiting near the side entrance to the building? That's tonight's audience. Drive up to that door and one of the attendants will park your car. The show is being held up 'til you cut Mister Skelton's hair."

As I pulled up at the curb, some gravel caused my tires to screech, causing the whole crowd to focus my way. I grabbed my tool bag and started to go with one of the attendants toward the stage-entrance door.

I heard a female voice say "Oh my God, it's %$&@%!" I never heard the name, but she might as well have said "Stampede!" for that's exactly what happened. I was literally bowled-over by the crowd and ended up on my back with a gal about my age on top of me, nose to nose.

"Who are you?" she asked, the question scrunching her nose and forehead.

"If you don't know, why're you on top of me?" I asked, the memory as clear as if it happened last Tuesday.

I remember seeing several attendants peeling people off me, a blue sky with puffy white clouds as a backdrop. They scooped me to my feet as five of them formed a cordon around me and led me through the crowd to the door. Once inside, they broke formation, all of us sharing a nervous bit of laughter.

"Is this a normal occurrence around here?" I asked no one in particular.

"Only for a big star," one of them replied. "Come on, I'll take you to Mister Skelton's dressing room."

We were in a dimly lit back-stage area, the ceiling way up there. We approached the more brightly lit area when I saw my first mobile dressing room, a large trailer on wheels, an object that became quite common to me over the next many years.

As we approached the dressing room, there were some director-type chairs and a couple sitting quietly, but I hardly noticed.

"Have a seat. I'll let Mister Skelton know you're here," the attendant said.

As I sat down, the man in the next chair asked if I was one of the guest stars for tonight's show.

"No I'm here to give Red a haircut," I replied, still shaking off the feeling of being mobbed and wondering who the hell all these people thought I was.

"Really! I'm looking for someone to cut my hair. Do you have a card?" he said with a pleasant tone.

As I handed him a card, he said, "Excuse me, my name is **Caesar Romero**. What's yours?"

It was only then that I saw that, yes indeed, there he was with that renown, wavy salt 'n pepper hair, Caesar Romero, alright.

"And this is our other guest star tonight, **Nanette Fabray**," he offered, being the graciously cordial gentleman he often portrayed.

Yep, double whammy. About the time I was mumbling something like, "Nice to meet...," Frank Novak beckoned to me from the dressing room door saying we could all chat later, that Mr. Skelton was ready for me and repeating that the show was being held until I was done with the haircut.

Know what really ticks me off? Outta space again 'n so much more t'tell. It'll be worth the wait. Promise.

Chapter 27.
Not Yet Ma, I'm Dreamin!

(Part 2 of 3)

How do you cut the hair of an Icon? With yer knees knocking, that's how. All my years in Hollywood fortifies the statement that the Biggest Stars have the Biggest Hearts. Here's s'more perfect examples as you will also meet Sammy, Billy and Johnny.

Lemmie see, I was recalling the time I got the hebejebees because my friend, costume designer **Frank Novak**, called me to go and give a haircut to a celebrity I definitely admired and the World's Favorite Clown, **Red Skelton**. As an added, totally unexpected bonus, I also met the handsome and gentlemanly **Caesar Romero** and the gorgeous and multi-talented **Nanette Fabray**.

In those few introductory moments, Caesar and Nanette made a major fuss over me, telling me what a wonderful job I always did on Red's hair and how fortunate I was to cut the hair of one of Hollywood's favorite and most highly respected celebrities. As Novak beckoned me to the door of Skelton's inner sanctum to do my deed, I didn't get the chance to tell the guest stars de jour that I was on my initial assignment to cut Skelton's hair. Ahem.

Frank Novak and I exchanged our hellos as I entered to find a surprisingly spacious interior that was tastefully appointed like the living room in an elegant home. Three men rose from a couch and an overstuffed chair to greet me, but none were familiar to me.

"Little Joe, say hello to **Sammy Kahn, Billy Rose** and **Johnny Mercer**," Frank introduced.

Wow, I thought, I'm flying in Hollywood's Stratosphere! They greeted me very warmly, one of them saying that my boss Cosmo had cut his hair many times over the years and another making a similar comment, saying that Nunzio Tringali was his barber and long-time friend.

A door to another room opened and out came **Red Skelton**.

I was surprised to see how tall he was. As we were introduced I said, "I'm very pleased to meet you, Mister Skelton."

"Call me Red," he said with a quiet smile and a firm handshake. "And I'm very pleased to meet you, too. Do people call you Little Joe?"

"Yeah, guess so. I like my name. My family and best friends call me Joey."

"Joey. I like that. It fits," Red said like he was tasting it. "Okay if I call you Joey?"

"Sure!" I said, amazed that his demeanor was more like a longtime friend rather than someone who was just introduced. "Of course," I said without skipping a beat, "you can call me anything but late for dinner." The instant the words were out, I wished they were never said, but the other three men got a good laugh out of it.

"Listen kid," Red said, not laughing and a sober look on his face, "I do the comedy around here, get it?"

For a split second, my heart fell, but the others let out a big laugh as did Red when he saw my face. Okay, I'd been had, but by one of the greatest whoever graced a stage.

"I'd love to do twenty minutes with you, but we're holding up several hundred people here and 30 million around the world, so we'd better get with it," Red said as he opened an accordion door to reveal a bigger than anticipated, well lighted makeup area with a large rectangular mirror surrounded by round, softball-size makeup lights.

Of course, I thought. If not him, then who?

Red sat down and looked me in the eye through the mirror.

"Y'ever catch my show?" His expression a caricature of someone who was worried that the answer might be negative.

I laughed and started to say something like "Of course," but he cut me off by putting up a hand. Novak, Kahn, Rose and Mercer were in the broad doorway getting a big kick out of Red having fun with me.

Many years later, mentally replaying this part of the story for maybe the millionth time, I detected that Red probably sensed that I was nervous and excited, and therefore was helping me relax into the situation.

Looking into the mirror, Red demonstrated that he needed his hair to do his characters, cautioning again to not cut it short. As he mentioned each of his creations; Freddy the Freeloader, Clem Kadiddlehopper, Cauliflower McPugg, he went into each one's characterization with different, appropriate facial expressions and hair arrangement, if you will. It was so funny! Tears of laughter were flowing down my cheeks. Red was very pleased at my reaction to his private performance for me.

Promising him that I would not cut his hair too short, I got started. The hair on the sides of his head was most critical to his act, so when I finished on his left side, I used my fingers to pick his hair out like he always did to demonstrate that he had the proper amount of hair to work with.

"Go ahead. See for yourself," I said.

He let me know he was pleased.

While I was working, Mercer and Rose - or was it Kahn and Rose? Hey! The two shortest of the three told Red they wanted to show him the routine they wrote and performed the previous Saturday evening at the **Friar's Club Roast** of **Sammy Davis, Jr.**

They went into a soft-shoe bit as Red and I watched by reflecting through the mirror to the area behind us. The two music legends, futzing with their top-hats and canes in sync, danced and sang one of the funniest and easily one of the dirtiest ditties I had ever heard. I was amazed that they were such polished performers, good enough to be on any stage, in my not-so-humble and positively prejudicial opinion.

As I was snipping the hair above Red's right ear, I noticed my knees were still shaking. They shook throughout the whole haircut, though I didn't feel nervous otherwise.

As a matter of fact, I was very confident. I was simply thrilled to be there, doing my thing with these giants of the entertainment industry who were going out of their way to make me feel at home.

When I finished the haircut I said, "Okay, check it out. Make sure."

Red went through his characters again, even his famous "featherlings," **Gertrude** and **Heathcliff.** He had all of us in stitches again.

"You're good, kid. You do good work," he said with words, but the smiling expression on his face is forever in my memory.

Red stood up, reached into his pocket and pulled out a wad of bills. "How much do I owe you?"

I had not thought anything about money. "I um, I don't want money," I heard myself stammer. "I want a picture, from you to me."

"Now wait a minute," he said, very serious now. "You're a professional, just like me. When I go out on that stage or perform anywhere, I give it my all, just like you just did, and believe me, I get a good buck. We'll get you a picture, but now, how much?"

As he was fanning the money in his hand, it seemed like most of the bills were hundreds. You'd think I'd have put it in a separate pocket, check it out later, but I didn't. I'm certain he was very generous. Maybe I'll ask my guardian angel one day, just for the fun of it.

"Would you like to stay and see the show," Red asked.

I hadn't thought of that possibility but of course I jumped at the invitation.

As we walked from his dressing room to the main stage, various members of his crew would call out to him. "Good evening Mister Skelton!" "Evening Charlie. How's Johnny?" He'd then lean over to me and quietly identify that Johnny was Charlie's eight year old son. "Hi Mister Skelton," another called out from high in the rafters. They all called him Mister Skelton and they all greeted him very warmly. I wondered about what I was witnessing as I had already discovered that Hollywood was mainly informal among those on the inside.

In all the years that I went to the studios, this incident was the only time I ever experienced crew members addressing the star as Mister and in a vocal tone that bordered on singing.

I mentioned my observation to Frank Novak the next time I cut his hair. He told me that Red was the most respected and loved star in Hollywood. That kid Johnny, and every other kid of all crew members, already had his college paid for by Red Skelton personally. None of the crew ever asked directly for anything special, but Skelton made it his business to know what was needed, and he took care of it. I was sworn to confidentiality but a lot of time has passed. I don't think any objections will be raised now that I'm breaking silence.

As we reached stage left, Red told one of the attendants to get me a seat in the front row.

Aw, come on, outta space again? Nutz! Don't go nowhere 'thout me.

Chapter 28.
Red Skelton; The Final Curtain
(Part 3 of 3)

A couple of years ago, Ginny asked me why I had never made a list of the Hollywood celebrities with whom I still have, or had, intimate contact. The answer is really very simple. I never felt a need.

Sometime after I started writing this series of columns I was having a challenge recalling the name of my late friend **Carroll O'Connor's** *wife,* **Nancy**. *To jog my memory, I started writing a list of celebrity-friends on a page of notebook paper.*

After the first column, I started a second column of names, then wrote a third followed by a fourth. In the days that followed, I'd go back to that paper and write additional names in the margins. I knew there were a bunch of people but the length of the list surprised me.

Of all the names on my list, some with Academy Awards and/or Emmys, Globes, whatever; I enjoyed my association with no one more than America's Favorite Comic, **Red Skelton**. *I believe it was the extremely positive human quality Red exhibited. Here was a giant among celebrities, an all-time icon; yet a man, a living, breathing physical human being who I had the privilege of witnessing as he reached out to others, certainly not out of obligation, but with a sincere desire to help.*

Of course, I am forever grateful for the way he treated me. Everybody I know who knew Red agrees that he seemed to love and care about everyone he encountered.

My personal observation is that the biggest, best known stars in Hollywood are among the most desirable people to deal with and know on a personal level. I am hard-pressed to think of even one celebrity I've known who is an exception to my statement, and I'm not going to push it right now.

☆

I Confess! I have no idea how anyone can ride through this particular section of Nostalgia Nook with dry eyes. If y'think you can take it, read the following.

At the conclusion of the previous column, Red and I had just arrived at the main stage area. He had asked one of the attendants to put me in the front row so I would literally have a ring-side seat. As the attendant looked out into the packed audience section, his expression spoke volumes, as all front-row seats were taken.

"I'd rather watch from here, Mister Skelton. My dad's an actor and I was born in a trunk, so I'm very comfortable back here," I said, sincerely hoping to remain somewhere backstage.

As Skelton said, "I'm Red, remember?" the attendant mumbled something about rules and the Fire Marshall. "So?" Red said to him. "Get Joey a costume if you have to, but just be glad he didn't want to watch from the catwalk."

Red used his elbow to nudge me. With a wink and a facial expression like his character, "Junior – The Mean Widdle Kid," he said something about always getting his way when it counted, especially where friends were concerned.

I watched from the wings.

The show was an absolute gas. Would you believe that I cannot swear that I specifically remember if Red's opening, outlandish costume was a duck or an exaggerated caricature of a circus clown, but I distinctly remember laughing myself silly on his every line.

At one point in the show Red came bouncing off stage, ran up to me and asked, "So, how'm I doin'?"

"Great!" I said as I continued to applaud and laugh.

"Oh wonderful!" he exclaimed. "I think I'll go out and do some more."

With that he leaped and turned around in mid air and goose stepped on stage but behind the downed curtain. He paused, looked at me with an expression of a person who was about to plunge into danger and dove through the curtain's middle fold onto stage center. The crowd let out a roar of utter delight without knowing that they missed the best part of his entrance.

His skits with **Caesar Romero** and **Nanette Fabray** were cute, memory saying maybe a bit trite, but as with so many other nights, the audience ate it up. Especially me.

I distinctly remember driving home that night by way of Laurel Canyon Boulevard, my top down and the wind rustling my hair. I had a childish fantasy that I had a loud speaker on my car so I could tell the whole world that I had just been the personal guest of Red Skelton at his show after giving the great comic a haircut.

I had further contact with Caesar Romero over the years, even went to one of his birthday parties in the early nineties with Larry and Norma Storch, but I'll save all that for another time.

Regretfully, I never had personal contact with Nanette Fabray again though I always felt a special pang of closeness whenever I saw her perform. Ditto for **Sammy Kahn, Billy Rose** and **Johnny Mercer.**

I did get my personally autographed picture, an 8 by 10 glossy, black 'n white, of Red as his inimitable character, Clem Kadiddlehopper. In the pose Red had a finger pointing up under his chin, he wore that goofy hat with his hair sticking out on both sides and definitely askew. Of course, his eyes were crossed. It has hung in the exact center of my work area for years and years, right up to and including now.

By way of an appropriate wrap, I'm lifting some information from a Red Skelton website, so no cops, please.

"I feel you would appreciate knowing that during his lifetime, Red wrote poetry, authored short stories and published full length books. He illustrated children's coloring books and wrote poetic definitions of each page. His "Gertrude and Heathcliff" book was a best seller.

Red also wrote several hundred songs and composed musical arrangements, including symphonies performed by Arthur Fiedler, The Palm Springs Symphony and The London Philharmonic Symphony Orchestra.

He is most widely recognized as a painter of clowns but he also painted landscapes and still life. After leaving television in 1971, Red performed on stage as many as 100 times annually in theaters across America. He lectured on Political Science at colleges and appeared in a Command Performance honoring the Queen of England. He had the honor of being a guest and entertainer of eight U.S. Presidents and three Popes. Red was a Thirty-Third Degree Mason and received the highly coveted and seldom awarded Gorgas Medal."

When I said good night to Red that wonderful evening, he invited me back to the show, "Anytime. Just ask Frank to set it up." Don't ask why, I don't know, but I never saw the Red Skelton show live again. This fact alone causes me to believe that anyone who says he would not change anything in the past if granted such a choice is either lying or being totally foolish.

If you'd like to take another virtual tour with me, use your imagination to visualize or picture this final scene. Squint just a bit and you will see Freddie The Freeloader, Clem Kadiddlehopper, George Appleby, San Fernando Red, Cauliflower McPugg, Willie Lump-Lump, Sheriff Deadeye and of course, the One and Only, The Man With The Golden Heart, the inimitable Richard Red Skelton. We are watching them take their final leave from the Skelton Estate in Rancho Mirage, California on September 17th, 1997. We see them boarding a Big Silver Bus accompanied by hundreds of Clowns of all size, shape and description with visible halos and – wait a minute – do I see most with large, white wings?!? And look who is driving the bus! It's Junior, The Mean Widdle Kid with those two goofy birds, Gertrude and Heathcliff seated right behind him! What a wonderful sight!

As Red always said at the end of his act, ***"May God Bless!"***

Chapter 29.
If You Knew Suzie...

Over the years, people have asked if I only had Hollywood celebrities as clients. While it has always been my policy to treat everyone as a Major Star, some clients had no professional connection to the entertainment industry. One person from this group accounted for easily my most unusual experience.

I Confess. Not all of my hair clients in Hollywood were people in Show-Biz. While none were mundane, one was unique. Take Suzie, for example. She walked into my salon one day to sell me advertising.

"Take my card, call for an appointment," I told her rather than the usual, "Hit the door."

An hour later she called, offering to buy me lunch at **Schwab's**. I learned that she usually introduced herself as "Sue, The Jewelry Lady," and that her advertising gig was something new for her. (It didn't last; the jewelry did.) I also learned that her wedding was a few months away.

Suzie had very long, thick, dark and wavy hair.

"My last haircut was more than seven years ago. I had just wanted a trim. I got a super-short, Sassoon-inspired radical cut. I cried for a year! (Sniff) And I promised myself I'd never get another haircut, EVER, in my life," she said.

Unfortunately, it's not an uncommon story.

Suzie would stop by occasionally to say hello. She would converse with my clients, male or female, star or not. She would talk to me, between clients, about the style of haircut I would recommend for her. She also sold me the Turkish-Rope gold bracelet I wear today.

One day Suzie came by, floored me. She wanted me to cut her hair for her wedding. She asked to be my last appointment on the Saturday she was to fly to New York on the red-eye and be married the following morning.

When she came in that evening, she was very excited. Me, too. She was going to give up her all-one-length hair for a layered top with the length basically unchanged.

Technically, there are two totally different ways to achieve a layered top with smooth, over-the-shoulder length hair. In one style, a "V" is cut into the top of the hair, encouraging a center part. The other method is to cut the top flat, no part. Suzie was undecided about which look she wanted.

Sitting for her haircut, Suzie was debating with herself in the mirror, deciding between the two looks. Finally, she chose the "V" top.

With my first move I made a flat cut at the crown of her head, cutting off hair that would be absolutely necessary to create the high points of a "V" top. I couldn't believe my mistake. I lit a cigarette. With my mind racing, trying to figure out how to overcome this huge technical mistake, I saw no solution.

I looked up "through" my ceiling and said, "Hey Boss, please, You gotta help me here! You're going to have to correct this, because I don't know how. I'm going to place my hands with scissor and comb above her head. Take over, please."

I watched my hands (I wasn't doing it, swear) pick up a section of hair next to my first cut and snip!, leaving the new cut just a millimeter or so longer than mine. I somehow did not yell, though it seemed that my error had just been compounded.

The next cut was just a millimeter or so longer than the previous one. By this time I was in a full-fledged, though silent, panic.

Several corresponding cuts later, I suddenly thought I saw a logical sequence. I told myself to keep watching without thinking or anticipating the next moves. Several minutes later the top was fully cut. It was gorgeous! I was going BANANAS but I had to keep quiet and act nonchalant. I completed the remainder of the haircut on my own and so help me, my feet were not touching the ground.

Finished, I said to Suzie, "Okay, shake your head violently."

When she stopped she looked into the mirror and literally SCREAMED with delight. She shook her head again, bent over, straightened up, looked into the mirror and smiled from ear to ear. She screamed, "I LOVE IT," lunged and gave me a bear hug that hurt for a week.

I told this story countless times over the next ten years and many more times since. Finally, I told Suzie. I never identified who I was talking about until I was finished.

"Naw! That can't be MY story cuz MY haircut was absolutely

perfect and EVERYONE complimented my hair the next day at my wedding, even my AUNT ROSE. You gotta be talking 'bout somebody else."

Of all the people I ever told about God's Haircut, Suzie was the only one who thought the story was a put-on. But believe it, I was just an observer.

The Boss sure does a great haircut!

Chapter 30.
Eddie Carroll; the Man with the Golden Career

I Confess! **Eddie Carroll** *and I have been friends 'n colleagues for YEARS and will be so FOREVER (per Sempre in Sicilian)! Eddie's Beverly Hills hair salon is called* **A Swinging Affair.** *Guess why, but don't blow it; only one shot per person. A bevy of Hollywood's Finest, many named here, have graced Eddie's place. Wanna great haircut? Call 310-271-6262. Tell Eddie that Little Joe sent you.*

GOING HOME can be fun and rewarding, contrary to the more popular saying. In my final analysis, the overall attitude and expectation of a given individual is often the paramount factor in determining the result of a visit to the place once called home.

On my recent trip to Los Angeles, I was able to spend decent time with Sam Russo, my good buddy and former partner. Sam and wife Theresa own **Beverly Hills Hair Design** on South Beverly Drive in the heart of Beverly Hills. Theresa, you may recall from a previous column, came into our lives when she was a fresh-out-of-school 19-year-old manicurist. She approached me at my salon in the **Century Plaza Hotel** for a job. I sent her on to see Sam. The rest, as we say in Hollywood, is history.

Currently, Theresa is having chemotherapy treatments. Her gorgeous raven hair has taken a beating, but clients haven't a visual clue as her attitude reflects her upbeat and positive posture. Theresa's medical prognosis is positive also, though "all prayers are gratefully welcomed," Sam told me.

This trip I was privileged to spend an evening with another long-time good buddy and colleague, Eddie Carroll. A small handful of people have earned the distinction of being known as Hairstylist to the Stars, with Eddie a prominent member of the group. Eddie's salon is named **A Swinging Affair**, a salute to his late friend and client, The Man, **Mr. Frank Sinatra**.

I learned during our dinner that Eddie was only 20 years old when he graduated from the **Hollywood Beauty Academy**, located on 42nd Street at the corner of Broadway in the Big Apple. In those early days he also worked at the famous **Paramount Theater**. That's where he met and developed a warm friendship with Sinatra and friends, including **Gillie** and **Joe DiCarlo**.

"**Tony Curtis** was a skinny kid in those days," Eddie related.

When Eddie first moved to Los Angeles, he set up shop on Crenshaw Boulevard in Baldwin Hills, a far more chi-chi area, then.

"I remember one time," Eddie said, chuckling, "I went to the **Coconut Grove**. **Bobby Darin** was performing. Frank and wife **Mia Farrow** were sitting in a more private, secluded area – we waved to each other – and when Darin was finished, Frank stood up and applauded and kept shouting 'Bravo!' That was the real Frank."

Vic Damone and **Jerry Vail** were a couple of other crooners of note who patronized Eddie. **Diahann Carroll** and **Lola Falana** were among Eddie's favorite female clients, along with **Nancy Kwan** and **Farah Fawcett**. **John Lennon** and **Yoko Ono** would draw more than casual attention.

"This is so different," Eddie said to me with his forehead scrunched. "I feel awkward talking like this, but I've read so many of your columns and we know each other all these years, so I'm gonna to tell you a story, but I don't want you to print it, okay?"

I put my pen down.

"**Betty Hutton**, as gorgeous as she was physically, she was even more beautiful inside. I don't hafta tell you she had more talent than – oh man, the right words escape me. Anyhow, there came a time when she was busted. Broke. What a shame. Shoulda never happened to such a quality lady. She hadn't come in t'get her hair done for too long a while, so I called her, told her I wanted t'take my picture with her, use it for a write-up. She bought it. It worked out for several visits, then she caught on, tried to stop it, but I truly loved her like a cousin, the heck with money, and she knew I was sincere, so we went on like that some more."

Later in the evening, I asked Eddie to let me tell the Betty Hutton story as most of us have a similar story, but often, the person is still around and might be embarrassed.

There are many talented artists in Hollywood I know who make good money, but their driving force is the love of their work and the love they feel for their people. Eddie Carroll is certainly a fine example of this truth.

So are Sam and Theresa Russo. I'm grateful to be able to put this information in public print.

So much more happened on my trip "home," several positive things that I can relate in upcoming columns. Perhaps one day I'll tell about my movie script that got a preliminary, positive nod.

I can hardly wait for my next trip home.

✯✯✯

Chapter 31.
Jiminy Cricket, it's Jack Benny!

Wow, outta all the celebs mentioned, I only knew Sinatra, Curtis and Joe DiCarlo. Hey, Hollywood's a big town!

✵

Here's another Hollywoodite named – are you ready for this? – **Eddie Carroll!** *How in the… Don't get jittery, their careers are completely different though their names seem identical and they both have prowled Glitter Gulch for decades. You'll get a big kick outta this can 'a pastafazool, too, I assure you and no, you can't have his phone number.*

O ne of my best buddies – all time – in Hollywood is **Eddie Carroll**, Hairstylist Extraordinaire, Sinatra's *tonsorial artiste* and about whom I wrote a column not too long ago. Another good-bud, this one a new friend and living in Encino with his lovely wife, **Carolyn**, is also, are you ready, named **Eddie Carroll**. Feature that!

Eddie Carroll, the one from Encino, teamed up with actor/writer **Jamie Farr** as a partner years ago. Together they formed **Carroll-Farr Productions** and wrote and sold ideas for TV shows, even pilot scripts, to **ABC, CBS, Screengems/Columbia** and **Hanna Barbera**. They created the *Man to Man* TV series and co-produced a full season of episodes for **MGM/TV**.

I'll bet you don't recognize Eddie, yet.

In high school, Eddie and **Robert Goulet** began their friendship as classmates. They were in plays together, even went to football try-outs and signed up on a dare. Both were members of the team that made State Champ! That was in Edmonton, Alberta, Canada.

No bells ringing yet, huh?

Oh, for heaven's sake! Eddie gets audiences to imagine/believe that he is **Jack Benny** in the wonderful play, *Laughter in Bloom*.

To quote from publicity, "This award-winning theatrical presentation is filling theaters, performing art centers and casino showrooms with wall-to-wall laughter, standing ovations and rave reviews…"

Eddie looks 'n sounds enough like Jack to fool **Mary Livingston**. I'll let you know when the show is coming to SW Florida, promise.

Still no clue, you say.

Ever since 1973, Eddie has been the voice, personality and exuberance of **Jiminy Cricket**. NOW you recognize him, right?

"But Eddie," I said to him, "I didn't think **Disney** was making funnies anymore."

He laughed.

"I have been working non-stop for the past 34 years portraying Jiminy Cricket." He then broke into the voice of the lovable bug. "There hasn't been a month that's gone by without my recording something, often a major project, and I don't have to wear those silly spats, either."

There, that did it. Everybody knows Jiminy. The whole country grew up on him. Why, he's actually more famous and a busier spokes-animation than **Mickey**!

Eddie still works as an actor, entertainer and writer. "I'm just about booked solid for the next year and I have bookings extending beyond three years from now."

Eddie told me his first public appearance occurred in the first grade. He sang and played a guitar his dad hand-made for him. It was at a PTA meeting. All the performing kids were waiting in the cloak room behind the chalk board on the wall in the front of the room. When it was Eddie's turn to come out, he experienced a severe case of stage fright.

"It was like my shoes were nailed to the floor. No matter how hard I tried, I could not get my feet to move. When the teacher called upon me the third time, I just started singing and strumming that guitar with tears rolling down my cheeks as I stood there in that dark room feeling like the only person on earth." The good news is that Eddie never again had a moment of stage fright.

"I want to tell you a story on my good friend, **Jamie Farr**. It happened years ago at a time when Jamie was on a very dry run. His last unemployment check had been cashed. Jamie was supporting his mom and was more worried about her welfare than his own. He decided to go to **The Church of the Blessed Sacrament** on Sunset Boulevard. Jamie approached the statue of St. Jude and knelt down to pray. He said that he was absolutely hopeless and had heard that St. Jude is the Patron Saint of the Hopeless in addition to being the Patron Saint of the Actor. He asked St. Jude to help him out of his dilemma and pledged to build a shrine to St. Jude in thanks.

"The next day, Jamie's agent called and told him that Jamie had been awarded a two-week role by director **George Stevens** in an upcoming movie. Can you imagine Jamie's elation? But as the day wore on, Jamie wondered if the part would have been his even had he not gone to see St. Jude the night before, so back to the church he went. Again he knelt before the statue and this time asked the Saint to give him an undeniable sign that the good fortune had been the work of the Saint.

"The next day, Jamie's agent called again, this time with bad news and good news. First he told Jamie that the two-week part was no longer his, but quickly added that the whole message was quite positive. The agent told Jamie that the previous evening, director Stevens had placed pictures of all speaking actors on his baby grand piano. Jamie's picture somehow fell to the floor. Stevens picked it up and placed it back on the piano only to have it again fall to the floor. The director was mystified as there was no breeze and no other picture even fluttered. Then Jamie's picture again fell to the floor. This time, Stevens picked it up, focused on Jamie's wonderfully featured face and concluded that he would rather have Jamie play one of the leads, a part that called for a one year contract.

"Of course I'm talking about the movie called, *The Greatest Story Ever Told*, the picture in which Jamie PORTRAYED ST. JUDE."

When Eddie said those last words, I let out a shout, just as I shouted again when my wife Ginny typed that last quote mark. (Yes, "Ginny at the keyboard" is a major part of my life.)

Eddie's wife, Carolyn, is his partner-partner, too. Carolyn is a Doctor of Psychology and has proudly been Mrs. Carroll since 1963. She retired from practice so she could be the Production Manager for *"Laughter in Bloom."* Right, she's the Boss, the Big Shot.

For more information about Eddie Carroll and his one-man show, *Jack Benny – Laughter in Bloom*, please visit his website: www. eddiecarroll.com.

✫✫✫

Chapter 32.
Aw'rite Louie, Drop d'Gun!

Okay, I Confess! Hollywood isn't all Glitz 'n Glitter and not everybody's named Eddie, either. This story would be forgettable if it wasn't so unforgettable.

*Tip o' the hat to **Jack La Rue**, one of Hollywood's Greatest 'n Most Gruesome Bad Guys. He also owned 'n fronted one of TinselTown's most swank Italian restaurants. (Shoulda tried the Steak Sinatra with fried green peppers, 'taters 'n onions. Holy Gastro... Gastric... eh,!)*

A big story came outta that fine eatery one night back-in-the-day as you will see as you feast yer beady eyes on this morsel. I shoulda called it "Moider, Wit-A-Twist."

San Francisco has a world-wide reputation for delicious food. Sumptuous dishes can be found in the many fine, expensive restaurants in the **Fisherman's Wharf** area. Food with great taste can also be found in many of the inexpensive hole-in-the-wall-eateries all over and around the Seven Hills. Food is only one of the reasons Ginny and I love to visit the Golden Gate City.

Hollywood can boast many fine restaurants, too. Back in the earliest days of my hairstyling career, my home was in the Granada Hills section of the San Fernando Valley. Good restaurants were all up and down Ventura Blvd., from Studio City through Van Nuys, Sherman Oaks and Encino, all the way to Woodland Hills, a stretch of some 20-plus miles.

Studio City was home to **Jack LaRue's Italian Restaurant and Steak House**. From Jack's front door you could throw a stone to **Republic Pictures** and **RKO Radio Studios**, catty-corner across the street and at the end of an entry road. Musta made a million Western movies there. Don't go looking; it's long gone along with **Tom Mix** 'n **Hoppy, Roy, Dale** 'n **Gabby**, my friend **Pat Buttram** and an eclectic assortment of **Wild Bills**. Yeah, La Rue's place, too, gone; kaput.

Anyhow, affable **Jack LaRue** was most always playing Host and Official Greeter in the restaurant that kept his name in lights. In the movies of the late thirties through the early sixties, Jack usually played the stereotypical growling gangster Bad Guy with his black fedora, menacing smile and penchant to be fast on the trigger. Sometimes, he played the cop. Then again, he was often seen in Westerns and yup, as the guy in the black hat.

LaRue's bartender, I'll call him Louie, was the friendly but quiet sort. He grew up on the tough streets of Hoboken. Jack LaRue's sister, a small-time actress who often mentioned that she dated Sinatra "back in the day," was Louie's girlfriend. It all appeared to be a congenial arrangement and without doubt, the food was of the homemade quality with Steak Sinatra and Saltimbocca the signature specialties of the house. The booze? It was dispensed free-pour.

"Food's good lotsa places 'round here. Free-pour is my marketing strategy," Jack LaRue once told me with a belly laugh. "Creates loyalty. I got a ton a people who come here three-four nights a week."

Bartender Louie had been my client for several years, starting at Cosmo's and following me to Russo's, Goomba Sam's place just off the corner of Santa Monica and La Cienega.

One Tuesday Louie called, wanted an appointment for the same day.

"Did you hear the news?" he asked over the phone. "I could get busted any minute. I'll tell ya when I come t'see you."

Later, as I was giving him an overdue haircut, he related that a guy entered his bar around 1:30 a.m. the Saturday just past, ordered a Scotch, neat. Fifteen minutes later, Louie made last call. The guy – said his name was Nick – ordered another. At 2 a.m., Louie started bussing glasses and closing out tabs. Nick was last to settle up, after which he made his way to the door. He stopped, started back, saying he forgot to leave a tip.

"I knew I was in for it, but I was too far away from my .38."

Nick pulled out a Lugar. He knew where the night's take was kept. Louie thought about holding some back, then had another idea.

"Don't try to follow me. I'm gonna wait outside for five minutes. If you come out, I'll blow yer head off." He slammed the door.

Louie immediately grabbed his revolver. He shut the interior lights before opening the door, not ten seconds behind Nick.

Out on the lot, Nick was just opening his driver's side door.

"Hey!" Louie shouted.

In one motion, Nick turned and fired. Louie squeezed off three of his own. In the next few minutes, an army of cops poured in, lights flashing 'n sirens blaring. Just like across the street on the back-lot. This time without cameras rolling

Louie, wouldyabelieve, was charged with murder. And convicted! The judge refused to honor the plea deal, gave him 15 to life.

About ten years later, Janet, my receptionist/manicurist, called me away from a client.

"Take line two. This guy will only talk to you, says he's a friend from years ago, but he sounds more New York than Cleveland."

It was Louie. He wanted my okay to make an appointment.

"I'm not going to stick around LA. Too different; feels strange." he told me during his first haircut in freedom. "Maybe I'll hit 'Frisco. Start fresh."

Never heard from him again. In my book, he's living proof that bad things can happen to good people.

At least I knew he'd be able to eat pretty good.

Chapter 33.
A Shave From Out of This World

I Confess! Out of the small handful of people who can honestly claim to be a Hairstylist to the Stars, I was the only one who had an Astronaut for a client. **Scott Carpenter** *was one of the Original Seven (those fabulous Right Stuff guys) who helped alla us (USA) to the Stars and Down deep, too, a fact most people don't know. You'll also meet the* **Calypso Team** *here. Scott had a positively eclectic personality and is "forever in the upper 1%" of my clients.*

In the Hollywood/Beverly Hills area, back when I first got there or even including more recent times, people visiting various hair salons, barber shops or beauty shops might see pictures of actors and actresses adorning the walls. Some of the people in those photos would be unknown, others would be in the "Oh yeah, that's What's-His-Name" class, and then there would be those who are easy-to-recognize celebrities.

In my salon over the years, I would display the pictures of those client-actors who gave me a photo and requested that I hang it on my wall. **Red Skelton** was a definite exception. His Clem Kadiddlehopper was prominently placed because I asked Red for the privilege. I also asked **Vic Morrow** for a photo. He gave me an 8 x 10 of him in his *Combat!* fatigues.

Many of my most prominent celebrities never were asked for a photo - nor did they offer one- as I knew they wanted anonymity. Today, I wish I had photos of several who held special significance for me. **Judy Garland** comes to mind. So does **Mama Cass Elliott**. (For accuracy's sake, **Sid Luft** was my client, not Judy, but she often told me how she appreciated the way I helped make her husband "...look so handsome." The ultra-friendly Mama Cass often came to my salon with her good friend and my client, Carol Rubenstein, but Mama did not have any hair-work done.)

Of all my hairstylist colleagues in Hollywood boasting celebrity clientele, I am privileged to be the only one who can claim an Astronaut. He was one of the original seven from Project Mercury, **Scott Carpenter**. I recall that people who patronized my salon would usually recognize Scott instantly. Even movie and TV celebrities would often show at least a crack in their composure upon seeing him. Oftentimes, when Scott realized that someone – celebrity and unknown alike – had recognized him, seemed to want to say something but remained silent, (if wide-eyed) Scott broke the ice by saying "Hello!" and extending his hand.

"What a Mensch!" I vividly recall one of my clients exclaiming, echoing similar meaning statements by others.

Scott had a rather quiet countenance, though as mentioned, I often saw him switch gears and be very personable. He demonstrated a high curiosity factor regarding various subjects when talking with strangers and an amazing memory when talking to people he had casually met previously. He seemed genuinely interested in the lives and opinions of people he met, as I was impressed to observe on so many occasions over the approximate 11 years that he was my client.

Scott Carpenter was the only Astronaut who was also an Aquanaut, a fact most people of today are surprised to learn. He established more still-standing aquatic records than accomplishments from outer space.

On the internet the other day while looking for a current address for Scott, I was surprised to learn that he worked closely with French oceanographer **J.Y. Cousteau** and members of his **Calypso Team.** (The article was covering part of the timeframe when Scott was my client.) The article also noted that Scott dived most of the world's oceans with the Cousteau people, even including dives under the Arctic ice.

Whenever they visited Southern California, the world renown Jacques Cousteau, his two sons and other members of the Calypso Team frequented my salon for a period of years, including when Cosmo owned the salon and continuing after I became the owner. Scott and the Cousteau gentlemen were visiting the salon in the same timeframe, but at that time all were unaware that we were associating with each other! Ain't that a hoot!

My memory indicates that Scott involved himself with few commercial products, but I know he had something to do with the introduction of the Track II Razor concept for Gillette. From our earliest getting-acquainted conversations, Scott knew that I shaved with a barber's straight razor exclusively. I related to him that I had taught myself the skill as a kid of 13 when I "borrowed" my father's straight razor for my first shave. Scott was aware that I had since tried various "safety razors," even electric shavers, but in my opinion those devices could not compete with a barber's razor for comfort or quality of shave.

I told Scott that the concept of the new Track II Razor seemed logical. He asked if I would consider shaving with the new razor so that I might give him my opinion as to its ability to compete with the shave of a barber's razor. He gave me a six-pack and promised a master case of blades if I liked the razor, a totally unnecessary gesture. My imagination still contains few scenarios wherein I would say "no" to a request from this man who I respect as one of the highest quality people I ever knew and one of history's major icons.

I was amazed at how favorably the "Deuce" - as I nicknamed the two-blade razor - performed against my pearl handled barber's razor, which I had years before dubbed "White Lightening." I used that first Track II blade for about five days before it lost too much of its comfort. The next blade performed comfortably for about a week. Impressive, indeed.

"It compares favorably to my straight razor," I told Scott. "But I don't like the cost of it."

Scott wanted to know how low the price would have to be for me to call it a good deal.

"You're asking the wrong guy that question," I told Scott. I went on to explain that my razor had been bought years before and would be usable for generations to come. I owned – and still own - a small collection of razors, some a century-plus old, all usable. Therefore, one cent would have been too much for me to call the Deuce a good deal, technically speaking.

I accepted the master case. (I shoulda asked for a *picture*!) By the time I went through those razors, I had pretty much made the switch. The Deuce didn't require stropping and allowed me to get through the shave a little quicker. Convenience can easily be called an All-American Achilles' heel, if you ask me.

I enjoyed my friendship with Scott Carpenter and the privilege of cutting his hair for all those years, our time together starting just about when I met Norma and Larry Storch. Scott and I lost contact when he moved to Florida. No, I don't recall exactly what part of Florida, but his move occurred in the early eighties, maybe 1984. According to info on the internet, he presently resides in Vail, Colorado. Wherever he is, may he know that we remember and we care.

Today I mostly use the upgraded three-blade razor, though once in a while I'll strop up 'ole White Lightening and give it a go. Funny, all these years later, most every time I shave, especially when using the straight razor, my mind snaps back through time... and I get to say a mental Hello! to my exalted friend, Scott Carpenter. It makes for a wonderful, positive way to start a new day.

★★★

Chapter 34.
Seems Like Only Yesterday

Coming up next you get to briefly meet my paternal grandfather, in whose honor I am named. Grampa Joe is just taking leave of this life, but you'll probably find the surrounding circumstances rather interesting. Many family 'n friends over the years have found my experiences outside the five senses to be fascinating, to understate the fact. 'Course, that's NUTTIN compared to MY reaction.

Far too many memories are rather flimsy-cloudy, thin and irritatingly just out of reach. Then there are those memories that remain vivid regardless of the number of years that pass. There is a certain memory, a very vivid and clear memory, of a major family event that occurred during the summer preceding my senior year in high school.

For practical purposes, it started on the evening of July 10th. I had just been to visit my paternal grandfather in Lakeshore Hospital. Grandpa Joe, for whom I am named, was not feeling or looking very good.

The whole family was at the hospital. Well, Aunt Mary and Uncle Pete had already moved to Arizona with cousins Gracie, Russell and Joey, but we still numbered about 35 or 40 people. Not bad, considering the family had only been in America from Sicily for about forty years. Anyhow, the nurse announced that visiting hours were over, that we'd all have to go. We all had come to know the routine, so we kissed each other and Grampa goodnight and it was *buona notte* all around.

I was driving alone that night. As I was leaving the hospital parking lot, I approached the traffic light at Lakeshore Boulevard. All the cars before me had made it through, so there I sat, staring up at the red light waiting for the change to green.

In that moment, a thought impacted me. It was another of those thoughts, the kind that did not originate within me. This time, like some of the others, the thought really made no sense at all.

"If you turn left, you will not see your grandfather alive again. If you turn right, you will see him one more time."

It didn't come to me in words, exactly; it came to me in *knowingness*. If that isn't exactly clear, don't fret; it took *years* for the messages to make sense to me.

Here's my dilemma. I was meeting some friends at a place where I needed to turn left on Lakeshore Boulevard. If I turned right, the road extended for four miles before I could turn around to head east. There was no road going straight. The hospital access road entered Lakeshore Boulevard with the option to go only east or west.

I was immediately angry. These "thoughts" had occurred to me before, each time warning of some imminent danger. When I followed the advice of the thought, everything worked out fine. When I went against the thought, many negative things happened including the deaths of people dear to me. If I were to tell somebody of the thought, everything was negated. No, I'm not exaggerating. That's the way it all worked since I was eight years old.

The real problem with these - what do I call them - Special Thoughts? The real problem with these Special Thoughts was that, often times, at first I wasn't sure if my imagination was fooling around with me or if I was experiencing one of "those" thoughts. Usually, after a bit of contemplation, I could determine the origin of the thought. Halfway, anyhow. Tonight, this seemed to be one of the Special Thoughts. Maybe.

I reasoned that if I turned left, as I wanted to, I might not get to see my grandfather alive again. Wow! Nobody told me his life was in danger! So what's with this Special Thought? Sure, I could turn right, drive the four miles and then do a u-turn. But that would take me a good half hour out of my way and I was already running late. Confused and unable to make a decision, I found myself wishing my '49 Chevy was some kind of jet-sled.

I was startled by a man banging on my driver's door window. As I rolled it down, I saw his face all scrunched.

"Hey buddy, you okay?"

"Sure. Why?"

"Why? You just sat through THREE green lights. Look behind you and see all the cars honking 'n piled up."

"Gee mister, sorry." With that, I jammed it into first and peeled some rubber as I turned left.

All the rest of that evening my decision really bothered me. I even told my friends about it, hoping to dispel my feelings and negate the message.

The next morning, after finding out that my grandfather had a rather restful night, I headed to work. At the time, my buddy Joe Mula and I were working as laborers for two scab bricklayers. I say scab to identify that they were not union bricklayers, though I do not mean the term derogatorily today.

See, union guys laid 300 bricks per day, not 299 or 301. These scabs each laid 1200 bricks per day. Wow, you say. Wow it is. We usually worked 10 hours a day rather than eight, for these men were independent contractors and Joe and I knew the deal up front.

Because these two men worked so quickly and efficiently, Joe and I evolved into a pattern where one day I would mix mud and he would carry bricks and the next day we reversed roles. Whenever one of us would fall behind, the other would jump in until all was running smoothly again. Often, one helping the other necessitated both of us doing the other job together until both ends caught up to the two bricklayers. God knows we were mostly spent at the end of a day.

The jobsite was a muddy mess. We had laid down some planks; otherwise the wheelbarrow hauling the cement could never have made it from the portable mixer to the partially-built home. Whoever was carrying the hod would also use the planks to avoid sloshing through the mud. Y'could lose a boot that way. When we both used the same planked pathway going in opposite directions, the wheelbarrow had priority.

I had just dumped my wheelbarrow and was turning to go back to the mixer. From behind me, I heard a loud BANG. It was more like a bowling ball making a hollow POCK! sound on a wooden floor. I wondered what could possibly have made such a noise. As I scanned behind me, I realized that no such sound could come from anything in sight.

Joe was just approaching my area with that 105 pound hod on his shoulder. I asked if he had just heard the loud noise. I can't exactly quote his response, not that I don't remember it, but suffice it to say that he used a lot of lip to tell me that there had not been any kind of loud noise.

"What time y'got?" I asked Joe.

"@#$@ "

"No really, y'know I don't wear a watch. What time is it?"

"@#$@ &^%@$# ! And we still have about two hours t'go."

There were more words. Friendly. Hey, we were buddies, still are. Anyhow, I convinced Joe that I needed to know the exact time, right then.

He balanced the butt handle of the hod on the wooden plank, almost loosing his load of bricks as he pulled his watch from his pocket. The time was exactly 4:20.

"Now what the hell difference does that make?" he wanted to know.

"Beats th'shit outta me."

Driving home we looked for the dog we had hit that morning. There were some kids playing in the yard near the impact area. We stopped. No, they didn't know anything about a hurt or dead brown dog.

At home, I found a message on the kitchen table. My mother's note said to pick up my sister at her girlfriend's and go to Granma and Granpa's house instead of the hospital.

I did my darnedest to shake off the negativeness that coiled me like a giant python as I showered and dressed.

Arriving at my grandparents' house, I saw family cars all over the place. Not good.

We went to the side door. I opened it and let JoAnn enter first. As she turned right and went up the three steps into the kitchen, my grandmother and my father were seated at the kitchen table, neither smiling.

"Hi Grandma! Hi Daddy," JoAnn said, seemingly oblivious to what I perceived to be an ominous scene. "How's Grandpa?"

"No more Grandpa!" Grandma exclaimed as she started to cry. My father also started to cry. JoAnn let out a blood-curdling scream. I turned and dove through the door, somehow without breaking it.

At a time like this, everyone is into their own head, their own thoughts, their own feelings. I was in a rage. Make that RAGE. I shouldn't have turned left! I was mad, damnit, ANGRY; and I was apologizing to my grandfather.

I was suddenly aware that my father was hugging me. My grandmother and my mother joined us as did other family members, creating a tight huddle.

"What's 420 mean?" I asked nobody in particular. Someone repeated 420, someone else tried to make sense of my question. "What room was grandpa in?"

"Grandpa was moved to the sixth floor after the procedure this morning. It had to be six-um..." Aunt Mel said.

"420 has to mean something," I said. "That was the time when I heard the loud bang."

"Oh, time! My father died at 4:20 this afternoon," Aunt Mel exclaimed.

Of course.

Now some of the things made a bit of sense. I really didn't want to talk about it right then, but some knew. My father and mother knew I had another one of "those." So did my Grandmother. They knew I would talk about it later, in private, and they would tell me that later was a better choice. All I really wanted to do right at that moment was light up a Lucky.

Y'know, I think I was addicted to the name as much as to the act. A little luck once in a while shouldn't hurt.

Memories. The older we become, the more precious, the more we live for them, the more they mean to us. This is a pleasant memory today, now that most-all of the questions have been answered.

It's rather hard to believe that all of the adults who were there that day have passed away. Aunt Mel and Aunt Jo are in assisted living. Uncle Ronnie, the youngest adult there, just passed away a few weeks ago. In that series of memories, I see and visit with them all. Yes, though bitter-sweet, it's a very pleasant memory.

Footnote: I got fired from that scab job. I found out when I called right after returning from Grampa's funeral. I still say that wasn't nice. Oh, the 'thoughts' that showed me future happenings? They continued for several more years, but I'll tell more another time.

Chapter 35.
The Surprise Guest Artist

I Confess! The Zigs 'n Zags that put a story together sometimes follow a plan of nobody on earth, apparently. An invitation to a party leads to a major crossroad in life; not at the party itself, but... Wait a minute! Let me just say that my old neighborhood followed me to Hollywood (Thank God!) and provided many benefits and I'll stop right there. You go on.

D ecisions, decisions....
     As I've noted in the past, sometimes making even a small, seemingly inconsequential decision can have an amazingly big effect. Like the time my neighbors invited me to a Saturday night party.

They were a married couple and lived in the building next-door to our apartment building on Woodman Avenue near Oxnard Street. Most of the people attending the party would be young married couples, I was told. Quite honestly, I wasn't very interested as I was still single. This was during my earliest days of working part time at **Cosmo's Hairstyling Salon** in Hollywood.

Something better would present itself for Saturday night, I was sure, providing a good excuse for not attending. Funny, nothing did. So along about party time, I decided to sneak away, go "somewhere special." But not to be. A '56 Crown Victoria was blocking my royal blue '57 Chevy convertible. (Shoulda kept that buggy, damnit.)

'Okay, okay, I'll go to the dumb party and then think of something so I could bow out gracefully' was my hastily conceived and not-too-imaginative plan.

One of the girls at the party had recently graduated from *Sanzo's*, a local beauty school in Van Nuys. I mentioned that I grew up with people named Sanzo in Cleveland. She told me that the owner, Mr. Sanzo, was also from Cleveland. Hmmm, interesting. I had been thinking about taking a color class, someplace, but I had no idea where.

I went to see him and to my surprise, Mr. Sanzo was from my old neighborhood in Collinwood. My name was not really familiar to him, but my mother's maiden name, Figer, caused him to startle, so I mentioned that mom's younger brother was known as Tubby.

"Would you like to attend my school?"

"Yes, if I could come part time, Mr. Sanzo. I want to learn how to cut ladies hair and I also want to know how to do color and give perms. I'd like to be able to offer those services to men."

"Do you have two dollars?"

I offered two one-dollar bills. "What's two dollars for?"

"That's to register you with the state of California. It's also your total cost of enrollment. Call it a free scholarship!"

Stunned? Try numb to the bone.

"I owe your uncle my life, literally. There's never been a good way to pay him. Not even now, but this helps."

Once, sometime later when I was giving Mr. Sanzo my special finger-cut haircut, I asked him to tell me more about him and my uncle. He simply said to never mind and shifted smoothly to another subject. He questioned my every move as I cut his hair, getting rid of the bulges on his sides and removing unnecessary length on top, giving him better coverage, making his hair seem fuller.

On another occasion I asked his neighborhood name, as almost everybody had one. He told me he was known as "Sonny Boy."

Later, I told my uncle and asked for more of the story.

"I'll have to tell Sonny 'thank you.' Like your grandpa told you years ago, you learn best with your ears open and your mouth closed. With Sonny, you have a great teacher. I'm grateful for his helping you."

And that, as they say, was that.

About a week later, the daily bulletin board announced that a ladies haircut would be demonstrated by a "Mystery Guest Artist" at 1 p.m. sharp. We were all anxious, other students telling me that Mr. Sanzo often brought in outside experts to demonstrate various techniques.

I took a front row seat and was somewhat surprised to see that the model was Mrs. Sanzo.

Mr. Sanzo gave the guest artist a major build-up. He asked everyone to pay close attention and explained the value of giving a precision haircut. He mentioned that the demonstrator would be using a uniquely developed finger-cutting technique.

Then he introduced me. Make that ME! I guarantee I was the most surprised person in the room though certainly not the only one. Some who had befriended me at first thought I was in on the gag, but I guess my expression and demeanor convinced them otherwise.

"But Mr. Sanzo," I whispered to him, "I don't know the FIRST THING about giving a lady a haircut."

"Yes you do," he whispered back. "Just cut away four weeks growth and improve upon the shape and balance."

Looking back, I am amazed to say that I understood him perfectly, for I had not yet fully realized that I possess God-given talent. That was easily one of the great lessons of my life and I have improvised on the concept ever since.

Thanks, Sonny Boy. Thanks for Everything. I'm sure glad I went to that party.

And see, a small decision, even one that seemed to be forced by circumstance, can have a life-long impact. I was right that night when I felt that I would be going "somewhere special."

Chapter 36.
Friends-a-Jillion – Hollywood Style

(Part 1 of 2)

*I Confess! Few people have strummed my heartstrings like **Norma** and **Larry Storch**. Here's a glimpse of our more than 30-year friendship. (The original column was written in just over the 1000 word limit imposed by the newspaper.)*

It has been said that to have one good, true friend is the ultimate definition of being rich. So how do you label someone who has an entire bouquet of good, true friends? Maybe that's a proper description of a multi-jillionaire.

For 30 years I have been blessed by a close, love-fueled friendship with **Larry and Norma Storch**. They came into my life just after I acquired ownership of **Cosmo's Hairstyling Salon,** having been referred to me by writer-producer-director, **Larry Sands**. (He became the first of two good friends I would lose because of a helicopter crash. The other, of course, was **Vic Morrow**.)

I was to learn that Larry and Norma first met in 1947. Sometimes, life teaches, even a rare, soul-mate type relationship gets off to an inglorious start; stops, and only once in a very blue moon has new life breathed into it. The Storches were wed in 1961.

In those days Norma was a lovely redhead in the **Lucille Ball** mold, retaining her great looks and demeanor through our most recent time together this past March. More importantly, she was also enthusiastic about becoming Larry's Manager, Confidant and Girl Friday-Saturday-Sunday.

Maybe I should throw in that Norma was his Savior too, as she was key to extracting Larry from the not-so-proverbial bottle.

"Of course," she once confided when we were sharing a quiet, private moment, "only Larry could accomplish such a feat, as all of us must exorcise our own ghosts, but I was there to spur him on, to encourage him."

For more than 60 years Larry has been recognized as an extraordinarily gifted actor, stand-up comic and celebrity-mimic. **Frank Sinatra** and **Dionne Warwick** often tapped Larry to be their lead act so he could use his unique talents to tenderize an audience for them.

In fact, **Sammy Davis Jr**. publicly acknowledged that he learned all he knew about being a successful celebrity-mimic from Larry Storch. Sammy told the story to my career-life-long good friend, **Casey Kasem**, during a broadcasted interview.

Larry is best recognized as **Corporal Agarn** on the popular TV sit-com, *F Troup*, which has been shown continually in syndication since it's original run in the late '60s. Then to now, Larry has also been a guest star on popular TV shows like *Married With Children* and *Columbo*, accumulating over 300 TV and Movie credits. And he's still counting.

Larry has spent these past several years performing around the country and on Broadway in stage productions such as *Oklahoma!* with **Jean Stapleton**; in *Annie Get Your Gun* with **Reba McIntire**; and in *Some Like It Hot* with 60 year good-buddy **Tony Curtis.**

Porgy And Bess is a classic movie out of 1959. It has also been a highly venerated stage production both on and off Broadway. The cast of the stage version has always been all black, except for the time they invited Larry to join them for a stretch. Small wonder Larry Storch is known and revered in millions of American households and who knows how many more worldwide, a celebrity's paramount reward.

Over the years Larry, Norma and I have had many memorable occasions in addition to a multitude of haircuts. Sometimes it was simply an evening out to dinner. That reminds me, they took me to **Caesar Romero's** birthday party around 1990 where I met their good friend, **Buddy Rogers**, the star of the epic 1927-28 film, *Wings*, winner of the very first **Academy Award**. I spent most of the evening kibitzing with Buddy. For me, a poignant memory.

I've always been like a kid in a candy store when sitting in a theater with Norma enjoying Larry on stage as he had the audience eating out of his hand. When we saw him in the Los Angeles production of *Oklahoma!*, the audience applauded Larry's every entrance and exit, a truly unusual display of recognition and appreciation.

There was a singular incident some 14 or so years ago. My parents came into my salon for haircuts just as Larry and Norma were about to leave. Larry and my dad had known each other for several years at that point as both had appeared with Tony Curtis in the movie, *Captain Newman, M.D*. It was the first time my mom and Norma had an opportunity to meet.

My mother handed me a large brown paper sack, advising that I "Better put this in the refrigerator." Norma asked if the bag might contain home-made spaghetti sauce, guessing correctly. At my mother's insistence, ("Joey can get more anytime") the Storches went home with the bounty. Next day Norma called, gushing compliments and wanting my mother's phone number. That began a period where each time Larry and Norma came by for a haircut, my mom made sure they also walked away with a quart of her delicious, authentic old-country-recipe sauce.

On our recent trip to Los Angeles this past September, Ginny and I were taken to Hollywood's still-fabulous **Musso & Frank's Restaurant** by **Tina and Joey Dorando**. (I met Joey during my first year while an apprentice at Cosmo's. Tina came along later. Joey's son Jimmy and my daughter Trina were born two weeks apart and have joked about meeting "prior to birth through tummy-graph.")

After we were seated, Tina said she was so sorry to hear of the death of my dear friend, Norma Storch. "Tina," I said, shock electrifying my body, "I just left a message on their phone before coming here to LA. You're mistaken, I'm sure."

With the gentleness of a true friend, Tina told me that the L.A. Times used a half page for Norma's obituary. I would have fallen had we not been seated in a booth.

Norma Storch, just a few years younger than my mother, is in my mind now sharing recipes and laughter with Mom, the two of them spearheading a group of extremely strong voices in my personal chorus of heavenly advocates. Hey, if you're gonna dream....

And Larry, what of Larry? Always the question at a time like this, isn't it? Toughest time in the world to take the ball and go out there and pitch, but you know what? I can hear Norma shouting encouragement. My mom and dad, too.

See, I really am blessed. Next week, I'll wrap up this friendship theme with another story that was born and still lives in Hollywood.

✮✮✮

Chapter 37.
Friends-a-Jillion, Two – Hollywood Style
(Part 2 of 2)

I Confess! **Theresa and Sam Russo** *are two of my most cherished friends. Sam and I have a massive history with Theresa right there in the front seat, as you are about to see.*

Hey, given this unpredictable world we live in, I wouldn't be surprised if we ended up working together again. I'd vote for that.

I looked up the word "friend" in my American Heritage Dictionary, 2000 Edition. It said, "1. A person whom one knows, likes, and trusts. 2. A person whom one knows; an acquaintance. 3...." (More of the same. Dull & Dry)

I've never been one to think that I could compete with a dictionary for definitions, but in this case, the above leaves a lot to be desired, (why'd they leave out the word 'love'?) so I'll continue to submit my case forthwith.

For a few years before I bought **Cosmo's,** I owned the hairstyling salon located in the still fabulous **Century Plaza Hotel**. At the time it was Los Angeles' newest and most prestigious hotel, the flagship of the **Westin** chain. Fortune 500 companies reserved suites the year 'round. The real plumb, by far, was the Federal Government, sole tenant of the 7th Floor.

One day she walked in. Just like that. Said her name was **Theresa Corea**. Talk about gorgeous – and every bit as sweet – she had a definite Eurasian flavor to her beautifully sculpted facial features and slicked-back-into-a-ponytail black, shiny hair. She was only 19, she said, and had just graduated from manicuring school.

I learned that her father was a Filipino waiter familiar to me who worked at **Trader Vic's Restaurant** in Beverly Hills. (I've called him 'Pop' ever since.) Furthermore, her uncle was **Leon Lompoc**, an actor and barber, the man from whom I bought my famous-at-the-time Filipino Shears, pounded out of blown-apart WW II Jeeps. Her mom, (explaining her exotic looks, somewhat) was Polish, she related, and in my memory a very sweet lady, indeed.

Did I need a manicurist, she wanted to know. Talk about timing. With all her wonderful assets, I would have been unfair to Janet Thomson and my other two manicurists, and Theresa, to say yes. But you know what? My goomba and best buddy, Sam Russo, needed a manicurist.

"Go see him," I recommended.

One of Theresa's sisters; Lana, I think – there are about nine of them, all gorgeous - told her to go see Bobby Russo, Sam's cousin, whose shop was located on Little Santa Monica, just down the street from where Lana worked. Lana didn't know about Sam or me, and the whole story didn't get connected for *years*.

Anyhow, Bobby had just hired a manicurist two days before, so what did Bobby do? Told her to go see his cousin Sam. (We lost cousin Bobby this past year. Very sad. I'll tell more another time.)

So why is the whole world trying to get me to go see this Sam Russo, Theresa has said she wondered. Getting a job as a manicurist was proving to be tough, but maybe this Sam....

Sam's place was named **Russo - Distinctive Hair Design**. It was located on the northwest corner of Santa Monica and LaCienega Boulevards. Yep, right next door to the infamous **Phone Booth**, where girls gyrated to hootchy-kootchy music and served watered-down booze that sold for three times a normal drink's price. Didn't seem to hurt or help Russo's reputation, but... Hey, we'll never know for sure.

Walking through the front door of Sam's, the reception/waiting area approximated a 20' x 20' space. A partition separated the working area with an archway entry in the right-side half of the wall. The reception desk was to the left and faced the door. Behind the desk was a glassless window so Sam could easily converse with those in the waiting room or the receptionist without leaving his work area.

The day Theresa walked into Sam's place, good buddy and fellow hairstylist **Phil Fayne** was seated behind the desk, minding the store while waiting for his next client. One look at Theresa and Phil leaned his chair back, rapped on the wall and said, "Hey Sambo, don't look now, but your next wife just came in the front door."

Steve was the porter in those days, a man maybe 25 years our senior and a **Nat King Cole** look-alike and no, he couldn't sing – or play center field – but so what?

"If you hire this young lady" Steve admonished Sam, "don't you go messin' with her." Sam didn't mess. He was already going through a thoroughly messy divorce. Fortunately for a jillion reasons, Sam hired her.

Sometime later, the situation was ripe for Sam and Theresa's first innocent dinner date. Even Steve approved. Guess what couple they chose as a double date.

The four of us went to my all-time favorite restaurant, the **Casa Vega** in Sherman Oaks, where the food still is authentic Mexican cuisine and delicious. The restaurant has always been dimly lit, offering a more romantic setting. Sometimes, entering from outside, a person needed a minute or so to adjust the eyeballs to the point of clearly seeing faces.

At the time, owner **Ray Vega** was my client, and Sam's client was the head bartender, **Chico**. A natural, understandable pick for the right place, wouldn't y'say? Just as the four of us were seated in our booth, drinking a double-margarita toast of good wishes for Sam and Theresa, guess who walked through the door.

Just as I saw Sam's new-ex-sister-in-law, she saw me and came bouncing over to our table with an enthusiastic "Oh hi Joe!" I can still hear the thud of her jaw dropping. Right on her tail was Big Sis, Sam's New-Ex. Thud-Thud. It was terrible. It also, thank goodness, ended without further ado, thank goodness. Yes, I know I said it twice. Still makes me shudder.

Next important date on the 2004 calendar will mark Sam and Theresa's 30th wedding anniversary. Among the many things, accomplishments or points of recognition that might be underscored here, I know they are most proud of their son, Justin, who graduated with honors from high school and just pulled a Ditto from UCLA. Justin now works for a highly regarded major medical HMO. Swings a mean golf club, too.

Sure Sam and Theresa shared a great evening and delicious dinner with Ginny and me when we visited L.A. recently. They took us to the new, extravagantly designed outdoor mall called **The Grove**, located where the old **Farmer's Market** parking lot once sat baking in the California sun on Fairfax Avenue and Third Street. Farmer's Market, by the way, is still there and located immediately South of the CBS Studios where I went so long ago to share a lifetime, one evening, with the inimitable **Red Skelton**.

Sam and I even got to play golf at **Balboa Golf Course**, our hacking yard for all those years. He shot 46 on the front nine to my 47. I shot 46 on the back nine to his 47. So what's new?

Sam and Theresa own **Russo's Beverly Hills Hair Design** in Beverly Hills, California. I bunked in, Ginny at my side, and gave a couple of haircuts one day this past September. **Casey Kasem,** recently officially recognized by the music industry as the Icon he has been for decades, dropped by for some chit-chat and some laughs as did **Janet Thomson,** the other manicurist I mentioned earlier and far more importantly, our good, true friend. All these years later, we're all together still. Always will be. Miles and years mean nuttin but good. It's a wonderful arrangement.

Part One of this column on Norma Storch is the most difficult I've ever written. I consider this part among the most pleasurable. Appropriate, huh? Good friends, truly good friends, are – to paraphrase a well-worn commercial – PRICELESS. Give at least one of your good friends a hug today. You'll make their day. And yours, too.

See, true romance can happen anywhere, even in Hollywood. It ain't all tinsel.

Chapter 38.
Spotlight on Coach Ed Ferris

(Part 1 of 2)

I Confess! I'm into lifting up the heroes who have graced my life, as if you hadn't noticed. How do you accurately portray a man who altered the Course of Life for so great a number of people? The question requires enough answers to fill a book. WHY do you portray... is more on point. So, Ladies and Gentlemen, meet The Coach!

Some people know what they want to do in life from the time they are young. **Mozart** knew almost from the cradle, as history tells us he was composing by the age of four. A goodly number of people, it seems, haven't a clue, often extending their indecision into college, many going beyond. For some uncertain people regardless of whether they partake of higher education, lack of decision can continue through varied portions of adulthood.

Nat "King" Cole was vehemently positive about what he wanted to do in life, right from the time he was a kid. He became, of course, one of the 20th Century's most famous entertainers, a true balladeer, even recognizable to a surprising number of the 'under 30 crowd,' though he died more than 40 years ago.

Two facts of Cole's life cause eyebrows to arch. He was the first Black entertainer to have his own prime-time TV shows; Specials, too. And the fact less well known, Cole wanted desperately, more than anything else, *to play center field for the Dodgers!* He applauded with tears-of-a-different-though-positive-kind when **Jackie Robinson** made the team... and the league... causing the country; yea the world, to be a better place in which to live.

(By the way, I regret that I never met Nat, but I met his beautiful daughter, **Natalie**. I'll cover that another day.)

The concept of determining Life's vocational direction at an early age comes to the fore as the result of feedback since I started writing this column. (Including my new friend named Jeni, but more on her later.) Did I want to write and cut hair, some have asked, or was it cut hair and then write? The honest truth is that as a teenager I knew for certain that upon hitting the age of 18, I was definitely going to drive a cement truck.

Yep, and furthermore, I was going to add a room above my parents' garage and fix it up real nice so I could have a place where I could roll around in all that dough I'd be raking in at the rate of $5 per hour. Man, I was going to have a ball and be rich, too! The company I anticipated working for had these big, red mixers, no small factor; then.

The dream of driving that truck was born when I was 13 years old and working summers and weekends in my Uncle Sam Negrelli's construction company as a carpenter's helper.

My life's new direction all started without my knowledge, consent or even wish, when I was a sophomore at Mayfield High School in one of the eastern-most suburbs of the greater Cleveland area. That was about the time that Life used a new young teacher and wrestling coach, Mr. Ed Ferris, as a prod to get me going down another path, for that's when he joined the teaching staff.

Actually, Mr. Ferris' duties began before the official start of school and classes that year, when he joined the football coaching staff. Ever so appropriately, final analysis reveals, I started calling him Coach from the get-go. (Football was my prime motivating factor for remaining in high school at that point in my life, a truth that caused me to blush for a time after high school and prior to maturity.)

At first sight I thought he was Italian. Picture Coach Ferris as a big man, though only average height, with dark, wavy hair and a totally disarming smile. I said big but don't think fat; he didn't have any. He was hard as a rock, so it was wise not to bump into him, let alone try to block or tackle him. I've hit some stone walls that were softer.

We learned that he was the NCAA Heavyweight Wrestling Champion out of Ohio University in Athens, Ohio, not to be confused with Ohio State, the Big Ten football powerhouse in Columbus. So his size had abundant credential, if you're picking up the drift.

Easily, Coach Ferris' most outstanding trait was his charismatic personality, once anyone focused beyond his commanding physical presence. My earliest studied impression was - and continues to be - that his heart and psyche decreed to him that people, their lives, ambitions and dreams constitute the most compelling subjects commanding his attention.

The theme of this column became a must-do-now for me since my recent trip to Cleveland. I spent a wonderful afternoon with Coach Ferris, meeting for the first time his lovely wife Pat, son Bill and daughter-in-law Jeni. Sometime during the three or four hours of non-stop warm and so-what-have-you-been-doing-lately conversation, Jeni pointedly asked why Coach Ferris is so special to me. I gave her a totally inadequate answer, but by the time I get to *Fini*, she'll understand with greater clarity, as will most everyone else, I trust.

Coach Ferris stayed after school and worked - unofficially and without pay - with a mere handful of guys during his first year, teaching them some of the basics of the age-old art of wrestling. I wasn't one of those first few, unfortunately for me, too caught up that Sophomore year with other teenage activities that snared my attention, the most noteworthy recalled being my association with a group of guys with whom I formed a club called the **Paisans**. (We wore blue corduroy jackets with a map of Italy and Sicily embroidered on the back with our club name scrolled and superimposed across the outlined map. I have a replica of the jacket, but little opportunity to wear it in our tropics-like paradise known as Southwest Florida.)

During the late-summer football season before my Junior year, Coach Ferris told me he was forming Mayfield's first official wrestling team. He asked me to join the team when wrestling season started in November, saying that he felt I was "probably a natural."

It has been said that flattery is a wonderful persuader. I'm living proof. I said "yes" even though I had no interest, desire or, quite frankly, intent of following through. And again, my recall piercing the Veil of Time, I can now clearly see that, for a teenager whose primary athletic focus was football, November seemed to be light-years away.

Next thing I knew it was November. Coach told me that a lot of guys were joining the team because I said I would be there, too. I figured he was blowing smoke until several of my peers backed up his story.

Time out. This is big; *tutto*, important.

My maternal Grampa, Dominic, who died when I was eleven, (I still love and respect him more than any combinations of words could ever accurately describe) had drummed into me that keeping my word is an absolute.

"When you give your word, keep it, follow through enthusiastically and you are aloft with the richest people on earth," my Grampa said with the clarity of this morning's conversation. "Those who go back on their word are without honor, they are bankrupt, for when you can't give your word, you have nothing worthwhile to give."

I had already learned the hard way that to defy one of his Pontifical Postulates, as I categorized his major pieces of old-country wisdom, was to invite wholesale disaster, for that's when the Golden Rule seems to rear back for a mighty WHACK!

With all that, the capper was Father Michael, my friend the Good, Old-Fashioned priest mentioned in an earlier column. He talked to me half the time in Sicilian, just like my Grampa and was enthusiastically supportive regarding my becoming a wrestler.

Given the formidable combination of mentors those three created, though all unknown to each other, meet Giuseppe the Wrestler!

Getting into proper physical shape and conditioning for wrestling proved to be far more difficult than for playing football, we were shocked to learn. Those of us who were in great football shape could not perform wrestling maneuvers for as many as 10 consecutive seconds!

Among the many early concepts to learn was that the apparent simplicity of maneuvers turned out to be quite complex, indeed. Fortunately, second wind finally arrived, allowing us to experience a considerable degree of fun before we all dropped out due to barfitis, or whatever other ailments might have come into play.

That first season, amazingly, we managed to win more matches than we lost while developing a rabid and large fan base, putting us alongside basketball as the next most popular sport after football. One of our guys, Bob Nolawski, our heavyweight and the only senior on the team, won second place in the State of Ohio Wrestling Championships.

At the Annual Combined-Sports Banquet and Awards Night held at the end of that Junior year, Coach Ferris announced that Bob (we called him Blimp) had been awarded a Full Boat Wrestling Scholarship to Ohio University! We were all thrilled, happy for Bob and certainly proud of him, especially me. I've said at least a million times over the years that I felt like I got hit by a Big Red Cement Truck that evening. In fact, that awards banquet I regard as being the setting for my personal epiphany.

What do I mean? How? Why?

Save all questions 'til next week, 'cuz guess who's outta space again.

★★★

Chapter 39.
Let's Make A Deal!

(Part 2 of 2)

No praise can be too much for truly deserving people. While all my columns were written with great care and directed to a broad audience, this one should be a positive inspiration for teachers and teachers-to-be.

The process of choosing a vocational direction can be a daunting experience, one that can take years to accomplish. For the rare people among us who appear to follow through on a singular declaration of ambition, there is no discernible process; rather, there seems to be a mystical knowingness. Most people who hassle with the challenge often turn to relatives, teachers, friends, even strangers, looking for a suggestion they can relate to, adopt and nourish, then assert as their own.

For a period of years while a teenager, I was certain that driving a cement truck was my future occupation. The plan felt like it was my destiny, as I was definitely looking forward to operating that rig with genuine enthusiasm.

One reason the big red truck was in my vision of the future was the idea that college was not available to me, a concept that later, mainly thanks to Coach Ferris – and a priest named Father Michael – proved to be as full of holes as a 20 pound block of Swiss cheese. You see, grandparents on both sides of my family emigrated to America from Sicily just before/after World War I. (I wish I knew for sure!) My mom and dad were each the eldest of six. Of my grandparents' combined 12 children, most of whom had reached adulthood during the Depression or early years of World War II, few completed high school and none had gone on to college, a fact not unusual for the time.

Sometimes, "evidence" can throw a nasty curve. Gotta be careful out there; don't wanna whiff on a big one.

The theme of life I thought I was born to fulfill followed a simple guideline that was common in our immigrant-heavy neighborhood's plan of action: Get out of school, get a good job with a decent future, work hard, keep your nose clean, get a car, get married, buy a house, raise a family. That is the concept I observed as being promoted, followed and admired by so many people around me; and therefore, the blueprint I was following.

Like some of my contemporaries, I sought the advice of many people, perhaps too many, as the combined recommendations led to greater confusion. I learned to discriminate, to seek guidance from only the successful people, but still, my plan for the cement truck seemed good and solid to me. The target time of 18 years old was simply a driver's license requirement. Since I was aware that a high school diploma was not mandatory for driving a cement truck, I was not in the least committed to graduating, or doing my best grade-wise.

The night of the Annual Awards Banquet at the end of my junior year was anticipated to be extremely exciting, for Coach Ferris was scheduled to introduce me as the newly elected captain of the wrestling team for next year, my never-thought-I'd-get-there Senior Year. At Mayfield, Captain was a Privilege, an Honor, with huge, profound, inviolate Responsibilities. Historically, guys with rough edges were noticeably transformed, rather instantly, into models of exemplary behavior; yea, even revered leaders. With all that, no way could I have predicted, or even dreamed, the other far more profound, life-altering milestone incident that was to happen that evening.

Finally, the stage belonged to Coach Ferris, who by now was renown and admired for his tasteful theatrics in front of an audience. Building it up, he made the startling announcement that our Heavyweight, Bob Nolawski, Mayfield's One 'n Only Blimp, had been awarded a Wrestling Scholarship; Full Boat, no less!

I went positively ape! And, Oh Boy, do I ever mean POSITIVELY. Everything inside me exploded; pulverized; disintegrated; transformed! Yes: *Everything!*

I could hardly wait for the formal festivities to end as I kept my eyes glued on Coach Ferris, our mentor, as we on the wrestling team individually and collectively regarded him. Over the course of the past season, we kidded him, called him "Camel Pusher" and he returned our affection by calling us his "Spaghetti Benders." They tell me such camaraderie is not possible today. How come, 'n sez who?!? Or is it 'whom'?

Finally, the formal shindig was over. Coach got up and made a dash for the nearest exit with yours truly in hot pursuit.

"Hey Coach, wait for me!"

I ran, caught up.

"Can you get me a scholarship, too? A Full Boat, I mean." Pant-pant.

Yes, Bob had done very good, second in the state and his grades had been decent. "How are your grades, Joe? What's your point average?"

"I get A's in English and Chorus," I replied enthusiastically, thinking that there really was more than just a chance. "The rest of my grades are average, maybe a little low, I guess, but what do you mean 'points,' Coach? What's points gotta do with grades? Far as I know, I don't have any points. Where do you get them?"

He started to laugh. "Sometimes, the things you say…"

He continued to laugh as he explained further, causing a very real fear to rise up and grab my throat.

"Your best bet is to place very high in the state next year," he said, the laughter still not completely under control. "You need at least a two-point, an overall average of 'C' for your last four years." He was calm now; and very serious. "The wrestling is very possible for you, and you're a natural, just like I thought, but only you can make you state champ. I'll certainly help, but you'll have to work hard, become better than you are now, but those grades worry me. They definitely have to be there."

That did it. Now I was full-blown scared. But if ever there was a time to reach back, dig deep and….

"Coach, you help make me State Champ, and I'll make Honor Roll, straight A's. I know I can do it; I just never had a reason. All guaranteed. We got a deal?" I was sincere, shooting the whole wad, but I was also choking off my fear and running full speed, looking for the daylight I just knew had to be there someplace, for the Gold Ring was nearer than ever before and much closer, *much closer*, than I ever thought possible.

He threw back his head and laughed so hard that tears sprang from his eyes and wet his cheeks. "That's what I like about you. Nothing's too tough." It took him a while to stop laughing, allowing me time to underscore my proposition.

Very important, here. Coach was not laughing AT me. Somehow, a true mystery to me, I would say something, a simple statement from my point of view, and Coach Ferris would laugh himself silly. If I could have done that to an audience…. The most important fact here is that I understood his laughter, knew he was firmly in my corner and definitely not undermining my resolve.

"Coach, do we have a deal? Guaranteed, remember. Don't make me work so hard in school to get straight A's if you can't keep your end of the bargain. Besides, the first grading period comes way before

November, so I'd have to come through with grades long before you'd have to do anything; so the heat's on me, really."

He was back to laughing again, but this time the laughter stopped abruptly.

"You get those A's next year," he said rather quietly, very pointedly and without pause, "and I guarantee you'll go to college if I have to pay for it myself."

We talked a bit more, putting more frosting on the cake, but all the cherries were in place, and you know me and my cherries.

The rest, as they say, is history. I got my A's, and more. The whole team won the Novice State Title with a still-record six (6!) of us winning individual championships! It was onward and upward from there, and certainly more complex than covered here. Hey, what d'you want, a book? Sure, Life's Road was still bumpy with dangerous curves and hidden potholes, always will be. But please, the focus is on the fact that several of us were forever fortified with much more confidence, desire to achieve and resolve than the average champion's dosage.

There are a whole gang of Mayfield alumni from over the years who point to Coach Ed Ferris as one of the pre-eminent influential people in their lives. He was a hell-of-a-lot-more than "just a Coach," as I'm sure you know by now. He was, naturally, a shoo-in for Mayfield's Hall of Fame a short while back.

Let's all raise our glasses in *Salute* to all the Coaches, Teachers, Parents, Friends and Strangers out there who made a difference in the lives of those people they touched, influenced and helped steer in a better direction; the maybe not-quite-so-ordinary people who made an extraordinary difference to some very fortunate souls.

Personally, lest there be any doubt, Coach Ferris put reality, substance and practicality into the sage-like teachings of my Grampa Dominic and the Good Priest, Father Michael. As a constant reminder to look beyond the obvious benefits at hand, on my workstation I keep a little toy cement truck.

So you see, Jeni, I owe him more than I can put into words. Go back and read between the lines if need be, but I'm sure you now have a better idea of why so many of us come by periodically for a visit and another clump of the bread-of-life sometimes referred to as chit-chat. And thanks for asking, Jeni; this was long overdue.

✵✵✵

Chapter 40.
The Ballad of Leona M. Pickard

I Confess! Yep, this is about another teacher; eh, Prof. This lady from College Daze saw a quality, a talent, that would not be fully-enough appreciated for years to come by her student.

Where would any of us be if others had not taken a profound personal interest along the way. No, it's not a question, for an answer would be impossible. Actually, the two previous sentences could be tacked onto several other columns, too.

E arly in my freshman year at Ohio University, Professor Pickard handed back one of my early compositions. It was marked "B –." A note asked that I make an appointment to see her. As class had not begun, I approached her desk.

"You want to see me? Was my paper that bad?"

She shot me a look. Cold.

"Mr. Micale, I am not in the habit of giving a 'B' for a bad paper."

As a freshman, I still felt uncomfortable being called "Mister" by my teachers; eh, Profs. I told her I wished she'd call me Joe and I asked if we might get together the next morning at 10.

She gave me another look.

"Tomorrow at 10 a.m. will be fine. Be sure to be there precisely at 10 a.m. as we have much to discuss."

Shucks, I thought. Musta been a bad paper or why would she want to see me? I got there at 9:50 a.m. No sense ticking her off some more.

"Ah, Mr. Micale," she said as I entered. There was no reception room as I expected, just an office. Shoulda knocked. "Come in and sit down," she gestured. "I've been looking forward to talking to you."

"I didn't think my paper was that bad, but…"

"Mr. Micale," she cut me off, "I told you in class that I am not in the habit of giving a 'B' on a bad paper."

"B minus," I corrected her.

By her expression, I knew I'd just made another mistake.

"Yes. I do not give a **B minus** for bad papers, either, but getting to the point, I can well imagine that the night before the assignment was due, you sat down at your desk and with pen in hand and fresh paper, you started to write, and upon concluding your thoughts, you stapled it and moved on to something else."

"It was that bad, huh?"

"Am I in the habit of giving a 'B minus' for bad papers?"

"No."

"Thank you!"

"But…"

"But what?"

"But why am I here if I wrote a paper good enough to get a B?"

"B minus." Her voice was flat.

"B minus." Nutz!

"Because I'm curious."

"Curious about what? You musta been a fly on the wall."

"I'm curious to know why someone with your immense talent for writing would settle for affixing your name to a paper that does not adequately represent that talent."

Duhhh. At least it didn't come out audibly.

"You see, Mr. Micale," she continued, "I have now had the opportunity to get to know you somewhat, so I have a good idea as to your capabilities when you put yourself to task."

"After *three* papers?"

"Two."

"Two?"

"If my memory serves me properly, you hold in your hand your second submission to me."

I almost dropped it. As the conversation continued, I told her that I wait for the "mood" to hit me before I write, that I wait for proper "inspiration."

"You cannot afford to do that," she said. "You must learn to write on a regular basis, a schedule. You must also learn to write according to a deadline."

"Why?"

"Why?" she questioned my question. "Because that is how professionals write. You must develop these habits now."

"What makes you think I want to be a professional writer? I'm an accounting major.

"Mr. Micale, I have been teaching at this level for more years than you have been alive," she said as she got up from behind her desk and walked to my side. "In all that time, I have had a mere handful of people with your gift for expressing yourself with the written word. It would be a crime for you not to write for a living. You can hire accountants to keep track of your money - and no disrespect intended toward accountants. And mood writer POO!"

I was thoroughly shocked by her comments, her compliments, but as I am rarely at a loss for words, I just let it all hang out.

"Look, first of all, my high school teacher told me pretty much the same thing. The problem is that I don't know how to relate to writing as a profession. It seems that I'd have to constantly be out looking for work; or, look for a job with a newspaper or magazine and get on staff somewhere, probably have to write about things where I have little or no interest, and honestly, that doesn't appeal to me. And I think one of the biggest drawbacks for me is that I KNOW I'm a mood writer, in spite of your saying POO!"

After a brief, thoughtful moment she walked back behind her desk.

"All right. I understand. Do you have fresh paper with you?"

I didn't.

"Here."

"What's this paper for?"

"From this day forward, you should never end a sentence with a preposition. Good training. Unless she's worth it, of course."

Not even the hint of a smile. Stone.

"Huh?" I asked. Then I got some of her meaning and had to laugh. "But what am I supposed to do with the paper?"

"Write."

"Write what?"

"Write anything. Tell me a story."

"Mrs. Pickard," I said with a sigh, "I'm not in the mood."

"Great!" Perfect! Write!"

"Write what?"

"Up to you. It's your story."

She went back to shuffling the papers she was working on when I first entered her office. I sat there like a lump. A few minutes later she looked me in the eye – she always looked me in the eye – and said, "You're not writing."

"My mind's a complete blank."

"OK, what is a common first word?"

"The."

"Don't tell me, write it," she said, pointing to my blank paper.

I wrote "The" indented, like I was starting a paragraph. And I stopped. Joe, The Lump.

"The what?"

I snapped as I said "The boy."

She pointed again.

So I wrote, "The boy...." and sat there.

"OK. What do you want to tell me about this boy?"

Completely frustrated, I wrote, "The boy in the red shirt was riding his bike down the street."

"Now we're getting somewhere. You say 'red shirt' and 'riding his bike down the street', not through a park or up a hill, or green shirt for that matter, so where are all these facts leading? You have my interest. Tell me more... on paper."

In my imagination I saw this kid on his bike and I followed him. I simply wrote what I saw him do. When I had written four, maybe five sentences, she asked me to read it and asked if I was happy with the context and construction.

A moment later I said, "Yes, but I don't know where I'm going with it."

"Very simple. Draw a line across the page. Now I want you to tell me again what you just told me, using different words, but without adding or deleting any facts."

I did as asked. This lady could read upside down! She said, "Good. Do it again." I did. She said, "Good. Again."

Ten paragraphs later, she asked me to put a number from 1 to 10 next to each paragraph corresponding to which I liked 1st, 2nd, 3rd....

After looking them over, I told her that any four could be number one, but actually all qualified. I also added that I felt that there wasn't a bad one in the lot, except that the first one was a bit simplistic.

"And you have been handing in your 'first one' for how many years now?"

Wow and double Wow! That hit me a ton. Coming off my epiphany somewhat, I was actually impressed with the work I had done.

"Joe, when you started to write, you said you weren't 'in the mood.' Are you in the mood now?"

Wow again, she just called me Joe! "I didn't even think about it. Yes."

"See what I mean? We get our 'moods' from our actions. Inactivity often gives the impression of no mood at all; and for many, inactivity produces a 'down' mood. So from now on, when you wish to be in a writing mood, start writing."

As it was precisely 11 a.m., she dismissed me.

I have never experienced writer's block. And more importantly, I recognized that she had given me the writing class of my life, but later, years later, I recognized that she had given me the Life class of my life.

THANK YOU, Mrs. Pickard! I am ETERNALLY GRATEFUL!

Chapter 41.
Freshman Frolics

What the heck, let's stay on campus. As we continue to focus on College Daze, there was an unexpected prank (Haircut, anyone?) that caused a major shift in my Life's Course... or were these Twists 'n Turns simply pieces of a Greater Plan known only to The Great Mysterious Planner? Okay, ya get a question mark on this one. (This 'Cause' was not recognized for several YEARS.)

The first year of living away from Mom and Dad can be dramatic, exhilarating, scary, wonderful, frightening, - okay, how far should I go? If that first time is also the freshman year in college, compound all adjectives by a factor of X to the 10th power.

Of all the profound changes that occurred in my life during my freshman year in college, the most far reaching, life altering event seemed at the time to be nothing more than a footnote. I started to give people haircuts. A means to an end, I thought. Earn a few bucks while in school. Put some loot in my boot. Scare up some *sordi*... a very loose translation from Sicilian is dollars.

Five years would pass before I realized that cutting hair would probably have a life-long impact on me, but that's putting the *carretto* before the *donkey*.

Sure, more Sicilian.

There was one night in particular, a night that started out with a mundane thud. My two roommates, Danny Mastro and Gary Dubin, and I were studying, me for an econ test the next day with Danny and Gary trying to speak French to each other. The "noise" didn't bother me a bit, just as music from the radio was not - nor is - a distraction.

Suddenly our door BURST open. Several guys came rushing into our room, all talking at once and excited, one of them telling me to get my tools so I could shave somebody's head!

I didn't know the guy who was giving me orders. The drift was that someone, call him John, had lost a bet and was to have his head shaved, but at 8 p.m. no hair places were open in Athens, Ohio. Heck, outside of the library, two burger joints and 738 bars....

Anyhow, someone in the group knew I cut hair in my dorm, Perkins Hall, so they came to recruit me. Abduct might be a more accurate term.

The ringleader said we were only going to the dorm lobby and I could be back to my studying shortly.

"So let's go get it over with," he said.

As we entered the lobby, there were at least 500 guys! They let out a mighty cheer, as though celebrities had just arrived. The group had already pushed all the furniture to the edges of the room and my "victim" was seated on a wooden chair in the center, shirtless. Seems the Student Council President, Pat Coschignano, (who these days is Dr. Pat Cosiano of Cleveland, Ohio) and the President of the East Green (Duhh, don't know, so I'll call him John) had a bet, who remembers about what. The President of the East Green was my victim, sitting there with a thick 'n fluffy full head of hair.

The mood of the room was jovial, just below riot level as I whipped out the one tool my father sent me that frightened me most; the electric clipper. I had already nicknamed it The Black Tractor as it removed a ton of hair in less than a gulp. No room for "oops" here.

The crowd did a countdown. Starting at John's forehead and ending at the nape of his neck, I zipped a stripe out of the middle of his head. Flash bulbs popped. Someone asked the name of the hairstyle and I replied that it was O U's first Reverse Mohawk. Doesn't seem so funny now but got me one of the best laughs ever.

When I had clippered John clean, I declared the job done, to which the crowd let out a negative roar.

"The deal is he's supposed to have his head shaved," someone in the crowd, maybe Pat, shouted, all others agreeing.

I reached into my pocket, retrieved a six inch oblong-ish case, opened it and held up a barber's straight razor.

"This is what I shave with," I said, using my best show-n-tell posture. "My father is a barber, that's why I shave with it, but I've never used it on another person."

All kinds of comments came back at me but the one I remember most is someone saying, "Use it on him or we'll use it on you!" I was sure they were kidding, but....

I lathered his head.

As I was about to take my first stroke, the crowd became deadly silent. The thought of the word "dead" made me kind of snicker, which caused the crowd to go into a ghoulish-sounding expletive.

After the first couple of strokes someone asked if flashbulbs would bother me. When I said I didn't think so, the room lit up like Christmas.

Finally his head was whistle clean. The spokesman asked for a big hand for John the victim. He got a Standing O.

Then he said, "And how 'bout a hand for Little Joe!" The chorus of BOOS made the walls rattle.

"You didn't even nick him," someone snorted and again, I think it was Pat, but don't fink, please.

The next day when the school newspaper hit the streets, on the front page was a large picture of me shaving John's head. The accompanying story was rather good, as I recall. The article contained a few flattering details about me, including the fact that I was attending Ohio U. on a wrestling scholarship. I was amazed at how a single write-up like that gave me instant recognition on campus.

Business really boomed. Everybody, it seemed, wanted me to cut their hair. About a week later as I was giving someone a haircut with several others waiting their turn, a man in a brown suit walked into the dorm john and told me I was busted. He gave me what looked like a traffic ticket and told me I had violated State Law.

My outwardly calm physical countenance belied the fact that I was experiencing a spate of petrifying panic as I found my way to the payphone in the lobby. I had been told, along with others who were on scholarship, that we'd best recognize that any breach of university rules or laws would almost certainly lead to a revocation of our scholarships.

"And there is no record of anyone ever getting his scholarship reinstated," we were told.

I made one of my life's most frantic phone calls, this one to my father. He listened, then asked the time.

"Six-thirty, why?"

"Because tomorrow night at exactly six-thirty, call me here and I will have an answer for you. And in the meantime, don't worry."

Right, don't worry. The next night, still shaking with the hebejebees, I called home at exactly six-thirty. I was told to mail the citation to a Mr. Russo.

"So who's Mr. Russo," I wanted to know.

"He and I lived next door to each other in Little Italy when we were kids," my Dad said. "Today he is the president of the Barber's Union for the State of Ohio. He also said not to worry. He's arranged for you to be able to cut hair while you're a student at O U."

I did get to meet Mr. Russo, a very nice man, indeed. At one point he started to laugh as he said, "I'd have put that inspector in the Boon-Docks, 'cept he was already there!" He then laughed himself all the way to tears.

Shifting gears, I want to tell about the incident that occurred about a week after my picture appeared in the Ohio U newspaper. I was given a note upon leaving one of my classes to call home.

"Oh Joey!" my Mom exclaimed. "Your picture is on the front page of **The Plain Dealer** shaving someone's head! And your Aunt Annie called from Pittsburgh, and Aunt Mary called from Phoenix, and your Godmother Muffie from California! You must be in every newspaper in the world!"

Moms sure do get excited some times, don't they?

I cut hair all the rest of that year, plus all of my sophomore year. Still, would you believe, I thought my haircutting was a minor factor that simply provided some very necessary and appreciated income.

Back home, I hardly mentioned my haircutting activity to friends. Had anyone asked, I'm sure I would have said something like, "Oh that? It's no big deal." HA! Funny how Time can change the significance of an event without changing the event itself.

Chapter 42.
Hollywood Spotlight on Harve Bennett

This story happened while I owned Cosmo's and after changing the name to "Little Joe's." Producer Harve Bennett, a client of the salon from my earliest days working for Cosmo, one day told me that the Man with the Golden Hair needed a Man with Golden Hair. What, too melodramatic?!? Hey, this is HOLLYWOOD! Anyhow, it all shook out to be Trina's Day.

One of Hollywood's most celebrated producers, **Harve Bennett** brought a lot of joy to the world. I met him when I first went to work at **Cosmo's,** the hair salon that became **Little Joe's** once I bought it from Cosmo. When I first met Harve, he was an executive with one of the three major networks.

Years later, I was surprised to hear that Harve quit his job to become executive producer of a new TV series called *The Mod Squad*.

In the theme of the show, police Captain Adam Greer, played by **Tige Andrews,** turned three street-wise rough-necks into an undercover police squad to infiltrate various criminal gangs. **Michael Cole** (also a Cosmo's client) portrayed Pete Cochran, **Peggy Lipton** was Julie Barnes and **Clarence Williams III** played Linc Hayes. Mod Squad premiered September 4, 1968 and last aired on March 1st of 1973.

During the last phases of *Mod Squad*, Harve became the executive producer of a project called *The Six Million Dollar Man*, starring **Lee Majors** as Astronaut Steve Austin. Three movies were made for TV before the show became the most popular science fiction TV series of all time. It premiered on January 18, 1974 with the last episode appearing on March 6, 1978.

The hook in the show has Colonel Austin being transformed from a legendary human astronaut to a bionic-machine-augmented super spy. The successful series spawned 101 episodes. Like the *Batman* TV series of the sixties, every actor in Hollywood clambered to be a guest star on *Six Million Dollar Man.*

During the latter part of the show's run, a new actor was hired to double for Lee Majors. From the back, the double and Lee Majors had twin physiques, with one glaring difference. The double had dark hair and Majors was a dishwater blonde, as we say in the trade.

"Joe, I have a problem," Harve told me while visiting my salon for his bi-monthly haircut. "Makeup tried to convert the double into a blonde but he became a redhead. Trying to get rid of the red, they made him orange. Bright orange. Tell me what to do to make him a blonde."

"Pray," I deadpanned. "**Billy Graham** was at the **Hollywood Bowl** last night. Get him to stick around 'n help for a couple of days."

"Very funny. Now give me a bottle of something. I saw you working on **Jerry Stiller** and **Anne Meara** not long ago. I know you have the answer."

I convinced Harve that I had to actually see the double before I could give an intelligent answer. To explain my presence at the studio, we decided that I would bring my daughter, Trina, on the set where we would both play visitor. I coached Trina on 'rules of the set,' like, stay 20 feet away from the star's chair, his sanctuary.

When Trina and I went to **Universal** that day, Harve told Trina that Lee Majors was a very nice man, but he often would not acknowledge visitors while he was shooting.

"So if Lee doesn't say hello to you, Trina, please understand that he is just maintaining character and don't take it personally," Harve instructed.

When Harve escorted us to the set where shooting was taking place, Lee Majors was stage center with actor **Richard Anderson** and the director. As we approached, Lee looked our way, looked away, then looked back again. When the director said "take five," Lee walked over to us, crouched in front of Trina.

"Hey gorgeous, where you been all my life?"

Trina, all of 13 years old, didn't skip a beat. "Well, I'm here now."

The whole set cracked up, Lee especially. Lee and Trina soon found that they shared a rapport that was so obvious. When the director called "places," Lee looked to the stage manager.

"Don't my friends get a chair?"

While a stage hand ran off set, Lee told Trina that she could sit in his private chair. First she looked at me, then went over to Lee's chair and sat, the Cheshire Cat personified.

A couple of days later, the double was a blonde. A dishwater blonde. Harve Bennett was all smiles and never forgot. But I think the biggest benefactor is Trina, on whose living room wall still hangs the personally autographed 8 x 10 glossy given to her years ago by one of TV's biggest stars, Lee Majors, the Six Million Dollar Man.

★★★

Chapter 43.
Love Letters from The Mark Twain Hotel

I Confess! I have 77 letters that create a virtual day-by-day chronicle of the efforts my dad, actor Paul J. Micale, expended while starting his acting career in Hollywood. This column is a very good synopsis for a book, now complete and ready for an insightful publisher with vision, panache, sav-wa-fair, deep pockets and a loose checkbook. Helloooo!

One of America's favorite films of all time is the 1939 classic, *The Wizard of Oz.* Gets my vote, too, for the many important life lessons throughout that marvelous film.

When Dorothy is preparing to return to Kansas, The Wizard, a.k.a. **Frank Morgan**, asks Dorothy, portrayed by a teenage **Judy Garland**, to tell one and all what she learned from her adventures in Oz. Among her many profound remarks, Dorothy states she learned that whatever a person really wants in life can often be found "… right in their own back yard." Amen; amen!

To relate one of my most memorable Back Yard discoveries, we first need to turn the calendar back to 1959. That spring my dad, Paul, had the lead in a play, *Wayside,* at **Theater Cleveland.** A **Columbia Studios** big-wig bought the rights, promising dad the lead role in the movie.

Labor Day that year, Dad drove fabled Route 66, "singing all the way." Shortly after arriving in Hollywood, he established residence at the actor-friendly **Mark Twain Hotel** across from the **Hollywood Post Office**.

Making friends with several other wannabee actors, dad set out daily to find an agent, to learn where movies and TV shows were being cast and to do everything in his power to get "discovered."

Each night when he returned to his hotel, he would write a letter to us, his family, describing the day's activities. He wrote in detail about the people he met, the places visited and the confusing array of freeways and congested traffic. The smog was no help, either. Dad always mentioned being entertained by the families of boyhood friends Nick and Joe Leo and Nick Germano.

Dad's letters were the highlight of the day for my mother, my sister and me. We wrote to him regularly, too, marking his days in a most positive way, as he always mentioned.

We finally joined Dad on December 21st, but while he was alone in Hollywood, we learned he was a very prolific letter writer. In one letter he said, "Sorry for the short letter of yesterday…" Yesterday's was 12 pages, and definitely not the longest.

Seventy-seven of dad's letters survive, wouldyabelieve! About two weeks ago, my wife Ginny and I, for the first time, started browsing through them and discussing the possibilities they present. We didn't take a lot of time to decide to develop a plan.

The book is tentatively titled, *Love Letters from the Mark Twain Hotel.*

Ginny is presently typing the letters into a computer file, copying dad's capitalization, underlining and other indications of emotion and/ or emphasis. I'll footnote his words, fill in the blanks.

Here's a clip from his letter of October 17th, 1959:

"… There is that word again, "Overnight." If people knew how long it takes, how many heartaches, broken dreams, insults, snobbery, disappointments, lonely nights, the feelings of uselessness, of despair – and on and on. If they knew how much of this it takes to reach that "Overnight success," maybe then the stigma that is attached to an artist would fall away and reveal not a "bum" or "loafer" who doesn't want to work, but a man with ideals, driving ambitions and the stubborn desire to create, to live, to sleep, to eat, yes to be the very source of entertainment, amusement and enjoyment of the people who look down their noses at him while he suffers all these indignations to accomplish this.

"My Darling, I'm afraid I kind of went off the deep end that time. Forgive me. I do not mean to distress you. I'm merely painting out a few things I've learned these past few weeks."

Not much to edit there, huh? Like that man said, you ain't heard nothin' yet. As some of you know, my father created a very large body of work and is best known for portraying Father Carmine, Rocky Balboa's favorite priest.

I'm in the process of engaging an agent who can get it to the proper publisher so that the print date can fall on or near the 50th year mark, a wonderful way to celebrate the letters' Golden Anniversary.

There are two other books ready to roll. One I call *Someday.* It is also in script form and in the hands of a Hollywood producer. The third book could be the spearhead.

The people of Cape Coral, along with various family and friends, have been most kind and complimentary toward my work over the past few years. Sharing this very personal information with you today is a grateful acknowledgement of your support.

The 'spearhead' book referred to above is the book you are reading now. When the right party reads this book and asks, "What else y'got?," I'll have at least TWO; plus ½ and ½ good answers, as I have two other fascinating projects in the early development stage. Yep, life is more exciting when y'keep movin' right along.

Chapter 44.
Play Ball!

A few years after moving to Hollywood, I became a part-time, eh, very part time beat reporter for the Koufax-led Dodgers. Well, the pertinent facts are below. And forget age, for when it comes to being a sports fan as a youth, growing up can take decades, if it ever happens.

Baseball is the trumpet of Spring. Here in Southwest Florida, the **Boston Red Sox** and **Minnesota Twins'** Spring Training base, local fans are joined by imports, many coming annually, to exercise their own idea of the Rite of Spring.

I grew up in Cleveland, home of the **Indians.** When I was about 11 years old, I met **Mike Garcia**, the Indians pitcher known as the Big Bear. Mike rented a house a few streets from my home in the neighborhood called Collinwood. I went to several games with Mike and got to meet all the players, like **Bobby Avila, Bob Feller, Early Wynn, Larry Doby** (the first black player in the American League), **Dale Mitchell** and the Shortstop-Manager, **Lou Boudreau**. They all called me by name. Talk about a thrill!

We moved to Hollywood about three years after the Dodgers shook up the planet by leaving Brooklyn. While keeping an eye on the Indians, the Dodgers of the sixties had legendary **Sandy Koufax** and a formidable array of greats like **Don Drysdale, Roy Campanella** (who served in a wheel-chair as Ambassador of Accomplishment), **Maury Wills, Tommy LaSorda** and too many more stars to name.

Starting in the mid sixties and for about two decades, I had a client - and good buddy - named **Stan Wawer**, Sports Editor of the **Burbank Daily Review**. When the Angels and Dodgers were both home, Stan gave me a press-pass so I could cover the Dodgers while he went to Anaheim. That was like giving a kid the key to the biggest candy store in town.

Sitting in the large Press Box one night, there was a commotion. Reporters stood and applauded. Wow! I never saw anyone get a Standing O from the press. I turned to the person behind me.

"**Casey Stengle** just walked in," I was told.

As I thanked the man behind me, I did a double-take. He was **Jim Murray**, Hall of Fame sportswriter and a Pulitzer Prize Recipient that

I still idolize. The seat next to Murray was empty, so I asked if I could sit by him.

"Sure kid, come on over. What's your name?"

Are you kidding? A Living Legend wanted to know my name? I must've smiled for a week, but I didn't let my emotions rob me of a classic opportunity. I interviewed Jim Murray right on the spot, which caused a few others around us to snicker. One guy about lost his lunch. Huh, bet none of those gigglers ever thought to interview Murray. Bet they wish they had now.

I was in the Press Box on September 3, 1969, the night **Willie Davis** extended his 31 game hitting streak by getting a hit in the 10th inning and beating the Mets, five to four. **Gil Hodges**, Mets Manager and former Dodger great, caught a lot of guff for pitching to Davis, but he just shrugged. "What the heck, we got him out four times tonight." I am holding the ball Willie signed for me that night. Ain't nobody got enough money to buy it, either, so don't ask.

There's a story I'll tell from my memory. As Casey Stengle used to say, you could look it up, but I won't.

It was his last start that season, 1966, I think. Koufax had just pitched another gem, win number 27, a 1-0 heart-stopper. Reporters stampeded, rushed to Kaufax's locker, stood 10 deep.

Sandy always talked softly, so people were shushing each other. I was shut out, bummed. As I looked around, no other player was being approached by a reporter. Not even **Maury Wills**.

I walked over. "Lucky me. Tell me about tonight."

He praised Sandy up and down.

"But Maury, you walked, stole second, then stole third and came home on an infield out. You manufactured that win, all by yourself, one-zip."

"Yeah, but Sandy had to hold 'em. He made the run stand up."

"So half the guys over there should be trying to muscle me out."

"Hey man, it's baseball. I'm not complaining."

I gave Stan my report, written as a column, like so many other times. Next time he came in for a haircut, Stan sheepishly told me he used my column verbatim. He apologized for not being able to give me a by-line, saying he felt like a thief. I thanked him for the honor, told him he could use my stuff anytime, that I felt privileged to have his confidence and approval.

That game turned out to be Sandy Koufax's last, his arthritic elbow forcing his early retirement.

Ah, but Spring; it comes back every year, renewing hope for the young at heart while giving some very fortunate people a chance to visit one of Life's great candy stores.

✫✫✫

*I Confess! I grew up a **Cleveland Indians** fan. A rabid Cleveland Indians fan. One summer day when I was about 10, I took a streetcar from my home in Collinwood all the way downtown to Municipal Stadium, getting there early enough for batting practice, per usual. I took up my position at the left-field foul pole, per usual. I would have tipped over the Terminal Tower for a ball. I think we all felt that way.*

*When the Indians were running to the dugout at the end of batting practice, 30 million of us kids begged the players to throw us a ball. I made eye-contact with **Allie Reynolds**. He saw I really, really wanted that ball. Oh my God, he THREW IT TO ME! But 10 feet over my head. I darn near cried. With all the pushing and shoving, somebody knocked me to my knees with my face on the cold 'n dirty cement. With continued shuffling, the ball rolled to me from my left. I pounced! 500 kids jumped on me, punching, kicking, some even swearing. But I held on.*

IT WAS MINE!

I held that ball all through the game. I'd let people see it, touch it, but I never let it go.

Of course I stayed for the last out, wataya, nutz? I didn't go for autographs that day, that would be too dangerous, so I started heading for the far away street where I would use my penny transfer to get back home to Collinwood, where I'd be safe, where everybody would protect me because it was MY neighborhood, the place where I belonged.

I had to cross a big, grassy area, big enough to hold two stadiums. Some boys, five, maybe six, were behind me. They were black kids. I'd have been apprehensive – make that scared – even if they were white, green or orange kids.

I started to run. Here they come! Now I was wide-eyed scared. Not for my life, my ball! Just as I got tackled, I heard someone yell.

"Stop that!"

Looking back from the safety of now, she was probably about my mom's age. She had a boy about six or seven by the hand. She told the kids to get off me, to leave me alone. They did. Y'hadda obey adults, even if you didn't know them.

She had been waiting for a streetcar heading west. My stop was still two blocks away. Heading east. She and her son walked me all the way to my stop, the attack kids following not too far behind.

When we got there, my streetcar was not due for about a half hour and the attack kids were maybe 50 feet away and getting boulder and more vocal. She verbally held them at bay.

Finally, my streetcar showed up. The kids made a move to board with me, but she stopped them.

Looking out the streetcar's rear window, I saw her start to go back to her stop and the attack kids turned and started walking another direction. I waved to her and she waved back. Her little boy, too.

For the Billionth time, THANK YOU LADY! I love you forever! Yes, I still have that ball.

Chapter 45.
The Boy Who Grew Up to be A Super Man

I Confess! Paul and Rana Petersen are the Cream of the Crop! May they have the Where-With-All (money is a great start) to fulfill their Mission in Life. Paul transitioned, with Rena at his side, from being Donna Reed's TV son, Jeff Stone, to being Champion for Kid Actors. So if you're looking for a worthy cause....

Last November I traveled to Southern California to cover the **Hollywood Celebrities and Collectors Convention** in Burbank. My objective was to spend some time with celebrity friends from the movie and TV industry and arrange interviews for future columns. I received an unanticipated bonus when I met **Paul Petersen**, best remembered from the popular '60's sitcom, *The Donna Reed Show.*

Paul and I had been in the same place at the same time on several occasions over the years, but I don't ever recall saying more than hello to each other. Given the friendliness we developed on this trip, people might think we were life-long buddies. Of the many attributes we share, it seems that neither of us is bashful and therefore, strangers can quickly become friends.

Paul was one of *Disney's* original **Mouseketeers** in 1955, when he was just nine years old. He appeared in dramatic TV shows like *Play House 90* and in a wonderful movie called *House Boat,* starring **Sophia Loren** and **Carey Grant**. In April of 1958 Paul, age 12, won the role of the son, **Jeff Stone**, for the **Donna Reed** pilot.

"I never expected the show to run for eight years, I was simply thrilled to get picked for the pilot. The most profound reward was being able to work for so many years with such truly great people."

Over the years Paul has been a recording artist, winning gold records, the Academy Award of the record industry. He has also written 16 books! In 1976, he sold a project to Dell called *Walt, Mickey and Me*, a fascinating and enjoyable biography of the Mouseketeers. (I am the proud owner of a copy.) That project raised Paul's awareness to the fact that being a child actor, for most people, is not the wonderful experience with a happy ending that the public perceives.

When Paul talked to **Jackie Cooper** about the plight of child actors, Cooper said there are three questions to ask about an individual. First, what is the family's composition. Second, what did the child become famous for, such as **Linda Blair** (who played a demon possessed child) and **Alfalfa**, known as the dufuss of the *Our Gang* comedies. And three, how old was the person when their career came to an end.

Sometime in the late eighties, Paul became acutely aware of the tragedies suffered by far too many child actors. By Christmas of 1990, three prominent child actor friends had committed suicide. **Rusty Hamer**, of *The Danny Thomas Show,* was a bright kid, a big star but later, he became overweight and bitter.

"I knew Rusty very well," Paul told me. "His brother John, too. I never checked on Rusty. If you really care about a person, in my mind you have an obligation to them. After Rusty died I sat down and wrote, *A Minor Consideration*, a book outlining many issues of children who work in the entertainment industry. After writing more than 1800 pages, I put it in a drawer in my desk, where it remains to this day." (My Bible has 1660 pages.)

Right, the book was never published. Instead, a non-profit organization was formed. I quote their website:

"A Minor Consideration is a non-profit, tax-deductible organization formed to give aid and support to young performers---Past, Present and Future. Children in the Entertainment Industry are subjected to unique pressures, and many times the images they create outlast the money and the Fame. There are consequences to Early Fame, and several generations of former child stars have joined together to organize the structure that surrounds the most visible children in our society. Solid Parenting can overcome most of the difficulties faced by young performers, but a Child Star must pick their parents with care. Family Education is the key ingredient and the members of AMC are always "on call" to assist parents and their professional children on a "no cost basis." By providing a strong emphasis on education and helping to preserve the money these children generate the members of AMC are always available to help in the tricky Transition issues that for many kid stars prove to be so troublesome. We've 'been there, done that.'

Please see what we've accomplished at www.minorcon.org/tenyearstime. html."

Today, that "nice, good-looking kid who appeared on TV and in the movies" has grown into a mature, caring man. With his wife, Rana, they have found their life's work, championing the cause of child actors and other children who do a grownup's work instead of enjoying childhood.

✯✯✯

Chapter 46.
Kathy Miller; An Earthbound Angel

I Confess! I love and admire Kathy Miller for who she is and what she does with her life. She takes care of kids. And kid's kids. Kathy is included here for your enlightenment and possible help. All positive actions are welcomed. Coulda said the exact same words for Paul 'n Rana.

Recently through my first newspaper publisher and now my personal friend, **Tonya Squibb**, I was introduced to **Kathy Miller**, Founder and Executive Director of **Lifeline Family Center, Inc.**, located at 907 SE 5th Avenue in Cape Coral. The center is a non-traditional, Christian maternity home for pregnant teens.

Going directly to the source, the following is taken from literature published by the Center:

"People sometimes think that only big things have the capacity to make positive change in the world. Big plans... big ideas... big contributions that affect the lives of many people. But at Lifeline... we know that changing the world in a big way can be done by touching just two lives at a time. Lifeline... is a non-traditional Christian maternity home modeling the love of God. We provide a safe learning environment for teen girls in crisis pregnancy, helping to turn around both the lives of the young mothers and their babies. At Lifeline... we offer so much more than a traditional maternity home. Our center provides support and services to birth moms and their babies from pregnancy until the child's second birthday."

Kathy Miller told me that the bench-mark beginning occurred in 1976 when she was a Crisis Pregnancy Counselor. During those early years, the objective was to help young mothers and/or mothers-to-be to learn how to use the welfare system.

"Using the Welfare System starts a cycle of poverty and dependence that is difficult – and in many cases, seemingly impossible – to break," says Kathy. "Also, the operating philosophy followed by most traditional maternity homes is to assist the new mother until physical birth, and shortly thereafter, the girls are released to the same environment that produced the problem in the first place."

Kathy realized that the help offered to young mothers, especially the teenagers with no family support, was organized failure. Here again we hear from the Center's published literature, which is equal to quoting Kathy, as she wrote the words.

"What if the only place you learned about family dinners was on TV? What if your introduction to sex came from being violated at five years of age by someone who should have been your protector? What if your only hope for the future was the hope that your father wasn't drunk and angry again when you got home from school and that he wouldn't become violent? What if you got pregnant and had nowhere to turn for help? These are some of the life experiences of the girls who come to Lifeline Family Center, Inc. If we only help them through their pregnancy and then sent them on their way, the chances are extremely high that they would repeat the same cycle of neglect, abuse and poverty with their own children. Instead, we give them the tools to break the cycle."

At Lifeline, young moms are coached and encouraged to build a positive future for their families by developing confidence, maturity and life skills. They are given a home to live in with a loving family atmosphere, transportation, food, clothing and taught the proper use of personal hygiene items. They are given education and career encouragement and guidance, including GED tutoring and evaluation for career training. The girls agree to obtain a GED and complete their career training prior to graduation.

Further, the girls are given spiritual direction, including character classes, bible study, prayer journaling and weekly church attendance at different Christian denominations. They are given life skills' training that includes classes on the important aspects of parenting, budgeting, etiquette and household tasks. The girls also receive weekly professional individual counseling.

Additionally, the girls receive child-birth classes, have the opportunity to work- out in their own exercise room and enjoy various recreational activities that often include members of the public. The center's current capacity is 12 girls and up to 24 babies.

Lifeline Family Center further believes that women are the second victims of abortion. They offer compassionate healing for those who suffer from post-abortion syndrome through P.A.C.E. - Post-Abortion Counseling and Education.

The complete story on Lifeline Family Center, Inc. cannot be told in one sitting, but it is important to underscore that the organization does not receive – or want – government funding. Let's hear it from Kathy again:

"How can we teach our girls to be self-supporting if they see our organization accepting government money? We demonstrate and teach them to rely on God's empowerment with the help of faithful volunteers and funds from businesses, civic organizations, private foundations, our NeXt Generation Thrift Store, and very importantly, the many Christian churches of all denominations in Lee County. Last but not least, the majority of our support comes from many caring local individuals who believe that positive change can be made in the world... two lives at a time."

Say hello to Jazmin. She's 17 years old, grew up in Camden, New Jersey and moved to Claremont five years ago. In April of 2007, with the help of a high school teacher, Jazmin found Lifeline on the internet. She talked to staffer, Dr. Sharon. Two weeks later she was a resident at Lifeline, but first she had to pass a drug test. She had to clear a police check showing that she had no felony charges against her. In talking to various counselors at Lifeline, she had to show that she has a good attitude and truly wants to change her way of life. At the time of this interview she was living at the home for one and a half months.

"I like it here," Jazmin said with enthusiasm. "It's a good home for teen mothers. It helps a lot. They teach us how to live in a Godly way. I have discipline now. Most days I take my daughter to nursery and then I go to the GED Lab and study. Of course, we go to morning devotions before GED. I need GED because I only got to the tenth grade."

Jazmin's due-date is September 25th. She knows he's a boy and that his name is Hezekiah. She said she found his name in the Old Testament of the Bible.

Sheree is another mother-to-be who is 19 years old. She grew up in Wisconsin and moved to the Cape when she was five. She lived in Naples for a short while before coming back to the Cape.

Sheree has lived at Lifeline since January of 2006. Her son, Josiah, was born May 19, 2006. Ever since she was a little girl she knew she'd have a son named Josiah. Sheree is also working on her GED. She is also working toward being a Certified Nursing Assistant. She will start by working in a nursing home before advancing to a hospital.

"This is an awesome place. It's a very Godly home that teaches me how to help my son and walk with Christ. I know it's one of the best things I could ever do. They have a heart for young women here."

For all the time spent at Lifeline, the only government assistance that is acceptable is Medicaid.

Stephanie is 22 years old. Her son, Malachi, was born in May of 2007. She pointed out that the name Malachi means Messenger of God or Angel of God.

Stephanie is currently enrolled in Edison College studying to be a Physical Therapist Assistant. At the completion of the two-year course, she will enroll in FGCU and participate in the program to become a Physical Therapist. Her intention is to work with home health care and focus on working with children. Stephanie already has her GED. She also found Lifeline on the internet.

"Lifeline has been very helpful, to say the least. If we apply ourselves, we can survive on our own and take care of our children. I couldn't ask for better child care. They love our babies here and we get to know the Lord. It's a good situation for mother and child. Mrs. Kathy is the Administrator but she also teaches two of my classes. She's like a surrogate mother."

For information or to help, please visit www.lifelinefamilycenter. org or simply pick up the phone and call **(239) 242-7238**.

Chapter 47.
Miracle on Ice – The Movie

*My dad, portraying **Captain Mike Eruzione's** dad, was in the original 1981 movie with lovable **Karl Malden** portraying **Coach Herb Brooks** and commemorating the Gold Medal 1980 USA Olympic Hockey Team. Here you can visit the movie set in production and get more than a glimpse from a ring-side seat behind the scenes.*

"Hey Joe," Ginny called out. "The movie, *Miracle On Ice,* the original from 1981 that your father is in, it's on TV. How 'bout we watch it?"

Ginny had never seen the movie and I hadn't seen it but once. The movie depicted the USA Olympic Hockey Team that competed at Lake Placid, NY in 1980. Our team was composed of young, inexperienced athletes whose average age was 22. The Russians at that time were thought to be superior to all the professional US and Canadian teams. You know the rest of the story, I trust. Our kids defeated the mighty Russian team and won the Olympic Gold Medal. They amazed the world, truly a 'Miracle' to many millions here and around the world.

I was thrilled that my father, actor **Paul Micale**, was cast in the commemorative movie and especially thankful that he portrayed the father of Team Captain and sparkplug, **Mike Eruzione**. Here, thanks to Ginny, was one more opportunity to visit with the image of my dad again.

As the movie started, I slipped back in time. One day during the filming, my father asked me if I'd like to visit the set at the Sports Arena in downtown Los Angeles. I always liked to go to dad's sets, meet the cast and watch them shoot.

I identified myself to the security guard at the Arena door. Off to my right I saw my dad wave to me while talking to a few people. As I approached, a man in a brown overcoat turned and looked my way. That was my first in-person sight of actor **Karl Malden**, who was cast as **Coach Herb Brooks**.

When my father introduced me to Malden, he shook my hand like he was pumping for oil, or maybe water, all the time saying how pleased he was to meet me and how much respect he had for my father.

"I always get excited when I know that Paulie and I are going to be working together, because we're two old goats who always know our lines and our blocking, so it's one take and we get on with the next thing. These younger actors, too many of them, need 20 takes and then they still didn't get it right."

My father had been cast, more than once, on *Streets of San Francisco,* Malden's successful TV-Cop series. I just looked it up; Four Times!

The last time he was on *Streets*, Malden asked dad if he was getting Star billing this time. When my father said probably not, Malden said he'd see about that. Sure enough, when the episode was broadcast, my dad had Guest Star billing.

Another person in the small group was Mike Eruzione, the captain and prolific scorer who was playing himself in the movie and doubling as Technical Advisor, or TA. As I reached to shake hands with Mike, he slapped my hand out of the way and gave me a hug, saying, "What's with the handshake, we're brothers!"

I had arrived just about lunchtime so I got to eat with the cast and crew. At one point, the Director, **Steven Hillard Stern**, approached me and asked me what part I was playing. I told him I was playing the waterboy. Sometimes I think I'm a comedian, God knows why, but I did get a big laugh that time.

Returning to present time, Ginny and I absolutely enjoyed watching the movie. Ginny got a kick out of hearing about the setup of a scene and a blooper committed by one of the actors. At one point I recalled that I colored my dad's hair so that he went from salt 'n pepper to pepper 'n salt. Just a basic Hollywood sleight-of-hand, nothing more, but the only time my dad had me alter his hair color.

Ginny and I get to see my dad on TV now and then, a real treat. At least twice in the recent past, I was not facing the TV when I recognized my dad's voice and turned around to intently watch the rest of the show.

More than a few times I've had someone tell me how fortunate I am that my dad can pop into my sight via the TV. I know what they mean as there is no chance to see my mom that way.

Like I've said a million times, I'm truly blessed.

★★★

Chapter 48.
The Bogus Teenager 'n The Italian Cricket

I Confess! Everybody wants to be an actor and I had my shot with the cutest blond 'Talian ever. Hey, two of these stars are still active... and as pretty – and bright – as ever! Now you get to meet them as they were emerging from their teens.

Okay, time to 'fess up. During my first year or so in Hollywood, like millions before and since, I thought I wanted to be an actor. I even had an agent, thanks to my Dad. **Mickey Harris** was a tall, attractive, **Rita Hayworth** look-alike, probably 40-something though younger looking and a former hoofer, just like Rita.

Mickey sent me out on several casting calls with one time in particular standing out clearly in memory. They were making a movie based on the life of **Rudolph Valentino** as a teenager. Frankly my dear, I don't remember who "they" were, but probably, it was one of the at-the-time new independent production companies rather than a major studio.

I could easily play a teenager into my mid-twenties, as I was constantly carded several years past 21.

The casting people paired me with an exceptionally pretty and petite blond gal who surprised me by saying she was Italian. We read together very well as I really didn't have to strain to say loving lines to her or behave like she caused me to have romantic feelings for her. We were called back for another reading, pumping everybody's blood on my side of the line.

One other couple was called back. She was also exceptionally pretty, a brunette, maybe 5' 6" or 7", sparkling eyes and an infectious smile. He was about 5' 10" with sandy blond hair. Half-way through the audition, the four of us were asked to change partners, even though the brunette was obviously taller than me. Sitting, I was told that we looked good together, size-wise.

Sometime later, Mickey gave me the low-down.

"They like you and the brunette best, even though you're not a good fit for her in both size and color contrast. To choose you, they would need to build runners like they do for **Alan Ladd**, but there's probably not enough money in the budget. With all that, they want to see you again." Mickey was happy and upbeat regarding my chances.

A third call-back causes everyone to have positive expectations. Mickey figured I had a decent chance for landing the other good role in the script if I didn't get the lead, so she told me to behave confidently, but not cocky.

At the third audition, I read with both my blond partner and the brunette. They also had me read the second lead, Valentino's buddy. By the end of the day, smart money was on the brunette and her sandy-haired partner for the leads.

As we were wrapping the day, my pretty blond Italian pulled me aside.

"If we don't get a role in this movie, don't let it bother you. They make decisions for all kinds of reasons, so just go on to the next one knowing you will get yours. Expect to win going in, but don't be upset whenever it doesn't work out."

Great advice. Many people not in show biz can benefit from such wisdom. Obviously, she lives by the words she shared with me years ago. Shortly thereafter she landed the lead in the TV show called *Hawaiian Eye,* where she was launched as a star playing the heartthrob character named **Cricket Blake**. I'm sure, paragraphs ago, several readers figured that I've been talking about the irrepressible **Connie Stevens**.

Last year I went to the **Hollywood Celebrities and Collector Show** in Burbank. Connie Stevens was a featured Special Guest. All weekend long I wanted to approach her. Finally when just a few people were around, I drummed up my nerve. I am not bashful, but my words to her were more stumble-bum than smooth. Nothing original, mind you, but something like, "…it was long ago… you won't remember… blah blah blah…"

"Yes I do remember and the girl who got the lead was **Stephanie Powers**, and she's as pretty today as back then. And you, I didn't recognize you at first with that belly…."

The reunion with Connie was a thrill because she remembered the incident, to my utter surprise. After all, given the long history of her personal success and the sheer volume of activity she has enjoyed, who woulda thunk?

Acting – like wrestling in high school and college - were part of my earliest years. My writing and hairstyling careers continue to be my one-two Pleasure 'n Joy. I've never considered either to be "work;" I've never considered either to be a "have to." Like right now. Telling this story is my greatest pleasure.

✮✮✮

Chapter 49.
A Salute To Veterans

Coming up is another "Special," commemorating the official dedication of the National World War II Memorial in Washington, D.C. on May 29, 2004. Have you waved your flag lately?

While growing up, the **Tom Brokaw**-dubbed **"Greatest Generation"** was in charge. They were riding out a reign that will be highly respected and favorably noted at least as long as America keeps its own record of history.

The Greatest Generation suffered a rude and frightening awakening at the hands of the Japanese Empire, no true American needs to be reminded. The record shows that the majority of Americans were not totally sure of the correct geographical or even hemispherical location of **Pearl Harbor** on December 7, 1941. However, by the morning of December 9th, men by the hundreds of thousands were lining up at their local military recruiting agency, offering everything. Countless thousands, like my father's younger brother Dominic, were teenagers, still too young to volunteer without official parental consent. All tolled, these men were zealous patriots; selfless; true heroes; though not by their own definition then or for most, not even now, unless they are talking about "...the other fellows...."

The women of the era were cut from the same cloth, possessing the matching (Guiding?) spirit, enthusiasm and resolve. The uniquely demanding period prompted the emergence of **Rosie the Riveter**, fostering her opportunity to get out of the kitchen and grab them there bulls, 'n ride 'em tough. Factories, in particular, will forever bear her imprint.

That entire segment of American Humanity will be most fondly revered and forever applauded, especially by those of us who are their direct descendants.

On Saturday, May 29, 2004, the **National World War II Memorial in Washington, D.C.** was officially dedicated by **President George W. Bush** with a crowd estimated at 140,000 present. Cameras and reporters visited with men and women who attended to represent and to honor the 16 million American men and women who donned a uniform and served. We are told that only 4 million U.S. Veterans of that horrific war are still alive, their number dwindling by slightly more than 1,000 per day currently.

Of all U.S. cities with populations of 100,000 or more, the two cities with the highest concentration of WW II Veterans are **Clearwater, Florida** and **Cape Coral, Florida**. Interestingly, since learning that fact, the feeling while driving on Del Prado Boulevard or Cape Coral Parkway has changed for me. Somehow, the sun shines brighter as the sight of gray-haired folks ambling to and fro causes a, how shall I say, a sense of appreciation, perhaps, that was not noted just a short week ago.

Once in a while I get to play a round of golf with a man who I'll respectfully refer to as Kenny, if you will. We've played together a dozen or 20 times over the past three or four years, so I called him and asked if he'd indulge me with some of his WW II experience.

I knew Kenny was a fighter pilot, but that was about it. He told me he joined the **Army Air Corp Aviation Cadets** on May 1, 1941, graduating from Flight School at Kelly Field, Texas, on his birth-date, December 12, 1941. (Hey, that's **Frank Sinatra's** birthday, too!)

The war came as a complete surprise to Kenny as well as many of his contemporaries, altering his plans to use the service to complete his college education. Instead he got to know the topography of the Pacific including the likes of Auckland, Australia, Tonga Taboo, New Caledonia and Guadalcanal flying in P-39s and P-400s, the plane developed for and rejected by the British, so our boys got them. The P-400 was hard to start in cold weather and had no oxygen, so it had to be flown at extremely low altitude.

Later Kenny flew P-38s and P-40Fs with Rolls Royce engines, including oxygen, using machine guns and 200/300/400 pound bombs including napalm as he and his squadron flew ground support. He flew 56 missions, then went back for about 50 more. The last two years of the war he was an instructor at Page Field right here in Ft. Myers, receiving his discharge in October of '45. As a civilian he was a retail merchant, his last business being a sporting goods and scuba shop.

"I didn't do a heck of a lot," Kenny said as we were wrapping up. "Others did so much more," he went on. "Look at all those who didn't come home. They are the heroes. Heck, I was just a small fry, so don't use my name. Please."

Sure, Kenny. Over 100 missions, any one of which could have ended with a splash. Instructor for two years. Small fry? Puts a whole new bent on "relative definition," if you ask me. And so very typical of so many of those who are bonafide members of The Greatest Generation.

I also had a long and very friendly visit via telephone with **Phil Phillips**. He was drafted in June of 1942 from his home in Cleveland and went to Camp Walters, Texas, one of a few northern guys among a group of predominantly Southerners. Our country and every aspect of our world has changed almost beyond the comprehension of most mere mortals in the past 60 years, but such a mix pre-war often led to real trouble. Phillips overcame the obstacles, went to OCS, came out a Second Louie and taught small unit tactics until the school was dissolved.

He was sent to Europe two months before D Day and later was assigned to the 83rd Infantry, Company E. At one point he was further assigned as a graves registration officer and at the same time was told to operate the PX when not fighting. He saw enough action to fill a book, so we won't attempt to do it here, but we do want to mention that he met up with General Patton for a while, got involved in the Battle of the Bulge and was awarded the Bronze Star for action in another phase of his story. His civilian career was likewise played out in the fast lane as he successfully climbed corporate ladders of a couple of America's more recognizable corporations, achieving the office of president. Mr. Phillips retired to Southwest Florida in 1985, living on Sanibel until last year when he and his wife, **Laverne Anne**, moved to their current home in Shell Point. The two met in high school and this August will celebrate 61 years of marriage. They each have earned recognition and applause for leading successful, productive lives, to which we add this all-too-brief salute today.

I had two long interviews with 22-year Sanibel resident **Gordon P. Schopfer**. He even prepared a full page of information as a special favor to help me get this all down on paper. One of his friends, who we must favor with anonymity, called Schopfer "...a most important cog in the European war effort of the United States." I honestly believe that Schopfer's story could make a movie that would compare favorably in content and action to classics such as *Flying Leathernecks* and *The Longest Day*.

I still haven't said a word about **Mark Rubin** or **Jim Dozier** or **Ted Tyson** and regrettably, I'm not going to attempt to use all the wonderful information they gave me as there is not enough space to do them and their stories proper justice. I make this simple reference to these fine gentlemen with sincere appreciation for their contributions to me.

I want to mention that I also had a great conversation with former Navy nurse **Jean Reed** who was on her way out the door to attend the commemorating ceremonies in Washington, D.C. the day I called. She asked that I at least mention that one of the most profound occurrences of the WW II era was the way the people of this country – civilians and military alike – pulled together, sacrificing personal desires in favor of common benefit. Entire books have been written expounding this theme, yet there is cause to wonder if those born after 1960 can possibly imagine that so many millions of diverse people actually behaved thus for such a long period of time.

One more and we'll call it a day. I spoke to **Rosie The Riveter**. This one worked in a sewing factory in Hoboken, traveling on two trains and a bus each way each day from and to the Bronx. She sewed together those heavy, prickly-material overcoats worn by the GIs in Europe, the coats that made her uncomfortably warm as she draped them over her lap while putting the stitches in place. Know what else she and her girlfriends put in each one? A note. A note in the pocket of each coat that said things like "Come Home Safe" or "You're In Our Prayers" or "Thanks Buddy. Come By For Coffee Sometime." For about the last 23 years, she has lived in Cape Coral and her name is **Lucy DiGiacomo**. Macular degeneration took her sight but not her spirit. After all, she, like everyone mentioned herein, is a bonafide member of The Greatest Generation.

There's an adage in life that cautions to be careful when wishing for something, for you might get it. I asked for this assignment to call attention to the commemoration of the WW II Monument and to underscore a few of the people who played an integral part in American life during the years of World War II. Tom Brokaw wrote at least three books on this era and said he felt he did not even begin to do the subject justice. I couldn't agree more. Maybe the best suggestion I can leave is to approach a veteran of that time and encourage him or her to have a private conversation with you. They're talking a bit more freely now. Such a conversation could change your life in positive ways that are beyond your imagination.

✯✯✯

Chapter 50.
Thanx for the Memories, 2003

I Confess! This next column focuses on only a partial list of Celebrities who passed away in 2003. Some I knew, some I didn't, but for sure I had special feelings for all people profiled. It is the only column I wrote that was a general, end-of-year memorial.

The movies have a tremendous impact on the lives of people all over the world, serving as a great source of entertainment, education and inspiration. Countless people are influenced when choosing their profession by a movie that piqued their imagination. In many cases, a motivating portrayal by a favorite movie star did the trick.

Movie stars like **Jack Lemmon** and **Jimmy Stewart** can become so familiar to us that we feel like we actually know them. Particulars and tidbits of their lives are of great interest to us. When these two died, many of us were immediately sad, for we felt the news on a personal level, much like the passing of a relative.

I had the privilege of being introduced to Jimmy Stewart by a mutual friend, **Dr. Eddie Cantor**, no relation to the great comic. Jimmy was on the quiet side but very friendly, looked me straight in the eye and impressed me as sincere when he said he was pleased to meet me. Over the years I would bump into him at the bank or on the walkway in front of my salon, owned in partnership with Sam and Theresa Russo, called **Beverly Hills Hair Design** and located at 9171 Wilshire Boulevard, as Jimmy had his office in the building next door. Once when I said "Hi" to him and he gave me a warm greeting with a handshake and smile, a lady walking by that I never saw before, or again, looked at me with saucer eyes, mouth literally wide open and said "Oh my God, you KNOW him!"

I met Jack Lemmon through my wife, Ginny. She knew Jack and his lovely wife, actress **Felicia Farr**, on both a personal and professional level before Ginny 'n I were married in 1995. Jack surprised me by requesting to read a movie script I had written. Extremely flattered, I told him there was no part in it worthy of his stature, "...unless you'd like to play one of the female nurses." If I could make everyone laugh like that....

Anyhow, he later sent me a note wherein he said something like his legs were no longer suitable for one of the nurse roles, but that he *would like to read anything I write in the future*. Jack Lemmon's friendship and interest in my writing will always be one the greatest compliments of my life. When Ginny and I moved to Florida, this all-time Hollywood icon sent us an unsolicited autographed photo "for good luck." The thrill is everlasting.

Every year about this time we see TV programs or read articles recapping the past year and those celebrities who died. I'd like to share some personal thoughts and feelings about some of the celebrities we lost last year. Please don't make too big a deal of the order, as in my mind, they're all worthy of being Number One.

The loss of **Norma Storch** was particularly devastating to me. Still is. Our friendship, our love for each other was as family. Norma will always be a true highlight in my life. A previous column titled *Friends-A-Jillion* was devoted to Norma.

Cartoonist **Bill Mauldin** was awarded two (2!) Pulitzer Prizes. When I was a kid, I read his fabulous book, *Up Front,* the collection of his cartoons starring his two very famous, fictional **WWII GIs, Willie and Joe**. Each cartoon brought a smile, and often, outright laughter. When **President Kennedy** was assassinated, Mauldin depicted the grief of the nation with his cartoon of the statue of **President Lincoln**, head buried in his hands, as he sobbed at the Lincoln Memorial. I can get that down on paper, but I never have been able to verbally describe the scene. So long, Willie and Joe, you'll never be cold, muddy or hungry again… and your sox will always be dry.

I never knew **Charles Bronson**, though I feel like I did. Many times I saw him in **Schwab's** but never even said hello. Big mistake, for perhaps we might have become friends.

Just a thought of **Art Carney** brings a smile to my countenance. I used to cut his look-alike, director-brother Jack Carney's hair, but I never knew the co-star of the "Honeymooners."

Also, unfortunately, lost track of brother Jack some years ago.

Ninety-one year old actor **Hume Cronyn** left us to join his actress-wife, **Jessica Tandy**, last June. Funny how 91 years can be considered as not long enough, huh?

Buddy Ebsen and my Dad, Paul, were friends, appearing in *Barnaby Jones* together a couple of times. Buddy was also the star of *Beverly Hillbillies*. Buddy was originally cast as the **Tin Man** in the 1939 classic movie, *The Wizard of Oz*, but the silver makeup almost killed him. They used different stuff with **Jack Haley**.

Buddy Hackett put on the funniest show I ever saw, this one in Las Vegas. I actually had to turn away from the stage and block my ears for fear of tearing my rib muscles from laughing too hard. He was just as funny on TV minus the unprintable words, if you ask me.

Katharine Hepburn. Twelve (12) Academy Award Nominations! Talk about STAR.

I'll always remember **Gregory Hines** at **Sammy Davis, Jr's**. last birthday party that was a TV Special. Hines invited Sammy up on stage to Tap. Sammy accepted to everyone's amazement. More dead than alive, Sammy out-danced the world. **Sidney Skolsky**, the famous writer who was my first steady client in the hair business, introduced me to Hines at **Schwab's** one day. We exchanged casual Hellos over the years.

Gregory Peck is mostly associated with **Atticus Finch** in the movie, *To Kill a Mocking Bird*, his Oscar role, but he is forever in my memory as **Colonel Savage** opposite the Academy Award winning performance of **Dean Jagger** in *12 O'Clock High,* one of the great WW II movies.

John Ritter. It was sudden, unexpected and way too soon. I think it appropriate to lift a line from President Kennedy's funeral when the Cardinal said, "We hardly knew ya, John."

Penny Singleton personified the comic strip character, **Blondie**, playing dits to the hilt and setting the standard.

The Untouchables TV show was, though unintended, a setup to the three-peat *Godfather* movie saga thanks to the vivid portrayal of **Robert Stack** as Eliot Ness. My father had the recurring role of **Little Augie from Detroit** in four episodes of *The Untouchables*. I was called upon many times to cut the hair of guest stars for the show, much like my association with *Johnny Carson's Tonight Show*. Now that Stack has departed, the Pearly Gates should be even safer, if I might share my fantasy with you.

Hail Columbia! Seven gifted astronauts, **Rick Husband, William McCool, Laurel Clark, David Brown, Michael Anderson, Kalpana "K.C." Chawla** and **Ilan Ramon**, took leave of this world last February 1st. Airports, highways and schools already bear their names. Very appropriate to helping us praise and remember.

David Brinkley had a long, eventful career as Anchor that brought him honor, acclaim and our heartfelt admiration.

Doctor Robert Atkins, diet and weight loss expert, continues to have a major impact on human health. Reminds me, time to drop ten.

Dr. Edward Teller, physicist. Regarded as "father of the H Bomb," he will be in the history books as long as civilization exists. Ginny got to know him during her 11 year tenure when she was Executive Assistant to

The Hon. Evelle J. Younger, former Attorney General of California and District Attorney of Los Angeles.

As a youngster, **Althea Gibson** was crippled by polio. She blossomed into a multi-talented athlete and became the first black champion at Wimbledon, inspiring millions.

Bill Shoemaker was the winner of 8,833 horse races, including four Kentucky Derbies! I know my partner, Sam Russo, is honored to have cut Bill's hair.

Then there was **Johnny Longden**, award winning jockey and trainer, and the only person to win the Derby as both. The little giant was also noted as a friend, colleague and competitor of Shoemaker. They were a great one-two punch in life and rather appropriately, exited together.

Herb Brooks was privileged to be the coach of the Olympic Hockey Team that took the Gold in 1980. **Carl Malden** portrayed him in the movie, *Miracle on Ice* along side my father, Paul, who portrayed Captain **Mike Eruzione's** father. Enough here for a future column, as mentioned before.

Larry Doby, Hall of Fame outfielder of the Cleveland Indians, will forever be honored as the first black player in the American League. When I was a boy, this kind man befriended me, called me by name. He also gave me a ball used in a game, a still-cherished possession.

Bob Hope. He was saved for last as he obviously is not least. Bob Hope journeyed from England to Cleveland to Hollywood, through Vaudeville, Broadway, radio, television and the movies, culminating at Icon many years before 2003. He is the only person in U.S. History to be given official status as an Honorary Veteran. Sir Robert was also awarded British Knighthood. He hosted the Oscars 17 times! Too many words would be needed just to list the highlights of one-line-zinger Hope's achievements. When in LA this past fall, we learned that he is laid to rest in Mission Hills Cemetery, the same place as my parents and just down the road.

This select group represents a truly large loss in both quality and quantity. Though I have conveyed only a micro-amount of the whole story in each case, each person has had specific importance and profound impact on my life, my perspectives, awareness and values. I appreciate being able to share these observations with you.

May this tribute deliver a measure of comfort.

★★★

Chapter 51.
Sid Cutler – Super Salesman

"Pour color onto a head? Naah, gimmie a brush."
Now just what does THAT mean? Witness a pivot point in history,
even though some might consider it just a minor blip. Whatever...

Alright class, open your history notebooks, please. Today we will learn some facts you never dreamed existed. Lucky you! Listen up; the test is next Tuesday.

Until the early 1980's, hair salons, barber shops and beauty shops were visited weekly by salespeople from various supply companies. Doesn't hardly happen anymore, certainly not in the big cities. And some people say we're more of a service economy!

For twenty-something years, I often bought supplies from Sid Cutler, a rare, bonafide Super Salesman. Sid was extremely knowledgeable, pleasant with a quiet demeanor and always respectful of the salon's clients' privacy, unlike others who easily shattered the obnoxious line.

In my early years as a hairstylist, the method used for applying hair-color, for both men and women clients, was to dispense it - pour - from a bottle. The applicator cap had a narrow, funnel-like spout. The objective was to flood the re-growth area without letting the solution bleed all over the hair shaft. Rots-a-Ruck on that one. Wouldyabelieve, many salons still pour, beats me why.

"Hey Sid," I said during one of his weekly visits, "do you have a brush for applying hair-color?"

"Brush? What do you mean, 'brush?' There's no such thing."

Sid Cutler had spoken. End of subject.

My thought was to "paint and whisk" the color on so the result would be a variation of color, allowing strands of the person's natural hair to remain exposed, rather than having every hair the exact same new color. I really liked the concept and wanted to experiment with technique, see if the result would be as imagined.

I went to **Koontz Hardware** in Beverly Hills. When someone walked into that huge store, an employee would greet the person and assist in the purchase. The employee would query the customer about the reason for the purchase and perhaps offer an alternative idea that might make everything go better. It was the kind of service many of today's young people would have difficulty relating to, from either side of the counter.

"Hey, here's a new one!" the clerk who approached me said to an older co-worker. "This guy wants a brush to paint HAIR!"

The concept caused everyone within earshot to smile. Finally, I bought a couple of paint brushes that we all thought might do the trick, though I was a quart low on enthusiasm.

There were a number of "I need something better" visits back to Koontz. Some brushes could only be used once. Some were reusable a few times, so I kept looking for "it."

Most importantly, the technique seemed to be valid. My clients and I loved the results, especially on men who wanted to "tone down" their hair by reducing the quantity of gray without having it all disappear. The gals loved the variation of color, a far more natural look. It also proved to be a great method for creating more sophisticated, natural-looking highlights without using foil or a cap.

I demonstrated the technique for some of the other stylists but only one was willing to give it a go. The result? Bonafide disaster!

One day Sid came in as I was painting out some silver strands on good-buddy and Top-Forty Countdown King, **Casey Kasem**.

"Where'd you get that brush?" Sid asked me when Casey was called to the phone.

Sid kept his distance while watching me intently. After going to his car, he waited for an opening, approached and asked if I'd like to try the brush in his hand.

"It's too wide. Where'd you get this one? What is it?"

He said beauticians used the brush to apply bleach. I cut off half the bristles.

"So give me a couple more and I'll cut 'em to size. I like the way these bristles feel."

Maybe two weeks later, Sid walked up to me with a broad grin. He held out a fistful of brushes, just the right side and shape.

"Where in the world...?"

"I had them made up, just for you." He said like a proud papa.

The color applicator-brushes of today are virtually the same brushes Sid Cutler had "made up just for... (me)" all those years ago. I hope he had them patented, if such was possible. The thought never occurred to me until too many years later.

I would not be surprised if other hairstylists around the country had the same idea at about the same time way back when. Sid Cutler was not the only Super Salesman on earth, either.

All that said, we had a fun time together living this footnote in our lives. And in case you're wondering, Koontz Hardware still thrives in Beverly Hills, California. And so does good-buddy Casey Kasem!

Chapter 52.
Goldielox Visits Hairdox

For a couple of years, my wife Ginny and I had license plates on our car that said, "Hair Dox." That explains half of the title. It's eight t'five you'll like Goldielox, too.

Sanibel and **Captiva** are adjoined islands that in many ways and instances are perceived as a single entity. Both are world renown for their natural beauty and their crystal clear atmosphere that allows for breathtaking, glorious sunsets at the end of each tropically-pleasant day. Of course, their picture-perfect beaches are noted for a mixture of sand and a seemingly limitless array of expended crustacean shells. Equally important, the islands are revered as one of the world's most abundantly endowed natural aviaries, featuring a wide variety of birds that range from the grandiose American Bald Eagle to the tiny birds of the Trochilidae family, those creatures with long, narrow beaks and brilliant, iridescent plumage known more commonly as hummingbirds.

Our Southwest Florida locale is also noted for its year-round playground weather, with summer daytime temperatures rarely exceeding 100 degrees and about equally rarely dipping below 70 degrees in wintertime. Small wonder that the population of our permanent residents is within 10 percent of the locally predetermined maximum, while our group of loyal annual visitors numbers in the thousands.

Debbie George was 10 years old when she and her seven siblings first started their annual trek to Sanibel from Ohio with their parents. These days, Debbie's siblings, with families in tow, come by at various times throughout the year. They take turns using Mom and Pop's place, which is reserved exclusively for family use, a rather common practice among many Sanibel residences.

Debbie and her husband, Dan, visit each summer with daughter Elisabeth, a reserved 16 year old; daughter Sarah, a "more outgoing" 12 year old, and six year old Danny the Dynamo.

During the George family's most recent annual visit to Sanibel this past Fourth of July week, 16 year old Elisabeth, as on previous summer vacations, walked the beaches, enjoying the solitude of sea-gazing while locked onto her own deep, private thoughts.

Occasionally, she'd pause to examine a shell, ever so infrequently deciding to keep one she deemed special enough to add to her limited collection back in Tiffin, Ohio.

Among Elisabeth's thoughts this year was her recent participation in the All Ohio Music Ensemble. This annual musical event features a highly selective group of young classical musicians who are accorded a special invitation to perform in the duet category based on recorded auditions submitted for preliminary judging. Elisabeth, who has been playing the piano since the second grade, teamed up with a girlfriend named Laura, the two girls playing their selection on the same piano. Then there was "the other thing...."

"This year's visit to Sanibel helped contribute to a truly unique and very special event in the George family's life, especially concerning Elisabeth," related Mom Debbie.

About six months ago, an episode of *OPRAH* featured two teenage girls who had donated their hair to be used for making wigs for youngsters who had lost their hair due to chemo treatments. Elisabeth told Mom Debbie that she decided to donate her thick, shoulder length blond hair.

"Part of me was a bit worried at first," Mom Debbie said. "But I saw this as her choice, and since it was for such a good cause, I wanted to support my daughter."

Consulting with Linda, the family hairdresser in Ohio, Debbie and Elisabeth were provided with a web site that gave instructions for making a hair donation. Linda was unable to assist further as she does not have the technical expertise or practical experience in any phase of hair replacement. This is very understandable as less than 1% of people in the hair business are in the hair replacement phase of the business.

I'm flattered and humbled to say that Debbie remembered having a phone conversation with me last year when the family made its annual trip to Sanibel. She recalled that we talked about my work with custom hair pieces and my geometric technique of haircutting, whereby the hair is cut to enhance the specific contours of a person's facial features.

On July 6th, Debbie, Elisabeth and Sarah visited our hair salon, named **Beverly Hills Hair Design,** just like my salon in Beverly Hills, California years ago. "An appointment we will probably always remember," Debbie stated. Before and After pictures were taken. The hair was divided into four sections; then each section was braided by Ginny, followed by the harvesting process. Elisabeth's remaining hair was then washed, conditioned and cut into a style to compliment her pretty face. During the process, Elisabeth's demeanor was calm and cool. When the work was complete, she seemed very pleased with her new look. As a final gesture, everybody hugged everybody.

Later that evening, Elisabeth told her family that she felt like a part of her was cut off, the statement reflecting a factual comment with no negative overtone. She was also surprised at the new sensation of her free flowing hair and the obvious loss of its weight.

The George family expressed surprise by the request for permission to publish this story. They gave the idea serious consideration.

"I'm allowing this story to be told as a possible inspiration for others to be attracted as donors," Mom Debbie stated.

Elisabeth is a very private person who has made a personal donation of a cherished portion of herself due to her compassion for others. Many teens would consider the donation to be an extreme sacrifice, a true challenge, especially if they were to consider going it alone. For many, enlisting family support would be a test of another color.

On July 7th, a teenager who lives in Cape Coral phoned my hair salon. "Can you cut my hair so that I can donate it to make wigs for cancer patients?" she wanted to know. Yes, but how did she know to call, she was asked. "You and your wife met my parents and me at a movie theater about four years ago. I've always remembered talking about the hair for kids thing, and I want to be a part of it." No, there was no connection between the two teenagers. None, certainly, that can be found using any combination of the five senses.

On July 8th, Lili Timmermann came to Sanibel and provided her beautiful raven hair for some very fortunate recipient(s). She too, was fascinated with this story, the timing, the similarities and the differences. Before our time together was concluded, we learned that Lili has recently received her letter of acceptance and will be attending Princeton University this fall.

"You think it's a trend?" I asked Ginny.

"I hope it's an epidemic," she replied.

Ginny and I are thrilled for the privilege of having a small part in assisting two lovely young ladies who are providing a most precious gift that will certainly bring great joy to other young people. Our commitment to enthusiastically participate has been in place from the inception of our careers and shall continue indefinitely.

For those with a desire for more information on the subject of donating hair for use in hairpieces for youngsters with medical needs, please log onto the following websites: **beverlyhillshairdesign.org** *and locksoflove.org*

Chapter 53.
The Gift

Jump on board my TimeMachine once more and take a trip to my childhood where I let the kid within tell a story that smacks of fantasy. Or could it be exactly as represented? Each reader's Belief System will probably swing into action, but lemmie tell you something... yer getting' the whole Truth 'n nothin' but the Truth.

Oh, one more thing. This following column was never submitted for publication, I now regret. I should have let the newspaper make the decision. Several friends enjoyed it immensely, asked a ton of questions. Other friends made no comment and I didn't push.

I enjoyed my childhood. Some people say they didn't enjoy theirs, a truly sad statement, but gratefully, my memories and feelings are heavy on the plus side.

I have a multitude of memories, like so many snapshots in their own large, leather-covered album, revolving around William H. Brett Elementary School. Brett school no longer exists, sad to say, especially since the school isn't the only landmark missing from the Collinwood area on the east side of Cleveland.

Several incidents from that time are worth telling, little slices of life as delicious as the taste of home-made apple pie, made from scratch, the likes of which kids of today may never know.

One incident in particular will always stand out. Maybe I was eight years old, maybe nine. That's when I worked in my grandfather's grocery store. I've told the story verbally a few times over the years, but this is the first time it's been put to pen.

It all started one day in Brett schoolyard. A few of us guys were having a discussion when first one, then a second friend, chimed in with the astounding declaration that they did not believe in God. I was shocked! Nobody had ever said to me that they thought God was "another lie grownups tell to keep us in line." The impact was like a blow to my chest.

"Look at that tree," I said, offering its existence as proof of God's handiwork.

"Yeah, I see the tree. Why, what do you see?" he said.

He went on to point out that the Tooth Fairy had a short stay in our lives and that the Easter Bunny was also a cheap shot with a short life. Santa

Claus was the major lie, making fools of us for all those years.

My best argument, sadly, was in the class of "Yeah, but...."

I was troubled all the rest of that afternoon. I was so upset that I didn't want to discuss it with anyone, especially my mom or dad. I hated to admit it, but the boys' argument had some weight; too much; and more than I would have thought possible.

Wow, could God be a lie?!?

So much of religious teaching is based on Faith, the stuff necessary when Proof is in short supply. Or non-existent. Like all the Miracles. Right from the git-go is Immaculate Conception. A Virgin giving birth! A Star that moved through the sky, leading three rich guys, smart too, coming out of Nowhere with Expensive Gifts. And on and on. Healing the Sick! The Blind! The Crippled! Even Raising the Dead! Walking on Water! And feeding the big crowd with a couple of loaves of bread and a few fish! Then the kicker: Dying a Horrible Death; and Rising Up three days later, ALIVE!

Man, if the whole thing was equal to April Fool, then it would be April Fool Forever! What would become of me? My parents? Everyone on earth? Without God, would there be Heaven?!? And if not, what happens when we die?

Poof???

Finally it was bedtime. The night light was on and my door was closed. Finally! Gotta get in touch with God so we can talk!

My tone was very respectful, as always. I didn't try to fudge with Him and wouldn't even have wanted to try. I was uncomfortable with the knowledge that He could read my mind, because I wanted to present my case step by step, so I plowed right ahead.

"God," I said, "I know You are All Powerful, All Good, 'n All Loving." I started to cry. I was really upset.

"I know You can do *anything*. Make a chair dance and sing. You don't, 'cuz; You don't fool around, but You could if You wanted to. I also know that miracles are as plentiful today as they were 2,000 years ago, maybe even more-so today, since there are more people. I have been taught not to ask for a miracle, unless asking for someone else."

I paused a bit. Did I have the right to do what I was about to do? So I'll ask, I figured. Yes and No are both answers. Besides, I didn't expect an answer that night. So I sucked up some breath. Guess I mean courage.

"Every miracle is a Big Deal, but over the thousands of years, You've probably done *millions* of miracles. Sister Cecilia said so, 'n I believe her.

This is not an idle request. This is serious. Those boys, my friends, they scared me today."

I was choking up, but I fought the emotion. I still had plenty more to say and I wanted the words to come out clearly.

"I don't ever want to go through that again. I didn't know what to say to them, God, but the right words aren't what I'm asking for." The emotion got the upper hand for the moment. I got mad at myself for my lack of control, but I got to the point. I had to.

"I'm asking You to help me to never doubt You again." I cried so hard that no sound came out. The pillow in my mouth helped, I'm sure.

Then, a calm, a quietness seemed to cloak me. "...and I don't care about what happened to Saint Peter right this minute. Not that I really don't care; understand, but if You'll do this for me this once, I can take this with me Forever. Now, I don't want a thunderclap, or lightening to hit the tree in our yard outside. That could be called a coincidence. Or weather." I was feeling better now, more confident in my quest.

"You seem to use Angels as messengers a lot. That's what I want. An Angel. Please send me an Angel so I know You are there and always will be, just like Sister Cecilia says." The last couple of words were drowned out, take that literally, but I was confident that He heard them clearly.

There, I thought. I got it out. I was exhausted. I signed off with an Our Father and a Hail Mary and quietly drifted off to sleep.

Oh, just so you know. At that time, my concept of an Angel was like the statues and paintings, beings with blond or light brown hair - maybe a bit long - with flowing robes. And wings. Big White Wings. The word Angel could also conjure up the image of St. Michael the Archangel, who wore battle dress and was, and still is, my *Padrone*.

The next morning I was working at my grandfather's grocery store. As I was sweeping one of the aisles, I looked up. To my utter amazement, I saw an Angel down at the end of the aisle! Already? I just prayed *last night!* And the other thing: He looked just like a man! No long hair and no flowing robe. And no Wings! But no doubt at all, he was My Angel!

I started to wave, but quickly withdrew my hand to my chest. Do you wave to an Angel?

He started to wave back, but stopped abruptly, following my lead.

I thought, hey, he's not leaving. Go up and thank him for coming. I started walking toward him. A slight tinge of fear hit his eyes, but not his face.

"I want to thank you for coming," I said, extending my hand.

The fear left his eyes as his face took on a Mona Lisa pleasantness.

"I am privileged that it is I who was chosen to come."

That really blew me away, to say so with my current choice of words, which probably were not available to me in those days. But all the same, his choice of words - an absolute quote - would not have been available to anyone in my old neighborhood, either.

I was so taken by the Promptness, the Profoundness of the whole situation, that I turned and started to walk away. Suddenly, I realized. He's *talking* to me! He could answer the most important questions on my mind! I should ask!

I turned. He wasn't there! Ratz! I shot around the corner; after all, he couldn't be more than a step away. Nothing! I ran around the other shelving. My Aunt Carmela was behind the counter near the register.

"Joseph. What are you doing?"

"The light-haired guy. Did he come this way?" Nutz! She probably didn't see him. I shoulda kept my mouth shut!

"What guy?" She looked toward the front door. "Nobody's been in here the past five, six minutes. Someone from the junkyard?"

"No-no, not the junkyard across the street. He's not from around here."

Aunt Mel looked to the back of the store. Uncle Sam was tidying up, broom in hand. "Sam, could anybody have gone out through the back door?"

Uncle Sam looked at the back door, then to Aunt Mel. He had a rather sheepish look on his face. "I forgot to unlock it," he said.

Aunt Mel gave me the third degree. I finally said I was daydreaming and got carried away. That wasn't the best or smartest tactic on my part, but what was I gonna say, 'I mean the *Angel*?!?' That would have gone over big. She finally let me off the hook.

I know, I know. I can make all the arguments against an Angel visit. A psychiatrist could say it more eloquently, I'm sure. But nutz to all that.

I got my Angel! God always was and always will be! Heaven too! And if I play my cards right....

I miss the old neighborhood. Brett school. Grampa's grocery store. Any wonder?

★★★

Chapter 54.
Philip Ahn; the Actor America Loved to Hate

*I Confess! **Philip Ahn** was my dear friend and a long-term client starting from my first months working for Cosmo. He was very easy to know, respect and admire for the obviously gracious man he was and the humble manner he presented to all people. Philip was a true Hollywood Star who was as lovable as he was successful, but only Hollywood insiders knew it all. Now, so will you.*

Sometime early in my first year working for Cosmo's, I acquired a haircutting client named **Poncie Ponce**, at the time one of the stars of the hit TV show, *Hawaiian Eye*.

As I recall, Poncie was Hawaiian born of Chinese extraction. His hair was ramrod straight with the sides sticking out perpendicular to his scalp. I used the Sicilian Razor Cut method as was taught to me by Sam Keston. Amazingly to both Poncie and me, his hair was far easier for both of us to groom and the hair would stay in place with less resistance.

Poncie told Cosmo how thrilled he was to be able to easily and effectively self-groom.

"I no longer need makeup put into my scalp for the show. Joe's razor-cut causes my hair to lay down controlled."

One day Cosmo booked actor **Philip Ahn** with me.

"You'll recognize him when he comes in," Cosmo assured me. "Philip has already had a great career, he's been a major star since the thirties. He played the bad Jap so convincingly so many times that the studio had to provide him with body guards for several years. He's also one of the most likable, gentle people you'll ever meet. He needs your razor-cut."

"Graciously polite" would be another way to help describe Philip Ahn. I recently learned that he has the distinction of being recognized as the first American citizen born of Korean parents in the United States.

Over the many years that I was privileged to cut his hair, he proved to be more than "just a client." When I was looking to buy my first home, he volunteered to show me homes near his home in Northridge, an upper middle class neighborhood in the San Fernando Valley.

"He thinks I'm a millionaire," I told Cosmo. "He showed me 4,000 square foot homes that cost $45,000. Too rich for my blood."

Ha! Shoulda jumped all over that one.

Philip and his sister, **Soorah**, opened **Phil Ahn's Moongate**, the Valley's most fabulous – and expensive - Chinese restaurant, located on Van Nuys Boulevard in Panorama City and across the street from Montgomery Ward Department Store. (A bit farther up and across the street toward the mountains was **Sanzo's Beauty School**, a story for another time.)

The Moongate had a Grand Opening, by invitation only, wouldyabelieve, with only one seating. It was like a major movie premier with search lights blazing in the night sky, the red velvet carpet and even uniformed attendants with velvet ropes holding back hundreds of people gawking at the many VIPs in all their glitter.

My group was a party of six, including Sam Russo and his wife along with my sister and brother-in-law. Soorah, decked out in full Asian regalia, seated us personally, telling our waiter with a flourish that we were special guests of Philip.

Oh boy, how great! As we entered the dining area, our names were announced to the applause of all.

The menu was fixed and fabulous, as was the thrill of exchanging nice-nice with Hollywood's Finest, seated to our left, right and all over the swank place. Some old lady, musta been 45, maybe 47, kept pestering me for an autograph. Thought she saw me in a beach picture and playing a guitar 'n singing on TV. She sure gave our table lots of laughs. No, I don't play guitar and no again, I don't sing, not even in the shower.

We each had our fill of exotic Asian libations. The waiter handed a bill to Sam. Sam laughed and gave it to my brother-in-law. My sister took a peek and reacted like it was a spider. Or mouse. At least she didn't scream. Laughing, my brother-in-law handed it to me.

The bill was for $206.00. Let me put that in perspective. The bill – in today's value - was $950.00. Fortunately, it was Saturday night. Sam had the salon receipts hidden in the trunk of his car. Nobody had to wash chopsticks. How gross would that be?

My brother-in-law decided to sneak out with one of the large, fancy drink glasses under his jacket. An elephant would have been less obvious, I'm sure. Just as our car was brought up, he – what'd you expect?

KA-SMASH!

Sometime later, Philip came in for a haircut. I started to apologize.

"What are you talking about? Did you enjoy the food? A glass broke? Heck, happens all the time. Anyone tell me? What for? Nobody was hurt, so why worry?"

See. Gracious, polite. Always with a smile.

We enjoyed several more years together and many more visits to the Moongate, most without my brother-in-law.

Philip worked with many of the greatest stars like **Crosby, Wayne, Cooper, Bogart, Lancaster, Sinatra** and even **Shirley Temple** and **Mae West**. On TV, you enjoyed him as the bald-headed **Master Kahn** in the ABC TV series, *Kung Fu*.

Philip Ahn died on February 28, 1978. On November 14, 1984, more than 400 friends and family members gathered at 6211 Hollywood Boulevard to witness the placing of his STAR, a fitting tribute to one of the most famous Asian actors in the history of motion pictures… and for always and ever, my dear friend.

Chapter 55.
The Pot Soldier

Here's a peek, just a peek, at one of my experiences while on active duty with the U S Army. Actually, I could write a book on my six month Active Reserve duty. In fact, I cover a bunch more in the book I call Someday, a novel standing by to answer the question: "So what else have you written?" Don't let the title – either my book or the one to follow - throw you.

I joined the Reserves shortly after graduating from Barber School (had to – the draft, y'know) and a million years (Actually about six months) before I ever knew I'd be working in Hollywood for Cosmo's and be known as Hairstylist to the Stars!

W hat choice? It was simple math. Getting drafted and leaving home for two years didn't appeal to me at all, so I signed up for the Army's six month program. Figured I could do 180 days standing on my ear.

Actually, it wasn't all bad. Just mostly. Take going for our Welcome To Camp Haircut, for instance. There were two guys using clippers much like I had seen in a movie-short of a sheep-shearing contest. The Army haircut took all of two, maybe three minutes. Even at one buck, it was grossly overpriced.

There was a third barber, if indeed any of them were licensed. Or formally trained. Number three was a girl. As I clearly recall, she was one of the most beautiful girls I had ever seen. She had an angelic face, body to match and long, flowing raven-dark hair. If that stretches your imagination, it fractured mine.

Most of my fellow recruits were waiting for Dark Haired Beauty. I'm not sure what they were looking at, but to me she seemed to be on a demonic mission. Her victims were not left with enough hair to accurately determine its color.

One of the male barbers finished, called "next." Nobody budged. It wasn't my turn but I stepped forward and sat in his chair, handing him a dollar as I did.

"You pay the cashier on the way out," he said.

I told him that the buck was for him and to please leave me with as much hair as the Gestapo would allow. His face was noticeably brighter than a DaVinci smile. I also mentioned that I cut hair for a living as a civilian.

Later, all the guys in my barracks were scrunch-faced over my 'do. What a crock! I rated it as the worst haircut of my life, though the color was not in question.

Army life is not complex, but it is the opposite of the American Way of Life. Just follow a few simple rules and things will go better, everybody knows. Like never be at the beginning or end of a line, no matter the purpose of the line. And never volunteer for ANYTHING. Did you see the word "never." Good. Now we can talk about an exception.

KP Duty started on Day One. (Only 179 to go, Whoopee!) When the initial group returned from KP duty that first night, they were dead tired and loaded with stories of do's and don'ts.

The Mess Sergeant asked for any squad leaders to step forward, as those soldiers got to take their pick. The leader of A Squad stepped forward and gave a "So there" grin to everyone.

"Anyone want to join him?" Sarge asked.

Two others stepped forward. They got their pick, too. The main sewer pipe alongside the mess hall was ruptured. The three of them were up to their butts in mud and muck, all day, swinging their picks and shoveling that stinky, gooey mess.

No job sounded good. The Mess Sergeant climbed all over everybody, handing out trouble with capital T's.

"Gimmie 10!" "Gimmie 20!"

They were doing pushups and sit-ups all day. And Super Windmills.

The worst job of all was cleaning pots and pans, all agreed.

"Anyone here like to work solo?" the Sarge had asked. Some Dufuss stepped forward. Most of the pots were big enough to sit in. After Solitary Sam had cleaned several, the cook, "a good ol' Southern boy" – his self-description - with a twangy accent and six stripes, walked over and started wiping his hand inside the pots, then throwing them all over the kitchen, shouting "Clean this mess" with each toss.

By noon, "Sam" was red-eyed and over-reacting to loud noises. Everybody listening to the stories that night seemed to think it was really funny, one guy saying he'd rather have been with the guys on the pick detail.

My turn for KP came soon enough. (175 days to go!) There were about 15 of us lined up in the mess hall that morning. The Mess Sergeant, a five striper who looked like an angry linebacker with a pit-bull for a father - or mother - was barking at us. He asked for any squad leaders. We had two. One brainiac stepped forward. Think maybe that broken sewer line was a ruse? I'd have bet a whole buck, but I couldn't find any takers.

Then the Sarge asked if anyone wanted to volunteer for anything. A couple guys almost lost it when I took one step backward and headed for the kitchen. I could feel the Sarge's glare on the back of my neck as he barked "Eyes front!" to the rest of the crew. When I got to the big sinks and the stacks of pots and pans, the Sarge said "Well now I've seen everything" and started to laugh.

First I thoroughly cleaned an area of countertop space. I started with one of the biggest pots. Scrubbed that sucker spotless. Put it on the just-cleaned counter. Picked another big one by using both hands. Ditto. I had noticed the ole' six-stripe cook sneaking a peek my way, acting like he was focused elsewhere. About the time I had cleaned my seventh pot, the cook approached. He looked into one pot, then another and smiled.

"You Eye-tal-yun, aint'cha" he said.

"Are you psychic or is it my curly hair, Sergeant" I asked, my smile and demeanor exhibiting my "hello friend" attitude.

"Helped your mama with the canning, dint'cha?" he said, still smiling. "Cleaned up them tomato-cookin' pots real good, I bet."

"One year," I said as I continued to scrub a pot, "Must've been eight, maybe nine years old, we lost a whole shelf of tomato sauce, 51 jars in all. I was just sick. Mom, too. She said one of us must have missed something, a speck, somehow. She never blamed me and it never happened again. And it won't here, either."

"Just made a fresh pot a coffee, in th'little pot," the cook said. "Wanna cup?"

I looked at all I had to do. Coffee sounded good.

"How ya drink it? I'll bring it by."

Don't get the wrong idea, cleaning pots, properly, is tough work. We fed 225 guys three times a day. Didn't leave time to lollygag.

Every time I went through the chow line after that, the Cook Sarge always gave me a nod, said hello, and asked if I was getting enough to eat. It wasn't heaven, but a friend, anytime, anywhere, ala the commercial, is priceless.

By the end of my six months I had learned all sorts of new things I have yet to use. One such piece of knowledge is that 180 days is far too long to do standing on anything as delicate as an ear.

And fortunately, I wasn't renamed **Cauliflower McPugg, Junior**.

Chapter 56.
Happy Birthday America!

I Confess: My Grampa Dominic was The Most Patriotic American of the 20th Century, even though he was never naturalized as he could neither read nor write. Notice is hereby given that visions of flags waving and sounds of marching bands playing enthusiastically have been reported by many otherwise sober and steady people who originally read this column in the newspaper. Left foot first now as we "Hup..."

It's that time of year again. July 4, 2004 is the 228th birthday of the United States of America! Happy Birthday, America; Happy Birthday, indeed!

Starting very early in my childhood, I began asking people about their feelings toward America. The resultant answers have run the gamut from positive to negative. I found the responses so interesting, so intriguing that my "survey" has continued through to the present time. Some people over the years have found the long history of my question surprising, even a bit curious, but my interest had a profound beginning.

When I was between the ages of five and seven, my mom, sis and I lived with my maternal grandparents, as my father was serving in the Army. My Grandfather, Dominic, and I had already established a very close relationship, so the move into his home forever solidified our camaraderie.

Grampa had a routine of going into the basement to smoke his pipe after supper, usually with me tagging along, hoping for another of his wonderful, interesting stories.

Hey, there was no TV then, or I would have missed plenty, for I don't ever remember my Grampa disappointing me. He never seemed to run out of subject matter.

I was to realize some years later in life that he had a distinctive story-telling style, but way back then, I was simply fascinated, often enthralled. He didn't repeat stories but would often link a story to something he had told me previously.

The theme of many of his stories was in praise of America. I distinctly remember the incident when he told me to always tip my cap to the Flag whenever I passed by in close proximity, even if it was displayed in a storefront.

"But Grampa," I remember saying, "I don't always wear a hat."

Not a problem, he assured me. "Just slightly bow your head to the Flag," he replied, demonstrating as he spoke his answer.

"Do I stop, or do I keep walking?" I wanted to know.

Paraphrasing him, he said to just keep walking, unlike the hesitation that was proper when passing by the church, when the tip of the cap was accompanied by a break in one's gait.

A pang of fear hit me for a moment, for I did not want to seem to disagree with my Grandfather.

"Grampa," I said, buying time to choose my words carefully. "I have been taught to make the sign of the cross when passing in front of the church, but nobody ever said to tip my cap, if wearing one, or to change my step."

Undaunted, Grampa rather nonchalantly said that when he was a young boy in Sicily, the custom in his town was to slightly genuflect and tip his cap when passing the church, or to slightly genuflect and make the sign of the cross if not wearing a cap.

When I asked if he tipped his cap to the Flag in the "old country," as we often referred to Sicily, he used my question to tell me for the umpteenth time that *"America is the greatest country on earth!*

"That's why we came here, like I've told you so many times," he continued with that definite air of pride he always exhibited when making a patriotic statement. "The Flag is the symbol of America. We are so very fortunate to live here, where you and your cousins can go to good schools and study hard, so that when you all grow up you can be anything you want to be. You don't realize, I'm sure, that if we were still in the old country, you'd probably already be serving an apprenticeship instead of going to school. This country, *la bella America*, is wonderful beyond my ability to properly tell you, but one day you will know."

Well Grampa, "one day" arrived for me a long time ago, sitting with you in your basement as you smoked your pipe and related to me, ever so eloquently with your thick Sicilian accent, that the United States of America is the most wonderful country on earth, notwithstanding negative commentary that too often these days hits the front page or makes the late-night news. Sure there is room for improvement, which I believe constitutes a major part of every good citizen's mission in life, but as somebody once said, don't throw the baby out with the bath water.

I am further grateful and proud to be part of the Sanibel/Captiva community and for the many wonderful people I've met here during the past four-plus years who have become dear friends and associates. Of the many enviable locales in this country, our islands are among the very top. Our visitors come from all over the world by the thousands, many on an annual visit, a true testament to our islands' venerability.

I know I speak for millions of people when I say I'm proud to be a natural citizen of this great country, working for a righteous today, a better tomorrow.

And thanx for the Jillionth time, Grampa, for the extremely rich legacy.

So again, Happy 228th Birthday, America! I tip my cap to you.

Chapter 57.
"Yo, Father Carmine, Let's Do V !"

I Confess that I love telling stories about my dad. If I said that before, call it an echo. Actor **Paul J. Micale** *portrayed* **Rocky Balboa's** *favorite priest,* **Father Carmine,** *in ROCKY II, III and almost missed V. This is the rest of the inside story of a Hollywood family's commitment to the axiom that The Show Must Go On! Enjoy mom's Rigatoni, too.*

Ginny and I went to see the movie, *Rocky Balboa,* on its opening day premiere in Southwest Florida. The movie is sort of a recap on the preceding five movies about boxing's best loved fictional character in which my father, actor **Paul J. Micale**, portrayed Rocky's favorite priest, **Father Carmine**. On the way home, I reminisced out loud to Ginny's utter delight, she said. Had you been in spirit sitting on the rearview mirror, you would have heard something like the following...

I love to eat dinner. Always did. Lunch has often been interesting, it could act as a nice break in the day, though it has historically been the most nonexistent meal given as many times as I worked through it.

Breakfast, once **Schwab's** was no longer of this earth, was enjoyed at **Factor's Deli** on Pico Boulevard at South Beverly Drive. I always looked upon breakfast as a real treat with my lox either on a toasted sesame bagel with cream cheese or scrambled with eggs and onions. You could ask **Enid**. She'd always take good care of me, telling the chef, ...eh, the cook... how to prepare them to my liking.

I especially enjoyed dinner with my parents, known to others as Paul and Pat, my mom also known as Pearl to family members. (When she was born, one of her aunts exclaimed, "Look at her skin; just like a pearl!") While we often went out to various restaurants together, the best meals by far were at my parents' home. They'd call me or I'd call them, there was nothing formal about an invitation.

"Are you doing anything for dinner tonight?" I heard my mom say maybe a million times as I remember one night in particular.

"Sounds like I'm with you," I remember replying. "We going out or your house?" This time she said to come over and asked if 7 o'clock was a good target time.

They made Rigatoni that night, my favorite, a true staple and always a delight. We were in the habit of exchanging news over dinner, so as I motioned for the cheese to be passed to me, I asked, "Eh, what's new?"

"Nothing much, really," my father replied.

With a kind of a smiling snort, my mom mimicked, "Huh, nothing new. Tell your son that Rocky called."

"Rocky! They gonna do another one? What'll this make, five?"

Man, that was exciting! Of the 300-some roles my father had over the previous 30-plus years, his portrayal of **Father Carmine** in the *Rocky* movies had brought him the most attention, the most world-wide requests for pictures and autographs.

"Yeah, they called alright, but I don't think I can do it this time."

Hold it. No one knew better than I that my father *lived* that role. "What-a-ya-mean?" rolled off my lower lip.

"It's shooting in Philadelphia again. I can't go with your mother recovering from bypass surgery."

"So? I'll come stay with Mom. I gotta work, but I'll stay close t'home otherwise."

"The shoot will take 10 days, maybe two weeks they said."

"So what if it takes three?" I answered as I rolled another meatball onto my plate. "Sounds like you'll have great exposure. How many lines y'got?"

By the time my dad was pouring our second glass of wine, it was all settled. I was free as a bird as Ginny hadn't flown into my life yet. The wine notwithstanding, the three of us began to get more than mildly excited about the positive possibilities of bringing Father Carmine back to existence one more time.

When my dad received his script, I helped him study his lines by reading the other parts with him. Father Carmine had *nine* SCENES. Wow! I always enjoyed helping my father study his part, as did my sister in years past. We did that with him ever since Dad was a stage actor back in Cleveland, seemingly a couple lifetimes ago.

This time was different, though. For the first time ever, Dad had a problem remembering his lines. Looking back, it was the major red-flag we now recognize as the beginning of Alzheimer's disease, but back in 1990....

He was in Philly about two weeks. I recall the shoot stretched a few days more than originally planned.

"One day on the set, an outside day-time shot on a Philadelphia street," my father related to us over dinner the night he arrived home, "… some young boys from a Catholic school, I could tell from the uniforms, maybe nine or ten years old, came by with an older priest to watch us shoot. When the director said 'Cut,' these kids rushed up, mobbed me. It was literally overwhelming."

The kids wanted autographs, not an unusual occurrence when a movie is on location. The boys all called Dad "Father Carmine" no matter how much Dad tried to tell them his real name and that he was "just an actor."

At one point, the white-haired priest sided up to my Dad, saying in Sicilian, no less, that it was okay the kids were addressing him as a real priest.

"No harm is being done," the priest added. "They respect your collar."

Later, one kid held out his Bible. "Father Carmine, please autograph this for me!"

My Dad looked around for the priest. Not seeing him, Dad signed the Bible as "Father Carmine, Rocky V, by Paul J. Micale."

The kid's friend then held the religious medal from around his neck in his fingers. "Please bless my new Saint Michael, Father Carmine."

Dad looked for the priest again. Nowhere in sight.

Dad was of a conservative bent, a respectful person. At his parish each Sunday, St. Elizabeth in Van Nuys, he was an usher, collected the offering. He loved taking an active part in the Mass, I can assure you. He had some question about his actions with regard to the boys' requests. Then he spotted the white-haired priest.

Dad told the priest how he signed the Bible. The priest obviously read Dad like a book, for he put his hand on Dad's shoulder and assured him that all was well and proper.

"And how did you bless the medal?" the priest inquired, speaking, my father realized, in the old Sicilian dialect of the town our family came from in the Old Country.

"I held Saint Michael in my left hand," Dad started, hoping he had done the right thing. Who was he to bless anything, he suddenly feared. "And with my right hand I traced the Sign of the Cross in the air over the medal as I said, 'I bless you in the Name of The Father, The Son, and The Holy Ghost.' The kid seemed pleased," Dad added.

"And why not?" the priest said, no English this time either.

"Y'know Paul, your blessing is every bit as good as mine. It's what's in your heart, not the cut of your collar."

My Dad got emotional, tears streaming down his cheeks as he was finishing his story.

"There's one more thing," he said, hesitatingly. "Those kids. Especially when they first rushed up to me, calling me Father Carmine. I had... I don't know what to call it... an illusion, maybe... eh, more a feeling, pleasantly eerie, and strong... I um, I felt that they were... they were really Angels! I can only say this to you, my family... others might not understand. Of course, I only saw kids."

Then he noticed that Mom and I had wet faces, too. We all laughed through our tears as we shared a hug.

That night Mom made linguini and clams, white. Absolutely delicious. After Dad topped off each of our glasses, he lifted his.

"Here's to those young kids and their priest who made sure my exciting two weeks had a special cherry on top."

A note before closing. In the script I helped my father study, as mentioned, Father Carmine had nine scenes. Plenty of good, meaty lines, too. Eight of 'em hit the cutting-room floor. The one scene they left in the picture was the very last scene of the movie. As credits start to roll we see Father Carmine waving good-by to the camera.

How Appropriate. It was Dad's last scene in his wonderful, highly successful Hollywood career.

Oh, by the way. I didn't tell the whole story, not by a long shot. I left enough to enjoy another time. Perhaps we'll finish up one of these days over a plate of *pasta 'e fagioli,* or as we pronounced it when I was a kid, *pastafazool.*

Ci rivedremo!

★★★

Chapter 58.
Hawaii, Helena and Ho

*I Confess! My first trip to the paradise formally named Hawaii (while I owned **Little Joe's Hollywood Hairstyling Salon**, formerly **Cosmo's**) was accentuated by the irrepressible HELENA and the effervescent HO. Yeah, yer right, but playing with you is a Ton a Fun. Be sure to feel the breeze and enjoy the deliciously different food accented with bites of pineapple.*

Like Hollywood, Shades Required.

The memory seems to be from last Thursday, but I know the year was 1976. My friend, **Bob Stonelake**, had put together a Hawaiian seminar for 325 independent business people.

Twenty-four hours into our ten-day stay, the word "Paradise" took on a new meaning for me. Looking at the sea rolling in on Waikiki Beach from our 17th floor hotel room, "the relentless waves" also became a phrase with an expanded definition and clearer meaning.

I couldn't visit the *U.S.S.Arizona*. Every time I cast my eyes toward the Memorial, my vision blurred. A few friends begged me to go with them, but I couldn't.

In five trips over the years, I've never gone. Maybe someday but don't take bets.

A small group of us visited **Punch Bowl**. Six arrived in my rented car. We marveled at the gorgeous, vast rolling-emerald-green terrain of the cemetery and the precisely aligned white markers.

We read the countless names on the Wall of Honor, reaching out to touch many. The six of us walked the grounds for more than an hour before returning to the car. We all were flabbergasted at the realization that no conversations took place between us, though we hugged and wept like children several times during our visit.

The daily seminars were fantastic, to understate the fact. "Be Responsible; Be Accountable, Make Up Your Mind and Go for It!" would have been an appropriate title. The lessons were life-sustaining.

Most everyone in our group went to the fabulous *Don Ho Dinner Show* one evening. The "room" he played seated 4,000 people who cheered like 40,000 when he came out singing his signature song, *Tiny Bubbles*. After a few bars, he stopped singing himself and directed the audience. Almost unbelievably, the audience sounded like a well-rehearsed chorus.

At one point in his act, Don asked for all grandmothers in the audience to join him on stage. A dear friend, Helena Sanchez, announced that she was going to join the group. Helena was no grandma, not at 28-ish. Helena was the life-of-the-party type, full of fun and mischief, "Of the Sanchez family of El Salvadore," she would say with a mixture of laughter-and-scream that is not duplicable. Helena was well over 300 pounds and had one of the prettiest faces on earth. Her effervescent, magnetic personality always lit up the room wherever she might be.

The grandmas formed a long line on stage. Don Ho approached each one, gave them a flower and a kiss, usually on the cheek or forehead. Some gave a kiss back.

Then came Helena. Don paused. The audience crescendoed into a roar, everyone recognizing that Helena was a ringer. She broke into her patented, irresistible ear-to-ear smile. Don Ho shot a sly smile to the audience, then gave an ear-to-ear back. The audience responded ghoulishly.

Don Ho put the stem of the flower into his teeth. Then he put one arm around Helena's shoulder and the other around her ample waist. He pirouetted and swayed her over backwards as he planted the Kiss of the Century on her.

The audience, as one, let out a roar of delight as they stood, stomped and screamed. When he put her upright, Helena had the stem of the flower in her teeth with tears of joy streaming down her beautiful, rosy cheeks. Don Ho also had tears flowing.

Looking around, everyone had wet cheeks. Hawaii is a deeply emotional and highly spiritual place with this moment the pinnacle of Love and Harmony during our trip.

When Helena returned to our table, everyone, even strangers along her path, rose to hug her, touch her, applaud her. She was the perfect princess and this was her shining moment.

Later, Helena asked me to accompany her backstage. "He invited me, but I need you to go with me, okay?"

I met him, shook hands, exchanged a few brief words. Still later, we asked Helena what happened.

"Let's put it this way. We exchanged autographs." Then she threw her head back and did her laugh-scream as only she could. Questions?

Save 'em.

I just read Don Ho's obituary. April 14, 2007. Ageless 76. Heart. That has to be a misprint. Don Ho's heart is his primary asset.

May Tiny Bubbles Effervesce Forever.

Mahala & Aloha.

Chapter 59.
The Teacher Gave Me A Golden Lemon

I Confess that I am about to expose the main BENEFIT received by my going to this particular barber school (there were several other schools, some a lot closer to home for me) for both my father and me. Ironically, the Life-Changing information was cloaked in a sarcastic, bigoted remark by the instructor named Joe. That irony isn't lost on me, either. Now, with the entire Universe listening, I again say, HEY JOE THE INSTRUCTOR; THANX A BUNCH!

Most people experience an incident in their life that originally seemed to be small and insignificant, but turned out to represent a major crossroad. In fact, many of life's major events seem to turn on what first appeared as a hardly noticed incident or minor decision.

Previously, I related how one of my instructors in barber school was making snide remarks about my "finger-cutting method." He suggested, tongue in cheek, that I go to work for Cosmo Sardo whose "hair saloon" was around the corner from Schwab's Pharmacy, the place famous as a Hollywood Hangout.

I have no idea if one of my instructors, a guy named Joe, ever knew that my dad went to work for Cosmo within a day or two after Joe's tainted remarks or that I also worked there once out of school. The job helped my dad's movie career as many producers and directors frequented Cosmo's.

Working for Cosmo was obviously a perfect start for me, too. Within my first year I was known as Hairstylist to the Stars. Heck, the benefits are almost too numerous to name. I've already related my great friendship with Sam Keston, my cockney English co-worker who taught me the Sicilian razor cut. I smile every time I think of Sam.

I've touched on my warm friendship with another co-worker, Nunzio "Johnny" Tringali, Cosmo's Sicilian-born cousin who established himself as one of Hollywood's most accomplished tonsorial artists long before my time. Among his clients were **Clark Gable, Robert Cummings, Donald O'Conner, Sandy Koufax, Cary Grant, Wayne Rogers** and quite accurately, many more stars than will be named here.

My first day on the job, Cosmo told me to watch Nunzio work without being obvious. Nunzio was a true master. He moved deliberately and seemingly without effort. He was quiet by nature, but we became friends over time.

Nunzio didn't have an ounce of brag in his being, but one day he told me about an incident, well before my time, when he owned the barber shop on the **20ᵗʰ Century Fox** lot. He was giving **Clark Gable** a haircut when "the old man" came in. Gable got up with the chair-cloth still draped on, picked up the newspaper and sat in a waiting chair. **Darryl F. Zanuck**, still chomping his ever-present huge cigar, sat in Nunzio's chair. When Nunzio finished, Zanuck, the cigar still in his mouth, got up, was dusted off by the porter and walked out the door. Gable then put down the paper and sat again in Nunzio's chair.

"During this entire episode, nobody said a word," Nunzio related to me. "No hello, no goodbye, not even a grunt!"

I laughed myself to tears. Sure I asked Nunzio some questions. None of the answers added anything to the story.

During my first year with Cosmo, there came a certain Thursday. The exact date is smudged in memory, but it was precisely 3:10 p.m. I was standing in the rear of the salon across from my chair, arms crossed and leaning against the mirrored wall facing the work booths. I was lamenting my unusual lack of clients that day while admiring all the others as they worked diligently, especially Nunzio. Even the people walking in without an appointment were requesting everyone but me.

I got to wondering how much calendar time would have to pass before I had a full clientele. Then my attention focused on Nunzio. I figured if I was going to dream....

Cosmo had told me that Nunzio was the absolute best, that nobody had ever challenged his volume of business. Thoughts developed into a committed plan. It was like someone was on my shoulder, whispering in my ear. I decided to put the plan into immediate action, starting with my next client.

I decided to treat each client as though he were my favorite, as if he were a $100 tipper. What a laugh! Nobody had ever given me a $100 tip and I'd have bet nobody ever would. (By Christmas that year, I'd have lost the bet several times over.)

I further decided to sit on my stool facing my client and discuss how I would change his haircut to better complement his features. The norm for most haircutters (me, too) was to have a brief few words with a client while draping and prepping them.

I pointed out that I would probably need two or three haircuts to get all the hair to blend into the desired look. I further decided to take an extra five or ten minutes to make "this time" a "show quality haircut." Very shortly after that, my objective became to always make "this time" the "best ever."

Six months later, I approached Cosmo on Saturday night and presented my total figure for the week. He had a wrinkled brow, so I asked him if my figure matched his.

"Yes, I have the same figure, but I still can't believe it. You surpassed Nunzio by $5 this week. While you have been close to his total recently, I didn't actually think you would do it. But tell you what, let's keep this between us. It will probably never happen again, so no sense mentioning it."

The next week Nunzio did slightly more volume than me. The following week, I again did more business, never again to be challenged. Six months after that, I doubled Nunzio's volume.

Please understand, *Nunzio was not competing with me*, but I was certainly using him as my monetary model. Also, I had to take appointments extra early and extra late while Nunzio worked at his methodical pace, quietly smiling at my efforts.

Some years after I bought out Cosmo, Nunzio told me he admired my ambition and my quality of work. It is impossible for me to receive a higher compliment.

Suppose that instructor, that guy named Joe, hadn't been smart-mouthing me that day back in barber school. Would another path have led to Cosmo's? I'd like to think so, but who's to say. Rest assured that I am extremely grateful that the small, seemingly insignificant and bigoted remark led my dad and me to wonderful careers starting at Cosmo's.

I think it's another classic case of making Lemonade out of a Lemon.

★★★

Chapter 60.
Guess Who Came To Dinner!

For most movie buffs around the world, it's great to learn for sure that a famous Hollywood nice guy is really a nice guy. I don't ever remember him playing a Heavy. Naah, wouldn't fit him at all. And with this offering, y'get more of my mom's pasta!

A happy surprise can convert an otherwise ordinary day into one that is labeled "special" from that time forward. A happy surprise day occurs when we unexpectedly meet someone new who becomes important to us, or when we buy a car when we really didn't think we would or on one of those occasions where we get dragged to a movie or stage-play that turns out to be a new favorite instead of what we thought was going to be a real bomb. Those kind of happy surprise days are the bright spots we live for, you might say. They are every bit as good, though somewhat more exciting, than when a well thought-out plan happens as designed.

Come with me on a little trip back in time, once again. My family in those days consisted of my father, Paul; mother, Pat; sister, JoAnn and me. We had been living in Mayfield Heights, Ohio – a suburb on the far east-side of Cleveland – for about six years. My dad worked as a barber and real estate salesman. He made a decent living, but if he really had his druthers, he would have been working as an actor – a movie actor. He'd get a gig as a radio actor once in a while, but not enough to quit his day job, which is not a thought I would have expressed out loud back then.

The Chagrin Valley Little Theater and the **Cleveland Playhouse** acting groups were – and still are, I'm told – two highly acclaimed theatrical groups known throughout the Midwest. **Tim Conway** had been a member of the Chagrin Falls group, as was **Milburn Stone** (Doc on *Gunsmoke*) before venturing to Hollywood. The Cleveland Playhouse can boast **Paul Newman** and producer **Ross Hunter** (*Pillow Talk*, and other **Rock Hudson** vehicles) among their distinguished alumni.

In a previous two-column set, I enjoyed telling how my dad, Paul, was a member of both theater groups. Movie actors would often join live theater groups around the country (still do) in the summertime to hone their acting skills, a practice referred to as doing Summer Stock.

At the time in focus, I was in my late teens. My mom asked me to be sure to be home for dinner one evening in particular as my dad was bringing a guest, an actor he befriended who was doing Summer Stock, visiting from Hollywood. The actor had been with the Chagrin Valley group for a week or so and had impressed my dad as a fine young person and highly talented actor.

His name was Alan, he was kind of tall (so who isn't?) and seemed to be a rather quiet, pleasant sort. He was at least part Italian and I'm sure he truly enjoyed my mother's fine Italian cooking. He even asked for seconds, my next clue. Alan seemed genuinely interested in getting to know each of us rather than talk about himself or Hollywood. There was no particular incident I recall outside of a very pleasant dinner and quiet conversation.

A few weeks later my father announced that Alan had requested a second invitation, as my parents had invited him to do. This time he was more relaxed and open, more friendly and talkative. The whole evening was very pleasant, indeed.

A year or two later we moved to Hollywood. A few years afterward, I attended my first Writers Guild Preview. The evening was an annual event, sponsored by the Guild to showcase TV shows that were scheduled to air during the upcoming season. The press was more than aptly represented, for each TV show would run about 15 minutes worth of clips from episodes past or upcoming, looking to make deals with writers, directors and producers who would be given assignments – read, contracts – to perform for a specific upcoming episode(s).

The evening was not intended for signing actors, so very few were on hand. Those who were present were helping attract attention to their series by making a brief appearance, usually pulling some kind of schtick.

The season before, *M.A.S.H.* burst upon the scene, looking every bit like a show that would run for 11 award-winning, highly entertaining years, but nobody, most notably their own publicity people, would have made such a brazen prediction.

Kojak was being ballyhooed, too, with good friend **Telly Savalas** conspicuously absent. Every so often a buzz would light up the place as word got around that Telly had just parked, but he never did show. Maybe it was the smartest tactic, who's to say.

Just as I saw Alan, the young actor from a few years before, several other people, mainly press and TV news people, formed a semi-circle with him as a local-celebrity TV newscaster was interviewing him. There was Alan, as pleasant as I recalled him being during those two evenings in my parents home, smiling and giving cordial responses as he also greeted various acquaintances who were off-camera.

Alan did a sort of double-take on me and started shuffling his feet, moving sideways as he, without contact, dragged his inquisitor, excusing himself as he passed people in the semi-circle. When he finally got to me, he put his left arm around my shoulders, concluded his sentence to the reporter and without skipping a beat he said, "I can't remember your name for the life of me, but your mother makes the greatest spaghetti sauce I've ever tasted!" He turned his full attention on me and we chatted briefly. Alan gave my dad – who just walked over to us – a big friendly hug, turned back to me and said to be sure to give his best to my mom.

Every media person in the place wanted my name and the complete skinny. The incident got mentioned as a minor item in **The Reporter** or **Daily Variety**, I forget which, primarily to play up Alan's good-guy image, but nobody offered me a contract. They didn't have to as I just got another happy surprise.

I really have not been trying to fool anyone and I'm sure I didn't. I've just been playing off the title to this column which I saw as too appropriate and fun not to use. I'm very happy to report that **Alan Alda** is every bit the nice guy and decent human being he appears to be.

Chapter 61.
Alex Stern: We Knew Y'was Here

I Confess that I really miss good ole 'Alex Stern, businessman extraordinaire, who helped create the first United States Men's Hairstyling Show and Convention and oh so much more. Alex has proven to be a Primo Character For the Ages. Where is he now when I need comic relief?

I'll always fondly remember **Alex Stern**. I met him when I first went to work for Cosmo. I always remember him as slender; in fact y'might even call him a scrawny man in his 60s with a full, thick head of disheveled white hair, a personality that some called loud and others called gregarious. He never entered a room quietly, so help me God.

He was the proprietor and star salesman of **Alex Stern Barber and Beauty Supply Company** on Melrose Avenue. Right, the same street that today is so chi-chi, a complete reversal of the lack of glitz during the early '60s.

Alex had to be at least 40 years my senior. He was always most complimentary of my work and especially, he liked the way I did my razor cut on his thick, wavy white hair.

The following conversation between us could have been called "Routine Six." Or was it number tree?

"Yer d'best in d'world, Giuseppe!"

"You say that to everyone who cuts your hair."

"Yes, but wit you I mean it."

"You add that line, too."

"Shuddup 'n gimmie d'mirror. I wanna see dis up close."

Alex was reportedly the number one distributor of **Clairol** products in the western half of the country. He always corrected the statement by saying, "The western half of the WORLD." He was one of the organizers, with Clairol, of the first Men's Hairstyling Convention in the USA that was held at the Hacienda Hotel, a major convention hotel near LAX.

The prime attraction of the convention was a hairstyling contest involving all male models, another first, with trophies and cash going to the top three contestants.

I called Alex to find out how to register as a contestant.

"Hey Little Joe, yer savin' me a dime!"

"Now what are you talking about, Alex?" With him, you never knew.

"Yer on my list t'call t'day. It's about dat big hairstyling convention comin' up. The highlight is da men's hairstylin' contest 'n we want you t'be a judge."

"Judge?" I wanted the trophy, the cash.

"Sure. I'm also gonna get Jay Sebring, your yonkle-doodle Sam Russo 'n Eddie Crispell. You four are da best in da worl'!"

Like I said, Alex was gregarious, at the very least. Also, Eddie Crispell was – is – a female; petite, blond and drop-dead gorgeous. When she entered a room, all heads snapped. She shoulda been in the movies, giving Marilyn fits. She and her husband, Nick, have remained good friends all these years.

A few years after that first show, Jay Sebring was brutally murdered. Also killed were pregnant actress Sharon Tate and Abigail Folger along with four other people. The case was sensationalized in headlines all over the world as the infamous Tate-La Bianca Murders masterminded by Charles Manson and his gang of misfits. The thought still haunts.

Sam Russo and I have been brother-close. He's Godfather to my Trina. We still get in a round of golf at **Balboa Golf Course** in the Valley at least once a year.

The turnout for that first convention was outstandingly successful, with several thousand paying their way in. Attendance and revenue exceeded the most optimistic estimates and prayers. I don't remember who won, but he's got my six foot trophy.

There were a couple of major follow-up events, also extremely successful, but cross-politics kept it from becoming an annual, stand-alone event. At one of the shindigs, The Weck Company, a manufacturer of razors and haircutting implements, had Alex present me with a 24 carat gold razor and name me the Hairstylist of the Year, a title in perpetuity.

I don't remember the last time I saw Alex Stern. I'd contact him now, except that I don't know how to reach John Edward. No, not the politician. If the right vibration should buzz my being, I'll do a sequel.

✯

Note: Not remembering when I last talked to Nick and Eddie Crispell, I called their 'old' phone number. Nick answered. To my horror, I learned that Eddie is no longer alive. Cervical cancer; a year ago. RIP, dear friend.

✯✯✯

Chapter 62.
"I'll Straighten That Hair Even If I Gotta…"

I Confess that I followed my Grampa Dominic's ears-n-mouth advice pretty good as I made sure I learned from that master processing stylist when he consented to teach me his most profound technical secrets. Hey, the guy made hundreds of people look great, including celebrities like **Sugar Ray Robinson, Sammy Davis, Jr.** *and* **Johnny Mathis**. *How's that for Star clients?*

L earning something new can be fun and exciting. Or it can be a royal pain in the neck. A new function or task can encompass the positives along with the negatives, but whether to pursue further depends to a great degree on a person's overall objective or personal philosophy.

I was given accordion lessons as a kid. I came to the conclusion that playing that instrument is not one of my talents. A year or so later, I was given trumpet lessons. I came away convinced that playing music – any way y'cut it - is not one of my talents.

Knowing when to push an objective or when to stop is finally a very personal decision. Remind me to tell the *Twinkle, Twinkle, Little Star* story sometime, but not when my lips are chapped.

Among my earliest clients at Cosmo's was a guy about my age named Alan. He had course, kinky-curly hair that could not be tamed, could not be blown into anything but a mess. He asked about hair straightening, but I didn't know the first thing about the process.

I found out about a black barber, Charles, whose clients included **Sugar Ray Robinson, Sammy Davis, Jr.** and **Johnny Mathis**. I called and asked Charles where I might learn the procedure. I was surprised when he offered to teach me. He said I would have to spend a day with him and the price was a week's pay. I readily agreed as Charles was the absolute best by reputation.

(My maternal grandfather, Dominic, was bonkers about "…Be Number One!" He also mentioned, many times, that learning something new from someone who was a Number One was worth a "…king's ransom…" so a week's pay seemed reasonable.)

I watched Number One Charles work on three different men. Two were getting a "re-do;" one was getting a "virgin." All three came out looking great! I remember thinking that the result was akin to magic. Charles sold me a jar of his straightening crème for today's equivalent of $100.

Next day Alan came in. I don't know who was more excited. Alan's hair didn't come out looking as good as Charles' clients, but for the first time his hair could be combed and be somewhat controlled.

The following day at about noon, Alan came by wearing a hat.

Uh–oh, I thought.

Uh–oh it was.

Half of Alan's hair was singed off and he had oozing sores on his scalp.

I don't know who was more upset.

Alan was a true friend. He was very considerate with his comments. Sam Keston, my English mentor and dear friend, was angry and suggested that I was not properly taught, as all I did was observe the procedure, not participate.

I called Charles and politely described my results. He suggested another "class." Same price. I agreed. Sam had a kitten.

This time Charles explained in greater detail. I bought another jar for another $100.

I offered a second good client the same deal as Alan: no pay, no guarantee. Like Alan's original results, his hair came out good. Sam watched me closer and said this time should be okay, though he had no experience with the process.

Another bedazzling failure! I had to cut this client's hair very short, but at least there were no oozing sores.

Charles listened intently. He asked me to come back one more time. "And leave your money at home."

Did Charles explain more clearly or did I understand better? He gave me another jar. No charge.

The third client's hair came out better, a lot better, than the first two. The next day he brought in his brother for a straightening. His brother was my first paying client for hair-straightening.

A few years later when I had left Cosmo and joined Sam Russo, **Casey Kasem** came in for a first visit. His course, curly hair was resistant to a smooth, undulating style. Sam asked me to use my magic crème on Casey. His hair finished in a style that was smooth and natural, a look that fit his desire. Casey and I have been good friends ever since.

Nobody can learn to play the accordion or trumpet in a day regardless of their desire level. A person doesn't need to be of any certain age to know when to push or back off. Desire to do well seems to be the most important criteria.

Since I don't know Charles' whereabouts, this is my Open Letter of Thanx!

Chapter 63.
"Ladies 'n Gentlemen, It's 'The Louis Lomax Show!' "

I Confess! It's time for another story on my pop. I'd tell you that it's one of my favorites, but honestly, they all are, even those not concerning dad.

Between 1964 and 1968, black author and journalist **Louis Lomax** *hosted a popular and controversial twice-weekly TV program on Los Angeles' station KTTV. My father went on the show, as himself, to profess a position foreign to him. I'm thrilled to report that through the magic of my memory, I'm going to transport you back through Time so you can see the show from the backstage perspective of the seat next to me.*

There must be a tape of this show someplace, but where? Lemmie know.

Okay, everyone who remembers *The Louis Lomax Show* on TV stand up and shout. I didn't hear anything. (Tap – tap – tap) Maybe it was a local show, in Los Angeles, circa 1968. Oh well.

Louis Lomax was a favored personality, a TV commentator and a writer. He broke ground as there were not very many black celebrities who had their own TV show in the 1960s. He had an interesting talk show, not quite up to **Johnnie Carson** (but what was, or is?) and certainly more entertaining than **Conan O'Brien**. Lomax loved guests who were controversial. He also loved t'make 'em squirm.

A podium was set up in the audience so people could address the guest and they did, often confrontationally. Actually, audience participants were pre-selected and rehearsed, a fact unknown to the home TV viewers and discovered by the live audience.

One show's topic hit a vital chord, challenging a long-standing custom. In American society at the time, barber shops were for men's hair cuts and beauty salons were for ladies. In Hollywood, someone had the audacity to open a men's hairstyling salon featuring all women "hair designers" and even a female boot-black! **The L.A. Times** covered the salon's opening with a huge spread.

Lomax had two of the lady haircutters as his guests. Make that two very pretty ladies. The audience was gruff, vocal and rather provoked, according to their collective reaction, but they also demonstrated interest in what the ladies had to say. Someone shouted that he suspected hanky-panky was an extra service. The ladies were mortified and responded accordingly.

My father and I were seated in the last row of the audience. My father, actor **Paul Micale**, was a barber by trade. He was hired by Lomax to challenge the two pretty ladies, dad's mission unknown to everyone including the ladies. Lomax had directed my dad to "give it to 'em good; make them sweat."

Dad was nervous. "I'm an actor. I'm used to playing a role, portraying someone else. Lomax wants me to go up there as myself, as a barber. But I don't object to them cutting men's hair. I'm sorry I said yes to this gig."

"So go up in character" I suggested.

Dad sat up straight, turned and looked me dead in the eye.

"Pretend you came to America on the boat 20 years ago. Use an accent. Now you're PAULO Micale, from the hills of Sicily. HE objects."

"Oh my God," Dad said, his smile expanding in two seconds flat.

"Oh, we have someone at the podium" Lomax said, interrupting the ladies who were defending their dignity.

"Tell the audience your name, please."

"I am-a Paulo Micale, Meester Lomax, and I am-a pleas-ed to meet you. Ah salute!"

The audience reacted instantly and shouted enthusiastically, wondering what was coming next. I was thrilled! Dad came up with a great opening.

"And what kind of work do you do, Paulo?"

The audience held its breath.

"I am a men-sa hair stylist-ta" Dad said with a flair, throwing a twisting hand in the air on "stylist-ta."

The audience went NUTZ! Then they "shushed" each other, not wanting to miss a word from "Paulo."

"I take it you object to these ladies cutting men's hair."

"Oba-jeca-ta!" I'm-a so mad-da. Why they no go work-a the beauty shop-pa down-a the street?" (heavy laughter-applause) "Or... or maybe, why they no go back-a to the kit, eh, kit, *cucina!*"

The joint fell out. Some man ran up and hugged my dad, shook hands with him, all on camera (and not planned) as security ushered him away from the podium. People were out of their seats; everyone had a comment, some pro and mostly con. And Wow, the noise! What the heck was keeping the roof on?

The audience was out of hand and seemingly heading for a riot, so Louis Lomax put up both hands. "Before this gets out of hand...." The audience slowly calmed down to a dull roar.

"Ladies and gentlemen, my dear guests," he shouted over the diminishing roar. "Say hello (his arm extended to the podium) to my dear friend, ACTOR... Paul Micale!"

The audience gave "Paulo" a raucous, standing ovation that reverberated endlessly. (Make that a minute, but oh brother!)

"Paul really was a barber, and as you just saw, he is a very fine actor, (major applause) and I know he bears no ill feelings toward these lovely ladies."

It was all so crazy wonderful. Everyone should be in an audience like that sometime. I was laughing with two gallons of joy-filled tears cascading all over my face.

Dad went up on stage and gave each lady a warm hug. On his way back to where I was standing on my seat, everyone gave Dad a hand-shake or a pat on the back. Attaboys flowed. Everyone wanted his autograph.

So just remember, whenever you see a star dancing in the night sky, if it isn't a UFO, it's probably just my Dad dancing the *tarantella* and reliving another memory from that glittering, shimmering place in the universe called Hollywood.

✭✭✭

*Did I ever mention that I write all my material longhand? I always have, even my scripts, then comes typing, usually by someone else whenever I could arrange it. Since the early '80s and upon the suggestion of my dear friend, **Gertie Horek**, I have written in spiral notebooks with blue covers. I have a large stack of filled notebooks and a larger supply of new, ready-to-go Bluebooks, I call 'em.*

*In '89-'90 I took the hypnotherapy course with the **Hypnosis Motivational Institute** in Reseda, California, founded by my late dear friend, **Dr. John Kappas**. I was the only person in a class of approximately 110 who was NOT studying to be a therapist; I just wanted to make sure* *that any fictional characters I created had logical psychological profiles. I got a lot more than I bargained for, (thanks again, HMI!) as part of the course focused on graphology, the study of handwriting. Cutting to the quick, writing longhand employs greater use of the creative half of the brain. (I know, a worthy subject for exploration, but gotta move on.)*

For several years in the early to mid '90s, I used a secretarial service in Santa Monica to transcribe my writing onto computer disks. Ginny became my transcriber when she came into my life in March of '95. Ginny, who can bang 140 wpm on the keyboard, also has natural Spell-check; I can't spell worth @#$%$#. In many ways, working with Ginny is a wonderful arrangement.

Chapter 64.
Johnny and the Kids

Oh boy, here we go. Let me just say that they laughed, applauded 'n stomped their feet at what they saw. As we observed them, we cried 'n laughed 'n applauded at what we saw. Huh? It'll all make sense, promise. Warning: One Kleenex will undoubtedly be insufficient.

One of my dearest friends EVER was **John Marc Gentri**. You just read the biggest, most profound understatement of my life. Though we had different parents, Johnny was my brother. Make that twin brother. I know, I'm repeating myself, but in this case it's worth it.

Johnny made his name in Hollywood as a producer, director, actor, stand-up comic, entertainer – and certainly not least – a writer.

"Never pumped gas," he was fond of saying.

Johnny won an Emmy for a TV documentary on heart attacks. Many other shows he produced won various awards for excellence. Ironically, a heart attack took him when all seven of his kids were still minors.

As noted in an earlier column, Johnny helped me get started as a professional writer. Our first collaborated work was for writing two assignments of Questions and Answers for the hit TV show, *Hollywood Squares*.

Those two projects showed us conclusively that we were a natural writing team. I never before or since found such a compatible writing partner. And optimist that I am… Please forgive me if I don't complete that thought. Gotta have Hope.

A Hollywood Pontiac dealer hired us to write a series of radio and TV commercials and newspaper ads. We thought we would be running an on-going campaign where we would write new copy periodically. We thought of the project as a great showcase for our creative abilities as well as a source of personal revenue that could be part of our financial base for years to come.

What was it that someone once said about the best laid plans of mice 'n men?

Well, plans, schplans!

The dealer said he wanted to "run with these for a while." Two years later he was still using our copy and layout without more than the original paycheck coming our way. On the one hand we were proud that our work was so productive and durable for our client....

Johnny and I had the privilege of writing and producing a documentary for **The Foundation for the Junior Blind**. We worked diligently to bring that project to life, but my most profound memory focuses on the kids' reaction when we held a private preview for them before the show was aired on TV.

Everyone gathered in The Foundation's auditorium. Our audience consisted of the blind kids - all were featured on the screen - their teachers, many of their parents and friends and a raft of network and production people. Huge crowd.

As we rolled the film, the teachers surprised me by adding narration, telling the kids seated immediately around them what and who was on the screen. One early example hit me a ton as a teacher enthusiastically exclaimed:

"And look! It's Charlie! Hey Charlie, look at you! And you're wearing your favorite red shirt!"

The kids cracked up with laughter and applause, pointed at the screen and Charlie and shouted comments directly at Charlie, who was both smiling on the screen and smiling even bigger in the audience. All the kids were showing tremendous joy and merriment.

That moment in time forever caused me to realize the absolute preciousness of the gift of sight.

Everyone can understand how to explain a puppy to a blind child who has never had sight. Explaining the concept of a house would be more challenging. But how in the world does one explain RED? Or BLUE? Or describe something on a MOVIE SCREEN?!?

Watching those kids that night as they so thoroughly enjoyed "seeing" that film and expressing ecstatic remarks when images of themselves and their schoolmates appeared was a personal pleasure and shock that is frustratingly difficult to accurately express here. I vividly remember their extremely positive reaction impacting my being.

I burst out a laugh, I thought, only to be shocked that I cried! I bawled so hard I almost fell on the floor. There was nowhere to hide as I was in plain view – of the teachers, parents and studio types– I abruptly realized.

I took a step to get out of the room. Johnny reached out, put his shaking arm around my shoulders and said, "This is beautiful. Look at them loving it!" Johnny was bawling like a baby, too. Then I realized, so were most of the sighted people present.

Except the teachers. They were enthusiastically narrating, teaching, enjoying with the kids. The kids were laughing with delight and often expressed shyness or pride as their teachers announced who was "in the center of the screen right now."

When I sat down to write this column, I intended to tell how Johnny and I conceived and wrote the pilot and several episodes of a TV show called *Boutique*. Obviously, we will table that idea for another day.

Sometimes, thank goodness, my pen takes off across the paper and goes seemingly on its own and tells something completely different than I had outlined. On these occasions, I become more a member of the audience than the writer. I always get a kick out of these excursions to a place that only exists in the Hollywood of my memory.

Chapter 65.
The Old Lady

Once when I was 14, maybe 15, I told my mom about a memory that had recently come to mind. I described a home, my home I sensed, and two little girls at play. I was able to describe details of the house and yard. I also had the distinct impression that the two little girls lived there, but I only have one sister and she is not one of the girls in this memory.

My memory was too fragmented to make much sense to me. I further described a scene in which I was being carried up some wooden steps inside the house by my father.

"Oh my God!" my mother exclaimed. "You're describing the house where you were born, but Joey, we moved before you were a year old. You can't possibly remember that far back!"

Later, talking with my father, we determined that I was indeed remembering something that happened prior to being one year old. The two girls were members of the Agresta family, one of whom was Louise, a schoolmate at Mayfield High! (No, Louise did not realize that we lived in the same house as children. She was likewise amazed when her mom confirmed the information.)

I also distinctly remember a picnic that occurred three days after my second birthday that we celebrated with extended family on the 4th of July.

Why do some people have memory that goes back to infancy while for others, memory excludes most childhood events? Gotta ask a shrink, cuz I ain't got a clue.

Following is the result of another memory from long ago.

My baby sister was really, really sick. My mom could hardly stop crying and my dad was also very upset. I could see both were really worried. Christmas was only three weeks away, but that didn't matter anymore. Baby JoAnn was born September 12th, so she was still really tiny. Doctor Fanelli came to our house yesterday morning and there we were, last night, just leaving his house, and it was later than when I usually had to go to bed. My memory goes way back.

Dr. Fanelli told my parents to give Baby Sis some of his special new medicine every four hours. He said he'd stop by our house the following morning. He sure is a grouch. He has a thick accent, just like my grampa, so he musta come from the Old Country, too. Maybe he'll learn to like it here in the young country. My grampa loves America, he always tells me.

As my dad started the car, I was sure glad this car had a heater that worked. Just about then, my mom started crying louder.

"Where are we going?" she asked my dad.

"Home. Put the kids to bed," he answered. He said it while softly crying. That scared me even more.

"What about the Old Lady?" my mom asked. I didn't know who the "Old Lady" was, but my mom had mentioned her earlier in the day.

"Maybe we should try the doctor's new medicine…"

Now my mother was crying even louder and Baby Sis was crying harder, too.

"If we don't go see the Old Lady," my mom sobbed, "and this baby dies tonight… I will never forgive you!"

Now everybody was crying. I was as scared as I was when the war started last year and I saw all the grownups cry, only this time I didn't look to the sky. The Japs never came over and neither did the Germans, at least not yet, but honestly, this was more scary. Until this moment I did not know that Baby Sis might die!

My parents said more words to each other as dad started to drive along the snow-covered streets. My mom calmed down a bit after my dad said we would go to see the Old Lady.

We got out of the car and knocked on her door. Even bundled up, it was really cold. A light came on inside. Then the porch light. She beckoned us inside without even knowing who we were or what we wanted.

I was wrong. She asked why we hadn't come earlier. Also, I do know her! She always comes to the Paisan picnics.

My dad said something but the Old Lady didn't seem to listen, she just reached for Baby Sis, gave my mom a kiss on the forehead and headed for the kitchen with us following. The Old Lady spoke with a thick accent but somehow, she is easier to understand. How come all the old people have accents? Will I have an accent someday, too?

She had my mom spread a blanket on the kitchen table and told mom to take off Baby Sis's clothes except for her diaper. Baby Sis was still crying hard. The Old Lady went to the sink and came back with a soup dish filled with water. She lit a candle, placed it on the table and shut the kitchen light.

My dad told me to go sit in the living room but the Old Lady said no, to let me stay, that I should watch.

"The boy represents God's Angels," she said.

Wow! No kidding? Even at my young age, I'm smart enough to know that all we really needed was one Angel and everything would be okay. I was told to remain silent, no matter what.

I know the Old Lady was praying, but I wasn't sure if she was speaking Sicilian, Italian or some other language. It certainly wasn't English. As she prayed over the soup dish, the water sort of quivered. I wonder what made that happen, so I backed off the table even though I was certain I had not caused the movement.

The Old Lady picked up the small bottle of olive oil that was placed next to the salt 'n pepper shakers and bowl of sugar. She put two drops of oil into the water. I let out a "Wow!" when the oil formed what looked like two eyes, each with a circle within a circle. Yeah, I got shushed.

As the Old Lady continued praying, the "eyes" got bigger and suddenly became so big they disappeared! Hey, this lady was good. I figured I'd try the same thing first chance I got.

The Old Lady got fresh water. She told me I was being a good boy. Good, I thought. Maybe that would make the Angel come sooner.

The Old Lady was praying over the water again. She had some white string and a pair of scissors but I didn't see where they came from. She snipped the string into three pieces and dropped the string into the water.

After more prayers, the string started to swim. Y'think that's something, the string had a front and a back. No, I didn't see a head, but each string had direction and swam just like a snake.

The Old Lady prayed louder and the string swam faster, splashing water out of the dish. Baby sis was screaming now!

The Old Lady Clapped! her hands and the string became string again, stopping dead.

"Quick," the Old Lady said to my mother. "Change the baby's diaper!"

My mom opened the safety pins on Baby Sis's diaper. Baby Sis had pooped muddy, lumpy poop that was loaded with maggots and worms! I'm not sure but I think I let out a yell.

"Clean the baby good," the Old Lady said. As she looked me straight in the eye, she smiled and said, "Your baby sister is fine now."

That made me so happy I gave her a big hug around her neck. She hugged me and lifted me right off my chair as she laughed and kissed me on both cheeks.

Mom and dad gave her and each other hugs and kisses, too. That's when I noticed that Baby Sis was fast asleep.

In the car, mom reached over and gave dad another big hug and kiss. That's when I realized that I never saw the Angel, but one musta been there. Boy, was I disappointed. But hey, Baby Sis was fixed.

The next morning, Dr. Fanelli was knocking at our door. Mom and dad both told me to say nothing of the Old Lady. I protested, told them that maybe Dr. Fanelli had other sick babies that the Old Lady could help, but mom said, "Not a word!" When she said it with that look, well....

When Dr. Fanelli saw a smiling, happy Baby Sis, he took off his glasses and turned and looked mom and dad in the eye. He was stern.

"What did you do to this baby?"

"We gave her your medicine like you said," my dad answered.

"Impossible, my medicine couldn't... "

"We prayed a lot," my mom said.

Dr. Fanelli was angry, but he didn't say much more.

After the doctor left, I asked my mom why I couldn't tell him about that wonderful Old Lady.

"I'll tell you when you grow up. You couldn't possibly understand at four and a half."

Chapter 66.
Benny 'n Moe

*I Confess! I don't know about you, but I love **The Tree Stooges**. (No, that's not a misprint, I simply said it in part-Italian. See, there is no 'th' sound in the Italian language, so 'th' comes out like the 'tr,' like in the English word, tree.)*

*Anyhow, back on point, lovable big **Benny Garcia** owned his hairstyling salon... Aw shucks, I almost gave it away.*

Watch yer nose.

I know the year was 1968. The month escapes me. **Benny Garcia** owned the **El Dorado Hairstyling Salon** on Vine Street, just a bit south of Sunset Boulevard in the heart of Hollywood. Benny worked in a private room just off the reception area. The balance of the salon consisted of four partitioned, semi-private self-contained haircutting spaces.

In the rear of the salon was another private room, the place I called home for about a year before I became the managing partner of the **Image Hair Salon** at the relatively new **Century Plaza Hotel** in Century City.

Benny was a gentle man whose manner of speaking was measured, quiet and rather deliberate. I was told that Benny grew up on the streets as a tough kid, a fast-fisted light-heavyweight who could and should have been the World Champ.

"Benny is the most gentle, most honest person I ever knew," according to my good friend, co-worker at **Russo's** and Benny's life-long amigo, **Ralph Trejo**. "He refused to take a dive for the Mexican Mafia, so he quit. And they let him! He's an old man now, but don't let it fool you, Benny can still kick the #&%@ outta any three people you can name."

My first Friday at the El Dorado, I walked out of my room after giving a haircut to good buddy (now the Brazilian music icon), **Sergio Mendez**. We were just saying goodbye to each other when the front door opened.

"Hello, boys. How y'doin?"

It was **Moe Howard**. He was a lot older looking than in **The Three Stooges** movies. He had Coke-bottle thick glasses and was wearing a hat that looked too small. He also had a whole lotta short-shuffle in his gait.

Sergio and I greeted Moe with our awe showing. I remember Sergio telling Moe that he and his kids loved the Stooges movies and watched them on TV "all the time." It was a truly moving, heart-thumping experience for both of us.

Later that afternoon, Benny and I were ready to call it a day. I asked how long he knew Moe. I was shocked when Benny answered that he and Moe were friends around 40 years.

"You're a young guy, probably been in this business, what, four or five years? Heck, Moe and I go back a long ways. We always joke about which one of us is gonna croak first. Moe says (Benny started to laugh) he won't croak until I pay him off."

Benny went on to tell me that a few years before, he was working for some guy. (Name? Maybe I never knew.) Benny said the guy was okay, but his personality was a little rough. One day Moe got mad at the guy and asked Benny why he never owned his own place.

"I told Moe the truth, that I never had enough money t'open a place of my own, but if I ever did, it would have to be a class operation." Benny smiled as he gave his place the once-over.

Moe asked Benny if $30,000 would be enough. Benny investigated and later told Moe that the salon could be done for "$26 to $27,000."

"I'll make you a deal," Moe told Benny. "I'll give you the $30,000, cash, but I want it back, $100 cash, every Friday afternoon. Can you do that?"

What interest rate, Benny wanted to know.

"Interest!?! Don't worry about no interest. Just gimmie $100 cash, every Friday, 'cept if you're in the hospital."

"But Moe, you'll lose interest that way," Benny protested.

"No I won't. Damn banks crashed in '29. I don't use banks, so I won't lose nuttin. Every Friday. Deal?"

"Deal," Benny said. "But I feel like I'm cheating you."

"Okay, okay. So gimmie free haircuts, but just 'til you pay me off. There's yer interest."

And that, as they say, was that.

Some weeks after I met him, Moe shuffled in the front door with a friend in tow.

"Hey, Little Joe. Say hello to my friend, Hymie," Moe said, squinting at me through those thick glasses. As I was saying hello to Hymie, Moe said to his friend, "This kid's the best hairstylist in the world. Benny says so."

I've had compliments from people I respect over the years, but never one bigger.

Oh yes, Sergio. I'll tell you about our many years together another time.

I think of my time with Benny Garcia often, but I had to work up the nerve to tell it publicly. The deciding factor is that I want people to meet the real Benny Garcia and his benefactor, Moe Howard, two of the best friends I've ever had.

Yes, the stars, the Big Stars, really shine in Hollywood.

One time my wife and I were having dinner at a rather posh Mexican restaurant, no longer in business, on Santa Monica Boulevard in West LA. It had to be sometime in the '70s, but beyond that, I haven't a clue.

After we were seated in the upstairs dinning room, we noticed that **Johnny Carson** *and his wife had a table about 15 feet away. I told the waiter that the Carson Show had been sending me celebrities for years to get haircuts, color, custom hairpieces, whatever. Giving the waiter my card to present to Johnny, I said I wanted to buy them a drink. The waiter got all flustered, saying he was ordered not to approach Carson with such requests, so I asked to speak to the maitre d'.*

The man came over, listened politely, looked at my card again and said he would try. He went to the Carson table and talked to them with his back to us. They each peered around him, one on each side, Johnny waving ever so slightly.

The maitre d' returned with a broad smile, saying that Johnny accepted, a first! He added that they already had their pre-dinner drink and requested an after dinner drink. Of course we were delighted.

Later, as we were informed that their drinks were served, they lifted their glasses to us and we reciprocated. No, we didn't approach them. The Hollywood Courtesy Rules taught to me years before by Cosmo Sardo have held me in good stead all these years. "When in Rome, do as…" And when in Hollywood; well, we have our etiquette, too.

✫✫✫

Chapter 67.
"Don't Mess With Them Cherry Trees"

(Part 1 of 3)

*Okay, coming up is a tree parter. (Get it? Relax, I'll quit.) Life truly is a Bowl of Cherries as the phone provides the initial contact with **Freddie de Cordova** and The Johnny Carson Show. Wait 'til you see the first person they sent in for a haircut!*

Like the man said, life is just a bowl of cherries. Proof is all around. Maybe those with veiled vision will need to blink three times – if only to clear things enough to allow an honest assessment. But for most of us, who can say what a new day will bring? Every day the possibilities are endless. Every day. Cherries galore.

There was this one day in particular, long ago. The memory recently came up in conversation, causing this whole chain of incidents to reappear. Only this time, it presented itself in fog-draped memory, offering another helping of contemplation. Popped me right in the proverbial noggin, it did.

As with a bevy of other days, I was tending to biz at my hair salon in the **Century Plaza Hotel**. I know, not much has been said about owning that place but really, only the surface has been scratched regarding my love affair with Hollywood, so please, stay with me. The curves are rarely sharp.

Anyhow, I was giving **Earl Nightingale** a haircut. I had just asked him to slouch again so I could reach the top of his head, some 6'4" or 6'6" from the ground and definitely way up there to me.

Most people remember Earl as the great motivational speaker who addressed and excited presidents and royalty worldwide. I remember him as a great guy with a formal if somewhat stiff, but decidedly dignified manner who exhibited a rather dry, though affable, sense of humor.

I had fun making him laugh, especially when pointing out the many practical differences between a guy his size and one who is at least a foot shorter.

"I wouldn't know what t'do with another foot, anyhow," I once told him. "I trip over these two as it is."

Are you laughing? He almost barfed with laughter, but maybe you hadda be there.

The phone rang. **Janet Thomson**, my receptionist/manicurist and adult-life-long-dear friend, put the call on hold and turned to me, bug-eyed.

"**Freddie de Cordova** is on the phone!" she said achieving an instant state of hyperventilation. "I didn't know you (pant-pant) knew him."

As of that moment, she was absolutely right. See? Big cherry. And I foresaw nothing beyond another business phone call.

Everybody within a thousand miles of Hollywood knew who Freddie was, still do, but for our not-so-familiar-with-the-Hollywood-crowd friends, I will expound. Freddie de Cordova cut his baby teeth as the motion picture and TV producer and/or director for the likes of – are you sitting down? – **Burns and Allen, Jack Benny**, now-100-years young **Bob Hope**, and – aw shucks – there's too much. You could look it up. Try the DGA.

At the moment in focus, if we may return, Freddie's operating title was – Ahem –

Executive Producer, NBC Productions: *The Tonight Show* Starring **Johnny Carson. Zeus** had to look up and squint out the glare just to cast eyes upon Freddie.

"He musta dialed wrong," was my initial thought as I picked up the phone.

"Hey, Little Joe, 'bout time we meet," he said with his smile glowing right through the phone. "You cut the hair of many of my and Johnny's good friends."

"Freddie," I interrupted. "My last name is Micale, M-I-C-A-L-E. There's another Little Joe whose last name is **Torrenueva**, good buddy of mine, but I can't spell it. He's up on Sunset Boulevard. We're much alike, except he's Filipino-American and I'm Sicilian-American. And we both work on a lot of your and Johnny's good friends."

"No. I got the right guy. You started with Cosmo, right? You cut **Casey Kasem**, **Vic Morrow**, gave **Rip Torn** his first Hollywood hairstyle. I heard all about your Convertible Cut."

Okay. So I'm not so tough to convince. I'll add that to my resume... and cover the Convertible Cut in another column.

Freddie was calling because he needed a favor. Now, you have to understand something. Some places are built on sand, like Florida. Some are built on granite, like various areas up north and out west. Hollywood is built on Favors. You can buy your way only so far with cash in La-La Land.

A Favor, a.k.a. Juice, is what gets a person from Merry-Go-Round to Gold Ring, only slowly for the novice. And here was the Ultra Powerful Freddie de wanting to make a Monster Deposit into my Favor Account! I could've given birth to a brick!

What time do I take my last appointment, Freddie wanted to know. Told 5:30 p.m., he asked for an appointment at 6:30 p.m. for "a very dear friend and politically powerful person," adding that his friend didn't want to run into any of the many senators who frequented my place.

"Senators?" I said. "Freddie, **Roone Arledge** and **Chet Forte** come by, but they cover all the teams, not just Washington."

After a hearty laugh, he shot back, "And what about **Senator Tunny**?" Here we were, shooting stuff back 'n forth like we knew each other for a hundred years. "I heard about him trying to take you up to the 7ᵗʰ floor."

Again, for those who don't know, the 7ᵗʰ floor belonged to the U.S. government. They even had a presidential command post up there with a wired-in Button, or so the story was told and believed.

"Freddie, you sending me The Boss?!?"

"Well no, but he's just a heartbeat away."

"Oh m'gosh, you want me to cut Agnew at 6:30 tomorrow?" Just what I needed, another tall one.

"No-no, not him, my guy's much more important. If you need a name, use Bill or whatever, and that's 6:30 *tonight*, not tomorrow," he said as calmly as if he were asking for a pizza, and hold the anchovies, please.

I had something really important to do that evening, but darned if I can tell you what it was at this late date. "Something big's popping for t'night, but I'll sweep it under the rug. Tell Bill to call me from the lobby, then I'll unlock for him."

At 6:25 p.m. sharp I let Bill in and Janet out. He was also kind of tall, but for me, who isn't? He was neatly dressed in a suit and tie, everyday garb for the time and was pleasant indeed.

At first we talked about his hair and how I could improve on the way he was wearing it. The balance of the time he wanted my personal impression of how the government was doing things, then he asked my observation of what clients of the salon seemed to say the most about the government's performance. Most specifics are foggy, but my habit is to answer frankly, as I'm sure I did. Numbers are gone, but I most assuredly recall that he was generous, very considerate of my staying late for him.

A spatter of time passed. A few days; a week, there-abouts. As I entered the salon that morning, Janet greeted me. Cherries were everywhere, but I didn't see even one.

"Hey Joey, your client's on the front page of the **LA Times** this morning. Did y'see it?"

No, I didn't, so I asked her which client, as it could have been any one of many.

Y'know, that 'Bill' guy you did late the other night," she said and, with considerably more impishness, she did a neat parry and thrust, finishing with a twist. "Hope you didn't take a check. He's no more named Bill than he's my grandmother."

I remember the headline was big. Maybe three inches tall. Bold.

"John Dean Blows The Whistle" or something close to that, as I endeavor to recall. Cherry juice all over the place, that's for sure.

John Dean. The night before, Washington, D.C., knew his name. This morning, the whole world knew. There was a large picture of him. Nice haircut, I thought.

Y'know, this is getting to be a revoltin' development if ever there was one. Outta space again. And I still have some cherries left. Same routine, next week.

Chapter 68.
Yesterday, It Was Always Now

(Part 2 of 3)

This time Freddie wants to send two famous red-heads so the Carson Show can go on as scheduled. Letting you in on the whole schmere requires a terd part, so hang in there. (You didn't really expect me to let up, didjya?)

When last we were together, we were munching on Life's cherries. Moving from one section of this vast country to another can play a large part in causing the psyche to use wide eyes on various aspects of life. That move from Cleveland to Hollywood helped me to consciously acknowledge the fact that, in my long-standing and kooky methodology of renaming otherwise everyday events, Life provides a daily dose of cherries, or situations that foster immediate and/or long-term benefits. Part of the lesson here is the understanding that the cherries usually do not fall into one's lap on their own; they need to be picked, much like the physical fruit called cherries.

It's kind of like snow, if you ever lived among the white stuff. Snowballs are not natural, but snow is. When there is sufficient snow, it's no big deal to make a snowball; provided, of course, that there is a conscious desire for snowballs.

During my teenage years, I started a life-altering relationship with a priest named Father Michael. (He was the Good, Old-Fashioned kind, not one of "those." I wrote a book about our time together called *Someday*, the same book previously mentioned that is in pre-publication.) The point here is that the Good Father and I had a particular conversation early on wherein he alerted me to the fact that "profound opportunities are available to each of us on a daily basis, if only we will attune ourselves properly." That conversation, I came to realize, was the seed of a greater awareness to come.

I acknowledge that my comprehension of the principal might not have been the same, or occur at precisely the same, 'early' time, if the cross-country move had occurred without the aforementioned conversation. Now that I have a seasoned perspective and a proper forum, I joyously present this before-now private experience to those who will use it for personal gain.

All that said, there is more to tell about the principal subject of this tree-parter, my late good friend who came into my life via the cherry route, **Freddie de Cordova.**

There was one day in particular, sometime in the '70's, after I had taken over Cosmo's and renamed it Little Joe's. The phone rang and Guess Who was on the line. Yep, Freddie and no, I am not blasé; the point is that I have lived in Cherry Heaven because I have been more aware, as I hope you will be from now on. And what d'ya mean, 'which year'? Why, somebody keeping score? Anyhow, Freddie asked me if I did color. Yes, and just like that, too: "Joey, you do color?"

I had to laugh. He always had that way of his to start a conversation; y'know, go right to the point, no frivolity, just wham! Pleasantly, though.

"Sure Freddie, you need a little color?" I was pulling his chain as I figured he was calling for someone else.

"No-no, not me," he responded through his laughter. "I got this couple, our guest stars for tonight, said they didn't have a chance to go to their hairstylist in New York before coming out, and they won't go on unless they can get their hair done. They're both red-heads, but not out of the same bottle, they tell me. You do red, don't you?"

I don't think I was on the floor laughing then, but I've had to dab my eyes more than once now while putting this incident on paper. With all that Freddie had said, I got a delayed realization of the word "tonight" in his comments.

"Hey Freddie, please don't tell me you have two people who want cut 'n color TODAY. It's eleven a-m and I'm booked solid ALL DAY."

"Joey, y'gotta help me on this one. They're serious about not going on unless they can both get color and a trim. You're the only one I can trust! I got the limo standing by. They can be there in 30 minutes."

"You say 'couple;' you mean a man and woman? They got names?" I asked, looking to get a line on the required time-frame to clear.

"Y'ever hear of **Stiller and Meara**?"

Now he was pulling my chain.

"Come on, Freddie; everyone's heard of Stiller and Meara. They're going to be with Johnny tonight? Wow, that'll be a great show!"

"Sure it will," he said. "If YOU come through. Otherwise I'm dead meat."

I told him to "stand by," that I needed to make some calls to clear up some time. What a dilemma! And that was the other quirk in Freddie's many requests over the years. The nature of his needs might vary, but the time frame was always "Now!" Think he'd call about tomorrow, or next week? Never happened!

I have few but very strong operating policies, my Cardinal Rules, that I follow rigidly. When up against a situation like the one being related here, I simply tell it straight and rely on the goodness of those with whom I deal regularly. The policy works so well I'm hard pressed to recall an exception.

The first person I called to ask to move over was my one o'clock client, an honest-to-goodness rocket scientist named **Bob Goldstein**.

"Any chance you can move over to one p-m tomorrow? I've gotta find room to do tonight's stars for the Carson show," I pleaded.

"Interesting," I remember Bob saying. "Who are they?"

"Jerry Stiller and Anne Meara. Ever catch their act?"

Bob asked if I was nuts, that probably everyone had caught their act at some time or another. Most importantly, Bob said he'd gladly move over on one condition. There was some pant-pant on my part, but needlessly. All he wanted was an autographed picture of them, addressed to him personally.

"Done, and Thanks! I'll have it for you tomorrow," I told him.

When I called the next clients in chronological-time order, I started by saying something like "How would you like to have a photo of Stiller and Meara, personally autographed to you?" Made me a big hero as all cooperated enthusiastically. Freddie was thrilled, too.

But you know what really ticks me off? I'm outta space. Again! How do I so often end up against this wall? Per usual, best part comes next week, promise. My first tree-parter.

✭✭✭

Chapter 69.
Freddie's Unforgettable Cherry-Tops
(Part 3 of 3)

So how do you say 'finale' in other words? Simple. Get Jerry Stiller and Anne Meara to mix it up with **Comic Chuck McCann, Nick "Coach" Colasanto, Ed "Officer Kirk" Peck** *and a bevy of Hollywood's Finest – oh, don't forget* **Jack Albertson** *– the motley crew that was hanging out at Schwab's that afternoon, just waiting for something to happen. And for good measure, chrow in a wise-acre New York Hairdresser. Mix. There, that should do it.*

N ot counting tangents that swing left and right, like cherries and snowballs, or the fact that **Father Michael** finally nudged his way into the column, I've been relating that the late, inimitable and very highly regarded **Freddie de Cordova** and I had wonderful, long-term association. Long term, indeed. I'd say the last 22 years of *The Johnny Carson Show's* run qualifies, eh?

The news of Freddie's passing on September 15th, 2001, put me in a deep funk, as if I - and so many of you - needed to be sent deeper. Funny how tears can coexist with smiles on those poignant occasions. I'm so proud to say that I had the trust of one of Hollywood's major contributors to several decades of tasteful laughter for this world.

When **Jerry Stiller** and **Anne Meara** disembarked - y'hadda *see* it - from **Johnny Carson's** big black stretch limo that bright 'n sunny day, they lit up the joint, a compliment they would certainly appreciate.

In my mind Jerry is currently the comedic backbone, character name **Arthur Spooner**, of the TV sitcom, *King of Queens*. Anne, remember, was one of the Stars of *Archie Bunker's Place*, headlining with good friend and former client, **Carroll O'Connor**.

Anne still takes on roles that appeal to her, especially something casting her alongside Jerry. In her own right, she has become an award-winning writer. (CBS's *The Other Woman;* and *After-Play*, written for the stage. For more, hit the Web.)

Three by-the-ways: Stiller and Meara, in their heyday as a comedy team during the '60's and '70's, appeared thirty six (36) times on *The Ed Sullivan Show!* A record? Dunno. Number two: Yes, **Ben Stiller** is their son. And Three: This year they celebrate 50 (FIFTY!) years of marriage! Mazeltov and 'ere's mud in yer eye!!!

Digressing a moment, an exercise I thoroughly enjoy as I'm sure you know by now, this is a perfect time to state that the brightest Stars of Hollywood, especially those who enjoy long careers, are almost always among the nicest people on earth. This statement is a fine example of how the word "nice" depicts its highest complimentary definition.

In the midst of my saying hello to them that day, Jerry looked me dead in the eye and said, "Hey kid, y'sure you know what you're doing? Y'mess this up, Anne'll kick me into next week." His expression was flat. Serious. Everybody laughed. No, it's not exactly a direct quote.

"Don't pay attention to him, Little Joe," Anne said with a smile. Flipping to a questioning expression, she asked if people addressed me as Little Joe, or what.

Jerry answered for me.

"They call him Joe, but his best friends call him Joey. Hey kid, lemmie see yer license."

Now I was laughing, too, with all the others and marveling at the accuracy of his dead-pan comedic savvy, if not my totally accurate quote.

"All right, enough already," Anne said. They were gratefully aware that I had created time for them, but now it was wise to get on with the business at hand.

"Do you have your formulas?" I wanted to know. They looked at each other.

"You need formulas," Jerry said without a question in his voice.

I told them not really, but I'd gladly call their stylist in New York if it would make them more comfortable.

The New York receptionist put their stylist on the phone so I could explain the situation to her personally.

"I don't give out my formulas, not unless someone wants to pay me $250," I heard her say.

"Hold on," I said into the phone. "Here Anne, you talk to her. Maybe she thinks this is a riff. She's asking for 250 bucks, but when she hears you, maybe she'll cooperate. In any event, don't agree to pay. I don't need the formulas."

"What!?!" Anne said a bit loudly into the phone after she snatched it from my hand. Anne was immediately serious; focused.

Ever hear two New York girls have a conversation where they disagree about the subject? Some of my staff, and some clients, scattered.

Others seemed to think it was great entertainment. I reiterated to Anne that I did not need the formulas just as she barked out an expletive and slammed my phone into its cradle. She then exclaimed "Oh nuts," or something like that.

At that precise moment, as if on cue from on high, Hollywood funnyman **Chuck McCann** appeared with a shout: "I don't BELIEVE this!" Anne, Jerry and Chuck practically leaped into a buddy-hug, all three talking at once, laughing with tears in their eyes as the three of them, as one, hopped up and down and slowly rotated in a tight circle.

Chuck McCann is a BIG guy, grew up in New York where he made his mark with a very successful kiddies TV show. Played a clown, I believe, though I never saw the show.

You've seen Chuck portray **Oliver Hardy** on stage, TV and the Silver Screen. At first glance, you'd think it was Ollie, himself. Chuck also portrayed a deaf-mute who was mentally challenged in a movie titled *The Heart is a Lonely Hunter*, co-starring **Alan Arkin**. I thought Chuck received an Academy Award nomination for that role, even wrote such, then looked it up and remembered that most of Hollywood seemed to be as shocked as I that he was passed over. No knock on the actual nominees, but he shoulda been added. Chuck was, for maybe 20 years or more, a favorite client, and obviously (news to me at the moment in the story) very dear friends with Jerry and Anne.

The pertinent facts of the day were related to Chuck in the proverbial New-York-minute.

"Joey's gonna do your hair? Shucks, you're in no trouble. Heck, he does **Shirley MacLaine's** hair, **Debbie Reynolds**, even mine!" Chuck said.

He lied about Shirley and Debbie, but yah-yah, ya-yah-yah, I didn't quote him exactly, either, so there! No Red Pencil's gonna get me, 'least not today, in spite of all these red cherries.

With pandemonium in full bloom, **Nick Colasanto** ('Coach,' the bartender on *Cheers*; before **Woody Harrelson**) walked in and the noise level shot up so high, this time I feared that my front plate-glass windows would burst.

Not even a crack. Whew!

We finally got on with doing some hair. Chuck went the 40 paces to Schwab's and brought back a whole hoard of Hollywood's Finest, predominantly former New Yorkers, to say hello to Jerry and Anne. Talk about noise level, but that's how it is sometimes when friends meet after a long interval, eh?

Bringing up the rear and waddling through my front door, his fog-horn voice blaring out a sound that would drown out the BURRRP! of a New Jersey tugboat was **Ed Peck**. Sure you know Ed. Think *Happy Days*. 'Member **The Fonz**? Who gave Fonzie all that grief? Ed Peck! Okay, you knew him as **Officer Kirk**.

Amazingly, everything turned out great, and yes, I worked out of different bottles. The two redheads looked stunning, they agreed, as they strutted over to Schwab's for a few command-performance bows before hitting their "Black Chariot," as someone dubbed it.

The Johnny Carson Show was an extra-special blast that evening, as I'm sure some people remember. Next day Anne called from Freddie's office with another bouquet of compliments.

She and Jerry are way up there in my memory. Oh, they did bring the personally addressed photos for Bob and the others they displaced. Please, someone, anyone, tell me why I didn't ask for a photo for ME! Missed that cherry, doggone it.

Oops, hold it a minute, Ginny says there's one last cherry t'nibble. I never did get to give Freddie a haircut, or Johnny either, for that matter.

"The makeup guy takes good care of us," Freddie told me. "You keep taking good care of our friends. It's a wonderful arrangement."

And you know what? It really was.

Say g'night, Ginny.

Chapter 70.
So, Y'wanna Make a Movie? Ask Forrest Gump

*I Confess, Hollywood makes a TON of movies year in, year out. I'll bet there are at least a hundred in pre and post production right now, and that only covers **Universal**.*

The following run-down will present some behind-the-scenes goings-on that will amount to just a glimpse of the intricacies involved in putting it all together using one of Hollywood's all-time favorite offerings as a model. Remember, this is just a for-instance; no two pictures ever come together exactly alike.

When I purchased my airline tickets for my September 2, 2007 flight to LAX, my primary purpose was to attend a Leadership Conference for a nutritional company. Five days before the flight, I received a phone call from the CEO and Executive Producer of a company called **REEL Productions**. They had been reading and evaluating my script that I titled *Someday*. They decided to produce my movie and wanted to talk turkey. We were both pleased with the fact that I would be in Hollywood five days hence.

Our afternoon production meeting extended into dinner and beyond. It was all very positive, very exciting. They want me to stay with the project through completion, which doesn't always happen for the writer.

I've shared the news with a few close friends, some of them jumping out of their skin with excitement and asking me how I, a normally high-emotional type, can be so calm. The answer is simply that I know the intricacies of taking a script all the way to and through production and then on to release and distribution. **Jimmy Durante** called this situation "da Pits!" too. Or did he mean two?

Remember the movie *Forrest Gump*? Great movie, millions agree. And **Tom Hanks**, in case you don't remember, won the Best Actor Oscar – for the second consecutive year – along with the Golden Globe, plus – PLUS, can you imagine - more than $70,000,000. (Yes, that's Millions)!

But wait a minute. Do you know that Tom Hanks was the EIGHTH Star contractually signed and paid money to portray Forrest Gump? From a reliable source whose name wouldn't mean jack-diddley to people outside Hollywood, I bring you the inside scoop.

When a production company wants a certain Star to read a script, they can go to extreme lengths. They might designate a certain person, maybe even hire someone outside the company with a special "in" to that star, to get, say Hanks, to agree to portray that role. The process goes something like the following.

Star: "For $20 million and 2 ½ percent of the gross, I can be available for this project between Monday, March 9th and Friday, July 13th in the year 2012." 2010? Maybe. Y'got more money?

If the production company agrees, they could say YES with a non-refundable payment of $3 million. The partial payment would buy an option on Hank's specified time in 2012, option time starting now and running through December 31st this year. The $3 million would be a portion of the contracted $20 million. On January 1, 2008, another $3 million could be due Hanks to buy another option for the originally specified time in 2012 leaving a balance of $14 million due to Hanks on or before the beginning/ ending date of May 9, 2012 or July 13, 2012. Percentage comes after release. Clear as mud? Don't feel bad, I didn't learn this concept overnight, either.

Now, let's say you have a signed deal with the Star and have publicly announced the deal. Good! Now the fun begins. Is the director of choice available for the same time frame in 2012? What about Cinematographer? Don't forget the pre-production facilities. How about the Studio (**Universal? MGM? Fox?**) sound stage time? Then there are Locations and Permits, right? Ho-hum, y'got Post-production facilities, yes? Other actors are not in Vegas playing, y'know. Is there a call for key props, like vintage cars? Everybody needs Wardrobe, especially period costumes and/or suits of armor. Got your Release Dates set? Distribution confirmation?

How's that for scratching the surface? Each of the key components can demand some form of pre-payment schedule, much like the Hanks example. From other circumstances, the same process might start with the Director, the point being, everything has to come together harmoniously. All must mesh perfectly.

So you wanna be a producer? Check for bats in belfry. Need fumigation? Personally, I'd rather write. And sure, the price of my script has been agreed upon while the legal jargon – and option payment - has yet to see daylight.

My Hollywood source, who is also a good buddy, went on to relate that Tom Hanks was definitely not the EIGHTH CHOICE to play Gump and that rumors insist that Hanks might have held down an earlier position to play Gump. But all the component parts couldn't be properly synchronized in the previous seven situations.

A production company can (and often does) spend millions of dollars without ever shooting a foot of film. In the early go, most professionals do not invest too much emotion along the slippery slope to making even a great movie like *Forrest Gump*.

Understand something. True professionals give a project their all whenever it is their time to perform. Because movies (TV shows, too) have a short and highly-defined life, professionals do their utmost on their current project with one intent being the use of this project to secure the next one. Producers check with producers, directors with directors, anybody can check with anybody, so nobody wants to make negative waves that would probably cut them out of a future project(s).

For your information, **Marilyn Monroe**, unique commodity that she was, lost several projects during her career. I know, that statement is contrary to public knowledge and in spite of denials issued by the publicity giants who knew the truth. Hollywood gossip, no matter how many supermarket rags print it, even with pictures, should not be confused with Truth.

So, am I excited about *Someday* being made into a movie? Of course. I'll just wait a little while before adding an exclamation point to my answer.

I just got a phone call. I'm flying to Hollywood next week. One objective is to cover the **Hollywood Celebrities and Collectors Convention**. I have an opportunity to set up interviews with some old friends. **Tony Curtis** and **Debbie Reynolds** will be among the gliterary. Will they or others consent to an interview? I'll keep you posted.

★★★

Chapter 71.
Authors Meet at 40,000 Feet

I Confess that the following is another of the unpublished columns that was in the wings when my newspaper gig came to a halt, so you get to see it first! When Columbus (nee Colombo) set sail in 1492, America was his Serendipity. Here's one of mine.

A few weeks ago, I flew from Ft. Myers to LAX thru Dallas so I could cover the **Hollywood Celebrities and Collectors Convention** in Hollywood. My main purpose was to talk directly to **Tony Curtis, Debbie Reynolds** and **Angie Dickinson**, among others, to arrange interviews so I could bring fresh, personal information to readers of my column. I remember wondering what other person(s) I might encounter for an interesting column.

After I buckled up, a couple became my seat partners. We exchanged a friendly hello and prepared for takeoff. I like to read during a flight, so I stuck my nose into a book. As the plane started its approach into Dallas, a conversation developed with the lady sitting next to me.

Linda Shelman is an attractive blond lady who is a Realtor. Husband **Eric**, also her partner as a Realtor, is the author of the book, *Out of Darkness, the Story of Mary Ellen Wilson,* published in '99. The Shelmans were on their way to a speaking engagement in Omaha arranged for Eric so he could discuss his book and child abuse with members of **The National Fellowship of Child Care Executives.**

As we deplaned, we exchanged business cards and agreed to get together soon. I saw the Shelmans head for their next gate as I turned and started to search for the terminal leading to my gate.

About 20 minutes later I thought I was seeing double or experiencing a form of deja vu. Linda Shelman, followed by Eric, was waving to me as I was about to enter an airport restaurant across from my gate.

"Our plane is delayed," Eric explained as we greeted each other for the second time in just a few hours. We ordered lunch as I heard more of Eric's fascinating story.

Eric admires the writing of **Dean Koontz** and **Stephen King**. In the early '90s and while writing a series of short stories, Eric was in the midst of seeking a storyline that he could develop into a supernatural thriller. He was searching for a true story that he could expand upon and weave into the horror fiction genre. That's how he came upon the Mary Ellen Wilson story.

"The story of Mary Ellen is so utterly fantastic," Eric told me. "The more I learned, the more I wanted to properly present the true story of her plight, her life. There was no need to make up anything, for all the fascinating elements are there; it actually happened, with documentation, but I had to discover it, put together little bits and pieces as I went along. Especially with the second book that came out in 2005, the story is all there. It is so spellbinding that I have been asked to speak to groups ever since. Several times, like recently, groups keep me for a lengthy Q and A session after a two hour presentation."

Eric's second book was given its title by the publisher: *The Mary Ellen Wilson Child Abuse Case and the Beginning of Children's Rights in 19th Century America.* Whew!

Mary Ellen was an abused child living in a foster home – circa 1870 – and was legally declared an animal so she could be rescued by the SPCA – yes, the **Society for the Prevention of Cruelty to Animals** - as there was no agency that could legally rescue children. That fact blew me away. I asked plenty of questions, probably the same that are going through your mind right now. But wait, there's more.

Eric had a co-author, **Dr. Stephen Lazoritz,** for the first book. Guess how many words Dr. Lazoritz wrote for that book. Zero! Then why….

"Dr. Stephen Lazoritz was passionate about the case, and the book couldn't have been written without his research" Eric emphasized as he related the history of the writing of the book.

"Dr. Stephen had done a wide-spread 10 year research of Mary Ellen's life before he and I met on the telephone. Interestingly, Dr. Stephen lived in the Hell's Kitchen section of New York, the same area where Mary Ellen lived, the area where all the negative action took place. Mary Ellen's mom worked at the **St. Nicholas Hotel,** very near the scene of the crimes. With all the information Dr. Stephen supplied, I was happy to give him co-author recognition. You might also find it interesting to know that Dr. Stephen and I did not meet face to face until a year and a half after *Darkness…* was on the streets."

Want more? The books are available on amazon.com. Or give the economy a pop; buy a home in Cape Coral, Florida. Call **Select Realty Associates** on Cape Coral Parkway, (239) 810-0203. Ask for Eric or Linda.

★★★

Chapter 72.
The Untouchable Paul Picerni

*I Confess, cuz I really would be a schnook to try to deny that my next title is not really clever, but I like it anyhow. Paul is a warm 'n wonderful person (don't you DARE tell him I said so!) and an extremely fine actor. Same can be said of his brother and my decades-long good friend, **Charlie Picerni**. Good! Now I made them both blush. Go meet 'em.*

Hollywood's many versions of the Cops 'n Robbers genre have always been a hot ticket. The Roaring Twenties era, the time of illegal booze, Dames 'n Diamonds and Cigar Chompin', Fedora wearin' Mobsters has caught the attention of a huge portion of the American public from the silents through the earliest talkies to last night.

In the spring of 1959 *The Untouchables*, a special, made-for-TV two-part program, splashed on the tube via the ABC Network. The **Walter Winchell**-narrated drama led to the TV series of the same name and ran from 1959 to 1963. In all, there were 118 episodes, each consisting of 50 minutes duration.

During the show's life-span, the most famous recurring stars were **Robert Stack** portraying Eliot Ness, **Abel Fernandez** was Agent William Longfellow, **Nick Georgiade** was Agent Enrico Rossi and **Paul Picerni**, who portrayed Elliott Nesses' side-kick, Agent Lee Hobson. The role brought Paul international fame as *The Untouchables* was one of the highest rated programs of all time.

Paul Picerni today is "85 years young and still a working actor. There's a lot more time between parts now, but I'm not complaining," Paul told me recently.

Paul's list of credits shows that he has been one of the busiest talents ever to hit that fabled place called Hollywood. To date, Paul has had roles in 63 movies and has been the spokesperson for **G.E., Rexall Drugs** and **The Webber Company**.

Not too shabby, you say? Paul has also guest starred in 455 TV shows, rounding out a formidable resume, indeed, "…and still counting."

Paul was attacked by the Acting Bug in the seventh grade. "I recited the poem, *Gunga Din,* while standing in front of my classmates. They gave me a Standing O. I was shocked at the great feeling that overcame me. That did it. I decided to be an actor."

Slightly more than a few years later, Paul was one of the many who volunteered to join WWII. He served in the Army Air Corp, earning a promotion to Second Lieutenant and Bombardier. Starting from Victorville Air Force Base in California, Paul flew 25 combat missions in a B-24 in the China-Burma-India Theater and was awarded several decorations, including the Distinguished Flying Cross. He wasn't a bit player there, either.

After the war Paul attended **Loyola University** in Playa del Ray, California, where he starred in many plays before graduating in 1949. About that time the **L.A. Rams NFL Football Team** hired Paul as their half-time Master of Ceremonies, a job he held for 30 years until the Rams moved to Anaheim.

Shortly after his Loyola days, Paul landed an important role in a war movie called *Breakthrough*, starring **David Brian, John Agar** and **Frank Lovejoy**. Paul's performance led to a seven-year contract with **Warner Brothers Studios**.

Once under contract, Paul had major roles in *Mara Maru* (**Errol Flynn**), *Desert Song* (**Kathryn Grayson**) and *Operation Pacific* (**Gary Cooper, John Wayne, Frank Sinatra** and **Lucille Ball**) to name a few. A Short time later, Paul landed the romantic lead in the greatest 3-D movie ever; *The House of Wax*, also starring **Vincent Price**.

I met Paul when he was one of the four lead stars on *The Untouchables* in the early '60s. Paul encouraged his brother, **Charlie Picerni**, to move from New York to Hollywood to be Paul's stand-in and stunt double.

(Charlie Picerni found his way to me at **Cosmo's Hairstyling Salon** while I was still new on the staff. Charlie and I have been dear friends, actually more like cousins, ever since. Charlie has won acclaim by climbing another Hollywood ladder, first as a stuntman, then moving up to stunt coordinator and then the rarified air as an accomplished director.)

Throughout Hollywood, Paul is referred to as the Buffet King, as hardly any time goes by that he doesn't get a request to M.C. some function. His answer is almost always yes.

While it is difficult to pick favorite TV shows from the vast quantity, Paul has been known to especially enjoy being associated with *Kojak, The Lucy Show, Playhouse 90* and *Alice*. Paul's favoring Kojak is to be expected as all Hollywood seems to know that Paul and **Telly Savalas** were best friends. In fact, Paul is working on a project that will chronicle Telly's life. That certainly has my interest as Telly was like family to my parents, my paternal grandmother and me.

In 1947, Paul was in a variety show named *At Ease* that was produced in one of Hollywood's theaters. Paul was attracted to a beautiful dancer named **Marie**.

"I'm still smitten by her, more now than ever," Paul said of wife Marie with a big smile. Together they raised four boys and four girls who in turn have created ten grandchildren and one (so far) great granddaughter. Hey, this is 60 years later. Who said Hollywood marriages don't last?

Speaking of family in the biz, get a load of this. Paul and Charlie have a sister named **Paula Picerni**, a precision stunt driver. **Paul Picerni Jr.** found his nitch as a property manager. Grandson **Rick Picerni** is an actor who appeared on *J.A.G.* Granddaughter **Katie Moran** is an up-and-coming actress. Another of Paul's sisters is **Eleanor Tamburro**, whose two sons, **Chuck and John Tamburro**, are well known helicopter pilots in the motion picture industry. Charlie also has two sons who are noted stuntmen.

More to come? "I would expect so," says proud papa Paul.

Paul wrote a book about his career titled *Steps to Stardom*. The book is available directly from Paul by writing to him at PO Box 88, Llano, CA 93544. To view Paul's official website, go to Google and type in "Paul Picerni."

Chapter 73.
Thanx a Million, Charlie!

I Confess! The following column is another making its premier appearance in print. I'm not sure where "Charlie" is today, but if he ever gets to see this, I trust he will be pleased to know of the huge positive affect he has had on my life. Every day I thank him with prayers of gratitude.

Okay, enough is enough. This story is too important to keep under wraps any longer.

There are certain positive incidences in life that happen in a moment but have a profound, life-long impact. The incident most often comes without warning, but the residue continues to grow and become more clearly defined with time. The life lesson, acted upon, helps to steer the course of a life-path to more positive events. The result of the original incident creates a cornerstone of a person's philosophy. For far too many people, there exists an unfamiliar axiom of life that states, "An individual's life path is determined by his philosophies." Of course, there is a negative application to this process, too, but we'll save that for another time.

Let me take you to the summer before my ninth grade year. I was hanging out with a group of guys who were two grades ahead of me. We formed a club, naming ourselves the **Paisans**. July 4th was the start of getting ready for football season, with daily but informal practices. On August 20th all high schools in our conference were allowed to begin formal practice with coaches, equipment and a schedule of practices and scrimmages.

"Charlie" was one of our coaches; a volunteer, but not a teacher nor part of the official high school staff. Charlie had been captain of Mayfield's football team during his senior year a decade or so earlier. Ever since graduating, he had worked in a machine shop and volunteered as an unofficial and unpaid football coach.

Charlie was knowledgeable and respected. He had specific duties when we practiced. During games, both home and away, only official coaches were allowed on the field in the team area, so Charlie was part of the three-person ten-yard chain-gang. Rain, sleet or snow, Charlie was happy and proud to be Mayfield's man for that all important game-time function.

Charlie was always pleased with his role on the team during all four years of my high school football experience. He was considered to be third in line of command though we had five people officially on the coaching staff.

My senior year was one of the most exciting of my entire life. In football, we were undefeated going into the second-last game of the year. Ditto our opponent. We were unexpectedly undefeated, I should mention, while our opponent was the pre-season pick to be county champions. The day of the game, the **Cleveland Plain Dealer** reported that we were two-touchdown underdogs.

The game was a gang war in cleats 'n pads, an understatement. I don't recall the name of the guy who played nose-to-nose with me on both offense and defense, but he went on to a major college and then to the NFL. He was at a disadvantage as I was much shorter than him, but that's another story for another time.

In the second half with us holding a definitely narrow and precarious lead, the battle became even tougher, more brutal. There were a few roughing penalties. Our opponent had the momentum and was driving. If anyone was cocky confident, he wasn't wearing Mayfield's green and white.

I was in on the sidelines from the action and kneeling next to our head coach, waiting for him to send me back with the next play. I was down on one knee, helmet on, ready to carry coach's message to our huddle.

Suddenly, THUD! Someone whacked me on my head. I was double shocked to see it was Charlie. For the only time ever, Charlie had abandoned the chain-gang to "fire up the bench." Only after the hit to my head did I realize that Charlie was going up and down the bench, admonishing each teammate to "Do your best ever! This is for the champeen-ship! When y'get in there, give it all y'got!"

As he whacked me, he said, "N'that goes fer you too, Little Joe. Put out a hun-nerd percent. No loafin'!"

Now if I say so myself, I didn't need anyone, not even Charlie, to egg me on. But as I at first tried to see who had whacked me, Charlie was backlit by the high bright lights that illuminated the Friday night field. I clearly saw that his eyes were bugged and there was spittle spraying and running down his chin. He was definitely out of his tree. The whole scene is forever burned into the screen of my mind.

In that moment I realized that Charlie was with us, at least in part, trying to reach back into his life to recapture a great (maybe the best?) part of his life. Without football, by his own admission, life had become rather mundane. At that early age I was thrust into understanding that a person's life pattern could be such that highlights could come early and the balance could be rather Ho-Hum.

Charlie moved on among my teammates, whacking other players and screaming like the madman he had become. I squinted into the darkest part of the sky perusing for a star. Ah, found one! Using the star as my not so long-distance focal-point, I addressed The Boss.

"Dear God in heaven," I started. "Thank you for where I am and all the great things going on in my life. I am really so very grateful, but please, Please, PLEASE, don't make this the highlight of my life."

At that precise moment, Coach Schmidt grabbed me by the shoulders, gave me the play and shouted, "Go get 'em!" as I raced back onto the field.

In the huddle, Joe Germano, our quarterback and still one of my best friends, asked for the message I brought from the sideline.

"Yeah," I said. "Charlie said we gotta kick the #@#$% out of these #^&O()'s."

Final score: Mayfield – 26; Visitor - 7. I know for sure; I looked it up.

Ever since, whenever a gain is acknowledged, I repeat the most important utterance of the entire incident: "Dear God... Thanx...and please, Please, PLEASE, don't make this the highlight of my life."

I'm convinced that's an important part of why life-altering highlights keep coming my way.

✯✯✯

Chapter 74.
Boutique! The First TV Magazine of the Air

*I Confess that we were the Zing and the Zang, the Yin and the Yang and oh what a ride it was! People ask if I have a favorite column. I don't, cuz I poured my heart and soul into alla them. But any time I'm writing – or thinking – of **Johnny Gentri**, my spiritual smile is ear to ear even if my physical face is only kinda bright. The memories of working with Johnny umpteen hours a day and too many days a week while writing this show years ago (seems like moments) is pleasure beyond description, unless you count that right now I'm also dancing 'n singing as Ginny bangs away at the keyboard. In any event, enjoy **Dick Clark** too, another Hollywood Mench.*

One day I met m'bro, **Johnny Gentri**, for lunch. The wrinkle on his brow had me somewhat concerned.

"I need to ask you something," he started as I was putting ketchup on my fries. "But I hope you will tell me 'no.' I'm going to write and produce the new TV show we co-wrote the pilot for, and as I promised, I'm offering you the job of co-writer, but before you answer…"

"Johnny, that's great! When do we start?!?" I said, almost spitting my Pink's Hotdog all over the place. (For non-Angelinos, Pink's has been recognized as the most audacious hotdog stand in the world. Still is.)

"Dammit, lemmie finish. There's a catch to it, a big one."

Johnny went on to tell me that the budget was tight and didn't allow for a second writer. The pay would be terrible. Make that miniscule. Also, the job would carry a production title instead of a writing credit.

Lousy money and no writer's credit. Bummer! Worse yet, the money was less than half my earnings as a hairstylist.

"I'll take it," I heard myself say.

Hey, it was a start. Many of Hollywood's biggest producers and directors started as "production assistants," a title meaning "gofer," with the pay just a buck-tree-eighty above bubkus. But like said, it's a start.

The first day on the set, by the compliments everybody paid me, Johnny did a great job of selling me.

As our first function, some 18-20 people sat around a long conference table. The executive producer - read The Big Cheeze - set the posture of the show. The name: *Boutique*. We would be a "magazine of the air," and a fashion magazine at that; a unique concept, Cheeze said.

We would be sponsored by **The May Company**, their first TV venture. We would be in the Los Angeles and Dallas markets. May Company would supply all wardrobe. If ratings were high enough, we'd go national on the **CBS Network**. **Pat Harrington** would be our MC with an unknown, **Susan Brown**, as co-host.

Again, the show would be all about fashion, not Hollywood, per se. So no actors, Big Cheeze said emphatically, unless they also had a "legitimate career in fashion."

We had three guest spots per show. The hosts had scripts to follow while the non-pro guests would be heavily coached to give a proper, off-script response.

Johnny and I worked on the first few scripts and presented our ideas to the "brain trust." Two made comments. Most just smiled and nodded. Just to let you in on the inner sanctum, we gave the main conceptual ideas to Cheeze before the meeting. He presented same as his brainfartz. That became the pattern, which I later found was the way it worked industry-wide.

A week before our first taping, **Pat Harrington** opted out. Everybody panicked. Almost.

"Hey John," I said in front of everyone. "Why don't you be the host?"

Big Cheeze gasped. So did everybody else. Almost.

"We wrote the stuff. John has the ability, God knows. Besides, at this late date, anybody got a better idea?"

Score one for the ratz.

I shoulda run it by Cheeze beforehand, but I was afraid that he would nix the idea, then I would not be able to openly defy him without cutting my own throat. On the other hand, there are reasons I have sometimes been called a Rebel. Y'just seen oneofem.

With John's many obligations as producer and host, I became the primary writer. Not by title or pay, just actually. Johnny often apologized for not being able to pitch in as I was no virtuoso on the typewriter, but then, a typewriter doesn't write. And I was THRILLED with the arrangement.

I wanted – and kept suggesting - **Dick Clark** as a guest to talk about the change in teens' tastes in music and clothes since his first TV show years before, but Big Cheeze kept nixing the idea. "It'll never fly," he kept saying.

We had a chance to feature a luxury yacht and a speed boat, so that entire show would be devoted solely to **Mike Reagan**, a boat designer and racer. He was also the son of the Governor of California. Right, **Governor Ronald Reagan**.

At the last minute, three goons – eh, executives – from CBS stormed onto the set. Reagan was out. The goons were afraid that all gubernatorial candidates would demand equal time. Talk about panic, the production clock was ticking at a rate of $1,000 per minute, with taping scheduled to begin in less than an hour. Nobody had a plausible idea.

"Well," I finally broke my self-imposed silence, "I could call Dick Clark, but I read he was in New York. I don't even know if he's back in town." Total BS.

Dead Silence.

Big Cheeze gnashed his teeth. "Call him."

Thirty seconds later I was talking to the voice that all America knew so well.

"You want me to grab some pictures off my wall and come over WHEN?!?"

In our makeup room, Johnny, Susan and I briefed Dick Clark on the flow of conversation. We were going without a script.

Yep, smooth as glass.

Of the 58 *Boutique* shows I wrote, the Dick Clark episode was BY FAR the highest rated. D'switchboard wuzza Christmas Tree. (The episode featuring **Ruta Lee** was another big draw. Cheeze didn't want her, either. How'd he ever get to be da Cheeze, anyhow?)

By the way; our production offices were on La Brea Avenue near Melrose, right next door to Pink's Hotdogs. So, whatta y'makea that?

And you know what? You ain't heard nothin' yet.

★★★

Chapter 75.
"And now, Ladies and Gentlemen, The Jackson Five!"

Now here's a HUGE STORY of a major Crossroad in my life. Looking back from today's perspective, I made a great choice. It is the subsequent choices I would alter, given a Magic Wand or Aladdin's Lamp. Got one? Send it by.

As I was enjoying my coffee and reading that the Dodgers, with **Joe Torre** and **Manny Ramirez**, were about to take on the Phillies for the league championship, Ginny read aloud from her section of the morning paper.

"Dateline: Hollywood, October 9, 2008. **Lloyd Thaxton**," she started, getting my immediate attention, "...an Emmy Award-winning producer and host of a popular Los Angeles TV dance show that went national in the 1960s, has died. He was 81."

My heart sank. I tried to swallow the lump. I know, for most people around the country it was probably, "Lloyd who?" Here's more from his obituary:

"Lloyd Thaxton was known for his comic lip-synching to rock 'n' roll songs on **KCOP's** *Lloyd Thaxton's Record Shop,* which launched in 1959 and became a hit despite its limited budget and cardboard set. He used puppets, costumes, mime and "finger people" he drew on his thumb.

"Three years later his show was revamped and renamed *Thaxton's Hop*, before going national in 1964. The show was eventually renamed *The Lloyd Thaxton Show* and featured teenagers dancing to records and guest appearances by top recording artists such as **Sonny and Cher** and the **Righteous Brothers**.

"He always signed off his shows by saying, "My name is Lloyd Thaxton," to which the teenage dancers would yell, "So what?"

"He also worked as an Emmy Award-winning producer with the consumer advocacy program *Fight Back! With David Horowitz* and **NBC's** *The Today Show.*"

In early 1968 I was writing a TV show for CBS called *Boutique*. The half-hour, five-days-a-week show starred my partner and Best-Bud, **John Marc Gentri,** as the Host. An attractive lady named **Susan Brown** was Co-Host.

Johnnie and I had co-written the pilot and, long story very short; he was also the co-executive producer, though not with me, with someone who had ties with **The May Company** and the **CBS Network**. The show gave me a production title instead of writer credit as they (the other exec) didn't want to pay me writer's scale, but it was a great entrée into TV writing, I thought at the time. Such shenanigans were common practice back then.

I was putting in five full days writing and shooting the show while maintaining my hair business on the run, taking clients before and after going to the office and on weekends. It was all so exciting that I never had a chance to get tired even though I often worked 20 hours a day and most weeks, all seven days.

Along about show #58, that other exec producer – read, the money guy – decided to bring in a new line producer to settle an argument with Johnny about who owned the show. The new guy brought in his own director, set designer and others, including his own writer. The whole schmear was very disappointing, to understate the fact.

The new producer called me in. He told me how much he admired my work and that he would prefer to keep me on, but there was not enough money, even if there was no ownership beef. He certainly didn't need to do so, but he leveled with me, saying that he and the new writer were unofficial partners. Sometimes the writer got the gig and would drag the producer in; sometimes it was the other way around.

"We're kinda like you and Johnnie; a team. But Joe, don't feel bad. You're a very good writer and for this kind of interview show in particular, I think you've got a better handle on it than my partner, but my hands are tied. I recommended you for another show, a new TV show, but that has to be kept quiet for now. I already told Johnnie, so let's keep it between the three of us. Capish?"

That part of the story has been a secret until now, God knows why. Anyhow, my agent was not much older than me and a protégée to Mel Bloom. He came to me like it was his idea and told me he had arranged an interview for me as the writer for a new TV show.

The name of the new show? *The Lloyd Thaxton Show*.

I met Thaxton's producer that very same evening around 6:30 p.m. at his home somewhere in the Hollywood Hills. It was a posh, ultra-expensive home that had a bird's eye view of the hills in and around Laurel Canyon. I brought along several of my *Boutique* scripts.

He took 15 or 20 minutes to read portions of several scripts, mumbling and smiling as he went.

"Yes, yes, you'll do fine. You're a perfect fit," he said as he again shook my hand.

"Here's the rundown," he started. He was pleasant and bottom-line business. My impression was that we could get along great.

"We're taking the show on the road to 27 cities in a nine-week production run. That will create our 27 week season. We'll travel with five acts, changing acts throughout as commitments dictate. When we get to a city, like Detroit for example, they will already have had a battle-of-the-bands contest, and their winner will be our sixth act. We begin our trip in five days. As agreed with your agent, we'll pay you $11,000 for the nine week run plus all expenses. Any questions?"

I was overwhelmed with thoughts and emotions. Looking back, I can imagine my eyes tumbling like images in a slot machine with whistles tooting and bells going ring-a-ding-ding. So much for literary license. I think I might have stammered a bit, too.

"Something wrong? I'll make it $15,000."

"Em…" Hey! I didn't want to use the word 'no.' "Let me tell you something, please. I have two kids with a third on the way. I was not able to be in the delivery room for the first two, but the doctor got permission for me to be there for the third. My wife is scheduled to deliver right in the middle of the nine-week run. Since this is our third, delivery is expected to be predictable. What're th'chances I could fly home for a day or two?"

"We're going to be a group of around 150 people. Only two are not replaceable. One is Lloyd and the other is you."

"Me?!?"

"Yes, you. Lloyd is a great host. In many ways he's extremely creative; some ways, well, left on his own, he'd do something like this; '*And now Ladies and Gentlemen, **The Jackson Five**!*' or '*And now Ladies and Gentlemen, **Nancy Wilson**,*' or '*And now, Ladies and Gentlemen…*' Got it? But as your scripts prove, you come up with unique and clever ways of introducing people. I didn't see any two intros alike in your scripts. So you pretty well better figure that you will miss the birth. $17,000 is the best I can do."

"I understand," I said. And I did. "Can I let you know first thing in the morning, say 9 a.m.?

"Yes. As a father, I understand, too. Whatever you decide, I support you one hundred percent."

Kimberley Ann was born in West Park Community Hospital in Canoga Park in the northwest section of the San Fernando Valley on September 9th at 11:50 pm. She weighed 6 pounds, 8 oz. I'm so glad I was there!

As life would have it, I never even met Lloyd Thaxton, may he rest in peace.

A wise man once said, "Sometimes in life, to realize something truly special, you must give up something truly special."

And to that I say, "Amen!"

Chapter 76.
Happy To Bring This To You

Now who the heck would have thought that ANYBODY would ever put this goofy incident in a publication of any kind? The following slice 'o life is akin to a tuft of broccoli. Of course, if the broccoli was graced with olive oil, garlic and a few other fixins like my mom or Ginny have been known to sprinkle, hmmm, not so bad after all.

Schwab's Pharmacy was easily the most famous celebrity hangout in Hollywood's long, illustrious and continuing history. At any moment in a day back then, stars of every stature and magnitude might be at Schwab's having a bite to eat, picking up a prescription or simply hanging out with friends.

Seemed like every new star-struck starlet-wannabee who hit town went to Schwab's, sat at the counter and ordered a chocolate soda, hoping to be discovered, just like **Lana Turner**. Of course, there were male-wannabees who showed up in droves, too, most also hoping for a glimpse of anybody recognizable.

Male or female, they shared a demeanor, a set of characteristics and used the same lines and questions to such a degree that it seemed they took and perfected a special class called, *How to Look 'n Act like someone who just fell off the same Turnip Truck.*

Cosmo's Hairstyling Salon (a.k.a. **Little Joe's** once I owned it) was less than a stone's throw around the corner from Schwab's and received a natural spill-over of the hangout's gawkers.

A particular incident stands out clearly in memory, at the top or bottom of the pile, your call. A man in his late twenties or so with a mop of hair covering his ears came bouncing in through our front door. He was all excited and loud enough that everyone throughout the 1500 square foot salon could hear him clearly. He told **Eileen**, the receptionist, that he wanted "the best hairstylist in the place" to cut and style his unkempt, mop-like hair.

Several of my staff and I exchanged glances. "Here we go again," describes our unspoken communication.

He had just come from a reading for a commercial, he said, his very first stab at stardom. I'll call him "Happy," as I have no idea how to more accurately designate him.

"Only three of us were picked out of at least 50 guys I saw t'go back this afternoon for another reading. The casting director told me t'get a haircut and gave me specific instructions. I just came from Schwab's where that actor, oh what's his name; he said to come over here. So tell me, who's the best hairstylist here, sweetie?"

(Later I learned he was referring to good buddy and noted chop-buster, **Nick Colasanto**, best remembered as "Coach," the bartender on *Cheers*.)

I excused myself from my client and walked to the desk, noting the subtle but definite look of relief on Eileen's face. Tony was 'up' next.

"You're in luck. Tony is available and the perfect hairstylist for you. He specializes in people who shoot commercials," I said, somehow keeping a straight face. Happy reacted as though this was truly a lucky omen.

Happy had to be one of the loudest people on earth and probably one of the most gullible. I was amazed that Tony spent so much time following Happy's every whim. Tony explained later that the incident was so far out that he just wanted to see how ridiculous it could be if he "let the string out as far as it wanted to go."

When Happy's cut and style were finished, he paraded around to each booth in the salon showing the other hairstylists and their clients the 'do' Tony had created. Happy repeated over and over again how happy Happy was with the result.

"Look at this, man, my hair is PER-fect! I even tipped that Tony tree dollars." Happy was easily history's happiest man.

Later that day, guess who came forcefully through the front door. Happy looked anything but happy.

He didn't get the part. He said that the casting director said his hair was too short. Now Happy wanted a refund. Okay, raise your hand if you need **Paul Harvey** to tell the rest of the story.

No, we were not unkind, just firm; and it was nobody's fault that Happy was more akin to grumpy when he left. Someone might think that this story contains exaggerations, but taint so. In Hollywood, cameras should be rolling on every corner. Well, certainly all up and down Hollywood and Sunset Boulevards.

Fortunately, the above incident is easily the most extreme example of dealing with the unprepared wannabees who came into our lives one day, never to be seen again.

The overwhelming majority of people and incidents logged in memory during all those years are pleasant, fun and, uhm, happy. Make that ecstatic.

Is there any wonder that I miss the good ole days of yesteryear?

Chapter 77.
Eight Thirty-Seven

I Confess, the following is a big surprise – to me. Ten years later this event is still fresh, though less raw. Somehow the Second Anniversary was the toughest so far. Once I put it all on paper, the load lessened, a process recommended for those very tough situations. Good thing I wrote it as there are some gem incidents that might have slipped through the Cracks of Time.

I never thought I'd tell this story. It's too personal, too private. But lately, I've felt compelled to write it.

That morning, January 15, 1999, though sound asleep, I heard the phone ring. Squinting at the clock on my nightstand with one eye, I saw the time was just past 2:30. 'It's Ginny's clients, those French guys,' I thought. They would call usually between 2 and 4 a.m. and dictate their report in English into the tape recorder so that Ginny could transcribe and email it back to them for editing.

Just passed 4 a.m. I awakened, and I mean Wide Awake. Weird, I thought.

I went to the family room in the other wing of the house and saw the blinking light on the answering machine. It wasn't the French guys. It was the night nurse from the Actor's Hospital in Woodland Hills, otherwise known as **The Motion Picture & TV Home**.

"Please call…" she said, slightly more than casually. The answering machine noted the time as 2:37 a.m. I wondered who was in trouble, my mom or my dad.

"Patricia succumbed at 2:30 this morning. I'm so sorry for your loss."

I'm the emotional type. I take after my maternal grandfather, Dominic. Tears come easily. This time; nothing. No reaction. How strange. "I must be in shock," I said quietly to myself as I hung up the phone. 'I wish I could have been there with her,' I thought. 'I wish I'd gone to visit last night.'

I love my mother very much. Always will. Ginny was a comfort beyond expression, but when you lose a loving mother, you feel alone in the world. I was more than able to cry with Ginny.

Mom had severe dementia. She was a petite 4'11" and down to 81 pounds. Caught a cold about a week earlier and was on a "no stat" that I lifted so she could get some help. Her nurse thanked me, said she didn't want to lose my mom over a cold. I had no idea the end was near.

9 a.m. I called my mother's sisters, Aunt Kay and Aunt Grace. She's better off, they both said, as if trying to convince and console me. They were sad. We had warm hugs, as much as a 3,000 mile phone line will allow. I also called Aunt Mel, my dad's sister. Very much the same.

I called the mortuary to make sure the system was working properly. Come in and sign some papers, they said. Grrr. I had already signed a ream of papers.

10 a.m. It's still a paper world despite computers. The man said direct burial would not happen before sunset as originally promised. "Can never get it done on a Friday," he feebly explained. Monday was Martin Luther King Day, a national holiday. That meant first opportunity for burial would be Tuesday.

I wondered if they were playing me for the $175 a day "holding fee." No, there would be no fee and they said, by the way, I needed to go to Mission Hills Cemetery and sign an authorization to accept the coffin and to open and reseal my parent's mausoleum.

What? Suppose I lived in Bacciagalloupe, New Jersey? I'd still have to sign, the man said, but in that case, the cemetery would accept a FAXed signature.

I went to the mortuary on my motorcycle, wearing my heavy jacket. Signed everything again. EVERYTHING! By 11 a.m., the jacket was much too warm. I decided to go home, a mile south, get my light denim jacket and head north to the cemetery.

Just as I was slipping my right arm into my lighter jacket, the phone rang. The doctor from the Actor's Home was calling. He told me that my father would not live out the day.

"What the $%#O you talking about, my mother just died," I heard myself say.

"Yes, I pronounced your mom. We're all in shock here, too. Close couples often follow each other within a year, maybe even several months, but never next day, not in my experience."

The doctor sounded genuinely sympathetic, maybe even a little shook. He told me that my dad had choked on his breakfast that morning, the food lodging in his lungs.

"Even if you were to ask me to save him, I couldn't."

I jumped on my Road King and headed for Woodland Hills. I've been on a 'bike since I was a kid of 14. I ride aggressively without taking chances. That trip I simply rode aggressively. I'm sure a shrink could explain it with labels. Funny thing; I think I understand it without the consultation.

I was aware on my wild ride that my mind was spinning much faster than the two wheels on my bike. Watching other people's parents die, I had wondered which of mine would depart first. That mystery was now solved and in a most appropriate way, I thought, a smile on my face. See, my parents were a genuine couple. They went everywhere arm in arm. Ask Sam or Theresa Russo. Or Janet Thomson. My mom never opened a door. And now, in spite of the fact that my father had more than a year ago lost all intellect – according to his doctors – my mom passed through the door of physical life and here was my dad, about to follow. Yes, how very appropriate.

On that ride, that day, I was invincible.

As I walked down the hall to my father's room, staff people offered sympathy, though nobody said a word. I entered my dad's room. He was propped up in bed taking rapid, desperate breaths. He was staring straight ahead, seeing nothing.

Shortly, as if on cue, the doctor came in and stood beside me.

"Did you give him morphine?" Now what the hell made me ask that?

"Yes."

I noted again that dad was breathing hard; labored. His eyes were open but I realized that he was not there. I sensed rather than saw that he was in pain, that there was a level of fear.

"I'm wondering if I should ask you to give him a mega-dose," I said.

"No need. I only waited for you to arrive. Why don't you go to the cafeteria, get a cup of coffee."

When Ginny joined me later she sat on the other side of dad's bed. My dad's nurse, a pretty black woman who reminded me of the secretary on the *Mannix* TV show of years earlier, came in. She looked sad. She said her son, around nine, was all excited to know that she was caring for the actor who portrayed **Father Carmine** in the *Rocky* series of movies.

"My son knows all of Father Carmine's lines from the *Rocky* movies by heart. He recites them all the time, especially since I took over as Paul's daytime nurse some time ago. I haven't told him anything and I probably won't, until he asks."

Above the headboard of my father's bed was a nicely framed picture, a still from *Rocky II,* depicting Dad marrying Rocky and Adrian, who were portrayed by **Sylvester Stallone** and **Talia Shire**. I took the picture down and handed it to the nurse.

"Tell your son that Father Carmine wanted him to have this."

"Oh I couldn't, could I?"

"Sure. For your son who honors my father with admiration."

A while later, it was Ginny and me, sitting there, each holding a hand. I told dad how much I admired him, how so many people back in Cleveland had changed their minds about his moving to Hollywood. Several people had told my father over the past years that they bragged that they were friends of his, grew up with him. Other showed their admiration by walking the other way when they saw him.

His breathing was still labored, not as deep now. I looked at him. They raised his bed so he was propped up, maybe at a 45 degree angle. His eyes were fixed; glazed.

A bit later, when I had just finished talking to the night nurse, I felt him squeeze my hand. Once. Medium strong. I looked back at him. To my amazement, his eyes were looking at me with his pupils normal; focused.

"Are you there?" I asked, knowing he was. He squeezed my hand again.

"I'll stay with you all the way, but you are free to go. You've done a wonderful job here. I'm very proud of you. You gave me a real shot at life, too. I could never have been hairstylist to the stars or written for movies 'n TV if you hadn't made your move. I'm very grateful."

An orderly came into the room, diverting my attention. After that, my dad's eyes were fixed again. His breathing was a bit more shallow now.

I looked up through the ceiling. "Hey Ma!" I said quietly but aloud. "I'll bet you're still here. Probably never left. Gimmie a sign."

No more than when the last word escaped my lips, I said "Hold it. Cancel that. I don't need a sign, Ma. I'm okay and I know you're here."

More time passed. Dad's breathing became more shallow. The doctor stopped by. That was a surprise.

"You on duty?" I asked.

"I'm always on duty," he said rather matter-of-factly. "I'll check back in a little while."

Just Ginny and me and Daddy makes three. I could feel myself smiling.

Breathing was real shallow now. Ginny and I made eye contact, no words, but it was time. We stood, one on each side, each holding one of his hands.

He stopped breathing.

Both of us were softly crying with smiles on our face, tasting the bitter-sweet, both thinking it was bottom-line good, that these last several hours like his last several years were not anywhere near as pleasant as they would have been if I could have written the script.

I looked up at the clock on the wall so I could mark the time; tell the doctor what to write on the death certificate.

It was **8:37**.

I let out a yell. Not loud. Brief. The kind of thing a guy might do upon sinking a 30 foot putt. I certainly recognized the significance immediately.

You see, when mom and dad got married, mom's address was *837 Whitcomb Avenue.*

Told you she was there.

I also knew that any time hence that I encountered 837 in any form, it would be my mom and dad saying hello.

And you know what? They flash me the numbers often. Ginny too!

There's more, but nuff for now. Let me catch my breath and I'll tell you about the funeral. The great Hollywood writer, **Milt Rosen**, my dear benevolent friend and mentor, couldn't have scripted it better.

★★★

Chapter 78.
"When the Phone Rings... the World Opens"

*When I recently went to the **Hollywood Celebrities and Collectors Convention**, my purpose was to arrange interviews with **Tony Curtis, Debbie Reynolds** and **Angie Dickinson**. While I'd had contact with each of them over the past 30 years, I expected that Tony and Debbie might call me by name, but Angie and I had only superficial contact, so I wasn't so sure. My serendipity this time was **Karen Cadle**, who proved to be a Gold Mine of the First Kind.*

At the **Hollywood Celebrities and Collectors Convention** held in **Hollywood** this past October, (2007) I had just finished visiting with **Eddie Carroll**, whose mimic-act of comic great **Jack Benny** is developing legendary status. I had asked **Carolyn**, Eddie's wife, if Eddie was better as Benny or **Jiminy Cricket**.

"Let me put it this way," she said. "Eddie portrays Benny; but Eddie IS Jiminy."

Walking around the room, I focused on the corner where **Tony Curtis** was seated. An attractive lady was sitting to Tony's left. As I approached his table, Tony looked up and said, "Hey, Hi!"

The lady turned out to be **Karen Cadle**. She had arranged for Tony and **Angie Dickinson** to be at the convention. I introduced myself to her and stated that I wanted to write a column on Tony. She gave me her card and invited me to call to set up the interview. Imagine my surprise when I discovered that Karen also is a great prospect for a Hollywood column.

Karen started in show business as a performer. After college she was in musical comedies, dancing and singing.

"But I needed to eat and pay the bills, so for my first job I went to an employment agency catering to people in the entertainment industry."

No such agency exists today, so forget the bus schedule. Through that now defunct agency, Karen landed a job as production assistance on *The Don Rickles Show*. She fell in love with the production side of the camera and working with celebrities on a personal level.

The life of a TV show is often very short, so Karen moved from one show to another until she found herself producing and directing celebrity pieces all over the world for various shows.

Remember *Lifestyles of the Rich and Famous*? Karen produced the last two years of the 13 year total run. That's much better than pretty good.

When Karen had the show, the interviews were deeper and more informative, not to take away from the previous shows. But to last that long, a show has to evolve by taking advantage of its stronger attributes.

As we were talking, Karen's other phone rang. With apologies, she answered. Kevin was calling. **Costner**? She didn't say. Karen gave him directions to someplace on Ventura Boulevard in Studio City. When she came back, she apologized again and told me she had a very busy afternoon with **Burt Reynolds**. Some life, huh?

About 10 years ago, Karen realized that she was rather constantly being asked to arrange meetings, interviews and even job proposals with various celebrities. Her Rolodex contained the private phone number of literally hundreds of Hollywood's most recognizable names, particularly the legendary stars such as **Paul Newman, Carol Channing, Elizabeth Taylor, Sophia** and **Doris Day**. Want more? Try her website.

Karen started booking stars literally all over the world. She formally opened an office called **Celebrity Access** in 1996. The name and focus changed and refined to become **Karen Cadle International** today.

"I never know what I'll be asked next. Often when the phone rings, a whole new world opens. It's all very invigorating, very exciting. Like a few weeks ago, I booked **Naomi Campbell** in Rome for an appearance on *Dancing with the Stars*. For one dance she received an incredible amount of money. Amazing, truly amazing."

Y'wanna book **Harry Belafonte**? Call Karen. **Linda Lohman**? Fergettaboutit. Karen only handles A-list talent.

Around Thanksgiving, Karen was in New York to do an autograph convention with **Katie Segal** (*Married with Children*) and **Patricia Neal** (from the original movie, *The Day the Earth Stood Still*). On Thanksgiving Day, Karen took a break and visited with **Delores Hart**.

Delores Hart starred in two movies with **Elvis** and also starred in the movie, *Where the Boys Are*. She was a gorgeous young actress who was being groomed to be the next Grace Kelly.

"At 26, she left it all and entered a convent. Now, 40 years later, she is Mother Superior at the Abby Regina Laudis, a cloistered convent in Bethlehem, Connecticut. She is the first movie star I met. I was 12.

"I spent the day with Mother Delores, even slept over in the convent by very special arrangement. What an honor! What a thrill! I think her story will one day be a movie. She is the most beautiful nun you've ever seen."

About a week after Thanksgiving, Kathy accompanied three stars, Tony Curtis, **Tippi Hedren** and **Carol Channing**, to a classic film festival in Palm Springs, known as **Star Fair**. The festival featured 26 classic films with at least one star from each film in attendance.

"At least 50 stars attended the festival, including **Margaret O'Brien** and **Rhonda Fleming**. Carol Channing represented *Thoroughly Modern Millie* and Tony Curtis was there for *Some like It Hot*. Of course, Tippi represented **Hitchcock's** movie, *The Birds*."

"I love them all. My client celebrities are business associates, but truthfully, I love each and every one of them. I find the big stars to be big of heart, almost without exception."

Karen told me a dozen anecdotes about her clients, but she plucked my heartstrings with the story about Tippi Hedren. Tippi heads an organization called **Shambala**, headquartered in Acton, California, about 40 miles northeast of Los Angeles.

Shambala is home for approximately 70 animals, including exotic big cats such as African Lions, Siberian and Bengal Tigers, Leopards, Bobcats, a Lynx and a Florida Panther. Most of the animals were born in captivity and then became orphans or cast-offs from circuses, zoos and private owners who could no longer care for them. They depend on humans to survive.

"It takes $75,000 per month to run Shambala. Tippi considers the overhead to be her 'glorious burden,' as she puts it. So I'm always anxious to book her whenever I can as the cost for keeping those rescued animals is pretty astounding."

There's oh so much more, but y'gotta go get it. Google these: www. karencadleinternational.com "Delores Hart" and www.shambala.org.

★★★

Chapter 79.
Spotlight on Labor Day, Past and Present

I Confess that what I have here is a perfect example of putting pen to paper and having that supposedly inanimate object take off on its own, nutz to the original outline. I started off with research notes on Labor Day and sat back 'n watched as that pen insisted on scribbling dis 'n dat about my Grampa Dominic. I became the guy who poured the coffee. By the last stroke of that pen, I hadda admit; nice goin'! I still have that pen and no, you can't have it.

Labor Day is a most patriotic holiday, holding hands with Memorial Day and joined by the fireworks that crown July 4th, officially designated as America's Independence Day. For many Americans and Canadians alike, Labor Day is another day of personal and collective recognition, as the day was set aside to salute the working people of our two great nations. By design, Labor Day falls on the first Monday in September and is officially celebrated by both the United States and Canada.

When I was in school, Labor Day also signaled the end of summer vacation and the beginning of the school year. It was usually a time for socializing with family and friends around backyard cookouts, picnics at a favorite park-lake-river-mountain or other recreational location. People still tend to look forward to Labor Day with positive expectations.

Labor Day was the target time for my family's move from Cleveland to Hollywood. My father, Paul, was originally scheduled to move to Hollywood the day after his 18th birthday, but Granma changed her mind, a story detailed in a previous column. So twenty-five years later, this time with a family of his own and on Labor Day weekend, Dad put his clothes and personal items into his new white '59 Chevy Impala four-door hardtop and headed west. My Mom, sis and I stayed behind to wrap up things while Dad went ahead to establish a foothold 3,000 miles away at the end of Route 66. Talk about an exciting holiday!

The thought of Labor Day also brings to mind my mother's father, Domenico, who preferred to be known by his "American name," Dominic. Grampa was born in Pace del Mele, Provincia di Messina, Sicilia, on February 15, 1885. (The town of "Piece of Apple," in the Province, like a state here, of Messina; in Sicily, an island that is a portion of Italy.)

Grampa came to this country and settled somewhere in Pennsylvania, sometime before World War One. I'm not being vague on purpose; I wish I knew exactly. My grandmother, Martha, was also born in Pace del Mele and came to America some years later where she became reacquainted with my grandfather. My grandparents were married in America and I'm certain my mother was born in Denora, PA, on July 21st, 1915.

During the latter part of World War II, my mother, sister and I went to live with grandparents Dominic and Martha while my father served in the army. My grandparents at this time lived in a two-story home at 837 Whitcomb Avenue in the neighborhood called Collinwood on the east side of Cleveland. Grandpa Dominic was a very patriotic American and was therefore very sad that Italy was "on the other side" for part of World War II.

There are two versions of how my grandfather emigrated to America from Sicily. One account was that he came through Ellis Island, where the family name, Ficarra, was "Americanized" to Figer, a familiar scenario, unfortunately, to many thousands of other immigrants.

In the other story, he was supposed to emigrate to South America; to Caracas, Venezuela, I was told and was somehow "diverted" to America, ostensibly by his older brother who was already here and "connected." How interesting. Maybe I'm really an Atlantic Wetback!

I asked my grandfather, way back then, which story was true. "The truth will die with me," were the first words out of his mouth, shocking me to the point of freezing the moment forever in present time.

"Y'need t'know WHY we came to America, not HOW."

I really wanted to know the *how* of it, but the *why* part was an unanticipated, curious wrinkle.

"Okay, tell me why."

His eyes grew wide as he focused on me. "WHY?" he repeated with a flavor of wonderment. "We came here for YOU!" he said with an inflection in his voice and a physical demeanor indicating that he expected that I should already know the answer.

"Came here for ME?" I shot back at him, my shock factor three levels higher.

"Sure, you, your cousins, aunts and uncles, EVERBUDDY!" he said emphatically, his arms making sweeping gestures to emphasize words or phrases.

He said that life in the old country was not as pleasant as he might otherwise have made it sound on other occasions. There were many times when "not enough food could be put on the table," or "they couldn't always keep the roof comfortably overhead." He said that "no matter how hard a man was willing t'work, there was too often too little work to do." A big part of the problem was that, "In the old country, you had t'do what your father did. If he was a stonecutter, you were a stonecutter; if he was a cobbler, you were a cobbler."

I had a hard time conceiving the picture my grandfather was depicting, not to be confused with his personal integrity, for he was above reproach.

"If your father had a brother, and if you had a brother or two, and your father would consent to loaning you to his brother, then you would be what your uncle was, do what he did. That was pretty much it," he explained patiently, wanting me to clearly grasp the message.

"South America, all of it, is just like t'old country. You have t'be whatever your father is. Ah, but here in America things are different, and much better." As he started to talk about America, his demeanor changed abruptly. His countenance lit up, he sat more erect and with the increasing brightness in his face, his eyes glistened.

"Here in America, you can go to school, the best schools in the world…" A tear wet the corner of his eye as he choked up a bit "…and the schools are free until college, and they will teach you to be anything you want to be! You don't have to follow your father or your uncles; you can be ANYTHING!" By this time, the tears of happiness were tracing paths down his cheeks.

"That's why I tell you t'pay attention in school, t'sit there with your hands folded across yer desk 'n listen to ever-thing yer teacher has t'say, t'learn all you can so that when you finish you can get a wonderful job with a great future. Here in this beautiful country, *La Bella America!* you can rise all the way to being the Best of the Best!"

Yes, he would have made a great *Secretary of Pride and Joy for the American Way.*

There is more to tell, lots more, undoubtedly a whole book's worth. My paternal grandparents were also wonderful people who were very successful in business here in America. They too emigrated from Sicily and always shared their knowledge and love with me unselfishly, as stated in past columns. I am truly grateful for my abundant blessings.

When I lived with my maternal grandparents, I was between the ages of five and seven. The quotes in this column were from a grandfather to his grandchild. The memory of this invaluable information has been with me continually; daily. I take great pleasure in sharing these intimate remembrances with you.

Happy Labor Day and May God Bless America!

★★★

Chapter 80.
Santa's Big Scene

A Christmas mystery is solved thanks to seeing it all through the perspective, eh, make that eyes, of a five year old. Again, I didn't plan to let the kid take over, but sometimes... Besides, if you've been reading from the beginning, I don't have many secrets any more.

To a child, Christmas often is an introduction to the concepts of family togetherness, holiday magic and a world filled with surprises. On Christmas Eve when I was a kid, we always went to my grandparents' home. Both sets. My father was eldest of six, Mom too, allowing for plenty of cousins.

While driving to Granma's the year I was five, (Make that five and a half. At the time that half was very important.) who should be coming up our street but Santa, his sack bulging as he walked with one of our neighbors. At my anxious behest, my father blew the car horn and Santa stopped in his tracks to wave to me. Wow, was I excited!

I begged my father to stop so I could talk to him, but dad said we'd better let Santa get on with his duties. I wanted to turn around, go home and to bed, so Santa would leave my presents under the tree. See, that year I was hoping for my first real bike and I certainly didn't want to miss out. My dad assured me that Santa would "come back later...." I wasn't really convinced, but what's a kid to do.

The evening at both grandmas' was fun and a drag, all at the same time. At midnight a couple of my cousins and I went outside to see if the dog could talk, but we were learning that you can't believe everything that's told in stories. After midnight we were allowed to eat meat dishes, though I was rather full from all the delicious fish we had earlier.

All the excitement caused me to get sick. Back home finally, Mom arranged newspapers on the floor next to my bed, asking me to try to use it, in case.

I woke up suddenly. The house was dark but I could see by the night-light in the bathroom next to my bedroom. There wasn't a sound. Slipping out of bed, the newspaper underfoot seemed deafeningly loud. I stretched beyond it and crept to the stairway leading down.

It was an enclosed stairway until the bottom three steps. A round mirror hung on the wall adjacent to the landing and facing the stairs. As I reached about halfway down, I saw an object in the mirror. Reflecting along the stairway wall of the living room to the Christmas tree was - and I know for certain as I squinted to make sure - the unmistakable image of a black boot with white fur trim on top and then the red pant leg of Santa Claus! The leg even wiggled a bit as though he was standing in one spot while doing something, like maybe, arranging my presents.

Joyous excitement and absolute fear hit me instantly. With a quick pivot, I tried to be quiet as I headed back up the stairs. Tip-toeing to my room, I heard the unmistakable sound of footsteps on the stairwell. Ohm'gosh, Santa's coming up!

I hopped into bed awkwardly, causing the headboard to bang against the wall. Wondering if I had given myself away but hopeful that I hadn't, I assumed my customary position of laying flat on my back with the covers pulled up to just under my chin.

Santa stepped into my room. He paused, turned and headed out. Then to my utter surprise, he turned into the bathroom and locked the door behind him! CLICK!

Shocked, I grabbed the pillow from under my head and stuffed all I could into my mouth. I heard Santa's pants drop. Then I heard some other sounds that made me wonder if the pillow and my hands would be enough to muffle my hysterical laughter.

The toilet flushed; the bathroom door CLICK!-ed open. I heard Santa pause at my doorway, then go back down the staircase. Whew, that was close.

Next thing I knew it was morning. Late, like 7:30. Down the stairs in a flash and there, under the tree, was my shiny red bicycle! And wow, also a bunch of presents with my name on them! Santa didn't hear me, after all; but I sure heard him.

My parents came down with new baby Sis, excited that Santa had brought me a bike and packages of other stuff, too. I started telling them what happened by promising that I would not make up anything. When I got to the part where Santa came upstairs, my mother started to laugh. When I told how he went into the bathroom and locked the door she was nearly hysterical. When I described what I heard and added sound affects, my mother laughed so hard she asked me to stop or said she would have an accident.

After church we joined family again at both Grandmas' houses. All of us kids were really excited. At one point Mom beckoned me.

"Tell all the grownups what Santa did."

Most of them behaved just like mom. In front of everybody, my Mom said that I was a good enough storyteller that **Jimmy Durante** would welcome me into "da act," if only he knew. Wow, keep that thought, Mom!

This strange but true story happened a million years ago, it seems, and even though I know better, *Yes I Did See That Leg In The Mirror!*

May your Christmas, this year and always, be filled with Love, Joy and Magic. And please, keep a light on in the bathroom. You never know.

Chapter 81.
The Wakeup Christmas

Christmas time is a state of mind, though some would call it a mindset, for there's an extra jingle in your step, a brightness in yer countenance and somehow, problems can behave like they took an aspirin or something. I choose not to focus on the Scrooges, someone else can do that, not to be confused with my making a recommendation. The people named here are top-o-the-heap of my life-long best buddies from childhood, and that continues right up to today. Uh – oh, now I am really in trouble cuz I didn't name at least 101 other Heaps as at least 108 of us show up every June for a golf outing somewhere in Cleveland. Maybe next June, insteada going to Cleveland, I should go to 'Vegas or somewheres else.

Christmastime often brings out the best in people. The Christmas Season has evolved into a time of millions of added bright lights, noticeably extra comings and goings of people and a dramatic change in the type and beat of music filling the airwaves.

We can sort the previous Yuletide Seasons by the people we shared time with, the places where we celebrated and the events that occurred.

There was a particular story this year, a news item. I saw it just about a week before Santa's Big Ride. A cache of donated Christmas gifts meant for underprivileged children was stolen. In just a few days, people not only replaced the gifts that took weeks to accumulate, they increased the original quantity several times over. The story gave me a profoundly good feeling, a sentiment I'm sure you share. The incident also led to a rousing of some profound memories of a Christmastime from my grade school days.

I grew up on the east side of Cleveland in Collinwood, a beautiful, well kept neighborhood, then. The Northeast YMCA was a major asset, providing a trustworthy place with programs to enhance the lives of the people of our community.

I fondly recall **Mr. Elmer Fairchild**, the Executive Director. He was one of the kindest, most caring human beings I have ever been privileged to know. His positive attitude, upbeat disposition and friendly demeanor personified Christmas all year 'round.

I remember walking into the "Y" one day after school, shortly before Christmas. I saw several kids wrapping new items in holiday paper, then placing the packages under the big, beautifully decorated tree. Mr. Fairchild invited me to pitch in, telling me these gifts, along with unseen food items, were to be delivered to needy families around the neighborhood. That was a surprise, somewhat. I wasn't sure what a "needy family" was, or where they might live, or if any of my friends might be on the list.

I learned the food and gifts were to be delivered in the evening time a few days before Christmas. I had to bring Mr. Fairchild a note from home saying that I could be part of the delivery team for the big evening, which would end later than usual.

In preparation for the delivery effort, several close friends and I met at the "Y" to put specific items into boxes and bags for each family we were to visit that night. I remember seeing large ham hocks, loaves of bread, bags of potatoes, jars of olives and pickles, cans of corn, green beans, peas; even fresh celery and lettuce; bags of apples and other fruit, and tons of other canned foodstuffs. The quantity boggled my expectation.

The "Y" had a former school bus, an old rattletrap that was painted dark blue. It often backfired, so we nicknamed it 'ole...' oh, never mind.

We loaded the bus with the carefully prepared boxes and bags of goodies, then placed each group of food and gifts in reverse-delivery order onto the bus, as our group counselor, Mait Purdy, had a charted route to follow.

We visited several homes that evening, one place standing out quite vividly in my memory. It was my turn to give the speech at the door.

"Good Evening! We are from the Northeast YMCA. On behalf of all our members, we wish you a Very Merry Christmas!" Right behind me were best buddies **Chuck Coletta, Eddie Maroli, Buddy Sivillo, Paul DeSantis, Danny Mastro** and the inseparable **DeLissio** brothers, **Brian** and **Henry**. They carried boxes and bags filled with goodies into the house. Okay, okay, stop twisting. I confess; we're still best buddies.

The house didn't look like any of those on my street. It more resembled a converted wooden garage.

A hunched-over lady had answered my knock. She seemed too old to have young children, but I was told later that she was indeed the mother. Her clothes were strange to me, not something like my mother, my aunts or my grandmother would wear; they were too ragged. Her hair was graying and askew.

When she saw the food and wrapped presents, her eyes opened as wide as her mouth dropped. I remember so clearly that she put her rather bony fingers to her cheeks and started to say "Thank you," and cry, revealing spaces where teeth were missing. I could swear she was laughing and crying all at once, but at the time, everything had become surreal.

The kids – there were four, maybe five of them – seemed to range between three and ten years old. They started to cheer, kinda like at a ballgame. One little girl began screaming and jumping up and down. They couldn't have been happier, memory tells me. They kept saying – no, make that exclaiming - "Thank you!" They said it over and over. And that little girl....

I haven't told this story very much over the years, maybe because to be completely honest, I'd have to admit that I couldn't get out of that house fast enough. Sounds terrible on my part, I know, but for all the joy that they blurted out, I couldn't take the heat of the reality; I couldn't take the pain of witnessing true poverty, especially at Christmas, the most joyous time of year.

See, up until that night I thought I came from a rather poor home. My parents grew up in the Depression. I considered them to be frugal, if I might use one of today's words. But that night a new reality, a new understanding, started to plow its way into my noggin.

By the time I lay down to go to sleep after saying my prayers that night, I recognized that our refrigerator, and our pantry, were never bare. We went to the grocery store regularly, a store owned by my paternal grandfather, and I knew Grampa'd give me anything! My whole family dressed nicely. My dad drove a decent, rust-free car. I would not dare go to school in dirty clothes, much less in those that were torn or tattered. And I never got up from the table hungry. I had a bike, a sled, roller skates and a basement full of comic books. That was the Christmas that I found out I was closer to being rich than I'd ever be to being poor. Made me want to jump up and down and shout "Thank you!" Again. And again. Still does.

So now really, how was Christmas? What are your prospects for the coming year? Tote it up again, but this time push the envelope a bit more. Think of and list all of the advantages on your side of the line. Then go have the best year of your entire life!

Buon Natale, Buon Anno, e auguri per Cento Anni ancore!

★★★

Chapter 82.
Hats Off to Carol Vittoria

Under most circumstances, following stories of Christmas would be a tough act, indeed, but not this time, 'cuz if you capish the main point of the following, you'll stand up 'n cheer and maybe even wanna help out a bit.

*I Confess, I really enjoy writing columns about people who are strangers to me so I can profile real people in real situations from a fresh, don't-know-anything-except what–I-see-and-hear point of view. Along the way I wrote a column about a 21 year old girl named **Arlene** who had a meningioma brain tumor. I was thrilled to report that after surgery, she had experienced a full recovery.*

*Because of that column a lady named **Carol Vittoria** contacted me. Her similar story had interesting differences, so I profiled Carol. A great footnote is that she and her husband Bob are now counted among Ginny's and my best friends.*

I like to write about residents of Cape Coral who have a story to tell that is fun, thought-provoking and on the light 'n bright side of life. The story on **Arlene Quezada**, published on March 3rd, 2007, told of a 21-year-old Edison College student with a 3.7 GPA and a very bright outlook on life, though she is also the survivor of a horrific brain tumor.

As a result of that column, Arlene received a bouquet of kudos. I even received a couple. Then I opened my email one morning and found the following:

"Dear Joe: ...Since I too am a brain tumor survivor, I was very touched by her (Arlene's) story. I moved to Cape Coral from New Jersey two weeks after my craniotomy for a meningioma (type of brain tumor). I suffered for three years from symptoms BEFORE it was discovered. If there is anything positive to say about my tumor, it is that it FORCED me to move to the Cape, which I wanted to do for five years. We were snowbirds, and I was living my life 'like I was dying.' Now, I do what I WANT TO DO.

"May 1 – 7, 2007, is National Brain Tumor Week. I would like to create awareness and raise funds for research here in the Cape and from my friends in New Jersey. I especially want to target the meningioma brain tumor, which has very little funds for research since it is a BENIGN(??) tumor. These tumors have doubled in the last 10 years and the cause is unknown. There is a tremendous need for education and research to find the cause and cure for these 'BENIGN' BRAIN TUMORS.

"How can a tumor that causes blindness, deafness, paralysis, seizures, stroke, tinnitus, memory palpitations, mood swings, financial bankruptcy, depression, suicide, divorce and DEATH be BENIGN?

"The treatment is the same for these tumors as for malignant tumors. Craniotomy (brain surgery), chemotherapy, cyber knife, radiation and all other forms of treatment come into play, yet there are very little funds for research to help eradicate this deadly disease.

"I am lucky to be alive, functional and have the ability to write this letter. Please help me create awareness and raise funds for National Brain Tumor Week through your column. Thank you. **Carol Vittoria**."

My wife Ginny and I met Carol for coffee at a local restaurant one afternoon. We found her to be very pleasant and upbeat while working on a cause that might understandably knock the pins out from under another person. Carol impressed us as being the type of person that people would enjoy meeting in a grocery store or while going about the Cape on life's many errands.

Carol provided us with a publication called *Brain Science Foundation Newsletter*. The cover sheet states, "The Brain Science Foundation is dedicated to finding a cure for meningioma and other primary brain tumors and to advancing the understanding of brain function related to these tumors. The BSF supports basic and clinical research, promising new treatments, and improvements in patient care."

The foundation has a complex website offers a tremendous amount of information for all people who want to raise their awareness and/or help either Carol or the foundation directly.

Last Christmas, Carol sent out a newsletter to her family and friends. It was a full page, neatly typed. The letter helped Carol raise $2000. I'll lift just one paragraph:

"I now belong to a club that no one wants to join, but I am so thankful to be a member. These people, all of whom are living with or who have survived brain surgery, are there for ME twenty-four hours a day. They help me with Post Traumatic Stress that EVERY survivor endures. We understand each other because we all wear the same hat to cover our scars. We are survivors with a purpose. We are all trying to make lemonade out of lemons. We all feel lucky, scared and want to PAY IT FORWARD. We want to help others."

Carol further stated that "All my friends and family know that I am going to periodically (every Christmas, for sure) ask for financial help till we wipe out this dreaded tumor."

Christmas in March; what a concept!

*UPDATE: As this book goes to print, you need to know that in October 2009 the Brain Science Foundation was invited to address the convention at **Harvard University** recognizing **Meningioma Awareness Day**, often referred to as **MAD Day**. The purpose of this day is to raise awareness — and research funds — through world-wide participation. So, if you want to help, Carol Vittoria can be reached at* louie8105@ yahoo.com.

Chapter 83.
Mickey Rothenberg:
Among the Heroes of United Flight 93

TA-TA-ta-ta-ta- DAAA! Read that tree times. That's the trumpets blaring, as promised.

*I Confess: We're rounding third and headin' home! This next column I wrote at the invitation of **Tonya Squibb**, the publisher of several Breeze Corporation's newspapers. As a result of writing this column, she and the executive editor, **Renny Severance**, (now my dear friend, golf partner and very importantly, my editor herein) asked if I would like to write a series of columns based on my experiences as Hairstylist to the Stars in the Hollywood/Beverly Hills area. So in reality, this next column was the beginning of the series of columns telling about Hollywood celebrities and other interesting people I met during my career as a salon owner in Southern California.*

Like I said earlier, I recognized that most of my inner thoughts and philosophies would be revealed over time, but I was many columns into the series before I realized that the series could also be thought of by some people as an abbreviated autobiographical record of my professional life.

*Mickey – a.k.a. Mark – was probably the first victim of the hijackers on **American Flight 93** that crashed into a field just outside Shanksville, Pennsylvania, on the now National Heartache date of 9-11-01. Here's a tidbit on my all-too-brief and warm friendship with **Mickey Rothenberg**.*

"**A** second plane just hit the **World Trade Center**," Ginny said as she came rather forcefully into my private haircutting room.

"Oh my God!" are the words I believe came from me. In that instant I was certain that two planes flying into the World Trade Center, virtually minutes apart, was neither an accident nor a coincidence. Through the adrenaline rush that evoked many emotional thoughts and feelings that lie on the dark side of thinking, I suddenly felt a pang of gratitude that the client sitting in my chair was **Pastor Dan Betzer** of **First Assembly of God Church in Ft. Myers, Florida**.

As the three of us held hands while Pastor Dan offered a prayer declaring faith and asking protection and mercy for all concerned, my thoughts shifted to admiration and wonder that, training and experience notwithstanding, anyone could be so mentally organized at a time of such extreme tragedy. In the countless times I've flashed back on that moment from just a short year ago, the frown on my memory has a touch of gentleness thanks to Pastor Dan.

Ironically, the atmospheric conditions on 9-11-01 were clear, providing a physically beautiful day throughout most of the country, but as we all came to know, there were more than ominous columns of heavy smoke clouding the ambiance of New York City, Washington, DC and Somerset County, Pennsylvania. Later in the day we learned that the airplanes used as living missiles creating death and destruction were regularly-scheduled flights whose destinations were San Francisco and Los Angeles, California, my home for 40 years before moving to Sanibel Island, Florida.

Many people I've talked to over the years have had, somewhere along the way in life, those illogical but unshakable prophetic feelings that something really bad was about to happen, or had already transpired. No matter the methodologies I employed to jostle my psyche, I felt certain that I knew someone on one of those airplanes.

About two weeks elapsed. I could not find a complete roster of the passengers on the four jetliners that crashed, a fact that is still true. Then on Friday night, September 28th, Ginny and I tuned into *Dateline* near the end of the program profiling many of the people on **United Flight 93.** Nice looking people, I thought. How very sad. As the next picture came into focus, I shouted "Mickey!" as my eyes darted to the name on the TV screen; **Mark Rothenberg**. That confused me momentarily, then as tears totally obliterated my view of the TV screen and everything else, I mentally transported 12 years back in time to our first meeting.

"Mark is my given name, but my family and best friends call me Mickey," he said with his warm smile and moderately firm handshake. That did it. From that point forward we greeted each other with a hug and became absolute friends. Forever.

Though he lived in New Jersey, I gave him many haircuts at my salon in Beverly Hills over the next several years. His business kept him flying cross-country with regularity, even going to the Orient, especially Taiwan, as many as 10 or so times per year.

I always looked forward to Mickey's visits, as did his manicurist, **Theresa Russo**, who is also Sam's wife, my partners in business for many years. Sam once told me he considered Mickey "...a perfect example of a *Mensch*." I couldn't agree more.

Mickey and I talked about very personal, even delicate matters, going beyond the line of subjects normally discussed between professional and client, keeping up on events and people in each other's lives. We discovered we were both hackers who loved to golf and kept promising each other that we would find time to play a round together. Didn't happen, darn it.

In the time that has passed since knowing that Mickey was on Flight 93, I've told several people that Mickey always flew first class and I know he actively resisted the terrorists. Of course, I certainly have no proof of my statements, nor will I ever. But I read the just published book, *Among The Heroes* by **Jere Longman**, (Excellent!; if heart-wrenching) that highlights the people and, as much as intelligent conjecture will allow, the events surrounding United Flight 93. Apparently, Mickey could have been the first casualty. My feelings are a sweet and sour mix of anger and sadness overshadowed, usually, with pride and enthusiastic, if silent, applause.

I abhor knowing I will not be able to hear his wonderful, melodious Brooklyn accent again while I'm flattered that I am privileged to have enjoyed sharing life with him for so many years. I've often thought about phoning his wife, **Meredith**, and their daughters, **Rachel** and **Sara**, none of whom I know or have ever talked to that I can recall. I'd like to tell them what they already know; that as my *compare* Sam said so well, Mickey was a perfect example of a *Mensch*. So why haven't I called? I'd never get the words out. Thank goodness Ginny gave me this wonderful idea.

★★★

Chapter 84.
Viewing 9-11-'01 From 9-11-'03

It's "The Rest of the Story" – I say again, with s'more hats off to **Paul Harvey***. The following column clarifies some of the events in the previous column and was chronologically the 24th column written in the original series. It was published as a First-Anniversary Column.*

C'mon, two years ago? Can it really be that over 700 days have passed since that surreal terrorist attack on our country? All those tears, the gut-wrenching anguish, I know, I know. My heart still aches, too. I can't think about it for very long. But it does seem more like a few weeks ago, maybe a month or two, an illusion fostered by the vivid video, with audio, whenever I slip and let some portion of the memories run through my mind. With that said, I must admit that all reality checks agree. It was two years ago.

For the past couple of weeks and until today I had been writing a column on **Red Skelton**. It's a wonderful, warm and funny recollection of a bouquet of zany incidents that make up a genuine Hollywood happening. While writing, I had paused, staring off into space when I realized I was boring a hole in the calendar on my office wall. As I came to focus, it hit me like a ton. It was time to turn my notebook page and start writing the "9/11 Anniversary" column.

I can't imagine that anyone needs a recap of the horrible events of that Black Tuesday. I'm sure that far too many newspapers, magazines and TV broadcasts will chronicle the events, complete with horrid pictures and heart-wrenching words. I'm glad I don't have the responsibility of compiling and recreating the events of the 9-11 Tragedy.

President Roosevelt called December 7, 1941, "A day that will live in infamy." There have been too many dates since that Sunday that could be grouped under the "infamy" umbrella, the most recent being 9-11-01. We all have a story to tell, as sharing the details of our personal torment helps to at least temporarily relieve the mental and emotional burden we find so difficult to carry.

One year ago I was invited by this newspaper to write something for the first anniversary of 9-11. I lost a good buddy, **Mickey Rothenberg**, on Flight 93 and this presented an ideal opportunity to take a bit of space and memorialize him. It started as a few words of honor and remembrance. I was anxious to see how the layout would look and I asked the paper to send a fax of it.

My wife, Ginny, overheard the conversation and told me our fax machine was not operating, she didn't know why, it looked okay; it just wouldn't go. Instead we arranged to have the fax sent to the *Island Reporter* next door and the publisher, **Tonya Squibb**, was kind enough to bring it by. The memorial turned into a column at her suggestion.

Writing the column, as it turned out, was my substitute for being at Mickey's wake. Thinking back, I do not remember if I wrote the column in my office, in our lanai room, if it was raining or sunny, or even if it was daytime or evening, for that matter. I do remember it was wet - the paper I was writing on, I mean.

That first column turned out to be a stepping stone to others when the editor, **Renny Severance**, agreed that bits and pieces about my Hollywood experiences could make for fun reading. When I tell friends and clients about people and events that I was involved with in Hollywood, they seem to enjoy the stories. It's a special kind of fun to know something personal that is first hand and never published about a celebrity.

This is column number 24. The first year truly turned out to be a labor of love. How wonderfully appropriate that my anniversary date is 9-11. There are probably a million themes, stories and angles that might have been chosen for this solemn occasion. I didn't want to open wounds that are not fully healed by talking about loss, death and destruction.

Today we again collectively pay our respects to those who were killed or injured in **The World Trade Center Complex, The Pentagon**, and the four aircraft. We acknowledge with eternal gratitude the people of the **NYPD**, the **FDNY** and all the other professional public servants who rushed to help as their final act on this earth. Of course, civilian Samaritans, along with all people who carry scars, both physical and mental, are also included here. We shouldn't forget the Red Cross, either.

Next week, I'll personally introduce you to one of the world's most loved and most soft-hearted comics, **Red Skelton**. It's a 100% happy story. The best kind.

As a final thought, I'd like to say a few words to my friend, Mickey Rothenberg.

It had to be you, Mick. I've been part of the Sanibel community now for three-plus years, and the only time my fax machine did not work was the day the paper was to send me the copy of my salute to you. Later that day, it worked just fine. Nice trick! Thanks for the nudge. It's just like you to reach out to others regardless of your own circumstances, just as you reportedly did on Flight 93 on 9-11-01.

I never "finished" writing my columns. Writing a newspaper column came to an end as the paper released several freelance writers, including me, to trim budget and editorial content. They then released several of their employees, their 'permanent' staff. All this reduction was prompted by a loss of advertising revenue due to the shift to e-information.

Employees are being terminated all over the country and by just about every industry. Good newspapers, even those with more than a hundred years of honorable service, are folding like thatched huts in a hurricane.

With all the stories I've told, all the Hollywood Celebrities I've profiled, I've only just begun. I have a ton more to tell, plus the fact that I'm still a member of the Hollywood Community and therefore able to interview many of today's celebrities. I'll look for a cue from Life – or a publisher - before I decide to pursue writing more columns.

In the meantime, I have several people about whom I fully intended to feature in a column. I made a list. I called my list, "Stardust," simply my Working Title that has become my Section Title.

Plan A was to write a line or two about each celebrity and put those "micro reviews" between each column. After a while, that idea proved to be cumbersome; ergo, the creation of an official Stardust Section.

I present my list in alphabetical order as not even I could line them up by my affection for them or by any other considered method.

So here for your enjoyment is a whole gang of Celebrities whose common thread is Hollywood and that we got to know each other through my hair salon(s) or my writing or; well, you'll see. Some of these people and I had or have a nice, tight, long friendship. A few are included because of my undying admiration and the fact that they help me make a point.

I'm starting with co-workers with whom I have had a profound connection. Answers the question, "What's Love Got T'Do With It?"

STARDUST

The following people who appear in this section had been, with a few exceptions, on my "Hollywood To-Do List" when the newspaper column was brought to a halt by the "downturn in publishing economics."

I thought that readers would rather have a brief glimpse into the how 'n why these people's lives intertwined with my own rather than no mention at all. As sometimes happens, my pen is known to take off on it's own and produce information beyond the scope of my outline. Anything beyond a few lines is a good case in point.

As I am fond of saying; Enjoy!

First, the original Staff when I started working at Cosmo's:

Cosmo Sardo, born March 7, 1909 – d. July 14, 1989 in Los Angeles, CA. For all practical purposes, my boss became, in affect, *My Godfather*.

Paul Micale, born in Little Italy in Cleveland, January 2, 1916 – d. January 16, 1999 in Woodland Hills, CA. My father shared the second chair with Cosmo in the original salon. (Nunzio was in the first chair.) When Cosmo remodeled and expanded, ten private booths were arranged around the 1500 square foot space in a horseshoe configuration. Cosmo, of course, had Booth #1 and Nunzio had #2. My dad had #5 and I had #6. On the left side of me was a walkway leading to the bathroom and the back entrance from the parking lot. I really liked my booth with its panoramic view of the whole salon and a great view of the front door, the reception desk and the waiting area.

My father moved to Hollywood to be a movie/TV actor, not to cut hair. Working at Cosmo's/Little Joe's was a major contributor to his getting work in the industry as so many stars, producers, directors and casting directors were regular clients of the salon. Familiarity and accessibility played a large role in securing more work for him over the years than he might have realized otherwise.

When I bought Cosmo's, we closed escrow around 5:30 pm on March 2, 1973. I called my parents to tell them that I'd like to drop by with some news. Believe me, nobody was more shocked than my mom 'n dad. I think my dad felt a little awkward at first, but he never showed it or in any way confirmed that being my employee was odd. That first Tuesday morning, I gathered all the staff and held a meeting with the very surprised crew. One of my biggest points was to tell them that my dad was an employee who did not have a penny invested or loaned and had no say-so about any decisions I would make. I think they understood that dad's focus was on his acting career and he really had no desire to be part of ownership. I think. In any event, it all worked out great.

Nunzio "Johnny" Tringali; born in Agusta, Sicily in October, 1911 – d. September, 18, 2008 in Granada Hills, CA. Johnny was (properly for the custom of the time) on the first chair. He's in my "Upper 1% All-Time." I'd almost have to write a separate book to tell all I know and experienced with Johnny, but then, I almost did throughout this book. To say that I loved him like an uncle starts to give you some idea of our deep friendship.

On November 22, 1963, I returned to work after a routine doctor's appointment just before One p.m. I was anxious for more news on the shooting in Dallas. As I changed my shirt, Johnny came out of his booth with his transistor radio pressed to his ear and said, "The dirty bastards just killed President Kennedy!" He turned back into his booth and wept. Somehow, from that point on, I understood Johnny's quiet demeanor better, maybe because this steady, gentle man showed such an uncharacteristic display of emotion. I cried so hard I almost lost consciousness.

Ludwig Fengel was born in Germany and spoke with a thick accent. (Ludwig died sometime in the mid '80s.) The Staff frequently kidded him about his being part of the Luftwaffe during WWII. Sometimes the 'kidding' got a little rough, verbally. I'm not sure Ludwig flew an airplane outside of his imagination. But then again, he said he flew "supply missions...."

John Forte was a Brooklyn transplant who was a typical neighborhood guy in mannerisms and demeanor. (He did not stay with us after the remodeling.) His son, John, was a couple of years older than me and visited the salon often and helped his French girlfriend, **Giselle**, get a job as a manicurist.

Sam Keston spent many years in London's Cockney area before coming to Hollywood and worked in the booth next to me my first couple of years at Cosmo's. That arrangement smacked of Devine Intervention. Sam is another person in my "Upper1% All-Time."

Lewis is the man I replaced when Cosmo promoted me from part-time to full. My dad told me that Cosmo and Lewis had a shouting match that caused Cosmo to fire him.

In early '63, as mentioned before, Cosmo took over a vacated store next door to the north and created the 10 semi-private booth salon that existed to the end of my ownership when the13-tenants business center was sold and demolished, along with Schwab's and three other parcels to make room for the building now on that site. In the larger salon, prominent Staff newcomers were **Gene Turner** from Pennsylvania and **Billy O'Connor**.

Gene Turner came to work at Cosmo's after the expansion from six to ten booths in the spring of '63. I liked Gene from day one. He was extremely conscientious; he tried harder than anyone else to convert from a barber and learn the secrets of the new concept of hairstyling. I convinced Sydney Skolsky to look to Gene for his shaves as a hairstyle could be done in the same timeframe at four times the cost. Gene, like me, was thrilled to have Sidney as a client.

Billy O'Connor. Billy was an enigma to me. I left Cosmo's in December of 1963 to join Sam Russo. I returned as only the second (and final) owner on March 5, 1973. In the ten years Billy was there, he would very rarely make his guarantee for the week. All other staff members had no problem earning the guarantee, often earning double or triple the minimum amount. Two weeks after I became owner, I overheard Billy trying to organize a mass walkout. I fired him, one of the few times in my life when the Heave Ho came into play.

The Staff at Russo's

Sam Russo. Given our long and intimate history and all that I've said about Sam throughout this book, even the term "Brother" hardly measures up. Y'want more? Wait till I publish *Someday.*"

Ralph Trejo. Ralph was about 25 years senior to Sam and me. We were all close, played some golf, had some great times in places like Sneaky Pete's and the Buggy Whip. Ralph played a mean Flamenco guitar. I asked him why he never went pro. "I don't remember a lot of those years" he told me. I didn't know him when he wasn't sober. But I know him from 1962. I never saw him take a drop. We lost him, still sober, in 2003.

Bobby Russo, Sam's cousin. Sam, Ralph, Bobby and I were the original crew of Russo's on Santa Monica at LaCienega. What a place! About 1966, Bobby left to open his own hair salon, called **La Barberia**, on Little Santa Monica in a building owned by one of his clients. It was a Sweetheart deal as Bobby paid just a fraction of what the rent should have been. In 2005, the building was sold and Bobby was told he would have to leave after all those years. He made a deal with our long-time good buddy, **Eddie Carroll**, whose salon, **A Swingin' Affair,** was located a few paces down the street toward Wilshire Boulevard. On Bobby's last day at his place, as he was driving to work that morning, he crashed. Police said he died instantly. Ironic. And very sad.

Phil Fayne. Phil joined us when Bobby opened his own place. We were a great mix. We all referred to our salon as a happiness place. Everyone was friendly and the work was superb. The four of us stayed intact until the spring of 1968 when I left to write the TV show called *Boutique*. I went to a hair salon called **Archie's** for about two months, then joined Benny Garcia at his **El Dorado Hairstyling Salon** on Vine Street.

Russo's Distinctive Haircutting was forced to close in 1978 and I was forced to close **Little Joe's Of Hollywood** on December 31, 1979. Our landlords refused to renew our leases, the details too repulsive to regurgitate here. Sure, lots of tears but Life isn't all Cherries 'n Cream. (I say that now, but it was a bitch!) On January 2, 1980 I joined Sam, Ralph and Phil along with **John Salter** and **Bernie Roberts** in a salon, called Russo's to avoid confusion, on the mezzanine level of the **ICM Building** on **Beverly Boulevard**. Life keeps moving one tick at a time with no Timeouts, no Waitaminutes, just gotta keep puttin' one foot in front of the other. Forget alternatives, y'wouldn't want to experience any of 'em.

The Manicurists

When I started to work at Cosmo's, the salon was open seven days a week, with 'regulars' – the full time guys - ideally wanting Sunday and Monday off. Only Nunzio had the ideal; everyone else worked one weekend day, taking another day – Tuesday, Wednesday or Thursday – off. All regulars worked Friday and Saturday, the two busiest days.

The original salon had six three-sided haircutting booths forming 8' x 8' cubicles. To my amazement, there were at least three manicurists on duty most days and never less than two.

Following are the cream of the crop, the very best of the best, the girls I will forever call family. I've arraigned them in the order that our working lives intersected.

Kitty Krupnick was working at Cosmo's from my Day One, having been there for several years. She was an attractive brunette in her forties (fifties? Naah!) who was always immaculate with her hair fixed in a short flip and makeup like she had it done at Max Factor's. She always wore a dress or skirt 'n blouse combo with heals and again, looked like she came right out of Central Casting. She was an excellent manicurist. Fast, too. She did a better job in 20 minutes than most others could do, PERIOD.

Kitty's husband, Bob, was a cameraman, a cinematographer, I believe.

Sometime during my first couple of days, Cosmo complimented the appearance of my hands and nails, then asked Kitty to give me my first manicure. Cosmo advised that I get a manicure every week and pay the manicurist a tip of ½ the price of a manicure. No, I was not charged for a manicure.

Kitty is the only person in this group who I did not associate with after our working days were finished. Unfortunately, she did not have a long life.

Janet Thomson. There is no P in Thomson. No bullshit, either. Janet is somewhat younger than me, I forget exactly. She was in her late teens when she first came to work at Cosmo's. I had only been there less than a year.

Did I mention that she was a drop-dead gorgeous redhead? With long slender legs like a racehorse? And a sultry gait? And a sharp wit?

She's always been the Queen of the One Line-ers. Everyone - the single guys, the married guys - wanted a date with Janet, but most usually got some smart lip instead. She was a great manicurist, too. And fast. We called her fast one a Zip Job (And laughed like hell!) like the kind she used to give when working at the train station in Philly, her hometown.

She and I hit it off like Brother and Sister – Cousins? – right from go. Janet too, could dress. Her makeup was ultra subtle, cuz she didn't really need any.

Janet has pro-quality talent as a writer of Country-Western lyrics. She's so good she had phrases, even entire songs, stolen from her.

On one occasion, I asked if she was going after a certain big name Thief.

"Rock 'em!" she said. "What goes around comes around. I'll get mine."

The first part of that quote contains more literary license than actual quote, but I hope lots of kids get to read this book.

I could sense that she and I could remain friends forever and I'm thrilled to report that we have done just that. We met again at Russo's. When I took over the salon at The Century Plaza Hotel, she was my first hire on the first day. Ditto when I bought Cosmo's. Ditto when Sam, Theresa and I bought the place known as Beverly Hills Hair Design. Ditto when we shut down and I again used my own name, Little Joe's, on South Beverly Drive, the last place I owned/worked before moving to Florida.

She's helped make my life beautiful; exciting.

Anita Kaye. I met her while working at Cosmo's. Anita was Bob Krupnick's younger sister. I found her beauty stunning. She started in the business as the receptionist at Russo's shortly after I moved there from Cosmo's. During that time she went to manicuring school and came out like she had 20 years experience under her belt. That's Talent, capital T earned and intended.

Anita has HUMUNGUS talent as an Interior Decorator. You

should see what she can do to a Christmas Tree! 'Nuff to bring life to 'ole Santa!

Anita also worked with me at The Century Plaza Hotel and again when I bought out Cosmo. We've put in a bit less time together than Janet and me, but not by much. All three of us are together forever.

One time Anita was having trouble with her landlord, the particulars lost to me in the passing of Time. One of Anita's long-time clients was so empathetic, he GAVE her a beautiful condo, free and clear. Strings attached? No way. Anita wasn't his type, but she was a dear friend in need and this man came up from scratch, so he understood.

And people ask why I love Hollywood!

Renee Edwards Right, another beauty. They all share that quality. Renee is the come-to-life Kewpie Doll of the bunch.

In spike heels, she was shorter than me. Renee was raised in the South and had a drawl that could melt steel. She had raven hair, dark eyes and thought she was grossly overweight if she hit 105 pounds.

If she liked someone, she called him "Dah-lin" with a heavy emphasis on the first syllable. If she didn't like someone, she called him "Dah-lin" and he knew to keep his distance.

Like the others, Renee gave a Top Notch manicure. When she applied the personality, which she always did, the clients simply couldn't get enough.

Renee, Janet and Anita were buddies from before I knew them. Especially since I moved to Florida, contact has been rather too infrequent for my blood. However, any of us can pick up a phone and find an excited, loving reception on the other end.

For a while, a year maybe, Renee dated my dear friend, Rudy Waxman. When they decided they weren't a couple, they remained friends.

I'd tell you that Renee could really light Rudy's fire, but then, she lit *everybody's* fire. All she had to do was say, "Hello, Dah-lin!"

Theresa (Corea) Russo. What more can I say about Theresa? We finally got together professionally when Sam and I lost our leases and reconvened at the ICM building, circa 1980, on Beverly Boulevard. When the building refused to renew our lease there, preferring to let in a convenience store that paid a large basic rent plus a percentage, I made a two or three year stopover until we – Sam, Theresa and I – all bunked in with cousin **Bobby Russo** on Little Santa Monica, maybe 60 paces east of good-bud **Eddie Carroll's Swingin' Affair**.

Some years later, Sam, Theresa and I bought the salon at 9171 Wilshire Boulevard and renamed it **Beverly Hills Hair Design**.

Eileen Walker. Okay, back up a minute. About the second year after I bought Cosmo's, I was having a kanipshin looking for a decent receptionist and another kanipshin looking for a decent manicurist. Both needs were fulfilled by Eileen.

She had spent previous years serving cocktails and food with the ability to remember the favorite drinks – quirks included, like 'tree' olives in wine – for hundreds of people. Successful as she was, she always wanted to be a manicurist. I'm convinced that contributed heavily to her being so good.

Eileen was a pretty dishwater blond that I converted into a bright honey-gold blond to better suit her outgoing, sunshine personality. I didn't have to do anything about her let-it-rip laugh that automatically got the whole salon going even though nobody else knew what or why they were laughing.

Our working together was short, maybe only five years, but we have remained friends, even though contact has been limited to a phone call here and there.

Oh yeah, she worked the phones like a bookie. Hmmm, maybe we missed the boat.

The Porters

Charles Grant. Chuck, like Kitty, was working for Cosmo's the first day I hit the floor as the Babe. That might have been my new handle except that "Little Joe" was tacked on from early grade school.

Before my first week was out, I asked Chuck for a shine. He shoulda been in the movies as it was a shine with a show. He'd snap that rag and do a shuffle-tap that caused ear to ear smiles all around. And shine? Oooeee!

When Chuck was finished, I held out some money. He refused, adamantly, sincerely, and told me he gave shines to all the guys who worked there, but never for money. The money in my hand was a five dollar bill, the only money I had on me that day and more than I intended to give him.

"Make you a deal, Chuck. I respect your policy, but just this once, take this fin. From now on, I'll only give you money if you ask for it."

He protested but I prevailed. He pronounced so many blessings on me that it now occurs to me that he possibly gave me my professional baptism.

Sometime later, maybe six months, my dad, Nunzio and I were casually hanging around the reception desk when Chuck went into his rag-slapping, shuffle-tap while giving a shine to one of his regulars. I mentioned that Chuck knew how to play that schtick that seemed to always get him a big tip; that Chuck was a lot sharper than most people probably thought.

Nunzio addressed his comment to my dad. "You did a decent job with this kid. He reads Chuck like a book."

When I bought Cosmo's, Chuck was no longer working there. I made a good but fruitless effort to find him, but I'll certainly never forget him.

Steve Thomas. Going from Cosmo's to Russo's had a bitter-sweet tinge. Steve helped smooth the sea. He was at least 25 years older than Sam and me with a smooth countenance, a fixed smile and with a voice and physique that reminded me of **Nat King Cole**.

No, he couldn't sing, but nobody ever held that against him. He knew how everybody drank their coffee. He knew everyone's car. He remembered everything anyone ever told him. I'm certain he didn't have a critic in the world, not even the biggest bigots, and I know we had a couple of real stinkers as clients.

Steve liked to read. I was amazed at the books he would comment on from time to time. I once asked him why he worked with us, for he was obviously over qualified.

He told me he chased his dream when he was my age and he was content.

"I have a wonderful wife, my house is paid for, so is my nice car and I don't have any pressure. You're all nice, clean-cut boys, Ralph is a fine gentleman, the people who come in here are by and large among L.A.'s finest. Hell man, I'm rich!"

Steve was always invited to everything we did as a group. He and his wife joined us many times. I'm sure glad. I'm a better person for having him as a friend.

General Junior McClary. Everybody called him "Mack." I inherited him as an employee when I bought Cosmo's. He's the reason I stopped looking for Chuck, for Mack was as good as they come.

Like Chuck and Steve, Mack was easy to get to know because he was friendly and open. At the same time, he was extremely quiet, though he'd always say hello 'n g'by to everyone.

He too could remember exactly how to fix everyone's coffee. In the six years he worked for me, he never raised his voice.

Like the other two, he kept the shop clean and sharp. I never asked him to so much as clean a mirror because he always had them – and everything else – standing tall, looking sharp.

Mack got jammed up by the IRS. They sent me a letter telling me to withhold 'X' on the 1st and 15th of the month and have the money in their offices by the 5th and 20th or I would be liable for a large fine.

I called the IRS for a little chit-chat. I told them I had a weekly payroll and it would be tough to figure just one person on a different schedule. I asked if they had a standard conversion for an employer with a weekly setup.

No, the IRS said, I'd have to comply with the 1st and 15th. We talked some more. I asked to speak to a supervisor. He said he was a supervisor and I had no choice. He forcefully reminded me of penalties and promised heartaches I would incur if I failed to comply. Mickey Cohen was nicer, more cooperative.

"Hey, what happened to MY rights? I was born in this country."

"You gave up your rights when you went into business."

Maybe he wasn't exactly representing IRS policy. Maybe he was just trying to get me to comply. What do I know?

"And you better not fire him, either, or there will be hell to pay!"

My old neighborhood had a mob element. Nobody in their right mind would mess with them. Ditto the IRS. I found a way to figure Mack's money on the 1st and the 15th. No, I was never late.

With tears in his eyes, Mack offered to quit. I told him to fergettit.

With all that, I miss Mack's friendship.

Following are the "Stardusters," the celebrities who had a Positive impact on me. Most were clients.

<u>**Nick Adams**</u>, **born Nicholas Aloysius Adamshock on July 10, 1931 – d. February 7, 1968**. Nick was my client in the early 60s and the star of the TV show, *The Rebel*. Nick is another celebrity with whom I had a good personal friendship. He was easy going and very frank in his conversation. I was shocked at his early death.

<u>**Jack Albertson**</u>, **born June 16, 1907 – d. November 25, 1981**. Jack was Nunzio's client throughout my experience at Cosmo's/Little Joe's. He had a natural wit and could seemingly deliver a zinger from a deep sleep. Funny man, lovable man.

<u>**Alan Alda**</u>, **born Alphonzo D'Abruzzo; New York, NY; January 28, 1936**... Read the column on Alan to get a more complete picture, but rest assured that he is a genuinely nice and a very considerate person.

<u>**Richard Anderson**</u>, **born Richard Norman Anderson in Long Branch, New Jersey on August 8, 1926**... We first met on Universal's *Six Million Dollar Man* set after Harve Bennett asked me to visit and offer advice on the hair color of Co-Star **Lee Majors'** double. Since that time I have seen Richard at a couple of Celebrities Conventions. If I ever resume my newspaper column, I will definitely feature Richard as he has had an extremely active career as a Lead Actor and we have talked about the potential. Unfortunately, he has never visited my salon.

<u>**Roone Arledge**</u>, **Sports, TV Executive; born July 8, 1931 – d. December 5, 2002.**
<u>**Chet Forte**</u>, **born Hackensack, NJ; August 7, 1935 – d. May 18, 1996.** Roon and Chet were clients at my salon in the Century Plaza Hotel and were serviced by other hairstylists. They most usually came in together. Both were very friendly and outgoing and enjoyed talking to other clients who recognized their celebrity.

<u>**Buddy Arnold**</u>, **born in NYC, NY on August 11, 1915 – d. March 31, 2004 in Vero Beach, FL.** Buddy was a Composer, Writer, Author and Producer. He was a graduate of CCNY. **Milton Berle** told me that Buddy was his head writer, but knowing Milt's schtick, I asked others and found that Buddy and Milt had a long and successful relationship. I enjoyed getting to know Buddy.

Frank Avianca, **born Frank Sardo; a Producer, Actor and Writer**. Frank produced projects in Europe and the USA. He was my client during the 1970s. He was easy-going, street smart and could easily have come out of my old neighborhood. Or been shot there.

Richard 'Dick' Bakalyan, **Actor, Writer, Producer; born January 29, 1931...** I first met Dick in the early 1960s when I went with my parents to a party at Dick's house. Dick found favor with **Frank Sinatra** and appeared in movies with him, notably, *Robin and the Seven Hoods*. He gave me a still – a photo taken on the movie set – that hangs in my salon. Dick is a fine actor who usually finds himself cast as a heavy.

Gene Barry, **born Eugene Klass in Brooklyn, NY on June 14, 1919. d. December 9, 2009.** Gene was the Star of two successful TV Series, *Bat Masterson* and *Burke's Law*. He has an impressive body of work in Hollywood. I often bumped into him at **Nate 'n Al's**, a famous Beverly Hills deli. I met him and his director son, **Michael**, at a Hollywood Celebrities Convention most recently in 2008. I remember my father appearing on Burke's Law as a waiter "with business."

Robert D. Bash, **Esq. d. 1992.** Bob was my attorney – and my dear friend – for 25 years. The last few years of his life we were avid golf partners. We were often joined by some combination of my father, **Sam Russo** and **Joey Dorando**. Bob had a tremendous influence on me.

Once, about the middle of our relationship, I chose not to act upon one of his suggestions. He said that maybe I should get another attorney if his advice was not taken.

I told him that his function with me was to offer suggestions and to cite possible gains or consequences. My function was to consider all potentials and proceed informed knowing that I would take or reject his suggestions, but I would always be grateful for his input.

I believe that too many people allow their attorney to make their business decisions. That's not an attorney's function. Legal advice is the attorney's function. The key word is ADVICE. Bob and I got along great.

I was shocked by Bob's sudden death. His minister used our relationship as the subject of his eulogy at Bob's memorial, a unique circumstance for me.

Today I often think, "What would Bob advise?"

Paul Benedict, **Actor, born in Silver City, NM on September 17, 1938 – d. 12/1/2008**. Paul frequented Cosmo's/Little Joe's for years as the client of Ludwig Fengel. Paul is best remembered for portraying quirky English neighbor, **Harry Bentley** on the TV series, *The Jeffersons*. Paul was a quiet and gracious man who was very friendly when approached.

Richard 'Dick' Benedict, **Actor, Director, Writer; born January 8, 1920 – d. April 25, 1984**. This fine actor also was a favored friend of Sinatra and appeared in several of Frank's movies. Dick was also a highly sought after director with a long list of credits for directing several of the most popular TV shows.

Harve Bennett, **born Harve Bennett Fischman on August 17, 1930, Television/Film Producer, Screenwriter**. Consult the column herein on Harve. He was one of the more interesting people I met in Hollywood due to his always being involved in more than one major project at any given time. He frequented Cosmo's/Little Joe's throughout my 20 year involvement with the salon.

Jack Berle, **Actor, Milton's brother, Deceased circa 1976**. Jack was another regular at Cosmo's/Little Joe's and was Nunzio's client. The entire staff was greatly saddened by his passing as Jack was very friendly and a very funny guy. In fact, I thought he was the funnier brother. Go figure.

Milton Berle, **born July 12, 1908 – d. March 27, 2002**. My wife Ginny's birthday is the same as Milton; July 12th. When she mentioned that to Unka Miltie at a party given by my dear friend and 30+ year client, **Joey Dorando**, Milt answered, in part, "… Bill Cosby, too…" Milton's snappy responses could be cutting and nasty and when challenged, vicious. He could also be civil at times. People learned to stay on guard around him.

Edward Binns, **born in Philadelphia, PA on September 12, 1916 – d. December 4, 1990, in Brewster, NY**. Eddie was also a client of Cosmo's/Little Joe's during my entire 20 year involvement. He was my father's client. Among his many Hollywood credits, he was a pilot in the movie, *Failsafe*. He and my dad were close personal friends.

Robert Blake, born September 18, 1933.... Several times our paths crossed. My impression has always been positive. One time at Schwab's, Bobby was paying his bill. I walked up on his left side and purposely bumped arms with him. When he looked toward me, I simply said, "You get me in a lot of trouble." He laughed and said he could see why. Many times during the run of the TV series, *Baretta*, tourists mistook me for him.

Pat Boone, Singer/Actor; born Charles Eugene Boone on June 1, 1934... I first met Pat when his secretary co-starred in a play opposite my father. The play was *Anthony on Overtime*, a light comedy. The entire Boone family was backstage on opening night but this time they were playing the role of "fans." While I met Pat several times over the years, I especially recall that he greeted me on the Red Carpet at the opening of the movie, *Funny Girl.*

Marlon Brando born Marlon Brando, Jr. April 3, 1924 in Omaha, Nebraska – d. July 1, 2004. Certainly Mr. Brando needs no recap for he is easily one of the world's all-time favorite actors. One night I was in the **Casa Vega**, for truth be known, I probably spent *thousands* of nights at the Casa Vega. No, I'm not a drinker, it's just that the **Casa Vega** was a great place to have dinner and kibitz with other regulars and interesting people, most in the entertainment world.

For more than 20 years, Willie – also known by his Spanish name, Guillermo – was the Head Bartender. One night I was sitting on my favorite barstool nursing my Mexican Coffee when Marlon Brando came in and greeted Willie with a firm handshake. "Hey Marlon, say hello to my friend Little Joe. He owns the hair salon next door to Schwab's." Mr. B was very cordial and complimentary, saying that I cut half his friends. I told him to send me the other half . At least we all had a good laugh. The man was friendly and displayed a great sense of humor with some back-n-forth jibes with me. At the time he was surprisingly heavy.

Fanny 'Baby Snooks' Brice, born Fania Borach in New York City, NY on October 29, 1891 – d. May 29, 1951 in Hollywood, CA. No, I did not have the privilege of knowing her, but when I was a child listening to RADIO, (TV? What's that?!?) she and **Red Skelton, Eddie Cantor, Lou Costello** and **Jimmy Durante** made me laugh my head off! I cried when each died, for I had lost a Very Dear and Personal Friend.

Snooks was the first to go. On her radio show that night, they played music. I cried the entire 30 minutes, so much so that my mom was worried about me. I really didn't like music programs very much before and I certainly didn't like them much after that incident. A carryover? Gotta be, at least partly.

Lloyd Bridges born in San Leandro, CA on January 15, 1913 – d. March 10, 1998. Here's another actor with a long, positive and successful history. Seems he has umpteen family members following in his footsteps, proving that Poppa's Shadow need not be a place to choke.

At one point, Bridges had a series where he played a beat cop. He often ended the show having a beer with his favorite bartender, Paulie. Paulie was my dad, Actor Paul J. Micale, who during that time was made an honorary member of the Bartender's Union for having portrayed so many bartenders that a group of them felt he deserved to be in the union. Sure, Pop got a big kick out of that.

One day my father and I entered Schwab's at lunchtime just as Lloyd Bridges was exiting. The two of them greeted each other with half shouts and a big hug. It's a great way to meet one of Hollywood's brightest Stars.

Joe E. Brown, born July 28, 1892 – d. July 6, 1973. Funny, funny man, he didn't need words to be funny. He had the most rubberiest face until **Jim Carrey**. He was taller than I expected. I met him in Schwab's one day but never really had the chance to know him.

Lenny Bruce, Comedian/Writer; born Leonard Alfred Schneider October 13, 1925 – d. August 3, 1966. Lenny was my first Outcall, not to be confused with that other profession. He didn't want to be subjected to the crowds that haunted him wherever he went. At the time he was doing a well publicized gig at the former location of **Ciro's,** called **The Comedy Club**. While I went to him more than once, his home was up in the Hollywood Hills but I don't think I could find my way there today. Lenny impressed me as a quiet, deep thinker who was interested in the opinions of others when not on the stage. I'm flattered to think that he was my friend, but for too short a while.

Lonnie Burr, born Leonard Burr Rabin on May 31, 1943... He's an Actor, Writer, Director and one of the Original Mousketeers. Lonnie was also my client for more than twenty years and my friend forever.

Pat Buttram, Comedian/Actor; Born Emmett Maxwell "Pat" Buttram June 19, 1915, Addison, Alabama – d. January 8, 1994, Los Angeles, CA. One night I was out with perhaps a dozen friends. Only God knows where we were earlier but we ended the night by going to the coffee shop in the **Beverly Garland Hotel** in North Hollywood for a snack.

Pat walked in with two other fellows, all were dressed in Western garb and fresh off a set. Some of the people in my party expressed a desire to meet him and I was chosen as the point man. I approached his table, extended my hand with apologies when he took over the introduction. Pat and his two actor buddies came over and joined our group and regaled everyone with stories of how a movie scene can go bad, especially when working with horses and other animals. I'd have a hard time naming people who were in that group, (Good-Bud **Clay Jackson**, for sure) but I'll bet every one of them still has a warm, glowing memory of Pat and his friends.

Michael Callan, Actor/Singer/Dancer; Born Martin Harris November 22, 1935... I met Michael while going out on casting calls during 1960-62. We would also bump into each other around town. I sincerely thought he would be a big star someday based on his displayed ability during readings, but in Hollywood, talent alone is not enough. Others have written several books telling what they think is enough, so I'll drop it here. I was always impressed with Michael.

Corinne Calvet, born Corinne Dibos; in Paris, 1925 – d. 2001. Matt Helreich has many titles, as you will see. Among them, Matt is known for throwing Thursday Night Dinners mixing Stars and Non-entertainment friends. That's how I met Corinne many times. She always impressed me as very quiet but friendly.

Rudy Campos Rudy seemed to always be cast as The Bad Indian or a Ruthless, Bloodthirsty Mexican. Actually, he was part Indian and part Latino and all fun while being very friendly. We knew each other from all over town and must have met at the **Casa Vega** a few hundred times. If you ever go to the **Casa Vega** in Studio City, on the right-hand wall by the bar is a great portrait of Rudy. Just ask Ricky or any of the staff.

Dr. Ed Cantor, prominent ENT in Beverly Hills, CA, Dr. Eddie is no relation to the great comedian. Eddie was a client of my father at Cosmo's/Little Joe's during my entire 20-year association with that corner. His clients included **Frank Sinatra**, **Barbra Streisand** and **Jimmy Stuart**, to name a few. Through Dr. Eddie I met **Tim Conway**. Through Tim I met **Larry Sands**. When you get to Larry's name on this list, you'll see the Stars he led to me. (Dr. Eddie also led me to **Dr. Larry Chusid**. That whole story is the prominent theme of a script and book I call *Someday*.) The last time I saw Dr. Eddie was after about a 10-year absence. It was like there had been no separation at all.

Jodi Carmeli. She played **Marilyn Monroe's** role in the stage version of *Some Like It Hot,* starring **Tony Curtis** and **Larry Storch**. If her name is one day up there with the Best of Hollywood, I won't be surprised. If she doesn't achieve that level of Stardom, again I say that talent alone is no guarantee, but oh brother, she gots it!.

Jack Carney. He was Art's brother and a Director in his own right. I had the privilege of cutting his hair for several years starting in the mid-sixties. I always looked forward to his visits.

Scott Carpenter, born May 25, 1925; Boulder, Colorado... While I have a revealing column on Scott, I'll say here that I enjoyed every moment of the several years when I cut his hair.

Jim Carrey, born James Eugene Carrey in Newmarket, Ontario, Canada on January 17, 1962... When I first started cutting Jimmy's hair, he was an unknown wannabe looking for the break that would take him to the Heights of Stardom he has now achieved, if he ever dreamed that high. Actually, I figured he was a shoo-in for stardom. He was a down-to-earth great guy who I really liked. He was under the wing of one of the major agencies and his personal agent, one of my clients, brought him to me. Jimmy was so quiet that nobody noticed when he walked in the door of my hair salon. Betchya everybody notices today!

Charlie Chaplin, Jr., born Beverly Hills, CA May 5, 1925 – d. March 20, 1968. I can almost say the same about Charlie that I did about Eddie G. except that I never knew Charlie to be an alcoholic. Both guys had a much rougher reputation than I ever saw. I treated both as good buddies and they responded in like kind. That's a lesson I learned much earlier in life. Grampa, again.

Dick Clark, America's Oldest Teenager - Born November 30, 1929 as Richard Wagstaff Clark... A protégée director of his production company was a client of mine for several years and told me of many positive insider incidents. Consult the column herein, but I have 100% praise for him. He really helped our TV series, *Boutique,* out of a jam.

Mickey Cohen, born Meyer Harris Cohen in Brooklyn, NY on September 4, 1913. According to FBI files, born July 29, 1914 in Brownsville, a section of Brooklyn, NY – d. July 29, 1976 in Los Angeles, CA. Da Feds didn't say nuttin 'bout how or where he died or if it was natural or unnatural, but stay tuned for updates. This Mick musta been scary with a gun in his hand cuz he didn't look poo-poo without one. I associated with tougher looking guys in gradeschool.

Dennis Cole, born in Detroit, MI on July 19, 1940... Dennis was a patron of both Cosmo's and Little Joe's. My dad, Paul, cut his hair. I'd like to compliment him by saying that he is another friendly and talented Actor whose Star should have shone brighter if talent were the primary criteria.

On April 9, 2009, Ginny and I drove to Ft. Lauderdale, FL, to meet several of my cousins for dinner. Dennis happened to be at the same restaurant, so Ginny got to meet him. He carries a bit more weight but he's the same friendly guy. I really got a kick seeing and chatting with him after all these years.

Nat "King" Cole, born Nathaniel Adams Cole in Montgomery, Alabama on March 17, 1919 – d. February 15, 1965. There is hardly a need to say that this great musician and entertainer is still well known more than 40 years after his death.

Natalie Cole, like her famous father, hardly needs an introduction. One night I was at a Christmas party hosted by **Jean and Casey Kasem** at their lovely home in Holmbly Hills. The guest list included hundreds of Hollywood's VIP Stars.

The food at the party drew a lot of attention as the Kasems served only Vegan food. At one point I approached the buffet table for another taste. I met a pretty black girl there who started a conversation like we knew each other. She pointed to a dish of food that she said had to be fried chicken. I pointed to another dish that I said had to be prime rib. We were having a good time making each other laugh as we both knew that every dish on the table was some kind of vegetable.

Later, Casey came up to me and said he noticed I was having a good time. "I didn't know you knew Natalie Cole," he said. Yep, the girl at the food table was Natalie, but I hadn't a clue. Later still, I told Natalie that I really appreciated the technique she employed to sing a duet with her father, saying, "I'll bet you heard that one a million times." She said she probably heard it five million times but that it thrilled her more each new time. During our second conversation she called me by name. I'm still very flattered.

Gary Collins, **born Gary Ennis Collins, April 30, 1938, Venice, CA**... I was sitting at the bar at the **Casa Vega** working on a writing project. The barstool next to me had a change of patrons. Willie the Bartender came over, topped off my Margarita and said, "Little Joe, say hello to **Gary Collins**." For the next while we enjoyed a wonderful conversation. Gary knew my writing partner, **Johnny Gentri**. I found Gary to be friendly and a very interesting person.

Nick Colosanto, **born January 19, 1924 – d. February 12, 1985.** A talented actor, "Coach" was also a very gifted director. He was a many-years client of Nunzio Tringali, but I am privileged to have given him haircuts from time to time. The number one adjective I associate with Nick is Brilliant. Number two is Creative.

Tim Conway, **born in Wade Hill, near Chagrin Falls, Ohio on December 15, 1933**... I met Tim through **Dr. Ed Cantor** around 1973. As most people know, Tim can drop a line and get an entire room full of people to laugh hysterically. He does that wherever he might be. He is genuinely funny, very bright and a very decent person. He introduced me to Writer-Director-Producer **Larry Sands**. Larry was my client for about a year before his untimely death in a helicopter crash while filming a commercial. Tim and I went to Larry's funeral together where Tim delivered a very moving eulogy.

Ben Cooper, **born September 30, 1933, Hartford, CT...** Ben is noted for being the fastest gun on film. I should add most accurate, too. Ben co-starred with **Burt Lancaster** and **Anna Magnani** (March 7, 1908 – d. September 26, 1973) in *The Rose Tattoo*. Ben was my client and good friend during the mid to late '70s.

Jacques-Yves Cousteau, **born in 1910 in St–Andre–de–Cubzac in France. Commander of the transformed mine sweeper "Calypso."** Jaques' team worked with the **National Geographic Society** and established many firsts in undersea exploration. Whenever the team was in town, they, including son **Felipe**, came by Cosmo's/Little Joe's for haircuts. They were all extremely friendly and polite. Their presence always caused a stir around the **Schwab's** corner.

Robert Cummings, **born Robert Orville Cummings in Joplin, MO on June 9, 1908 – d. 1990 at The Motion Picture Hospital in Woodland Hills, CA.** He was not as 'stuffy' as Cosmo made me think. We had a limited but enjoyable friendship.

Mike Curb, **born December 24, 1944; Savannah, GA**... Mike was a guest on the *Boutique* TV show that I wrote with **Johnny Gentri** and **Susan Brown** as hosts. In addition to Mike's achievements in the music world, for a time he was also Lt. Governor of California.

Jimmy Webb, **born Jimmy Layne Webb in Elk City, OK on August 15, 1946...** Jimmy Webb and Mike Curb appeared on the same episode of *Boutique* together. In this case, I think one of them requested to be put on the same show, rather than my stacking them, a function normal to me. Both knew **Casey Kasem** and perhaps Casey suggested one or both. Again a normal circumstance where I would consult with various celebrities for candidates to fill upcoming categories of guests. In any event, Jimmy was a major coup for the show, as we aired in Spring of 1968 and as good as Jimmy Webb's future looked at that point, he went forward to such successes and acclaim that he is today mentioned in the same breath as **George Gershwin, Richard Rogers, Cole Porter, Barry Mann** and **Burt Bacharach.**

WOW! Way to go, Jimmy!

Tony Curtis, **born Bernard Schwartz, June 3, 1925, Bronx, New York...** Tony is well chronicled in the columns including my rather-life-long good-buddy **Larry Storch**. I've always enjoyed bumping into Tony over the years. Check out his paintings sometime.

Patsy D'Amore, born January 12, 1902, d. August 15, 1975. Patsy owned 'n operated the famous 'n fabulous **Villa Capri Restaurant** in the heart of Hollywood just off the corner of Highland and Hollywood Boulevards. The food was delicious and expensive. The crowd was VIP and dressed to kill. There was plenty of heat on one of the nights when I was there as I counted several of 'em. Guys w/heaters, that is. Patsy's daughter, **Filomena**, my new friend, is gathering data for a documentary and book on her father's life. To contribute, contact filomenadamore@ca.rr.com. Tell her Little Joe sent ya.

James Darren, born James William Ercolani, June 8, 1936... My first memory of Jimmy is seeing him at casting calls for movies in the early '60s. He came to see me for a haircut in the mid '60s, telling me that his stylist was away for a while and had recommended that Jimmy see me. When non show-biz clients approached him, Jim was very cordial and friendly.

Gray Davis, born Joseph Graham "Gray" Davis; December 26, 1942... I first met Gray around 1983 when he was the client of another stylist. I gave him a few haircuts over the years and came to know him on a friendship level. I've always admired him and feel he got a bum deal when he was Governor of California.

Roger Davis, born Jon Roger Davis in Bowling Green, KY on April 5, 1939...
Jaclyn Smith, born in Houston, TX on October 26, 1947... Roger and I go back to when he was a star of a TV series called "Alias Smith and Jones." While he has had a very busy acting career, I also know Roger to be a developer of real estate properties. I'd love to own a home he designed as he has a tremendous and exotic imagination.

Several years ago when he was married to **Jaclyn Smith**, Roger became extremely ill. For a few days the medics were unable to diagnose his ailment before discovering that his appendix had burst. Roger went from 185 pounds to 80 pounds and was at the doorway to death. During this time he was not allowed visitors, but Jaclyn let me in an emergency entrance to the hospital late one night. She and I sat next to the bed of the mostly unconscious Roger that evening. Roger is easily one of my favorite friends of all time.

John Dean, born in Akron, Ohio in 1938… I'd call John if I knew his number to tell him how much fun I've had the past 40 years telling of the time I gave him a haircut. I really do enjoy my encounters and associations with the movers 'n shakers of this world.

Freddie de Cordova, born Frederick Timmins de Cordova on **October 27, 1910 – d. September 15, 2001.** With all that transpired between Freddie and me, I was extremely saddened by his passing. Though I only covered the tip of the iceberg of events between us, suffice it to say that many smiles during my Hollywood career can be traced to Freddie.

Frank De Felitta, born August 3, 1921 in New York, New York… Frank was my client for several years in the mid/late 70s. I knew he was an investigative reporter who became an author, a script writer and a movie director. Among his many accomplishments, Frank wrote the Best Seller book, *Audrey Rose*. He also wrote the script for the movie of the same name starring **Marsha Mason** and **Anthony Hopkins**. The hit movie was produced by one of Hollywood's all-time greats, **Robert Wise**.

Audrey Rose is a story revolving around reincarnation and based on true incidences that occurred mainly in New York City during the '60s and '70s, culminating in a court case in New York City.

I found the story incredible. I asked Frank if he actually used his investigatory skills and found the concept of reincarnation to be a fact of life. He asked if I was casually interested or if the answer would have special meaning for me. I told him that the answer would have an absolute impact on my life.

"Then do your own investigation and come to your conclusions independent of me or anyone else," I recall him saying.

I told him that I have many subjects of extreme interest, but I find there are not enough years in a lifetime to master all. I said that we need to look to various experts to get a comprehensive idea to explain many of life's questions.

Frank agreed with me "in all areas but this one. Each person should come to their own conclusion without undue influence by another."

I didn't like Frank's answer. I wasn't angry; I just didn't want to conduct a comprehensive study, for I had started such a study years before and came away frustrated and without satisfaction. I originally flipped off the subject by telling a friend that "in my research, I bumped into Cleopatra one time too many."

Several years after my association with Frank, I walked into a store that was the first one I experienced that billed itself as a New Age store. I picked up a book that caught my eye. That act, unknown to me at the time, started a major project that lead to my search for answers to many questions.

What do you think? Your best answers can be found somewhere into your own investigation.

Frank told me another reincarnation story that totally blew me away, better than the Audrey Rose story, but I do not want to betray a confidence. If I can contact Frank...

Raymond De Felitta, born June 30, 1964 in New York, New York... One day Frank De Felitta brought his 11 year old son Raymond for a hairstyle. I discovered very quickly that Raymond was not a typical kid. He didn't want to talk about school or sports; rather, he preferred a person-to-person mature conversation. Nothing off-beat here, just good conversation.

For the next couple of years, Frank and Raymond would come in on a tandem appointment. Raymond became a great personal friend as we developed a compatible interest in each other's lives.

When I left my Crescent Heights location due to the center being sold and torn down, I don't recall Frank and Raymond following me. I think I became "geographically estranged," as one of my other clients phrased it. The down side of a location change is that some people will be missed. Here are two perfect examples.

Today, the Internet tells me, Raymond has become a successful screenwriter and director. No surprise here!

Angie Dickenson, born September 30, 1931, Kulm, N. Dakota... I am certainly a long-time fan of Angie. If I ever write more columns on Hollywood, she will be one of the very first people I will again ask for an interview. She is an accomplished actress and more importantly, I know from my brief encounters and mutual friend, **Matt Helreich**, that she is a wonderful person.

<u>Troy Donahue</u>, born Merle Johnson, Jr. in New York City on January 27, 1936 – d. September 2, 2001 in Santa Monica, CA. I knew Troy to be rather quiet and unassuming. I enjoyed our friendship and still count the movie, *A Summer Place* among my favorites.

<u>Joey Dorando</u>, born in New Jersey on February 24, 1932...
<u>Art Aragon</u>, boxing's original Golden Boy, was born in Belen, N.M. on November 13, 1927 – d. March 25, 2008. Joey Dorando became my very dear friend and client sometime in 1962, about a year into my career with Cosmo's. I want to emphasize that he became my friend immediately. I'm sure we played golf more than a thousand times (no exaggeration!) often with **Sam Russo** and/or my father **Paul** and/or **Bob Bash**. There is no way to estimate how many times we shared lunch or dinner together, but it was four or five times the number of golf outings. We often went to **The Friar's Club** for lunch or dinner.

Joey followed me from salon to salon as I was forced to move more often than I would have chosen. Four times when my lease came due, my landlord would try to raise my rent so exorbitantly that I was money-ahead to go through the expense of moving.

Joey told me to be sure to spell his name correctly.

As if I don't know how to spell J-O-E-Y!

Joey was a great boxer as both an amateur and professional. He quit the professional "sport" when The Mob told him to take a dive against a lousy but connected pug. And they let him retire, too, just like **Benny Garcia**. I guess it was early signs of the Mob getting soft.

Joey became a bail bondsman. Joey and Art Aragon were close friends, the reason they are here in tandem. Art, a natural, extremely funny comedian, was Ralph Trejo's client, so we saw plenty of Art over the years. Art also became a bail bondsman. Joey's business motto was "Gentlemen Prefer Bonds." Very classy, I told him. For Joey's website, go to joeydorando.com.

Art's motto was "I'll Get You Out If It Takes A Hundred Years." Boy, that's Art for you! Just Google Art Aragon.

<u>Harry Drucker</u>, born in Romania in 1907 – d. May 13, 1998 in Los Angeles, CA. When I started at Cosmo's on August 27 of 1961, the other top salons were, in no particular order, **Drucker's**, **Rothschild's** and **Sebring's**. I left Cosmo's in December of 1963 and joined **Sam Russo** where we started THE FIRST men's hairstyling salon that offered

100 percent styled cuts.

Harry heard of my move and called me, saying to call him if I wasn't happy with my decision to join Russo's. I told Harry that I would talk to him only if he was open to partnership or selling out. He jumped at partnership but said he had no intention to sell, so we made an appointment for a dinner meeting.

I went to his salon at Harry's suggestion. One of the barber's was giving a haircut to **Ronald Reagan**. I enjoyed meeting the popular actor, but who knew he would become Governor of California and *President of the United States?*

Harry and I went to **Trader Vic's** in Beverly Hills. While there, **George Raft** came to our table with a back-slap for Harry who said, "Oh hello, Georgie, say hello to my future partner, Little Joe."

When we got down to business, Harry proposed that I give him $5,000 in cash now, work for him as an employee for six months to test our compatibility, and after "...six months or so..." we would discuss partnership percentage and price. I couldn't believe my ears.

"Harry, if I was schmuck enough to accept that facockta offer, would you be willing to have such a schmuck as a partner?"

No, I didn't want any dessert or an answer, I just wanted to leave. And no, he picked up the tab, I guess. I was disappointed but not angry. I just figured that Life had a better offer waiting as I had nowhere to go but up.

So God Bless Harry Drucker; we both came out just fine.

Angelo Dundee, **born Angelo Mirena, August 30, 1921, Philadelphia, PA...** I met Angelo while I owned the **Image Hairstyling Salon** in the **Century Plaza Hotel**. Once when I was giving him a haircut, I asked if he could arrange for me to cut The Champ's hair. Angelo used a lot of words to tell me that **Muhammad Ali** had someone close to him cutting his hair and not to count on a positive response. Quite frankly, meeting The Champ was privilege enough.

Clint Eastwood, born May 31, 1930 in San Francisco, CA. I'm thrilled and privileged to say that Clint was the First Star to sit in my chair for a haircut. "What a way to start," Cosmo said! Yep, Cosmo got that right.

Jo Hymes was a highly talented lady writer who moved to Hollywood from Brooklyn. She and Clint were close friends, which is why she is mentioned here with Clint. Jo died very young. As I knew the situation, she was paid $85,000 for the story and first draft of the hit movie, *Play Misty For Me*. That was huge money for a movie script at the time, especially for a woman. Before the movie was released, she forced the studio to eliminate her name from the credits and all publicity. As Jo was my friend, I asked her if what I heard was true. She told me that the studio changed her story so much that it hardly resembled the original. I said I thought that a credit for any legit movie was a positive. She replied that they could shove it and in fact, she gave very graphic instructions. While I didn't and still don't agree, I love that Brooklyn attitude, as long as I'm not on the wrong end of it. Further proof? My wife Ginny!

Vince Edwards, **born Vincent Edward Zoino, a twin, in Brooklyn, NY on July 9, 1928 – d. March 11, 1996.**
Linda Foster, wife. I met Vince sometime in the mid '60s due to the fact that his wife Linda was my sister's best girlfriend in high school. (Grant HS in Van Nuys where **Tom Selleck** – January 29, 1945… - also graduated.) Vince was a quiet, private man and through his demeanor expressed a preference for a minimum of conversation. I found him to be polite but formal. **Linda** was the personification of a living doll, as sweet a person as she was pretty. She came to America as a child from England with her family and never fully lost her accent, thank goodness. She had a short-lived TV series but chose to be a mom. Getting accurate info on her has been tough.

Mama Cass Elliot, **born Ellen Naomi Cohen, in Baltimore, on September 19, 1941 – d. July 29, 1974…** Mama Cass graced the shop known as **Little Joe's** a few times shortly before her very untimely death. She would come in with my client, **Carol Rubinstein,** and rather take over the place. Mama was extremely open and friendly, oftentimes introducing herself to someone who was silently looking her way. She was easily one of the most friendly people I ever met.

Nanette Fabray, **born Nanette Ruby Bernadette Fabray, San Diego, CA, October 27, 1920…** The only time I had direct contact with Nanette was the time I went to CBS to give **Red Skelton** a haircut. I remember her as a very gracious lady and someone I would have loved to get to know better. Every time I saw her perform, I felt like I was watching a dear friend.

<u>Peter Falk</u>, born Peter Michael Falk, September 16, 1927.... I never had the pleasure of knowing Falk, but greatly admire his work. During the early '70s, a hair client and I took an evening script-writing course at **Hollywood High School** taught by veteran screenwriter **Bill Koenig**. Bill had been the head writer for the hit TV show, *Dragnet,* in previous years. For my project, I chose to write a script for the TV show, *Columbo*. That's when I learned how to time a show and write the script to fit a tight, specific format. That intimate contact caused me to feel a great kinship with Columbo/Falk over the years.

<u>Grampa Dominic Figer</u>, born Domenico Ficarra in Pace del Mele, Provincia de Messina, Sicily, Italy, on February 15, 1885 – d. December 11, 1949 in the Collinwood area of Cleveland, Ohio. My grandfather taught me so many of Life's Principles.

"The Golden Rule is 100% true 100% of the time. Obey that one and all the rest will be served."

He also admonished me to be NUMBER ONE in whatever I chose as a profession. I asked why number one, wasn't number five or 10 acceptable. He said that the NUMBER ONE person never got laid off. I asked him to clarify how to become a NUMBER ONE.

"If you could bring 100 bricklayers into this room," he started, "and line them up according to their ability, someone would have to be NUMBER ONE, the very best, and someone would have to be NUMBER 100, the very worst. Most people will tell you they want to be average, or normal, which means that most people are focused on being number 50, though many don't realize that fact. Some ambitious people will say they want to be in the upper 10%. That means they want to be NUMBER 10. A few people, more-ambitious, will say they want to be in the upper five percent. That means they want to be NUMBER 5. But almost nobody says they want to NUMBER ONE because they fear scrutiny, falling short and failure. Go for NUMBER ONE, Joey, there's NO COMPITISH!"

And one more: He told me to be very careful when giving my word to someone.

"Always keep your word, even if circumstances change. A person who doesn't keep his word is bankrupt. If circumstances change dramatically and you have to question your obligation, apply the Golden Rule."

One more time once. Regarding 'shortcuts.' "The only shortcut is do it right the first time." End of discussion.

Was it good advice? Works for me. Don't worry, you haven't heard the last of Grampa Dominic. He's in everything I write.

Mike Garcia, born Edward Miguel "Mike" Garcia in San Gabriel, CA on November 17, 1923 d January 13,1986; Pitcher - Cleveland Indians. Mike was my dear friend when I was a kid. As he was of Mexican-Indian decent, I asked him if he spoke Spanish. When he said 'no' I guess I had a surprised reaction. He then asked if I spoke fluent Italian and when I said no, he asked how come.

"I was born here in the USA," I answered.

"So was I, in California" he told me.

He brought me to several Cleveland Indians games over about a two year period. After one game, I was in the locker room waiting for Mike to dress so we could go home. The Indians had lost that afternoon to the mighty Yankees. Manager/shortstop **Lou Boudreau** came storming in and started shouting for the guys to gather 'round. He then chewed them out using the vocabulary of a drunken sailor. When he suddenly noticed me, he glared at Mike and said, "Why didn't you tell me Joey was here?" He didn't wait for an answer, just shot me a look and said, "Sorry, kid," and said to the team, "Pick it up tomorrow!"

I remember thinking, 'Wow, *Lou Boudreau* knows my name!'

When the movie came out named *The Kid From Cleveland*, I thought Hollywood missed a good bet as they should have told MY story, cuz mine was a lot better. I haven't changed my mind and my gratitude for Mike's friendship has grown over time.

Alan Garfield, born Alan Goorwitz in Newark, NJ on November 22, 1939... Alan was my client for about 30 years and my friend much longer. I was invited to his 50th Birthday Party held in a lovely restaurant for a select group of about 50 friends. When 'saying a few words' that evening, he expressed his love for those present by telling a story on each of us and how we individually fit into his life. Like I told him, I will copy that pattern one day, the most sincere form of compliment. Alan has more talent in his little finger than most people have in their entire being. As I told him, I'd love to do a scene in a movie with him.

<u>Judy Garland</u>, born Francis Ethel Gumm in Grand Rapids, MN on June 10,1922 – d. June 22, 1969 in Chelsea, London, England, UK.

<u>Sid Luft</u>, born 1916 – d. September 15, 2005.

Sid became my client in the early 60s when I was working for Cosmo and followed me to Russo's. Many times he would bring son **Joey** and/or daughter **Lorna** when he came in for his appointment.

On several occasions I had the opportunity to talk to Judy on the phone. She was always sweet and complementary, telling me how gorgeous I always made "my Sidney." Wouldn't you think that somewhere along the way I would have asked for an autographed picture? Duhhh!

One more thing. I have always admired and loved Judy Garland, one of the Very Greatest to grace Hollywood, All-Time. She was so abundantly TALENTED, loving and lovable.

Her movie, *Wizard of OZ,* is my All-Time Favorite just a half-blip off my All-Time Number One Favorite, *It's a Wonderful Life*. Both flicks score at the pinnacle with me due to the humongous life-lessons in each.

In *Wizard*, the key scene for me is Judy's answer to the question: "What did you learn from your journey to Oz?"

Of all she said in that short speech, to paraphrase, "…and whatever you really want out of Life can usually be found right in your own back yard."

Blows me away as the concept became a guidepost for me.

<u>Errol Garner</u>, born Erroll Louis Garner in Pittsburgh, PA on June 15, 1921 – d. January 1, 1977. When I met the great musician in **Sherry's** a few doors from **Cosmo's**, we finished our drink and had another as he kibitzed with Sam Keston and me. We probably spent the long side of an hour together but we shared a lifetime's worth. We agreed to meet again on his next trip to Hollywood, but somehow, it never happened. Shucks!

<u>John Marc Gentri</u>. I've called Johnny Gentri my twin for at least a thousand reasons and maybe a thousand times just in this book alone. From our introduction we had an immediate bond, far greater than anything before or since. From the first time we sat down to write, we discovered that our minds melded into one. We constantly spurred each others creativity. His lovely wife Joannie was amazed at our instant rapport and immediately blended with us. Over the years, Johnny pulled me in on several of his assignments.

In one major project, we were to develop a new TV comedy series written especially for an established male comedy star. Two other writers were given the same challenging assignment, with the writer of the winning concept to be the head writer(s) for the new TV series.

We decided to write a half-hour sitcom with two male comedy leads and we proposed the co-star to be **Don Knotts**, who was then on *The Andy Griffith Show* portraying **Barney Fife**. Our story was about a nutty professor and his know-it-all-from-books next door neighbor (Don) who was the town (Buona Fortuna, California) Librarian. Half-way through the Development Time, the network called a halt, saying "keep what you have as a spec property." They were fed up with the unidentified Big Star and from that day forward, he was very rarely seen.

Johnny took the mostly completed script and literally threw it in the trash can.

"John, what are you doing?!?"

"You want it? It's yours."

"But John, it's a great concept. It's the best we've ever done."

"Sure. Two male comedic leads. Which two comic-stars would you cast in it? And what dimwit would dare pitch it to which network?"

Sometime later, Johnny took Joannie and the kids back to his family's home in Greenwich, Connecticut. About two years after I bought Cosmo's, my receptionist called me to the phone. I heard a young voice say, "Uncle Joe, my Dad just died." It was Johnny's teenage son, John.

"Devastating" is an inadequate word here, they all are, but for most people, no further attempt at explaining is necessary. Or possible.

He is my twin and I'm so blessed.

Betty Grable, born Elizabeth Ruth Grable, St. Louis, Mo., December 18, 1916 – d. July 2, 1973, Santa Monica, CA.

Harry James, born Harry Hagg James in Albany, GA March 15, 1916 – d. July 5, 1983 in Las Vegas, NV. The first time I went to Las Vegas with my parents in the early 60s, my father wanted to look up a boyhood friend known as **Peanuts** who worked at the **Desert Inn**. My father reached Peanuts initially by telephone and arraigned for us to meet him after work in the lounge at 2 a.m.

When we arrived the lounge was dark, but in less than a minute a bartender appeared and said Peanuts would be along shortly. The bartender seated us at a large horseshoe shaped booth and poured us all a drink.

As we were about to toast, Peanuts came through the door with a loud "Hello, Paulie!" The two embraced and mentioned that it had been at least 20 years since they were together. Peanuts was very friendly and had plenty to say about his experiences working in Las Vegas.

At one point Peanuts raised his hand and beckoned someone from behind me to come join our table. It was **Betty Grable** and **Harry James!**

Harry pulled up a chair and straddled it while Betty slid into the bench-seat beside me. They were curious about us like we were the big stars, letting us know that Peanuts had briefed them about the relationship that began in childhood.

If all that sounds incredible, you don't know the half of what I felt. It was truly a night to remember, just to wrap with an understatement.

Art Graham, born in New Jersey in 1923 – d. October 24, 2001 in Hollywood, CA. He fronted the Art Graham Trio when not working solo. Art was trained from his youth as a classical pianist therefore giving him a polished style especially when playing jazz numbers. Art was an entertainment fixture at **Sneaky Pete's**, a fine restaurant/nightclub on the **Sunset Strip** for at least 10 years, coming in contact with all of Hollywood's Royalty including regulars **Johnnie Carson** and **Ed McMahon**. The Art Graham Trio provided the music for the TV show I wrote called *Boutique*.

Gary Graham, born Gary Rand Graham, June 7, 1950, Long Beach, CA... I first met Gary in the late '70s before his star had risen very high in the Hollywood Sky. I've always enjoyed the friendship we share and I'm pleased to see that his talents are widely appreciated. He wrote a book called *Acting & Other Flying Lessons.* I enjoyed it; so might you.

Coleen Gray, born Doris Jensen, October 23, 1922, Staplehurst, NE... Coleen has a very impressive list of movie credits, having starred opposite John Wayne, John Payne and too many to list here. Try Google. I met Coleen in the mid '70s and was surprised at her classic beauty and polite shyness. I've seen her among people she does not know and in spite of her reserve, she is very friendly and warm. I feel very privileged to call her and husband Fritz my friends all these years. Her picture hangs prominently in my private cutting room in my hair salon.

Harry Guardino and **Eddie Guardino**. **Harry, born Brooklyn, NY, December 23, 1925 – d. July 17, 1995 in Palm Springs, CA.** Of the four Guardinos, I knew Harry and Eddie best. Harry was the senior of the two and achieved a definite measure of Stardom. I don't believe Eddie ever did very much of note as an actor. They both were friends and qualified as part of the group of actors known as "Schwab's Cowboys."

Huntz Hall, born Henry Richard Hall, NY City, August 15, 1919 – d. January 30, 1999. He was the 14th of 16 children and a featured member of **The Bowery Boys** with **Leo Gorcey**. One day my father introduced him to me in **Schwab's**. Like so many others, he was a quiet man off the set. I really got a kick greeting him over the years and having him respond warmly, for he was an idol from my youth.

Mickey Hargitay, born January 6, 1926, Budapest, Hungary – d. September 14, 2006 Los Angeles) Zolton Hargitay/Mariska Hargitay (Zolton born 1960; Mariska born 1964. I always liked Mickey and met Zolton as a child. I'm not sure if I ever met Mariska, but I'd love to so I could compliment her as a fine actress and tell her, as many have I'm sure, that her Mom was a wonderful, thoughtful person.

Pat Harrington, Jr., born in New York City, NY on August 13, 1929.... I met Pat through the TV show called *Boutique* that I co-wrote with **Johnny Gentri**. I have had casual contact with Pat over the years. I would really like to work with him some day.

Mariette Hartley, born Mary Loretta Hartley, Weston, CT... She was a featured guest on the *Boutique* TV show. While I did not get to know her as well as I would have liked, I found her to be friendly and open.

Paul Harvey, born Paul Harvey Aurandt in Tulsa, OK in 1918 – d. February 28, 2009 in Phoenix, AZ and buried in Chicago, IL. *Stand by for TRI-BUTE!*

Ask me when I first heard of Paul Harvey and I'll ask when you first heard of Santa Claus. He was as good, proud and patriotic an American as my Grampa Dominic. There was another guy cut from the same cloth known as sportscaster **Bill Stern** who I'd like to recognize here. **Walter Winchell**, oft-times called WashyerWindshield in my old neighborhood, was 'up there' if not equal to Paul and Bill.

PAGE TWO. But really, my fellow Americans, like Santa, there really was only one Paul Harvey, and now we gotta make it on our own without him. OH, WHOA is us! He would only advertise a product we could count on and believe in with a Money-Back-Guarantee by Paul Harvey, Himself. What can we buy – fearlessly – now? And tell me, who will hold the politicians to task? Who can we count on to report the Unwashed Truth? Who will tell a story, a rather ordinary story, in such an extraordinary way that the two minute vignette will make our heart jump? Maybe even cause our eyes to spring a leak on occasion, too.

PAGE THREE. Twenty-five Million People Per Week of us are hung out to dry – FOREVER! NO ONE has so far been able to stand up to Paul Harvey's level, not even his son, but please don't blame the boy, as the best of the rest in the business fall flat on their collective faces trying to tell it Paul Harvey's Way. Someone ought to call **Casey Kasem**, the only positive possibility in my mind.

PAGE FOUR. Sometime in the 1980s, some minor moguls wanted me to do a marketing job for them regarding their eight month new Mini-storage facility, but they didn't want to pay very much. Through some bantering – haggling? – I found they wouldn't agree to cough up $3000 to begin a job worth more than ten times as much. So I proposed that they pay me a commission based on number of units leased for a percentage scale I allowed them to create. Well, they were happy and I was ecstatic. Gimmie a percentage <u>ANY</u> <u>DAY</u>. Then I got lucky, according to Losers, Inc. See, a loser includes everyone who believes in the concept of LUCK. Rhymes with another nasty word. Anyhow, I discovered that I could get exclusive sponsorship rights to *Paul Harvey's Rest of the Story,* the five minute, million-year-old award-winning radio program. In six short months, tons of leases were signed and the Big Shot discovered that he paid me a total of $41,000.00! That's FOURTY-ONE-THOUSAND DOLLARS. Ha – HA!

Only now, dear friends, you know - The REEEST Of The Story. Good DAY!

Peter Haskell, born Peter Abraham Haskell in Boston, Mass. on October 15, 1934... Peter was **Sam Russo's** client in the '60s when we were all at the beginning of our careers. Peter is very friendly and outgoing and appreciates the people in his life. I love bumping into him but it only happens once in several blue moons.

Matt Helreich, former Personal Manager of Michael Landon, Charo, Hogie Carmichael, Betty Grable, Telly Savalas, Fabian, Natalie Wood, Jayne Mansfield, Robert Mitchum, Cher and oh, so many more. Matt befriended my father and me during our earliest days in Hollywood. He is a walking encyclopedia on events, places and especially the people of show business. Matt has been a career-long friend and client.

Matt created the "Thursday Evening Dinners," an informal gathering of some of the biggest names in Show Business along with people who would never see either side of a camera in action. Often, Hollywood personality **Sid Silver** would be co-host. Each dinner could have made a great column. Matt was my client for several years, right up until I moved to Florida. We keep in touch by phone and get together whenever I visit LA.

Michael Shawn Herron, born December 18, 1972... Mike is my nephew, the third of my sister's four sons. He put himself through Cal-State University, Chico where he majored in Communication with an emphasis in Film Production. Mike's wife, Corinne, gave birth to twins, Brooklynn and Breyden, on December 11, 2008.

Mike started in Show Biz as a Production Assistant in 1996. Read "Gofer" and understand that being a PA is a great entry level for a young person, especially if he/she wants to be on the business side of the camera.

Moving up, in 1999 Mike served as actor **Treat Williams'** assistant during filming of the movie, *The Deep End of the Ocean.*

Moving up again, in 2000/1, Mike became a Digital Video Assist Operator and worked on the movie, *Ready to Rumble.* Mike attaches his equipment to the lens of the camera and records the action exactly as seen through the lens. When the Director says "cut," he can immediately view the just-shot scene. The process saves a production a ton of money.

Along the way, Mike worked with director **Ron Howard** on the 2003 movie, *The Missing* and with director **David Fincher** on the movie,

Fight Club. I visited the set of *Fight Club* and enjoyed watching Mike work. Director Fincher was nominated for the 2008 Academy Award for *The Curious Case of Benjamin Buttons.*

Mike also worked on *The Prestige* with director **Christopher Nolan**, who also directed the last two *Batman* movies. I read where *The Dark Knight* broke $1 billion in revenue. Heath, we hardly knew ya, but oh boy, we will remember you forever!

The last movie Mike worked in 2008 was *Drag Me to Hell*, directed by **Sam Raini**, who also directed all three *Spiderman* movies and is geared up for *Spiderman 4* in February, 2010, with Mike as the Digital Video Assist Operator.

I wouldn't be a bit surprised if Mike turned out to be a great director on his own one day. To follow Mike's progress through the industry, go to **IMDb** and type in Michael Herron.

Charlton Heston, born John Charles Carter, October 4, 1923, Evanston, Ill; - d. April 6, 2008. His name is a combination of his mother's maiden name, Charlton; and his step-father's name, Chester Heston.

I had the privilege of sharing a very special incident with one of Hollywood's most recognized international Stars. **Johnny Gentri** was to produce and write a telethon to raise money for the Pasadena Playhouse. He brought me on as co-writer and stage manager. As happened with *Boutique*, producing occupied the bulk of Johnny's time, leaving me rather solely responsible for putting the show in script form.

Our host was **Victor Jory**, always a highly respected actor in Hollywood and a many years member of the **Pasadena Playhouse**. Movie buffs remember many of Jory's roles and especially that he portrayed the father of **Helen Keller** in the movie, *The Miracle Worker*.

Probably the most famous name on the Celebrity Guest List for the telethon was that of **Charlton Heston**. I was on stage cueing actors to take their place on camera along side Jory to make their pitch for the cause when word permeated the set that the great Heston had just entered the Green Room.

I had a four-line speech especially written for Heston in the hopes he would show up and participate. I truly felt a rush when introduced to him as the writer of the show. I had written the speech on a strip of paper. As I was handing it to Heston, I said, "Mr. Heston, I wrote this for you…"

He interrupted me and said, "Call me Chuck and I'll call you Joe." He smiled, took the paper from me and quickly read through it before putting it in his pocket.

Other actors entered the Green Room and caught Heston's attention. While performing my tasks, I managed to keep an eye on my new friend, Chuck. At one point he went over to a chair, sat down and again quickly read the paper that he had put in his pocket. When it was his time, he took center stage and said my words *verbatim* as though he made them up on the spot! It was the most impressive act of memorizing and delivery I have ever been privileged to witness.

Later, saying goodnight, he complimented me and added that I used words in the appeal that I wrote for him that he would have used himself. I had nailed him and I was delighted.

Moe Howard, born Moses Harry Howard in Brownsville, Brooklyn, NY on June 19, 1897 – d. May 4, 1975 in Los Angeles, CA. When I met Moe Howard that first time at **Benny Garcia's El Dorado Hair Salon**, my knees didn't shake, but they should have. I walked **Sergio Mendez** to his car that day with the two of us commenting on the moment, for Sergio was as thrilled as I to meet one of the great icons of comedy. For the next year it was my privilege to have many friendly conversations with Moe. I really got a kick out of our friendship.

Howard Hughes, born on December 24, 1905 – d. April 5, 1976. For what should be obvious reasons, here's an unpublished tid-bit. Many of my best friends and clients will be surprised or even shocked to read this along with people I may never meet.

About six months after buying **Cosmo's Hair Styling Salon** in 1973, I changed the name to **Little Joe's**. I found no need to keep the place open seven days a week as Cosmo always did, so our work-week became Tuesday through Saturday.

I developed the habit of going to the salon on Mondays to do the books and monitor a cleaning crew. Or *be* the cleaning crew. One of those Mondays when I entered from the back door, I did not lock it behind me as per usual. About five minutes later, a man entered. I couldn't believe my eyes. It was **Howard Hughes**.

He greeted me by name and in a very friendly tone of voice. He said he had wanted me to cut his hair "for a long time." When I told him he lucked out, that I was really not open for business, he said, "Yes I know, that's why I'm here now."

I told him that I preferred to cut freshly washed and conditioned hair. He said, "Sure, let's get to it." Shock!

Whenever I started to ask something about himself, he would rather fluff it off and ask me about myself, my career, my family. He obviously knew pertinent facts about me. I don't remember exactly how much he paid me, but I remember that he was very generous.

The next day I swore **Nunzio Tringali** to confidentiality and told him of cutting Hughes' hair. Nunzio was incredulous. He raised several arguments against such potential. I told Nunzio I agreed with his arguments.

Maybe two months later, Hughes again came to my salon, this time on a regular work day and accompanied by two young men. Nunzio was flabbergasted and said he wouldn't have believed it if he hadn't seen it himself. My dad, **Gene Turner** and **Ludwig Fengel** also recognized Hughes and were equally shocked. I never even thought about a camera.

I'd love to end this segment by telling you that Howard remembered me in his will, but if he did, I'm still waiting for his lawyers to call.

James Hutton, born Dana James Hutton in Binghamton, NY, May 31, 1934 – d. June 2, 1979.

Timothy Hutton, born Timothy Tarquin Hutton in Malibu, CA on August 16, 1960... Best I recall, Actor Jimmy Hutton was a client of Cosmo's from my earliest employment until his all-too-early passing. I really enjoyed his friendly visits over the two decades. There were times when son, Tim, would accompany his father.

One time in particular, shortly after Tim appeared prominently on the Silver Screen, he came into my salon as his father was completing his haircut. It was the end of the workday and I was doing my bookkeeping when Jimmy called out to me and apologized for keeping me late. I assured him that I had work to do and if he and his son wanted to continue their conversation, they were welcome to do so. I guess that sitting there talking privately was more desirable than going to **Schwab's** or someplace else. I was very happy to offer my hospitality.

Norman Jewison, born Norman Frederick Jewison in Toronto, Canada on July 21, 1926... I had the privilege of cutting the great director's hair for a while in the early '80s until he went on an extended trip to Europe. I really liked him; enjoyed his visits.

Arte Johnson, born **Arthur Stanton Eric Johnson in Benton Harbor, MI on January 20, 1934**... For several years, Arte was a client of **Bernie Roberts**, first at the ICM Building and again at **Beverly Hills Hair Design**, the place I owned in partnership with Sam and Theresa Russo. When Bernie retired, Arte became my client and stayed with me until I moved to Florida.

He and wife, Gisela, have sent us postcards from all around the world, some funny as %$#@$#. We have maintained our friendship nicely-nicely, thank you.

Victor Jory, born in **Dawson City, Yukon Territory, Canada on November 23, 1902 – d. February 12, 1982 in Santa Monica, CA**. Continuing the story about the benefit for the **Pasadena Playhouse**, Victor Jory was our host. With the great lineup of Hollywood Stars, we knew it would take someone strong to be our Host and Master of Ceremonies. We made an excellent choice.

Hours into the show, fatigue became evident. Several members of the crew noted that Jory was tiring and his call for donations was strained, but nobody wanted to approach the great actor to correct his delivery. I had developed a good rapport with him, I felt, so I volunteered to carry the message.

I said something like, "Mr. Jory, you're doing such a wonderful job here and the pledges are rolling in, but some of us noticed that perhaps the lights are bothering your eyes, uh..." He put his hand on my forearm and said, "Thank you, son, I appreciate your kindness toward me."

He then went back on camera totally refreshed with a pleasant countenance. There was no need to direct him further.

Alex Karras, born in **Gary, Indiana on July 15, 1935**... Alex was my client in the '70s when I owned **Little Joe's** (formerly **Cosmo's**). He was a killer in the **NFL** and a Teddy Bear in Hollywood. Football was my favorite team sport to play before wrestling came along, but devoted interest in wrestling ended with college. I've always loved watching college football and the pros on TV, so I always looked forward to Alex's visits. Great guy; down to earth.

Casey Kasem, born **Kemal Amen Kasem in Detroit, MI on April 27, 1932**...

Jean Kasem, born **Jean Thompson in 1954 in Portsmouth, NH, married Casey in 1980**. When I met Casey, I had been in the hair business about three years and was working with Sam Russo at his shop on Santa Monica Boulevard.

Casey already had worked as a DJ in his hometown of Detroit, then moved on to Cleveland, then to New York and was making his name in Los Angeles as a DJ at **KRLA Radio**. Hands down, I have had Casey in my chair more than any other two – maybe any three – other people combined, as we'd get together weekly and more. Most usually we met at my salon(s) but we'd often meet at a Studio or Casey's home.

When all of my three kids were born, Casey did a Dedication on his *Casey's Top Forty Countdown* program. I've always had great appreciation for his thoughtfulness. Casey had three kids before he and Jean were married in 1980.

Jean is a fine actress in her own right, especially as a comedian. She and Casey have a miracle baby named **Liberty** who today is approaching adulthood. So to say Casey and I have been through a lot together is another of those confounding understatements.

Casey and Jean have been known for hosting several of Hollywood's most Star-Studded and Glamorous Holiday Parties of all time. Hollywood's brightest VIPs came by Invitation Only and security was ultra tight. One year, when I was in the reception/security-check line, I found myself behind **Sid Caesar** and in front of **Caesar Romero**. All up and down that line were other recognizable people from the entertainment world. Someone made a crack about me being Little Caesar and the three of us representing the Royalty of the party. The two Caesars and I laughed with the rest of them but right now I can't figure out what was so funny. Guess y'hadda be there, and remember it verbatim.

A major feature of the Kasem's parties is that they served only Vegan food. Make that DELICIOUS Vegan food. And, EVERYBODY in Hollywood wanted to be invited.

If I were to tell you about each party they threw, the only thing that would change would be the celebrities in front and behind me in the reception line.

Casey is still on over 500 radio stations across the country with a couple of different recorded programs from years past. Ginny and I get to hear him every Sunday morning doing Top 40 Countdowns from various years. Casey's son, **Mike Kasem**, is the host of the show.

On July 4, 2009, (daughter Liberty's birth date) Casey formally announced his retirement from Show Biz.

There is plenty more that could be said about my relationship with Casey, but in truth, it would take a separate book. With all due respect to everyone else, Casey is my all-time favorite celebrity client and friend.

Scott Kaufer. Early in my career, my dear friend, producer **Paul Leavitt,** referred his good friend, **Matt Kaufer,** to me. Matt is extremely easy to like as he has a quiet and friendly personality. He mentioned that he'd like to bring his son in for a "decent haircut." He made the comment several times over maybe a year.

One day a young kid came in and sat where he could watch me work. No, he didn't want a haircut, nor did he want to go to the waiting area; could he just watch?

I finished one client and then another. The young man approached me.

"You almost lost me with that first guy, you cut his hair so short. On the second guy, you left him with full hair. That was much better."

"I cut both guys according to how they want to wear their hair, not necessarily how I wanted it. I follow what each client wants."

"So if I told you to take off only a half inch all around, you'd do that? Show me a half inch with your fingers."

That's how I met **Scott Kaufer.** He wanted a haircut right then, but I had appointments, so I booked him for another time.

"Are you getting a haircut for a school play?"

"No, I'm making my Bar Mitzvah and I promised my mother I'd get a haircut, but I never said how much I'd have cut."

Some noive, and only thirteen.

Scott was my client for all those years until I moved to Southwest Florida. I can't count the Dodger games we attended. He'd often call and offer his tickets when he had a conflicting event.

Scott became a Writer/Producer and has developed TV Sitcoms. **Casey Kasem** told Scott that I have a story that should be a movie, so Scott encouraged me to write the story I call *Someday* as a script.

Later, encouraged by **Milt Rosen**, I wrote the story as a novel. I've had two unacceptable offers on the script and have not attempted to publish the book, yet.

Remember the TV Series, *Murphy Brown*? Yep, thank Scott. Y'like *Boston Legal*? Scott was Executive Producer the first two years. He's liable to announce another new series any day now, but I have to stop tootin' his horn. Not his style.

On a recent visit to LA, Scott, Sam Russo and I went to dinner and a Dodger game together. Long-term friends are special, indeed.

Josh King. Josh was a DJ at various stations in and around Los Angeles from when I first met him in the early 60s through the 80s. Josh was a deep thinker and well read. Josh introduced me to **Edgar Cayce** through the book, *There is a River*. I am eternally grateful to my friend Josh.

Burt Lancaster, born Burton Stephen Lancaster in New York, NY on November 2, 1913 – d. October 20, 1994 Los Angeles, CA. There was a time in the very early '60s when I "apprenticed" makeup under the watchful eye of **Claude Thompson**, Head of Makeup, Worldwide, located at NBC in Burbank. My friend and client, **Paul Leavitt**, owned **The Player's Ring** on Santa Monica Boulevard just east of La Cienega Boulevard. The Ring was arguably Hollywood's most prestigious live theater, laid out in the round. During one production, I was doing makeup for the show. On opening night just before curtain, the word spread that **Burt Lancaster** was in the House. After the performance, he came back to meet cast and crew. A couple of years earlier, I was up for a part in a movie that starred Lancaster. I don't know if he ever put the two incidences together, but I sure did.

Don Lane, born Morton Donald Isaacson in New York City, NY on November 13, 1933... I knew Don as a fun-loving, outgoing naturally funny person. One day in the early '60s he came into **Cosmo's** for a haircut and told me he had just come from lunch with his agent who had booked him for several stand-up-comic gigs in Australia. Don said he had casually mentioned to his agent at a previous meeting that he would like to go to Australia "sometime."

Don said he protested to his agent that he was awaiting word on a couple movies and TV shows, so the timing for going to Australia seemed awkward. His agent told Don that he hoped calls would come in for Don to appear in USA movies and TV shows during Don's absence as the price for Don's future appearances would increase.

Instead of returning to the USA after a month, Don stayed on and became *the Johnny Carson of Australia!* Amazing where and how Life takes us sometimes, isn't it?

Paul Leavitt, d. 1968. Paul was one of my earliest clients and a dear friend who was with me during my first eight years – every other Friday morning at 9:00 am, with a manicure. He introduced me to fishing in the Pacific Ocean as we enjoyed several outings together, catching sea bass and sheep's-head, a red-n-black fish indigenous to the Pacific.

Paul was going to take me to Europe as the head writer of his next TV series after *Tarzan* when his untimely death occurred. Maybe some day I'll tell that whole story, but right now I just want to say that I've missed his friendship. He serves as a great example for those people who leave an indelible impression that lasts forever.

Francis Lederer, born Frantisek Lederer in Czechoslovakia on November 6, 1899 - d. May 25, 2000. Francis was a European stage actor who came to America to perform on Broadway around 1932. His talents were recognized by Hollywood where he had starring roles in the early days of talkies. I was privileged to become acquainted with him when he was a guest on our TV Show called *Boutique*.

Ruta Lee, born Ruta Mary Kilmonis in Montreal, Quebec, Canada on May 30, 1936... I became acquainted with this movie and TV Actress when she was a guest on *Boutique*. She did our show a major favor by flying back to L.A. from Palm Springs in a private plane to fill in for another guest who had an emergency health problem. For many years, Ruta has been very active with **The Thalians**, (with **Debbie Reynolds**) a charitable organization supported by numerous Hollywood celebrities.

Jack Lemmon, born in an elevator in Boston, Ma, as John Uhler Lemmon III on February 8, 1925 – d. June 27, 2001. I met Jack through my wife, Ginny. She had a business relationship with Jack and wife **Felicia Farr** that became quite friendly.

One time when Ginny and I were delivering the shooting script called *Someday* to **The William Morris Agency**, Ginny suggested that we go next door and drop in on Jack Lemmon and his partner, **Connie McCauley**. I asked Ginny if we dare drop in and she said no problem, she had done it many times.

Both Jack and Connie greeted Ginny with warm hugs. When Ginny introduced me as her fiancé, a lot of that warmth was directed my way, hugs included. I was really blown away.

When Jack and Connie found out that we were delivering my script to William Morris, Jack asked if he might be able to read the script. I of course said yes and quickly told him that there was no part in the story for a star of his magnitude, unless he wanted to play one of the female nurses.

Later, when the script was returned to me, the note from Jack and Connie said he'd pass on the role of the nurse as his legs were not in great shape. He also said that from that point forward he wanted to read everything written by me from that time forward.

Can there be a better compliment? No, not this lifetime.

Tommy Leonetti, born Nicola Tomaso Leonetti in Bergen, NJ on September 10, 1929 – d. September 15, 1979 in Houston, TX. Tommy was a singer, composer and performer who I first met when he was featured as a guest on *Boutique*. He had plenty of talent, enough to become a major star. Tommy later became my friend and then, my hair client.

His life was cut short, if I may.

Buddy Lester, born January 16, 1917 – d October 4, 2002.
Jerry Lester, born in Chicago IL, 1911 – d. March 23, 1995 Miami, FL. The Lester brothers were both very popular comics who were with me as clients on and off throughout the 1960s and '70s. They were always a lot of fun and very friendly with everyone.

Greg Lewis, born somewhere in Chicago sometime in the 1930s... and still going strong, last I heard. We have been friends since the 60s and like other true friends, years apart are bridged in less than a twinkling when next we meet. I also cut wife Roberta's hair, the boys and Anastasia's hair and a host of other family members.

They lived on Stanwell Street in Chatsworth when I lived on Minniehaha in Granada Hills. (For a couple of years, John Elway was the QB at GHHS, but that's another story.)

Hey, I just took another look and found Greg's website. I sent an email but it came back. Maybe it's his latest joke but I don't get it. Somebody find out and get back to me on that, please.

Joe E. Lewis, born Joseph Klewan in New York City, NY on January 12, 1902 – d. June 4, 1971 in New York City, NY. We asked if we could meet Joe E. after we had our time with Sinatra at the Sands that night and were told he was "sleeping it off" and that he'd probably walk the casino floor "in a couple of hours or so." I remember thinking that his timing on stage was impeccable. In a couple hours or so, we were all fast asleep, so we never got to meet him. @#$%!

Jerry Lewis, born Joseph Levitch in Newark, NJ on March 16, 1926. I met Jerry sometime in the early 60s at a bowling alley in the Granada Hills area. He was there to watch a team he sponsored as they played in their league. He was very friendly and approachable and we had a brief but very friendly chat. There are different stories, both positive and negative, about meeting Jerry in public. I think that sometimes fans forget that actors – big stars too – are people first. We all go through nice times and rough times, so a star's reaction can be as different as someone whose never seen the inside of a studio.

Louie Lomax, born in Valdosta, GA on August 16, 1922 – d. July 30, 1970. I saw several of Louie's TV shows, some from backstage, and I always found him to be friendly, courteous and thoughtful when dealing with people, even those he challenged. He treated me great, as though I was a star.

Eddie Maghetto. Eddie was one of the most talented and suave hairstylists (also the <u>First</u>) I ever knew. He came to Cosmo's about six months after Cosmo hired me. Shoulda been a column but I cover the big splashy story very completely in my as-yet unpublished book that I call *Someday*.

Eddie demonstrated the technique of hairstyling for the assembled arms-folded-across-chest-and-face-scrunched staff. Except for me as I was fascinated. Some on the staff called me "naïve" but not for long.

Eddie worked in an expensive suit, tie and long-sleeve shirt with flashy cufflinks, even shampooing his client without rolling up his sleeves or getting them wet. He then cut the hair wet and applied Jeris Tonic and used a huge pair of Filipino Shears. He used a hand-held Oster blower to dry the hair when he was finished with the haircut. (Another first as I had never seen a hand-held hairdryer.)

All that he demonstrated was foreign to the staff, including me, and contrary to methodologies taught in both barber AND beauty schools of that era.

Eddie had recently moved from San Francisco to L.A. He told us he had flown to New York and paid a stylist $2,000 for a one week experience to learn the hairstyling technique. (A new car, like a loaded Chevy or Ford, could be had for about $2000!) The New York stylist had previously flown to Paris and paid someone $1,000 to learn the technique.

Privately, Eddie offered to teach me for free. Why?!? He said I had the best reputation of all the people at Cosmo's and he needed someone (me) who could take his overflow as he expected to be too busy to accommodate all who would want his type Style Cut.

At first, I thought Eddie was blowing smoke at me. I rated myself a babe compared to everyone on Cosmo's staff. And take his overflow? Babe or not, I had never looked for someone's overflow. I was building my own following nicely, thank you. However, I loved Eddie's RESULT and if he was willing to teach me – especially FOR FREE! – well, I'm no fool. I jumped in with both feet.

If Eddie scratched his nose, I wanted to know why. Also, I had a distinct advantage of adding the Sicilian Razor Technique. I offered to teach Eddie the razor, but after giving him a demo, he refused, saying I had a special God-given talent that he could never learn.

At first, again, I thought more smoke. In time, I learned that he NEVER blew smoke at me.

I am eternally grateful to Eddie Maghetto for his friendship and all he taught me. Now THERE is an understatement to chisel in stone. Make that Black Italian Marble.

Lee Majors, born Harvey Lee Yeary on April 23, 1939 in Wyandotte, MI... Lee impressed me – and my then 12 or 13 year old daughter Trina – as warm, friendly and sincere. I believe the stories of his coolness towards visitors on the set of *Six Million Dollar Man* has quite a bit to do with maintaining character with as few invited distractions as possible. Many actors do not want to be involved in frivolous conversation on the set especially, as every reasonable person should understand.

Karl Malden, born Mladen Sekulovich in Chicago, IL on March 22,1912 – d. July, 2009. Meeting the *Streets of San Francisco* star was a pleasure almost beyond expression. He made me feel like he was sincerely looking forward to meeting me and you know what? Maybe he was. The man impressed me as genuine. As I've said many times, the biggest stars are often among the most gracious people one could ever hope to meet. Here's a perfect example.

Jayne Mansfield, born Vera Jayne Palmer in Bryn Mar, PA on April 19, 1933 – d. June 29, 1967 in Slidell, LA. I really liked Jayne, for those who like understatements. She was always very sweet and friendly with me, going out of her way to make me feel special. Our sincere friendship will last my lifetime.

Rocky Marciano, born Rocco Francis Marchegiano in Brockton, MA on September 1, 1923 – d. August 31, 1969; plane crash. The Original **Rocky** and **Andy Granatelli** were best of friends and business associates, which is why Andy is following after this spot where I'm highlighting the Brockton Blockbuster, the ONLY Undefeated Champ in Boxing History whose record is forever 49 – 0!

Do what you have to so you can view one of Rocky and Andy's STP commercials. Talk about priceless!

When I was 16, I worked for **Foodtown**, a grocery chain with a store in Mayfield Heights, my neighborhood during the last seven years that we lived in Ohio. One of the regular customers there was a man named Mr. Napoli. He would come in every Friday, take two wire basket-carts and go pushing and pulling through the store. He always wanted the same cashier and me to pack his groceries and then be his carryout. Just before the cashier would hit the register's total button, Mr. Napoli would give her a figure that included tax. Ninety-nine percent of the time he got it right to the penny. On the few occasions where the total was off, they'd go through the whole list again and he was almost always proved correct.

One day Mr. Napoli had an especially large order. He very excitedly told me that the Heavyweight Champ, the great **Rocky Marciano**, would be visiting his home. Mr. Napoli and Rocky were in the Army together and became *Compare* as Rocky was Godfather to Mr. Napoli's son.

"You wanna meet the Champ?" Really, what a silly question!

I waited by the phone all day Sunday. I wouldn't do anything that would take me out of earshot of that phone for the call that never came.

The next day Mr. Napoli showed up at **Foodtown** and was very apologetic. No, he hadn't forgotten, it's just that there was so much business going on that the right time never came. But he offered me the next best thing, an 8 x 10 glossy of Rocky throwing the knockout punch on **Jersey Joe Wolcott** in the 13th round on September 23, 1952, making Rocky the Heavyweight Champ of the World! The ballpoint pen inscription reads, *"To Joey Micale, Best Always, Rocky Marciano."*

What do you think that photo is worth? No, it ain't for sale.

Andy Granatelli, born Anthony "Andy" Granatelli on March 18, 1923… I met Andy when I owned the **Image Hair Salon** at the **Century Plaza Hotel** (1968 – 1973). Andy was a client of one of my hairstylists and a most pleasant person who was polite to everyone.

One time when he was paying his bill, he noted two hand-held hair dryers, one more powerful – and more expensive - than the other. He asked me to explain the difference.

I told him, "Andy, you'll FEEEEL the difference," a take-off on his popular commercial for STP, the oil additive. Everyone got a good laugh; especially Andy's Marketing chief who was with him that day.

If you're under 30, ask someone over 50.

Dean Martin, born Dino Paul Crocetti in Stubenville, Ohio on June 17, 1917 – d. December 25, 1995 in Beverly Hills, CA. One time in particular, I was having dinner in an Italian restaurant in Beverly Hills. The owner, Tony, was a many-years client of my Compare, **Sam Russo**. The next time Tony came in for a haircut, he let us know that Dean wanted to know about me as the two of us ran into each other more than occasionally. Over the years I felt strongly that I could have easily approached Dean, but as a member of the Hollywood community, I chose to respect his privacy. I could say likewise for others who I never got to meet directly. **Mel Gibson** comes to mind. So does **Patty Andrews**. Another is **Zsa Zsa Gabor**, and you can tchrow in **Eva** and **Magda**, too. Tchrow 'em somewheres.

James McArthur, born James Gordon McArthur in Los Angeles, CA on December 8, 1937…One day sometime in the 70s, James walked into my salon on Crescent Heights Boulevard, walked right up to me and said, "Hi Joe! Can I get you to cut my hair?" We went to the front desk and I gave him the next available appointment. When I was cutting his hair, I asked how he came to see me. He was very complimentary but I don't recall his answer. It was all very friendly. Recently, on his birthday, I sent him an email, though I'm not sure that I have a correct e-address.

<u>**Gardner McKay**</u>**, born George Cadogan Gardner McKay in Manhattan, New York on June 10, 1932 – d. November 21, 2001.** Gardner was the star of the TV show, *Adventures in Paradise,* about a guy who would sail from port to port and have adventures. He was my client in the early 60s and extremely quiet though very friendly. And very tall, so I always asked him to do what his mother told him never to do and slouch. Some people y'gotta ask over 'n over, but I enjoyed knowing him.

<u>**Sergio Mendez**</u>**.** Sergio is either two years younger than me or two years older, I'll have to ask sometime. **Herb Alpert** brought Sergio to the USA from Brazil around '64 or '65. Hey, it's a long time ago and just a minor fact though a major, life-changing event for Sergio.

Sergio's haircuts were paid by his manager for about the first six months that he came to me. Then Herb shocked the music world with the **Tijuana Brass**. The recording was a major hit with the public, which demanded a live concert. The way I got the story, the recording was mostly synthesized, so Herb had to be doubly creative and put together a live group of musicians who could perform like the recording. Some people said that the live performance was "electronically enhanced" but I was there, backstage, and I don't think that part of the story is true.

Herb decided to use the Tijuana Brass' debut as a double-debut by opening the show with the then-unknown group, **Sergio Mendez and Brazil 66**. I was there to groom Sergio and all the guys in '66. Seems like EVERYONE, every celebrity in Hollywood, came backstage to say Break-a-Leg and then, after the show, they came to offer congrats. The evening is one of the most exciting in memory.

A year later, on January 30, 1967, Sergio and Brazil 66 opened at the same **Greek Theater**, but this time and for the first time, as Headliners!

Sometime later, Sergio returned from a month's visit to his hometown in Brazil. He came directly from the airport in need of a haircut and for the first time, he requested a shave. I mentioned that I had studied makeup at NBC some years before and offered to "thicken" his sparse beard.

When I finished he was so impressed he said he'd like to show his wife, so he walked out with his new beard. Before going home he stopped at **A&M Records** to say hello to Herb. As he entered Herb's private office, Herb jumped up shouting. Sergio ducked 'n turned to see who might have followed in behind, but nobody was there. That's when Sergio realized that Herb was shouting, "That's it! That's it!" while holding thumbs and forefingers in a square.

"That's it! That's it!"

"That's WHAT?!?"

"Your BEARD. We have been looking for an icon for you, like a flower in your lapel or a colorful vest or ... We couldn't come up with that SOMETHING that could be your signature. But your BEARD, THAT'S IT!" Yep, see the pix on Sergio's first album, taken the next day.

A few years later when Sergio came in for a haircut, one of my regular non-show-biz clients was amazed and thrilled to be able to actually meet Sergio. He complimented Sergio on his music – and his beard.

"Compliment Little Joe" Sergio said. "Because of this son-of-a-gun, I gotta wear this beard all my life."

Beard trim, anyone? Ladies?

One more, 'cuz I love this vignette almost as much as I love my friendship with Sergio. Coming in for his appointment one day, Sergio asked me to step outside for a moment. Parked in front of the salon was a new Silver Cloud Rolls Royce Convertible.

"Oh m'God, Serg, is this YOURS?!?

He smiled, ear to ear, like a proud Papa and put an arm around my shoulders. "Joey, you remember when I came to this country? I couldn't even pay for my own haircuts. Well, you're the first to see this and I'll tell you something. I paid CASH."

It was one of the happiest moments I ever shared with a friend. We both had wet eyes.

"Only in America..." as my Grampa Dominic would have said.

Robert Middleton, **born Samuel G. Messer in Cincinnati, Ohio on May 13, 1911 – d. June 14, 1977 in Hollywood, CA.** I always remember the movie, *Friendly Persuasion*, and the buggy race with Gary Cooper, whenever I think of Robert Middleton. I know you've heard this one before, but one day when my father and I were walking into **Schwab's** to have lunch, we bumped into Robert Middleton. He and my Dad exchanged very friendly hellos with a hug and slaps on the back. We had some friendly chit chat with other Hollywood personalities popping in and out of the conversation. He always remembered me after that first time. It is one of those casual friendships that seems to stay fresh in memory forever.

Mark Miller, born on November 25, 1925 in Houston, TX... Mark became my client while I was working for **Cosmo's** and followed me to **Russo's**. Mark was the star of the successful TV series, *Please Don't Eat the Daisies*. There was a time when Mark was going on location in Africa to shoot a picture. The shoot was scheduled for nine months. He asked if I would be willing to go along and work makeup and hair for him personally. I explained that I could not be away from my business – or my family – for such a long period of time. He jacked-up his generous monetary offer. While I don't regret my decision, I still haven't seen Africa. Ungowa!

Rick Monday, born Robert James Monday, Jr. on November 20, 1946 in Batesville, Arkansas... I remember April 25, 1976 like it happened yesterday. That day I took all my kids – for the one and only time – to see a baseball game, this one between the Chicago Cubs and the Los Angeles Dodgers at Dodger Stadium. Trina was two months short of 12 years old, Joey was eight and Kimberley Ann was six. Our seats were in the left field foul-pole area, maybe 20-25 rows up from the playing field.

Early in the game with the Cubs in the field, two men (both looked adult-age and scruffy) ran out onto the left field playing area, one carelessly carrying an American Flag. The Flag was thrown to the ground and something liquid was squirted on it from a can (lighter fluid?!?) by one person, then one of them was obviously attempting to light a match.

I started screaming, yelling my head off, - and I wasn't the only one - but imagine my frustration as I realized that I was too far away to even attempt to stop them.

Then I saw Cub centerfielder Rick Monday running from his position toward the men, seemingly picking up speed with every step. I yelled louder! I would have clobbered both of them if I were able to be Monday. But thank God, Monday instead grabbed the Flag on the run and sprinted away with it and finally, he handed it off to Dodgers Pitcher Doug Rau. I also remember Dodger third base coach Tommy

Lasorda running toward the two men as were three or four stadium security personnel. (I didn't really have to be told later that Lasorda was screaming every profanity invented by man. Good ole Tommy, you gotta love him.)

From the beginning of the incident, many other fans realized the severity of the scene unfolding in left field. By the time Monday grabbed the Flag, it seemed like everyone in the whole stadium recognized his feat and was cheering him.

I started to explain the incident to my kids but such was not necessary, not even for Kimberley.

The first time Monday came to bat, Dodger Stadium gave him a Standing Ovation! I was thrilled! I yelled louder than anybody, just ask my kids. Monday's next at-bat and the next, he received extra applause, but not enough according to me.

By Monday's final at-bat that day, the kids and I had relocated to just a few rows up and behind the Dodgers' Dugout. I was the only one standing, shouting and applauding. Okay, that's an exaggeration, but not by much.

During the off-season, Rick Monday became a member of the Los Angeles Dodgers Baseball Team. No relation to the incident, the LA Times reported, though the incident was by then recognized as one of the 100 Most Memorable Incidents in Major League Baseball History. The incident had nothing to do with the trade? Yeah, right, and I got this bridge...

Today, more than 30 years later, Rick Monday is still part of the Dodger family, serving in the broadcast booth these many years. And even Kimberley remembers the incident.

PS: All baseball nutz will want to know that Doug Rau pitched nine years for the Dodgers and played his last season with the Angels. He was 16-12 for the Dodgers in '76, his best season, with a 3.35 ERA. Doug was 81-60 lifetime. This tidbit courtesy of career newspaper man and decades-long good buddy Stan Wawer.

Marilyn Monroe, the Most Famous Female of the 20th Century, was born Norma Jeane Mortenson in Los Angles, CA on June 1, 1926. – d. August 5, 1962 in Brentwood (a section of West LA) CA. Some people understand that if it wasn't for **Sidney Skolsky**, the world might never have known her. The same can be said of a select few other people in Marilyn's life without diminishing Sidney's role. By the way, according to the latest figures, Marilyn made more money in the year____ than any year previously. If you filled in the blank with "last year," give yourself a bright, shining star! And Oh Yes, her death - - Oops Overdose or Something Sinister? Think we'll ever know for sure?

Terry Moore, born Helen Luella Koford in Los Angeles, CA on January 7, 1929... A career in Hollywood is very delicate. Terry is an excellent case in point. Her career was much shorter than projected. We became friends through our mutual friend, **Matt Helreich**, who is famous for his "Thursday Night Dinners," mixing celebrities and non-showbiz interesting people. Terry and I always give each other a warm hello and enjoy each other's company. If I were to resume my newspaper column, Terry would receive one of my first calls.

Vic Morrow, born Victor Morrow in The Bronx, NY on February 14, 1929 – d. July 23, 1982 in Indian Dunes, CA. My good friend Vic was the quiet, reserved type when not acting in a TV show or movie. One time he came to see me for a haircut and said that just before he left the *Combat!* set that day, he shot a scene where he had just opened a door leading from one room to another. Vic said when he returned to the set the next day, the first shot would be of him finishing crossing the threshold from the previous day. "I'm desperate for a haircut, but please don't make me look like I got one while crossing the threshold." A few days later he called to say "Mission Accomplished!" Vic also referred actor **Johnny Gentri** to me. There are no human words to properly express my gratitude.

George Murdock, born in Salina, Kansas June 25, 1930.... George is one of Hollywood's foremost character actors whose face is familiar while his name is rather obscure except to the most avid movie and TV fans. George was my client off and on over the years, a statement that can be made by several of my colleagues. George has an extremely long list of credits. I've always enjoyed our conversations and I especially enjoyed bumping into him around town.

Stu Nahan, born in Los Angeles, CA on June 23, 1926 – d. in Studio City (LA) CA on Dec 26, 2007. One day in the fall of 1968, I went to Cosmo's to have lunch with my dad. That's when I met Stu

Nahan, the new sportscaster for KABC-TV Channel 7, who was getting his hair cut by Gene Turner. We had a great conversation as we struck an immediate bond of friendship. Everybody who ever met Stu knows what I mean. He was that kind of guy, a for-real person.

Shortly after meeting Stu, I went to Dodger Stadium as a writer "reporting" for the Burbank Daily Review's Sports Editor – and my buddy and hair client – **Stan Wawer**. Stu was surprised to see me, to put it mildly, and offered "to show me the ropes."

"O'Malley treats us scribes to dinner and we each tip the waiter a buck. Not two, now, but just one. Don't screw up the works here; we're all on the same team."

A while later I was doing marketing research for a company that developed a Swimming Pool Alarm System. Using a transducer (an underwater microphone) the device would convert underwater sound into an electrical impulse. Reading the pattern, the device could separate a thunderclap or other loud noise from the sound created by a live (human or animal) unauthorized entry and set off a high decibel alarm.

I took a System to Stu's new pool at his home in Studio City. After a brief demo, he became very excited and declared that the company would sell a million devices.

Stu alerted the news department. Fred Anderson met me at a pool in the Valley where I had an 8-year old girl help me with the demo. Three times I asked her to sneak into the water without setting off the alarm. Three times she was no more than one foot or one hand into the pool when the alarm sounded, bringing neighbors from their homes.

Between the 6 o'clock and 11 o'clock newscasts, the alarm was given 11 minutes of coverage. We had a winner.

I must have bumped into Stu a few hundred times over the years. Every meeting was an improvement on our introduction. It's hard to accept that I won't get to see his smiling, happy face on my next trip to L.A.

Earl Nightingale, **born in Los Angeles, CA on March 12, 1921 – d. March 25, 1989**. I had listened to Earl on radio and via cassette tape long before I ever had the privilege of giving him haircuts. He became my client when I took over operation of the **Image Hair Salon** in the **Century Plaza Hotel**. Earl was a very tall man, perhaps four or six inches above six feet. I made a joke about our difference in height during one of our early meetings and struck Earl's funny bone. From then on I made sure to throw in a dig, sometimes playing on the fact of his height and sometimes playing on my 5' 4" frame. We had a wonderful friendship.

David Nelson, born in New York City, New York as David Oswald Nelson on October 24, 1936... David was a client of stylist and good-buddy, Bernie Roberts, who was on **Sebring's** original staff. Bernie started working with Sam Russo, Ralph Trejo, Phil Fayne and me when we banded together for the second time in 1980 after Sam lost his lease on Santa Monica and I lost mine on Crescent Heights. Yep, another long story, but that's when we all became acquainted with David, who had gained fame on TV with brother Ricky and Mom and Pop, **Ozzie and Harriet Nelson**. David always had a very quiet demeanor. A few years later, 1988, Sam, Theresa and I bought the salon we named **Beverly Hills Hair Design**. Bernie joined us again, bringing along **David, George Peppard, Mel Torme, Arte Johnson** and so many more who will cut off my nose for not including them here. Had y'goin', did I?

Frank Novak. Even using the internet, I can only find information confirming that Frank was on the Skelton show's costume staff. How disappointing! As my search continued, I came upon information leading me to the very recent widow of **Frank Novack**, long tome CBS Producer and Executive. Mrs. Novack acknowledged knowing of Frank Novak, the costume designer for **Red Skelton**, but she pointed out that there is no "c" in his name. Nutz! I'll keep looking in case I write a sequel to this book, something I would only do if encouraged by popular demand.

Warren Oats, born Warren Mercer Oats in Depoy, KY on July 5, 1928 – d. April 3, 1982 in Los Angeles, CA. Warren, one of my early clients when working at **Cosmo's**, often played a heavy in the movies. He did a marvelous portrayal of **John Dillinger** and also starred in the movie, *In The Heat of The Night*. In person he was rather quiet and reserved though very friendly.

Carroll O'Connor, born John Carroll O'Connor in Manhattan, NY on August 2, 1924 – d. June 21, 2001. Like Warren above, I started cutting Carroll's hair early in my career at **Cosmo's**. Carroll would come in with his lovely wife, **Nancy**, most times and thank goodness, too. She and I would have wonderful conversations on any subject you can name while Carroll would read the paper or a magazine as I cut his hair.

I remember seeing the movie, *Julius Caesar* in which Carroll had a featured role. Using all the diplomacy of which I was capable at that time, I told Carroll that he was a major star just waiting to be discovered. I predicted that his level of talent could not be kept in the dark for much longer. I know Nancy was extremely grateful for my comment by her verbal response. Carroll's reaction displayed mild surprise and humble gratitude for my opinion.

Years later when I owned the hair salon at **The Century Plaza Hotel**, I chanced to bump into Carroll walking alone through the lobby on his way to meet friends for dinner. By this time the world knew Carroll as **Archie Bunker**. We stopped and had a warm conversation wherein I reminded him of my prediction. His answer to my suggestion that he was on top of the world was to say, "Yeah, and as a bigot, too." Hollywood knows he was anything but.

When Carroll died, dear mutual friend, **Judy Rosen**, widow of **Milt**, flew 76 of her White Doves during his funeral services. I'm sure I'm wasting ink to tell you that Carroll O'Connor was easily one of Hollywood's best loved and most respected members.

Donald O'Connor, born Donald David Dixon Ronald O'Connor in Chicago, IL on August 28, 1925 – d. September 27, 2003 in Calabasas, CA. He was Talented with a capital T and as gracious as they come. Please don't tire of me stating that so many Hollywood Celebrities I've associated with are "nice people" and other words to that affect; for when it is true, I want you to be informed by someone with personal knowledge. Most of the crap published and sold in convenience stores and supermarkets are just that – CRAP. Those rags are there because dummies buy them. Grrrrr!

Jess Oppenheimer, born in San Francisco, CA on November 11, 1913 – d. December 27, 1988. Jess was a Writer, Producer and Director for so many greats of the industry like **Lucille Ball, Fred Astaire, Jack Benny, Al Jolson, Fanny Brice, George 'n Gracie** and too many more to name here. Lucy called him "the brains of *I Love Lucy*." Good Nuff! Now you know why I am so grateful to **Debbie Reynolds** for going out of her way to introduce me. Thanx again, Deb!

Freddie Otash, **born in Massachusetts on January 7, 1922...** Research tells me that Freddie is still walking the earth someplace, so I'll just shout, HEY FREDDIE, GIMMIE A CALL!

I first met Freddie during my earliest days at **Cosmo's**. For whatever reason, the first time he sat in my chair for a haircut was after I bought the place in 1973. Freddie is the former L.A.P.D. officer who became Hollywood's favorite private eye. He was the person along with **Frank Sinatra** and **Joe DiMaggio** who knocked down an apartment door in Hollywood one evening looking for **Marilyn Monroe**.

Freddie is noted for a thousand capers that would make one heck of a book if he and I can ever get together. At one point during my time as owner, money was somehow disappearing from my cash register. During a haircut, I told Freddie of my dilemma. He said he would tell me who the thief was by the end of his haircut. I thought he was pulling my leg.

At the end of the haircut as Mack the porter was brushing him off, Freddie leaned over and whispered to me. "It's the receptionist." He taught me how to lay a trap and sure enough, before the day was out, I caught my thief. When I later asked Freddie how he knew, he said it was her body language. No, he didn't charge me a fee, just gave me a memory that will last through the ages.

Jerry Paris, **born William Gerald Grossman in San Francisco, CA on July 25, 1925 – d. March 31, 1986 in Los Angeles, CA**. Jerry was an actor and maybe better known as a director. He played the role of **Jerry Helper**, the dentist and next-door neighbor of **Rob and Laura Petrie** on the hit '60s TV sitcom, *The Dick Van Dyke Show*, where he directed several episodes.

Jerry also produced and directed many episodes of the TV hit series, *Happy Days* and before my time in Hollywood, he appeared in the movie, *The Wild One*, starring a young **Marlon Brando**. He also had a recurring role in the first season of TV's, *The Untouchables*.

To me he was a fun-loving friend and client.

Ed Peck, **born in New York, NY on March 26, 1917 – d. September 12, 1992 in Hollywood, CA**. I had the privilege of cutting Eddie's hair for more than 20 years. Eddie was a big guy with a foghorn voice who loved to bellow his hellos and goodbyes. You best knew him as **Captain Kirk** on *Happy Days* where he seemed to be constantly giving **Fonzie** fits.

In case you didn't know, he was very active with the kids who participated in the Special Olympics. That part of his life became his true passion. He often told me how absolutely flattering it was to be approached by these children who held him in such reverence that he couldn't tell me about it without tears rolling down his cheeks.

Early on, Eddie asked my favorite booze. I told him Scotch. From then on, every Christmas he would bring me a bottle of Johnny Walker Black. At the time my favorite brand was Haag n Haag Pinch, so I never opened one of Eddie's bottles until the last one. That's when I discovered that I *really like* JWB. Ever since, much as I might want to try something else, Ginny and I go with the JWB and the delightful memories of my very dear friend Eddie.

George Peppard, born in Detroit, MI on October 1, 1928 – d. May 8, 1994 in Los Angeles, CA. At the pinnacle of George Peppard's Hollywood career is the movie, *Breakfast at Tiffany's*, also starring **Audrey Hepburn** and two TV series, first *Banacek,* then later, *The A Team*, that also starred **Dirk Benedict** and **Mr. T.** George has many more accomplishments.

I met George in 1980 after being forced to walk away from the salon called **Little Joe's** that was formerly **Cosmo's**. I had once again joined my compare, Sam Russo, along with his wife Theresa and Phil Fayne, Ralph Trejo, Bernie Roberts and John Salter in a salon simply called **Russo's** in the ICM Building on Beverly Boulevard in Beverly Hills.

Bernie had been cutting George Peppard's hair for several years at that time. On more than one occasion, George and Bernie talked of plans to retire together to a large ranch that George had developed. Unfortunately, neither one lived long enough to fulfill that intention, Bernie's death preceding George by about a year.

Bernie was among the most talented hairstylists in Hollywood and a dear friend. I met Bernie during my first year or two in the business.

George Peppard was basically quiet in public, but he always initiated or acknowledged a "hello." When George would come in for a haircut his demeanor was cordial and sometimes even friendly. I always felt that George was a deep thinker who would focus so intently on his thoughts that he was oftentimes only peripherally aware of his surroundings. Just the way it was and everybody (the staff) seemed to understand.

That salon had a brief life, long story short. In 1988, Sam and Theresa Russo and I bought an existing salon at 9171 Wilshire Boulevard in Beverly Hills and named it **Beverly Hills Hair Design**. George and Bernie were with us again as was John Salter, plus others. Ralph and Phil had moved on but stayed family with us.

Paul Petersen, born William Paul Petersen in Glendale, CA on September 23, 1945... I would think that most everyone remembers Paul as **Jeff Stone** on the TV series, *The Donna Reed Show*. Today, Paul and his lovely wife, Rena, are fulfilling a most admirable mission of helping others, most pointedly, former child actors. We can all help them by spreading the word of their marvelous work and perhaps dropping them a check now and then. It is my privilege to call them friends.

Charlie Picerni, Stunts, 2nd Unit Director, Actor, Director, Crew, Producer, Writer - From 1961 to Present. His vital stats are hard to come by, but most importantly, Charlie was my friend and client from my earliest days at **Cosmo's**. Charlie was brought to L.A. by his brother, **Paul Picerni**, to be Paul's stand-in on the TV series, *The Untouchables*. Charlie made it big in his own right as a stunt man, a second unit director, an actor, a director and a producer. Charlie also owned some of Hollywood's most popular restaurants. Best of all, he is my long-time good friend.

Paul Picerni I feel like I covered Paul rather completely in the column I wrote on him. I'll say again that Paul has had one of the most fantastic careers of anyone in Hollywood's history. For me, the best part of Paul's story is the quality of human being I have always known him to be. As far as I know, I have not met Paul's wife or other family members except brother Charlie, but there is always tomorrow.

Bobby Pickett, born 1938 – d. April 25, 2007 in Los Angeles, CA. Bobby was my friend and client from my earliest days at **Cosmo's**. I guess everybody has heard the hit specialty song, *The Monster Mash*. Bobby got a big kick out of being the **Boris Karloff** – imitator. Like most people I've encountered throughout my career, Bobby was a very warm and friendly person who enjoyed being in the entertainment world.

George Piscatelli, a.k.a. George Perry George's vital stats are hard to come by, but I'd lay five to eight he died in 1968... or maybe it was early '69. I know for sure that I was one of his pall bearers.

At first I thought George was a "rounder," a term for guys who were always hanging around Hollywood, especially the nightlife. He loved my haircuts, eh, hair*styles*. He also loved how I could make his hair appear after a shampoo, conditioning and blow-dry. He came in three and even four times a week for a shampoo 'n blow. For a period of time, I saw him more often than Casey Kasem. But it was all over far too soon.

I was never clear about George's business life, but I was told that he was "a movie producer." Through others I was told that he was known to push a little dope around town. He also was supposed to have financed a madam and her bevy of girls. I do know that he and a guy I only knew as Gino went to an apartment house supposedly to collect a debt and as George knocked on the door, the guy inside shot five times, right through the door and into George's heart. I seem to recall that the shooter got away with a slap on the wrist, but I hope my foggy memory is incorrect.

I was very upset when told that George was dead. After all, he and I had become friends and he was also a good client. I called his wife to express condolences and heard myself volunteer to give George one final do... in the box, wouldyabelieve. That was a first.

Me and my big mouth! The mortician welcomed me and led the way to the Prep Room, I think he called it. George was already in his casket and in no position for me to do much of anything. The mortician said he'd be in his office and opened the door to leave. I was right behind him.

"Where are you going?" he asked.

"Wherever you're going is fine with me," I answered. Hey, I was uncomfortable in that room as George apparently had a roommate about 20 feet away, so the mortician, unable to stifle his chuckle, agreed to stay with me while I did my work.

"They won't hurt you, y'know," he said.

Right, 'cuz they won't get a chance.

It was a good thing he stayed as somebody had to lift George enough for me to even begin. In about two minutes flat I was spritzing hairspray and ready to go.

After the funeral service, the procession made its way to Mission Hills Cemetery at the corner of Sepulveda Blvd and Rinaldi Street. We pulled up to a prepared gravesite by a large tree. The pallbearer to my left I knew as Hollywood Mike and to my right was George's attorney. During the graveside ceremony, Hollywood Mike started saying "Hey you, get outta there. Ain't you got no respect?" He repeated it two or three times. I looked up but couldn't figure out who Mike was talking to, so I asked the attorney why Mike had stepped forward and was now shouting.

"Look over by the tree," he said.

I saw a man in a dark blue suit with a movie camera on his shoulder. The attorney said the man was FBI.

"FBI? Why is he here?"

The attorney told me to look behind me. There were sound trucks from all the major networks and hundreds of people. Off to my left was another camera man and to my right was another. Neither was wearing a suit.

The next day George's widow called to tell me I looked really sharp on all the networks' news shows. I half expected a visit from the FBI, but as far as I know, nothing ever came of it. Whew!

All these years later I still miss George, known as GP to us in his inner circle.

PS The internet tells me that George was sitting with Mickey Cohen and Sam LoCigno the night Jack "The Enforcer" Whalen bought the farm at Rondelli's restaurant. Whoa, news to me.

Michael J. Pollard, born Michael John Pollack, Jr. in Passaic, NJ on May 30, 1939… Early on I asked Michael the name his friends used to address him by and he told me "M J." Somehow I had one heck of a time remembering those two initials. I think he thought that was really funny because every time I would stumble, he would laugh. That incident alone convinced me that M.J. has a very strong self-image. We lost track of each other once I moved from Crescent Heights, I'm sad to say. I admire his deep talent and consider him a personal friend.

Poncie Ponce. I wanted to present an update on Poncie, but my research has been fruitless. I recall that he told me he was moving back to Hawaii when the TV series, *Hawaiian Eye*, closed. So wherever you are Poncie, I think of you often and pray for your happiness.

Stefanie Powers, born Stefania Zofia Federkiewicz in Hollywood, CA on November 2, 1942… I still smile, big time, when I think that years ago I actually played some love scenes with Stefanie Powers. Needless to say, I followed her career over the years and especially enjoyed the work she did with **Robert Wagner** in the hit TV series, *Hart to Hart*. She is another celebrity at the top of my list if I were to resume my columns on Hollywood.

Vincent Price, **born Vincent Leonard Price, Jr. in St. Louis, MO on May 27, 1911 – d. October 25, 1993 in Los Angeles, CA**. Vincent Price was a guest on the TV show *Boutique* that **Johnny Gentri** and I always called "our show." Vincent came on the show as a gourmet cook. He prepared a cooked meal for the entire crew of 150 people.

His idea, certainly not mine, was to be in the midst of cooking and describing what he was doing while having some food already prepared so that our host and hostess, **Johnny Gentri** and **Susan Brown**, could taste and comment on camera.

Vincent had his own portable cooking ovens and stoves that he had delivered to the set at his expense. He brought four big stainless steel appliances that were trucked by a vehicle just smaller than a semi.

The show was a major hit with our TV audience and an even bigger hit with the crew. We made his segment the last of the day so that everyone could sit down to a wonderful meal. Vince was open and friendly with everybody, treating all as though they were years-long friends. During the meal he was also the head waiter, pouring wine and bringing more bread. Talk about fabulous! Gracious hardly begins to describe the gentleman the world knows as Vincent Price.

Joe Pyne, **born December 22, 1924 – d. March 23, 1970.** My good-bud Joe Pyne was a front-runner of the concept of having a TV talk show where the host could easily become confrontational. Over the years I have heard plenty of talk about doing a movie or TV series based on the life and demeanor of Joe Pyne. Maybe the idea has been too good and has therefore not sprouted wings. That's a dig on the Networks that have tried to fly some obvious turkeys while passing on winners that showed up later – sometimes.

Joe was my client during the first few years of my career that I worked at **Cosmo's.** He was very friendly and cordial with everyone in person, contrary to his TV image. One time comic **Soupy Sales** came in to get a haircut from Nunzio and started a banter with Joe where Soupy was faking giving Joe a hard time. I thought it was the funniest shtick I ever saw Soupy do. Joe didn't pull any punches, spitting back four-letter words on a tit for tat basis. Hey, no TV cameras were rolling, so they just let it fly. Shucks, no film at eleven.

<u>**George Raft**</u>**, born George Ranft in Hell's Kitchen, NY, on September 26, 1895 – d. November 24, 1980, Los Angeles, CA.** I only met Georgie that once but what a thrill! Hey, I didn't say anything before, but he was BALD. I almost lost my lunch. Didn't look so tough anymore, either.

Georgie, Cagney, Bogie and Eddie G. were atop the greatest mobster-portrayers of my youth, God Bless 'em. Hey, y'don't think they were all... Naah, couldn't be.

<u>**Alan Reed**</u>**, born Teddy Bergman in New York City, NY on August 20, 1907 – d. June 14, 1977 in Los Angeles, CA.** I'm sure you'll recognize Alan if I quote his most famous line, so I'll shout, "YABA – DABA - DOO!"

Right, he was the original voice of **Fred Flintstone**.

He was also a regular at **Cosmo's** and Ludwig's client from my first days working there and continuing through my ownership up to his passing. I once asked Alan if I could take him to lunch and pick his brain for the memories of his career. He answered that with such a purpose, he would take ME to lunch.

That lunch lasted 3½ hours and at the end he wouldn't allow me to even pay the tip. He didn't just tell me his story, he DRAMATIZED it and had me and the waiter laughing so hard I came away with a case of sore ribs. I only regret that I did not bring a tape recorder and capture some of the gems he shared with me that day. He put a smile on my spirit that will last through eternity. Wish youse were there.

There is nothing on the web to replicate that lunchtime performance.

<u>**Barron Richard Rennick**</u> When I started working for Cosmo, the first wigmaker I met was Richard Rennick. He was always Richard, never Dick, though he did not insist that I or anyone call him "Barron." The title, he told me, was primarily for Hair Shows and visiting royalty.

Richard designed and manufactured men's hairpieces that were the first I ever saw that were truly undetectable. You could see into the front hairline for up to three inches instead of the heavy "rug" thickness that was – and still is, for the most part – so common with far too many other so-called designers.

The front base of Richard's hairpiece was constructed using lace netting that was extremely delicate and would tear easily. On a movie set, especially in a studio or interior shot, the hot lights would cause the lace to lift, but makeup was right there, so it was not the problem like when out in public. The person had to be very careful and aware. Very recently, lace fronts have been developed that solve the problems of years ago and allow for the same undetectable quality that Richard first created. I use the lace front method exclusively.

Richard lived on Hollywood Boulevard in a large home that was tastefully and expensively decorated. His furniture was French provincial with twenty-four-carat gold inlays and plush carpeting that I was reluctant to walk on. The home was very near Hollywood Boulevard's termination at Laurel Canyon Boulevard, the road beginning at Sunset Boulevard and winding north through the Hollywood Hills to Studio City in the San Fernando Valley. Laurel Canyon Boulevard is the continuation of Crescent Heights Boulevard, the name change occurring after crossing Sunset Boulevard.

When I found a client who wanted a hairpiece, I would make an appointment for us with Richard. We would go to Richard's home and enter a large room created as a one-chair hair salon with beveled mirrors in large, ornately carved frames and sans carpet, of course. Richard had several hairpieces tastefully displayed on male manikin heads/busts to show samples of his custom designed hairpieces – today often referred to as "units." In that room Richard would make a mold of the client's cranium so that the finished unit would fit the person's scalp precisely. I always watched Richard work with pure fascination as he would explain the intricacies of his design.

Once the unit was ready for delivery, the client and I would return to Richard's so I could do the cut-in. Most times over the years, the client would come to me at Cosmo's – or later, wherever I was working - often as my last client of the day. Richard would also send me his private clients for the cut-in, telling them - and me quite often - that I was "the best cutter in the world."

My association with Richard continued for about 20 years. I really don't recall exactly when we did our last collaboration. I do recall that sometime in the seventies, after I bought Cosmo's, Richard said it was about time that I became the designer.

"Why?" I asked, shocked. "You're the best designer in the world, Richard."

"Has it ever occurred to you that I'm 30 years your senior? Besides, I might decide to retire to Hawaii next year. Then what?"

So he drilled me on the intricacies of design with the next client who I'll call Tom. A few weeks later I brought another client to Richard's, this one named Jim. Richard walked out of the room as he told me I was on my own. Confident? Don't be silly.

Richard returned as I was finishing my design. Without checking it, he accepted the mold and shushed us out the door.

When the unit was ready, Jim and I returned for the initial fitting and cut-in. When we were finished that evening, Jim was as happy as any client I ever knew. After he left I had questions for Richard, but I didn't really get much of a chance.

Richard told me that he DID check my design before he shushed Jim and me out the door the night I made the mold.

"If I didn't know better, I'd have sworn that I made the mold," Richard said with his best smile. "When the time comes, you won't miss me."

Bullfeathers. Every time that I make a mold or simply clean a unit, Richard is right there with me. I'm in great hands. And grateful for a lifetime.

Debbie Reynolds, born Mary Francis Reynolds in El Paso, TX on April 1, 1932... She's been called America's Sweetheart. Gets my vote. She has always been very gracious and considerate with me. So much has been written about her that I might have a challenge adding anything new if I were ever to do a column on her, but I'd sure love to give it a go. I honestly think she'd bring out my best so that I would paint a very honest and beautiful portrait of her.

Bobbie Rhea, born circa 1956 – '58
Gene Kelly, born Eugene Curran Kelly in Pittsburg, PA on August 23, 1912 – d. February 2, 1996, Beverly Hills, CA. Here's another two-fer-one deal. Gene Kelly had a Ton of Talent. Ask anybody. My direct contact with him was in 1967 when he starred in *Jack and the Beanstalk*, a made-for-TV movie special. Surfing the web, NBC aired the show on February 26, 1967.

Gene's co-star was my client, nine year old – or was he eleven? – **Bobbie Rhea**. Bobbie was a great-looking blond kid who could act, sing and dance. And oh boy, could he dance! I went on the set several times to make sure Bobbie's hair was just so.

One day in particular, Gene and Bobbie were performing an intricate dance routine, leaping to and from obstacles all over the set. Gene slipped. The director called "Cut!"

Okay, from the top. After some leaps and jumps, the two almost collided. "Cut!"

Okay, from the top, again. Dancing along, Gene went this way and Bobbie went yonder. "Cut!"

Now Gene's anger burst forth. He mumbled something about "... kids on the set." The air was suddenly heavier than water.

"I'm sorry, Mr. Kelly" Bobbie said. "Let's do it one more time. I'll get it right this time, promise."

From the top, one more time. Ahh, perfect. "Cut!"

I stood there like I'd just been hit by a tree. How could a kid, maybe nine, maybe 11, have the maturity, the MOXIE, to apologize **when every step he took that day was PERFECT?!?**

Kelly, at his angriest now, stomped off the set. Not a word. Just sullen.

I was as disappointed with Kelly as I was proud of Bobbie.

I visited a web site recently featuring the "...Beanstalk" movie starring Gene Kelly. Nice. Except, there was no mention of Bobbie Rhea. Nada. The video was no longer available, either.

Yes, I've been known to sometimes go where Angels fear to tread. Lowers my blood pressure. Maybe Kelly was having a bad day or a middle-age crisis, who knows. Did the market take a dump in 2/'67? Aw, fergettit. Like I said, they're all human, even the Bigs.

And please, ask Bobby t'call me. If I knew his or Mom Jackie's number, I'd do the calling, for sure.

Tony Robbins, born Anthony J. Mahavick in North Hollywood, CA on February 29, 1960... I met Tony at one of **Jean and Casey Kasem's** Holiday Parties circa 1992 – '94. Tony is as comfortable one-on-one as he is in front of a group of thousands. I had heard about him and his seminars that teach The New Science of Personal Achievement. Two acquaintances have successfully gone through his Fire Walk, a 20 foot long shallow trench of burning charcoal.

Tony was kind enough to send me his audio tape course called Unlimited Power. I know we are the product of the experiences that we have related to the influences around us that we have put into thought or practice, so I again thank Tony Robbins for all I gained from his teachings.

Ronnie Robertson, born Ronald Robertson in Brackenridge, PA – d. February 4, 2000 in Fountain Valley, CA. When I met him during my first months with **Cosmo's**, Ronnie was the Star of the Ice Capades and a former Gold Medal Winner in the Olympics.

Ronnie was so blond that his hair seemed to disappear while performing. I suggested a Light Ash Brown hair color. He protested, saying he did not want to be considered anything except a blond. That was the end of my use of words that could be misunderstood by him or anyone else.

On his next visit I suggested Ash Blond hair color. He agreed. A few days later he called to say that he had seen new film on himself and was extremely pleased at how his blond hair was now visible under the harsh spotlights. He and I were equally thrilled.

I used exactly the same color on his hair that I had suggested earlier, but this time the name was more acceptable to him. "A rose by any other name…"

Edward G. Robinson, Jr., born Emanuel Goldberg, Jr. in Los Angeles, CA on March 19, 1933 – d. February 26, 1974 in West Hollywood, CA… Eddie had a rough reputation and was reportedly an alcoholic. Eddie was my friend in the late 60s – early 70s, I am proud to say. For some entertainer's children, being in the shadow of a celebrity parent is a very heavy burden, especially when the parent is a Mega-Star and the child has little or no entertainment talent like in this case.

What I say is no knock on Eddie, as my observation is that no one has any control over his own talent. I believe that everyone is born with talents, but maybe not the specific talent(s) desired. Skill can be developed, but that skill will not be able to equal a well developed talent-based skill.

Buddy Rogers, born Charles Edward "Buddy" Rogers in Olathe, Kansas on August 13, 1904 – d. April 21, 1999 in Rancho Mirage, CA. We only met that one night around 1991 at **Caesar Romero's** birthday party. We had about three different conversations, but I am richer for the experience. He impressed me as a kind and gentle person.

Buddy was honest to the point of saying he was impressed that someone of my age actually knew who he was and knew some of his accomplishments. Isn't it curious and amazing how so many actors can appear in several movies and/or TV shows and then disappear from public view though still alive? Fortunately in Buddy's case, his movie, *Wings* is one of Hollywood's all-time greats, so we will have Buddy forever.

Wayne Rogers, born **Wayne M. Rogers in Birmingham, Alabama on April 7, 1933...** One of the stars of the extremely popular TV show, *M.A.S.H.,* Wayne was more than a client to Johnny Tringali; he was a friend and business associate in real estate investments. "Mr. Friendly," he came in weekly for many years. Wayne was always friendly and cordial.

Caesar Romero, born **Cesar Julio Romero, Jr. In New York City, NY on February 15, 1907 – d. January 1, 1994 in Santa Monica, CA**. We had brief encounters over the years. Nunzio told me that Caesar had called **Cosmo's** wanting to book an appointment with me shortly after the time I met Caesar on the **Red Skelton** set, but Cosmo tried to get Caesar to book with him instead of me. Nunzio didn't spill the beans until sometime after I bought Cosmo's in 1973. I do not doubt Nunzio nor do I feel anything but gratitude toward Cosmo. After all, Cosmo and his sister, Maria, favored me greatly and gave me countless people who would have taken anyone on the staff. I came out way ahead.

Mickey Rooney, born **Joseph Rule, Jr. in Brooklyn, NY on September 23, 1920...** During my early years in the hair business, Mickey was my father's client at **Cosmo's**. Mickey was very friendly, very outgoing, lighting up the entire place when he came by for a haircut.

Mickey, like others mentioned throughout, would look someone dead in the eye when talking to them. He would listen and respond, often with humor, showing a sharp wit. I remember noticing that quality about him in his earliest movies.

That quality is shared by every successful actor I ever met, a blanket statement that might seem hard to believe, for it is so profound, but I am hard pressed to think of an exception.

"Nice" people are kind to other people, strangers too; not too many buffoons make it to the top and stay there.

Milt Rosen, **born in 1923 in Poland – d. August 11, 2000 in Northridge, CA**. With all I've said about Milt, there's still more. The love I have for him is akin to the love of a nephew for his favorite uncle. He taught me to constantly be aware in my writing that even a good story is presented to people who have no prior emotional connection.

"Connect them by making your reader co-author with you by not describing every last detail."

And;

"Always play to the intelligent reader; let someone else talk to the eighth graders."

The co-author thought was profound. Writing for the intelligent reader was confirmation of a years-earlier commitment. Another biggie was when he said;

"Genuinely enjoy the experience of writing the story. If some parts make you laugh and some make you cry and other parts invoke other emotions and/or cause you to stop and rethink, then your readers will probably feel likewise. If a story doesn't move you, why write it? Probabilities are that it won't move anyone else, either."

He also said,

"Of all the millions of people out there, if 100,000 buy your book, you're a Best Selling Author. Don't try to please *everybody*; please yourself and YOUR audience will find you."

Thousands of people were fortunate enough to experience Milt's wisdom and advice over the years. Now, to a degree, so have you. Make good use, please. And above all, enjoy!

Joe E. Ross, **born Joseph Roszawikz in New York City, NY on March 15, 1914 – d. August 13, 1982 in Los Angeles, CA.** He was the short, chubby co-star of the TV Sitcom, *Car 54, Where Are You?* Joey was also my friend from the late 60s until his death. He was very easy to know and like. He delightfully established his character of **Patrolman Gunther Toody** of New York's 53rd Precinct after a very successful run with the great comic **Phil Silvers** on his TV show.

Joe died while performing on stage. Had he survived, I can just imagine him going up to everyone in sight and making a big joke of the incident.

Jacques Roux Jock was a French-born character actor who I'm guessing to be twenty-something years my senior. He for sure had baby-fine hair and was definitely a gentleman's gentleman. We met very early in my career and I believe he was with me at least ten years as I fondly remember him with me at **Cosmo's** and continuing as a client at **Russo's**. He was always very gracious and behaved with a friendly formal personality. I always enjoyed his visits over the years.

He was in the movie, *The List of Adrian Messenger*, released in 1963, playing the role of **Raoul Le Borg** in an otherwise mainly all-star cast. On the internet, this is the only movie credit I found. No TV. Well, the net is great, but even the info on my father is highly incomplete.

Lauro Salas, **born August 28,1928 Monterrey, Mexico** Lauro Salas won the World Light Weight Championship from **Jimmy Carter** at the Olympic Auditorium in Los Angeles on May 14, 1952, several years before I moved to Los Angeles. He lost the Championship back to Carter in his first title defense in Chicago on October 15, 1952. I've heard some stinky stories about that Chicago fight, but bottom line: What the @#$%$ do I know?

I really enjoyed the friendship we experienced while I attended **Mohler's Barber College**. I can't believe we didn't keep in touch over the years.

My good Bud, **Joey Dorando**, said he knew Lauro when both were in the Boxing World. You'd think Joey 'n I might have invited Lauro to lunch, maybe asked him to join us at the Friar's Club, but we didn't. Mistake.

While expressing regrets from that era, I also had a great friendship with another Mohler's student whose last name was **Salazar.** I called him Sal and he called me *conado*, Spanish for brother-in-law. He had enrolled with a few of his Buds from East L.A. I feel I had an easier time at school because of our friendship. I didn't stay in touch with Sal, either, another change I would make if ever I can fix my %$#@O^ TimeMachine.

Larry Sands Larry was a Writer, Producer and Director. He was my friend and client for a year, maybe a bit more when he was killed in a helicopter crash while filming a section of the Feather River in 1973 or '74. **Tim Conway** referred Larry to me and Larry referred **Scott Carpenter** and **Norma and Larry Storch**. When I thanked him for his referrals, he said he planned to send me enough people to force me to work another day per week.

Scott Carpenter was with me for 11 years, I believe, until he moved to Florida around 1984.

As stated many times, I enjoyed a wonderful personal and professional friendship with Norma and Larry until Norma's death in 2003. Ginny and I stay in touch with Larry with cards and phone calls now that he is retired and living in New York.

From our first meeting, I felt that Larry Sands and I would be friends forever. I expected our time together to be measured in decades. He has never left my thoughts.

Joe Santos, **born Joseph Minieri in Brooklyn, NY on June 9, 1931...** One morning, as happened too many times to count, I met **Sam Russo** at the **Balboa Golf Course** at 7 a.m. for breakfast. We had a tee time around 7:45 when we would meet the other two people we would be assigned to play with that day. One of those people one day was Joe Santos, who had co-starred with **James Garner** on the TV series, *The Rockford Files.*

One of the nice things about playing golf in Southern California is something I've come to call Celebrity Surprise. Even the biggest stars will show up on a public course to play a round. As might be imagined, it's a great way to get a glimpse of someone's off-screen personality. I never met a grouchy celebrity that way.

Joe Santos was like a thousand other guys in that he was friendly and open and made it seem as though we had all known each other for several years. Like I've said many times, the more recognizable the celebrity, the more likely he will be a friendly person.

Telly Savalas, **born Aristotle "Telly" Savalas in Garden City, NY on January 21, 1924 – d. January 22, 1994 in Los Angeles, CA.**
George Savalas, born in the Bronx, NY on December 5, 1924 – d. October 2, 1985 in Westwood, CA. I really liked Telly Savalas very much. George, too. Both were super down-to-earth. And **Mama Savalas** was the BEST!

One Thanksgiving, maybe '62 or '63, Telly, wife (Marilynn?) and six weeks old daughter, **Penelope**, celebrated the holiday with us. I think Mama was there, too, but I'll not swear. They were all great people. Like family to us.

Telly, like my Dad, started his career later than the norm, by far. Then Telly really made it BIG, as the whole world knows. At one point he was the highest paid star in Hollywood.

I remember a conversation with a few people, tough to name any except my dad, when someone asked Telly if massive success had changed him any, in his opinion.

"Yeah," he said, surprising me with an affirmative. "My bets are bigger."

Sure, everybody got a good laugh, but some wag said Telly lost enough to buy half of the San Fernando Valley. I don't know, sounds like a Hollywood exaggeration to me.

There is no formula for "making it – becoming a Big Star" in Hollywood. "Talent" has to be there, you'd think, but there are exceptions. There's the thing about "getting the right role and really slamming it," but that's been done with a THUD for follow-up.

Another wag I know put it this way. He said "Achieving success in Hollywood is like a rocket ship to the moon. There's a million moving parts and you have to get enough of them humming in unison or you'll fall into an abyss." I'd identify the source, but I don't remember who said it.

I really miss Telly, George and Mama, dear friends all.

Leon Schwab, Leon was born in 1911 and I think he came from NYC, but the numbers, ya gotta ax somebody else. Leon Schwab, the Managing Partner and one of the four Schwab brothers who owned the famous **Schwab's Pharmacy** that was known as Hollywood's Hangout, was my friend from Day One. When I went to lunch that first day working for Cosmo, I forgot to grab my money from my Levi's at home. As I went to pay the check I had a kenipshin. No, I didn't do anything outwardly and no, I'm not sure how to spell kenipshin, either. Leon happened to be at the register, THE ONLY TIME IN 23 YEARS THAT I EVER SAW HIM AT THE REGISTER, and he saw me fumbling, searching every pocket I possessed and guessed my dilemma.

"Yer the new kid, working for Cosmo..." he said rather than asked. "Don't worry, pay me tomorrow."

And that, as the saying goes, was that. I never told Cosmo or my dad, cuz I felt like a schmuck, as Sam Keston would say.

Johnny Seven, born John Anthony Fetto in Bay Ridge, Brooklyn, NY on February 23, 1926... Johnny was my father's client at **Cosmo's** all during my time there both in the very beginning and through my ownership. Johnny was a very friendly and bright breath of fresh air. I last saw Johnny in 2008 at the **Hollywood Celebrities and Collectors Convention** where he agreed to be interviewed for my newspaper column. Shortly thereafter, the column assignment came to an end, thus the interview was not completed.

Frank Sinatra, born Francis Albert Sinatra in Hoboken, NJ on December 12, 1915 – d May 14, 1998 Frank Sinatra had plenty of publicity in his lifetime, quite a bit of it on the negative side, as he fought with most of the media. All that negative stuff is contrary to my impression of the man. I heard the same from most people I knew who were acquainted with The Chairman.

There is no dispute regarding his immense talent. Some organizations named him the preeminent singer of the 20th Century. His charitable side has never been properly explored mainly due to his desire for and insistence upon anonymity. Good buddy and fellow hairstylist **Eddie Carroll** "loved the guy." He was friendly to me and the people with me the evening we sat and had a drink and some conversation with him.

Stata buon! Good-e-nuff fer me.

Red Skelton, born Richard Bernard Skelton in Vincennes, IN on July 18, 1913 – d. September 17, 1997 in Palm Springs, CA If I gush any more over Red Skelton, the Whitecoats are gonna look me up, so I'll just point out one more thing.

On Sunday nights for more than three years now, I have been the host of a Multi-National Telephone Conference Call focusing on Health and Nutrition. For almost 200 calls so far, I end the call by saying, **"Good Night and God Bless."** I'm copying – mimicking - the one and only, the inimitable, one of America's most patriotic, God Loving and favorite funnymen of all time, **Red Skelton.**

If you see any a them Whitecoats approaching, lemmie know.

Sidney Skolsky, born in New York City on May 2, 1905 – d. May 3, 1983 in Los Angeles, CA. Sidney was my Dutch Uncle, if ever there was one. I am Forever Grateful for his friendship and favors. He anointed me Hairstylist to the Stars and kept Hollywood Celebrities coming my way. The love is mutual, Thank God, and everlasting.

Slash, born Saul Hudson on July 23, 1965... One evening when I walked into the **Casa Vega**, I took a seat next to a guy with a huge mane of hair. As Willie the bartender approached me, he said, "Little Joe, say hello to Slash."

While the name was not really familiar to me, I sensed that he was a rocker, so I asked if he played bass guitar. Quite frankly, I don't remember his answer but I do recall that we had a nice, friendly conversation. I think he got a kick out of meeting someone who didn't know him or his music.

After a while, I went into the men's room to use the public telephone to call my daughter **Trina**, who by this time was living in Alaska. I told her I was sitting at the bar next to "a guy named Slash, I think he plays guitar."

Trina almost came through the phone at me. She chastised me for not keeping up with great groups like **Guns N'Roses**.

After a few more laughs with my eldest daughter, I went back to the bar to discover I had a new neighbor. What the heck, this one was a girl. Pretty, too. And I was single at the time. What happened? Beats me.

Jack Soo, born Goro Suzuki in Oakland, CA – d. January 11, 1979 in Los Angeles, CA. I first met Jack in the early sixties during my earliest days at Cosmo's. The first time I clearly recall cutting his hair was after I took ownership in '73. Jack was a warm, talkative guy. He also had a great sense of humor and could laugh easily. He was always very complimentary of my haircuts, saying that when I used my "magic razor," it gave him exceptional ability to control his hair. The entire staff was deeply saddened by his passing.

Connie Stevens, born in Brooklyn, NY on August 8, 1938... I'm proud of the fact that Connie and I once portrayed some romantic scenes together for costarring roles in a movie. She is at the top of my list of the interesting people I would like to profile one day.

James Stewart, born James Maitland Stewart in Indiana on May 20, 1908 – d. July 2, 1997 in Los Angeles, CA. Since his office was in the building next door to ours on Wilshire Boulevard, I would often bump into him on my way to or from lunch or ditto the bank or simply walking along the sidewalk. Jimmy and I would always say hello and most times stop to chat. He really did have difficulty hearing. I felt a true sense of friendship with him.

As I mentioned in another space in this book, Jimmy's movie, *It's a Wonderful Life,* is my all-time favorite movie, just a snip above *Wizard of OZ.* The life lessons have consciously affected me, and I do mean daily.

Everyone has impact on other people. Everyone is unique and necessary. And I firmly believe that Angels appear as 'ordinary' people on occasion to help fulfill a mission. Maybe you encountered one recently. Maybe you are about to, again. Think about it. Screwing up at a time like that would be unthinkable, hey what? Don't wanna whiff on THAT one, for sure.

<u>Jerry Stiller</u>, born Gerald Stiller in New York City, NY on June 8, 1927...

<u>Anne Meara</u>, born in Brooklyn, NY on September 20, 1929...I haven't seen either of these lovely people the past several years, but I look forward to the time when our paths will cross. If another column were to come about, I'd ask them to give their version of the time I gave them both a cut 'n color, but not out of the same bottle.

<u>Larry Storch</u>, born Lawrence Samuel Storch in New York City, NY on January 8, 1923... <u>Norma Storch</u>, born Norma Greve in Pocatello, ID on April 6, 1922 – d. August 28, 2003 in Manhattan, NY. As you know if you've been reading and not pretending, these two are among the best friends I have ever had. Another fact of interest is that both Larry and Norma are animal people. I don't know if they ever went on the road without at least one of their cats. (I know, but it's hard to use past tense with Norma.)

<u>Barbra Streisand</u>, born Barbra Joan Streisand in Williamsburg, Brooklyn, NY on April 24, 1942.... Though I do not know her, I admire Barbra for her many profound talents. I rate her the greatest female entertainer EVER - nudging m'honey, **Judy Garland**; and further, I respect Barbra for the very reason some others in Hollywood hold her in contempt.

When starting a movie, Barbra is reputed to gather EVERYONE involved in the project, regardless of job-title, and announcing that she will give EVERYTHING in her being to make this project better than anything accomplished here-to-date, telling all that she expects an equal commitment from EVERYONE, or "Hit the %$#@& door, never to return and don't let it hit you in the ass!"

Yep, my kinda Gal! Our philosophies are amazingly similar.

Vic Taback, born in New York City, NY on January 6, 1930 – d. May 25, 1990. Vic was a dear friend of first my father, then me, for 30 years. It seemed that Vic was either on a movie/TV set, at **Schwab's** or at **Cosmo's/Little Joe's** when away from home, but I'm sure that's an exaggeration.

It's no exaggeration to say he was always friendly with a big smile for friend and fan alike. In 1990, he and my dad co-starred in a play at one of Hollywood's famous live theaters. The play closed earlier than originally intended due to the fact that my dad had to fly to Philadelphia to once again portray Rocky Balboa's favorite priest, Father Carmine in the movie, *ROCKY V*.

I went to the final performance, a packed house, loaded with lotsa movie people. Backstage, a gang of people converged on Vic, so I reached through, he grabbed my hand with a "Hi, Joey!" to my "Great job, Vic!" and I let everyone else have a moment with him. After all, I could talk to Vic most *anytime*. Funny, I almost regret that I didn't make a bigger deal of my congrats that night, but honestly, I'd play it the same way if I had known. The smiles we exchanged were the familiar warmth we shared for so many years.

While on that movie set in Philly, another actor offered condolences to my dad on the sudden death of Vic Taback. My dad was so shocked that he collapsed at the news. Ironically, the play my dad and Vic shared was the last for both of them. How's that for a great way for friends to bow out?

Mel Torme, born Melvin Howard Torma in Chicago, IL on September 13, 1925 – d. June 5, 1999 in Los Angeles, CA. When the Russos and I opened **Beverly Hills Hair Design** in 1988, Bernie Roberts again joined our staff. Among Bernie's clients was Mel Torme, easily one of the most open and friendly people on earth. He loved telling stories about the old days with **Frank Sinatra** and **Sammy Davis** and so many more. I was privileged to cut his hair a few times when Bernie was unavailable.

Tracy Torme, Mel's son, is a successful Writer/Producer in his own right. He was also a client at Beverly Hills Hair design, so we got to know each other somewhat. Having a famous name might open a few doors, but the talent better be there. Famous name kids are often held to a higher standard. I know for a fact how proud Mel was of Tracy.

Rip Torn, born **Elmore Rual Torn, Jr. in Temple, TX on February 6, 1931...** I was the unofficial hairstylist for the ultra-successful TV series, *The Untouchables*. One of the producers, I'll call him John, had become my client and had me cut the hair of many of the Guest Stars and various other cast members. I say unofficial as I never asked for nor received screen credit for my work. Funny, at that time, screen credit was not important. I never thought about bragging rights forty years later.

One day Cosmo beckoned me to the phone. He always did everything in his power to not call any of us to the phone, so I knew this had to be special. It was John.

"This jerk thinks I can't book an appointment for you. He says he MUST talk to you directly." Cosmo didn't really think John was a jerk; John gave Cosmo plenty of Extra work, with business. Cosmo's temper would flare, but two minutes later; poof.

"Little Joe, I've got a situation that I don't think even you can handle," John started. "We're bringing in a New York stage actor, gonna give him a big career shot. He's going to be the Guest Star in our first two-parter. In part one, he's a stone killer who is right off the street, doesn't know how to dress, his hair is unkempt and everything he does shows no sophistication, shows him as gruff. In part two, he's the Don, having shot his way to the top. Now he dresses in thousand dollar suits. In one scene he's getting a manicure, one girl on each hand and his hair is dapper, not a strand out of place. The problem is we have to shoot part two first due to sets that are to be demolished. After shooting part two, the next week we shoot part one. So first he has to look really chic, then a week later he needs to look like a bum. Oy vey, think you can do something?"

"Hey John, not to worry. Bring him in and I'll give him a Convertible Cut."

"What the hell is a Convertible Cut?"

"Simple. I'll make him look like a million bucks; then I'll show him how to make himself look like two cents."

(You'd think I'd have told John that I'd have to be on the set to make everything work out, but that's not me. I knew his hair would look great without my being there.)

When I hung up the phone, Cosmo had this scrunched, quizzical look on his face.

"What the hell is a Convertible Cut?" Cosmo unknowingly echoed.

"Beats the %$#@ outta me. I'll figure it out when he gets here."

That might have brought out the biggest laugh from Cosmo, ever.

Oh, when I was setting the appointment with John, we agreed on 3 p.m. that day as I recall.

"What's the New York actor's name?"

"**Rip Torn**."

"Oh sure, and his dinner date tonight is **Gail Storm**, I guess."

"Joey, put down any name you like. We'll see you at 3 p.m."

Rip had never had his hair styled, he had only been to barbers. I talked him through the whole process so he would understand the 'why' along with the 'how.' When I blew his hair into place, he couldn't believe the transformation.

"Now watch this," I said as I completely destroyed the styled look by scrubbing my hands through his hair. He actually let out a yell. I handed him a brush.

"Here, you put it back in shape."

He took the brush and ZIPPP! Lookin' good again! Over the next few weeks, Rip sent me several new clients, mainly his transplanted actor buddies from New York.

Though the public sees Rip Torn portraying several different characters from show to show, his non-horror rolls contain much of his personal friendliness and warmth.

I can hardly wait for his next performance. I wonder who's doing his hair?

Regis Toomey, born John Regis Toomey in Pittsburg, PA on August 13, 1898 – d. October 12, 1991 in Los Angeles, CA. Regis was a regular client of Cosmo's from the early 60s. He had been a regular on *Burke's Law* and is fondly remembered as Uncle Arvide of The Salvation Army in the film version of *Guys and Dolls*. He was always very friendly and easy to approach. I wish I had developed a closer rapport with him.

Ritchie Valens, born Richard Steven Valenzuela in Pacoima, in the North San Fernando Valley, CA on May 13, 1941 – d. February 3,1959, Clear Lake, Iowa, *The Day The Music Died*. (Earnestine Reyes, his aunt and I had lunch one day). I am forever greatly affected by the deaths of **Ritchie, Buddy Holly** and **The Big Bopper**. All three were rising Stars of the music world, I'm sure most people (50+) know, Ritchie the newest and youngest among them. I was driving my car through snow-draped Cleveland when I heard of the plane crash while listening to either **Bill Randal** or **Joe Finan** on radio. I had to pull over.

Buddy Holly seemed a Sure Thing to have a major impact on music for decades to come.

The Bopper had been hot, a favorite for a decent run of time.

Ritchie was the *Kid Phenom*, not yet old enough to drink. Some career; all of what, eight months? Go turn on yer radio and chances are, before long, here comes *La Bamba!* or *Donna*. Same goes for Buddy's many hits, especially *That'll Be The Day* and *Peggy Sue*.

Every time I hear of a reference to that incident, I get a lump in my throat, @#$%-faced and often, my cheeks get wet. The death of those three affected me like few other celebrities.

Recently, **The Broadway Palm**, a local Southwest Florida live theater, produced *Buddy!*, a salute to the three. At first I told Ginny I didn't want to go, that NOBODY could do a decent job portraying Buddy Holly. Somehow, I changed my mind. The guy playing Buddy was TERRIFIC. Once, trying to hide my tears, I looked around at the audience. Right, not a dry eye in the house. Live on, ye merry jesters! Like the song, especially written for them, says, now there are *Three New Stars in Heaven*.

<u>Dean Valentine</u> of Symbolic Action, LLC. Dean has been my friend and client since he was referred to me by good-bud **Scott Kaufer** in 1980. At that time Dean was working for **NBC** and just a few years later, he went to work at **Disney.**

I wish I knew his whole story but he's the quiet type when it comes to his work. I learned more about Dean's accomplishments through Scott over the years than from Dean.

Disney made some curious zigzag moves that seemed to flush several millions into thin air, but it's a pretty big entity and at the time no negative affect was visible to most of the entertainment-loving public. In the meantime, Dean received one of those offers he couldn't refuse and became the Big Gun at **UPN**.

An up 'n coming comic decided the time was right to set the record straight, but she needed approval and cooperation. Dean decided to pull the trigger and give his consent to allow **Ellen DeGeneres** to lift the curtain from her personal life. Ellen's popularity skyrocketed while threats on Dean's life caused extreme safety measures to be put into affect.

One consequence was that I started going to his house up in the hills to cut his hair. One day I pulled my motorcycle up to his property entrance. I rang the bell and announced my arrival.

As I gave the bike some gas, it stalled and I fell over onto my left hip, bike pinning me down. The curbing hit my shift lever and put the bike in neutral. My left leg was trapped under the bike and my foot was pinned between the bike and the curbing with just enough clearance that my ankle was not feeling any pressure or pain.

It was almost funny. I wasn't hurt in any way, but with my leg and ankle pinned, I could hardly budge that 540 lb. bike. I knew Dean would come looking for me, but I felt silly just lying there. I figured he'd get a good laugh and help me.

I managed to lift the bike about an inch, but it rolled back. Nutz! I held the front wheel hand-break with my right hand and lifted again with my left. Fergetaboutit. Impossible.

Then I remembered. With the Good Lord, NOTHING is impossible. I said, "Please God, help me!" as I gave it all I have.

The bike POPPED UP so fast I thought it might put me on my right side, but it went straight up and STAYED THERE.

I whipped around to see who... but of course, nobody. I immediately realized that even a gorilla couldn't have helped from behind.

Tears of joy and gratitude burst from me.

"Why?!?" I asked. "I wasn't in any real trouble."

I don't hear voices and I don't see non-physical things, but I got the message loud and clear.

BECAUSE YOU ASKED.

I kicked over the engine with my thumb and made it up the driveway with no further incident. EVER.

Once inside the house, Dean offered a cup of coffee, per usual. Sipping the brew, I told him what had just happened. After a moment, Dean asked if I was okay now.

"Never been better in my life."

If anyone can explain it better than I just did, I'm all ears.

Dick Van Dyke, born Richard Wayne "Dick" Van Dyke in West Plains, Missouri on December 13, 1925... I've mentioned that in the early 60s I had thoughts of becoming a makeup artist. I was referred to **Claude Thompson**, head of makeup, worldwide, at **NBC**, by good-buddy **Jimmy Kantrowe, Johnny Carson's** AD the last 19 years of the show.

Claude helped me set up my makeup kit and would allow me to bring female models to NBC where Claude would coach me on various glamour makeup techniques.

I'd bring my model, generally the wife or girlfriend of a client, go to the makeup department and prepare my model. We would often encounter **Dick Van Dyke** being made up for his show. He was always friendly and personable, greeted me by my name and made a pointed effort to remember my models' names, too.

I decided against makeup as the studios were getting rid of their makeup, wardrobe and other support services as independent production was replacing studio production and independent producers would prefer hiring their own services.

One more thought on Dick Van Dyke. He's another perfect example of comedians with a massive heart. Seems like it's almost a rule. They love people and seem compelled to make 'em happy and keep 'em smiling.

Val de Vargas, born Valentin de Vargas; played Suarez on Hill Street Blues. It seems Val was an off 'n on client from the '70s through the '90s. I've always liked him as a person and admired his acting work.

Robert Wagner, born Robert John Wagner in Detroit, MI on February 10,1930... Wagner and I met by telephone several times over the years. He was a client of my good friend 'n colleague, **Joe Torrenueva**, who started his career working at **Sebring's**. He has also been known as Little Joe, the link to this story.

When Wagner would want to make an appointment to get his hair cut, he would call information and ask for the number for "Little Joe's." Well, my last name is Micale and since M comes before T, he kept getting my number. Please don't blame Bob Wagner, I received lots of calls intended for "Little Joe T." I had my receptionist post Joe T's phone number near the desk phone so we could give callers the correct number.

I was pleased one day when Joe T called to thank me for properly directing his clients. Joe informed me that a third guy was calling himself "Little Joe" and trying to get clients from both of us. Joe #3 had actually booked and worked on some of the people referred to Joe T. One person in particular, the Star of a new TV show, was given a cut and color that was terribly botched. The whole mess caused Joe T a lot of grief until the truth became known.

Somebody, maybe Wagner, maybe someone else, asked why I didn't try to steal him. I answered that if I wanted to be a thief, I coulda joined my Unka Louie in Cleveland when I was in my teens. In fact, that's always been my standard answer to the Thief questions.

Ask Wagner, I bet he'll remember.

Ray Walston, born Herman Walston in New Orleans, LA on December 2, 1914 – d. January 1, 2001 in Beverly Hills, CA. When the Russos and I opened the salon we called **Beverly Hills Hair Design**, a lady stylist on our staff was **Ann Brown**, originally of **Sebring's.** One of Ann's clients was lovable **Ray Walston,** star of the TV comedy series, *My Favorite Martian.* What a great guy! He was like everyone's grandfather, a compliment intended to make his family proud. He was on the quiet side but very personable, friendly and easily approached.

Burt Ward, born Bert John Gervis, Jr. in Los Angeles, CA on July 6,1945... I started cutting Burt Gervis' hair while working at Cosmo's. He followed me to Russo's. Burt was a nice kid ('kid' does not really fit as he was a young adult who looked much younger) on the quiet side who lived with his family in Trousdale Estates, a section of Beverly Hills that is in a beautiful hilly area.

As I recall, one day Burt was throwing a ball around with a neighbor friend who was about Burt's age. The friend's father, a TV producer, pulled into the driveway, so Burt and his buddy went to say hello.

The producer asked Burt what he was up to, what he intended to do with his life. Burt said he wanted to be an actor, even surprising himself. The producer asked if Burt was enrolled in an acting school or attending one of the professional actors' workshops around town. Burt said not yet and asked if he might try out for some project the producer could recommend.

The producer mentioned that he was working on an upcoming new TV series based on Comic Book characters **Batman and Robin**. He offered to arrange for Burt to read for Robin, but he also warned that Burt's chances were extremely slim given his lack of experience.

Some of the rest of the story comes from long-time supporting actor and sometimes associate producer, **Jimmy FitzSimons**. Jimmy who, you say? Remember the gorgeous redhead A-List movie star, **Maureen O'Hara**? She and Jimmy were sister and brother. Jimmy also had the recurring role of a cop on the *Batman* TV series. (Just for clarity, sister Maureen was not part of the project.)

When Burt read for Robin, everyone was aware that his reading was arranged by The Producer and that Burt was highly inexperienced. Burt's reading was understandably stiff, but he also showed that he was anxious to follow directions.

At the end of the day, the executives evaluating the many candidates wanted to narrow the competition down to about three actors. As they were voicing their opinions, someone suggested that Burt be included in the final group. The suggestion was considered off the wall by some others, but the point was made that Burt's lack of experience could be an asset in a production that was going to portray comic-book icons in a totally tongue-in-cheek fashion. Burt seemed to be prone to strong direction.

As the world has known for decades, Burt won the day and will forever be associated with the Boy Wonder.

The show became High Camp with the public – and with Hollywood. Famous actors – and actresses – jockeyed for a shot at a unique caricature creation unavailable in 99 percent of Hollywood productions. Remember **Caesar Romero** as **The Joker?** Or **Burgess Meredith** as **The Penguin?** Or ravishing **Julie Newmar** as *Catwoman.?* YeeoOOooww!

ZOWIE! BAMM! ZAP! Holy Moly, Batman!

Sure was a lot of fun. I was thrilled to be on the 'in,' many times going on set to assist Burt.

Rudy Waxman, born July 3, 1926; d. May 9, 1974. For about 12 years starting in the early sixties, Rudy was my dear friend, client and Mentor. He was born into a very wealthy Jewish family. Rudy and his only sibling, a one-year older brother, Kurt, were driven to school in the family Mercedes Limo by the chauffer. A butler and his staff provided a comfortable home for the Waxman family.

Rudy's father, Fritz, operated (owned at one time?) a mill that specialized in converting used metal into steel. The railroad was the main carrier of metal to and from the company yard. The steel mill was located in pre-WW II Germany in the town of Oppeln (today called Opoel) and was visited by high-ranking government officials; most notoriously, **Heinrich Himmler**, the head of the Gestapo and the architect of the Final Solution.

Rudy's father was confident that his family was safe as the steel mill was essential to the needs of Germany, but one day the SS arrived in force, took over the huge complex and arrested Rudy's family like common rubble. Seventeen year old Rudy was never to see his mother or brother again.

In the political prisoner compound where Rudy was sent, he and another young man, a look-alike, were put into a cell together while undergoing brutal interrogation. One night English Commandos raided. During a bloody battle, they liberated both Rudy and his cellmate, an undercover spy not yet discovered by the Germans, as the raiders were unable to determine which of the two prisoners was their target. By the time the Commandos reached their hideout in a small village beyond the forest where the true spy could be identified, Rudy's cellmate had died of his wounds. Rudy was ordered to be executed to maintain security.

Rudy surprised his captors as he spoke to them in an excellent British accent. He convinced them of his superior geographical knowledge of that region of Germany and volunteered to help the Commandos with their operations.

Amazingly, the British accepted Rudy's offer. Rudy would be captured again and believe me, you ain't heard more than 2% of the story.

For the first five years of our close friendship, I never knew that Rudy was a Survivor (and not a born-here American) until that hot summer day when I saw the numbers tattooed on his forearm. When I asked, he smiled and said, "Aren't we all survivors?" At least three years passed before the subject would be broached again.

I'll give one last fact before I call it quits. Rudy died on May 9, 1974, the 29th Anniversary of Germany's WWII Surrender to the Russians. Ironic? Maybe. Just? Absolutely. After all, there is no such thing as a coincidence.

Yes, you had an opportunity to meet him.

When **David Wolper**, the famous documentarian, focused his creative energies on the Holocaust, he interviewed several Survivors to better present their all but unimaginable experiences. Wolper and his staff were profoundly impressed by Rudy Waxman's accounts and especially with the fact that Rudy was able to decipher unidentified photographs taken during the war by German photographers. Wolper even commissioned Rudy to appear in the documentary on camera and narrate several minutes worth of film and photos.

I am eternally blessed and grateful for all Rudy taught me during the experiences and years we shared. I am a much better person due to his teachings and influence on my thinking.

<u>Footnote</u>: Rudy had a daughter named **Susan** who was about twenty at the time of his death. Maybe a year later, I discovered that I could no longer contact her.

Writing this section on Rudy, the final section written in this book, I again consulted the internet looking for info on Rudy, though prior attempts over the years had proved fruitless. This time more than 5000 pages came up. Fergettit!

But somehow, I hit my keyboard a couple of times (What did I do? Beats me.) and the names of Charlotte and Rudy Waxman came up. Who dat? Never heard of her. I followed some other prompts (?) and called a phone number in *Cleveland*, the city where I grew up. Funny, I thought, but what's been said about every six or seven people?

I left a brief message and my phone number on the voicemail. Having second thoughts, I called back to leave my e-mail address. This time a lady answered. It was **MY SUSAN!!!** I know I shouted and I think she did, too.

I fly to Cleveland three weeks from now with a ticket purchased *two months ago*. Some will say, "What a nice coincidence!" The rest of us know better.

UPDATE: Had a five HOUR LUNCH with Susan on June 4, 2009. In a Deli, of course. We are family *per sempre* – which, like I said before means 'forever' in Sicilian.

<u>Jesse White</u>, born Jesse Marc Weidenfeld in Buffalo, New York on January 3, 1917 – d. January 9, 1997. I remember seeing Jesse hanging out at **Schwab's** during my earliest days at **Cosmo's**. He was Nunzio's client, but I also remember seeing my Dad cut Jesse's hair.

Both memories are probably accurate as all haircutters on the staff would help each other's clients from time to time with no animosity like might be found in other haircutting establishments.

When Jesse got the **Maytag** gig in 1967, everybody was happy for him. Getting a commercial for a major company could often give an actor enough income to relieve basic financial worries for a while. They didn't all rake it in like **John Wayne,** who had enough left over to buy a WWII minesweeper and convert it into a yacht, y'know.

. With all due respect, I think Jesse was the best Maytag Repairman ever. He did more with a facial expression than many other actors could do using words to fortify demeanor. Jesse held the gig until 1988, research confirms. That's <u>22 years</u>, when a 13-week commercial contract was considered the norm.

An actor's career can be hampered by being too closely associated with a product. Nunzio asked Jesse about that affect one day when there were a few people within earshot. Jesse's answer was along the line that he hadn't had to worry about the rent for the past few years. Everyone laughed. I believe he was speaking figuratively and literally.

I know that Jesse could portray the gregarious type on screen, but in person he was more on the quiet, reserved type. I know he and my father worked on screen together in either *Gomer Pyle* or *Love American Style*. My Dad told me that on the set, Jesse was as quiet as when in my place or Schwab's, but when it was time for the cameras to roll, Jesse became whatever character he was portraying.

Billy D. Williams, born William December Williams Jr. in New York City, NY on April 6,1937... My father introduced me to Billy D. Williams at **Schwab's** one day. They had met on the movie set of *Lady Sings the Blues*, I believe the only movie in which both had worked as actors. Billy, like the huge majority of actors I met in Hollywood, was friendly and open. He would undoubtedly remember my father easier than me, but I will always fondly remember his warm smile and friendly personality.

<u>Tom Williams</u>, Producer of the hit TV Series, *Adam 12*. Tom became my hair client and good friend in the early '70s, like maybe shortly after I assumed ownership from Cosmo on March 5, 1973. He remained my client until we moved to Southwest Florida.

Tom is a wonderful actor and comedian in his own right. He still does a ton of voice-over work, too. Tom can imitate a baby's cry as well as any baby I ever heard, so he does that quite a bit for movie and TV shows. Cats 'n dogs, too. He also does a variety of birds like cockatoos and parrots. Monkeys? I'll get back to you on that.

Treat Williams, born Richard Treat Williams in Norwalk, CN on December 1, 1951... We were aware of Treat Williams' talent long before Ginny and I met him in 1999. My nephew, **Michael Herron**, was Treat Williams' assistant when Treat filmed the movie, *The Deep End of the Ocean.*

During the filming, another of Treat's films, this one called *Deep Rising*, premiered. One night the entire company of "...Ocean," with families and friends, were invited to a screening of *Deep Rising*. It was a fine night as Treat was a great host.

Nephew Michael is today a Digital Video Assistant Operator. He is profiled herein just before **Charlton Heston**.

Just to prove it's really a Small World, when Ginny and I moved to Florida and set up our hair salon we call *Beverly Hills Hair Design*, just like back in LA, Ginny one day gave a haircut to a "Mrs. Williams." Turned out to be Treat's mother, who was visiting **Sanibel Island** with Treat's dad. Both were surprised by the simple but unexpected connection.

Jonathan Winters, born in Dayton, Ohio on November 11, 1925... I had limited but profound contact with Jonathan, one of my all-time favorite comics. One day late in 1968, **Johnny Gentri** and I visited the set of Winters' TV show. We were scheduled to meet with one of Jonathan's producers – I'll call him Al – to discuss our upcoming telethon to benefit the **Pasadena Playhouse**.

The previous night, Winters' son, Jonathan H., about 18 years old, had been in a horrific auto accident. His passenger, the son of another Hollywood celebrity, had been killed. Jonathan H. was in critical condition in a local hospital. The segment of the Winters' show being taped that day was scheduled to be broadcast within days and therefore could not be postponed.

A direct-line-phone had been set up in the backstage area, just 20 feet from Stage Entrance Right. Winters was on the phone, slouching with his head down, talking inaudibly to his wife, we were told, who was at their son's hospital bedside.

A young man from the production staff approached Winters, stopping maybe 10 feet short.

"Ten seconds, Mr. Winters," he said just loud enough.

Within three seconds, Winters placed the receiver on the counter next to the phone. Still slouching, he turned and walked slowly, head down, to Stage Entrance Right. Upon getting his cue, he crossed the threshold onto the stage where his posture, demeanor and facial expression all took on new life, doing a complete 180, perfectly in character.

Everyone knows zany Jonathan Winters, so when I say he was Vintage, Typical and Rocked the live studio audience, believe it.

As I looked out from my backstage vantage point at the upward, smiling faces of the people in the audience, I could see that they had no idea something was tragically wrong, an observation later confirmed by Producer Al. Winters was hilarious, per usual.

When Winters made his exit to an appreciative, Standing O, he stepped across the threshold and like *Shazam!* he slumped like he was hit in the gut, his head dropped and his back bowed, coming back 180. He made a shuffling beeline for the phone. He uttered no audible sound, but his body language said he was listening and talking.

Winters guest star that day was someone I'm going to call **Twinkle Toes**, because I'm going to tell it just the way it happened, so you figure out which Hollywood bas..., eh, *Star* personified a schmuck that day.

He was on stage in front of the orchestra doing a solo. He wore a black Tux with Tails 'n Top Hat, with Stick. At one point in his soft-shoe routine, he allowed the Top Hat to tumble down his arm so he could catch it in his fingertips to the drummer's rim shot; but oops! a misfire.

They reset. "Take it from the eight-bar lead-in," the music director said.

Dum-da-dum-dum. Ooops again! This time Twinkle Toes lost the hat halfway down his arm.

One more time. A third Twinkle Toes Goof! One-hundred percent (100%) HIM.

He turned to the orchestra and thrust his index finger to the drummer. "Get that @#$% drummer outta here!"

The audience gasped, groaned.

TT snapped around and GLARED at the audience.

"Don't you DARE do that or I'll walk outta here and never come back!"

The audience gasped anew.

I was appalled! Everyone could see that the drummer was not at fault. And never before – or since – have I seen a Big Star - or a spear-carrier - turn on a live audience in anger.

The drummer left the stage. Someone took his place.

"From eight bars…"

Twinkle Toes got it right this time. The "applause" sign lit up. The response didn't rate lukewarm.

"Do you know how to applaud?!?" Twinkle Toes *screamed* at them!

The applause sign lit up again. The audience gave it up, but don't think "wildly."

Twinkle Toes made a dramatic, over-exaggerated deep bow before exiting Stage Left.

The audience didn't Boo him, thank goodness, or I shutter to think of the possibilities.

How could he, you say. He knew that Jonathan Winters was experiencing the worst day of his life.

Later, watching Twinkle Toes mingle backstage, he behaved like nothing extraordinary had happened. I wondered if that was the best acting of his schmaltzy career.

Jonathan Winters, given his "ten seconds Mr. W…" he went out as before – *Shazam!* took the final curtain call, then - *Shazam!* – back to the phone briefly and out the door to a waiting car to join his family at the hospital.

Some readers might review this account with dry eyes, but living through it all was gut wrenching and sometimes quite wet.

And yes, Jonathan H. recovered, Thank God.

Robert Wright, born Robert Craig Wright in 1914… and his partner…

George Forrest, born George Forrest Chichester in Brooklyn, NY, 1915 – d. October 10, 1999 in Miami, FL. For today's moviegoer, Wright and Forrest are probably not very familiar names. In my first years at **Cosmo's**, the two of them became my regular clients. They were highly talented music composers who wrote the hit Broadway stage play that became a wonderfully entertaining movie called *Kismet,* released in 1955, well before my time as a pro, but they were still in Hollywood making movies and became my clients during my first few years in the business at Cosmo's.

Burt Young, born Jerry De Louise in Queens, NY on April 30, 1940… One night Ginny and I were out to dinner with **Matt Helreich** and a few other friends. We went to a tastefully decorated and moderately priced restaurant on La Cienega Boulevard owned by Burt Young's brother. As we were finishing our meal and enjoying our coffee, Burt dropped in.

Matt introduced us to him. Burt let me know how much he enjoyed working with my father on the *Rocky* series of movies. He offered condolences on the passing of my parents and mentioned the shock of seeing that my mother and father passed one day apart.

I told him I considered their passing together a blessing as they were so very close. The incident put a warm glow on the end of a very enjoyable evening.

Burt Young impressed Ginny and me as being so much like neighborhood guys we grew up with who hardly changed in spite of massive success.

✯✯✯✯✯

When I started writing my newspaper columns, I only intended to tell stories about many of the Hollywood Celebrities who graced my life. I told about incidents where I was involved with them; I was not just recounting general facts or accounts that another writer might entertainingly portray.

I never intended to write an autobiography, and I haven't, though part of my life story is in the pages of this book. See, there are too many important people and facts that are either absent or simply not here in enough detail for this to be a truly representative autobiography.

Now that I've confessed all over the place, anyone who has paid even the slightest bit of attention has to know that I'm sincere when I say I rate myself among the most fortunate people on Earth. I have never, EVER, said or felt; "Shucks, I don't wanna go to work today."

While there were days when I had a partial idea of things to come, I was – hundreds of times – surprised by events that were absolutely unpredictable right up to the moment they occurred. That was part of the beauty of living as an integral part of a community like Hollywood where ANYTHING could occur ANYTIME. Imagination stands no chance against reality when it comes to the unimaginable, especially in such a make-believe and ever-so-real place like Hollywood!

Once, seems like yesterday but can't be, back in the day when talking to dear friend Milt Rosen about the subject of good things happening, I asked, "Why me, Milt? Does it make sense to you?"

"So why not you," Milt said with a shrug as he offered to ladle me s'more matzo ball soup.

Okay, Milt. You win. So why not?

I'll end by again thanking The Boss and All Heavenly Beings who pitched in from time to time… and so many times…. Tell me you're still there. Hel-looo!

And just think: The Best is Yet to Come!

Benediga e Salute!

All that put to bed; I think a truly appropriate ending, with a Tip-o-the-Cap to Warner Bros. Pictures, is to pay homage to their iconic Hollywood Salutation by shouting…

"Th-a-th-th, Tha, uh That's All, Folks!"

To order *autographed copies*
of
First Edition - Author's Copy of this book,

Confessions... of a Hollywood Hairstylist
by *Little Joe Micale*

Go to: www.littlejoehollywood.com

**THIS OFFER IS FOR A LIMITED TIME, VALID
THROUGH JULY 31, 2010. EXTENSIONS OF THIS OFFER
ARE AT THE DISCRETION OF THE PUBLISHER,
*BUONA FORTUNA PUBLISHERS.***

ALSO

Copies of the book may be ordered through
www.amazon.com

Books to be Published
by
Little Joe Micale

Little Joe is currently conducting research for a book on the history of the Network Marketing Industry. The book – as yet untitled – is scheduled for Summer/Fall 2010 release.

Buona Fortuna Publishers (bfpublishers.com) is proud to announce that two books by Little Joe are awaiting their publishing release date. One is titled, *SOMEDAY*, the story of a young man and a priest, and the other is titled, *LOVE LETTERS FROM THE MARK TWAIN HOTEL*, containing parts of 77 letters written by Little Joe's dad, actor Paul J. Micale, as he made his first attempts to start his Hollywood acting career. A synopsis of both books follows.

SOMEDAY
Synopsis

SOMEDAY is the heartfelt story of how a young man was befriended, guided and coached on the road of life by a priest. No, you haven't heard this one before, promise, and it has nothing to do with the negative, headline-grabbing, sordid accounts of pedophile, pulpit phonies.

Time: It's the early '60s. We see Italian Joe Minnetti, about 25 and his mentor - looks Italian, too – a priest named Father Michael, late 30s - early 40s, parking near Cantor's Deli in the heart of the heavily-Jewish-populated Fairfax District of Los Angeles. They are on a mission "to obtain a proper memento." An elderly Hasidic man helps Joe find just the right item, a Silver Menorah; Sterling, no less. Father Michael is delighted while somehow, the elderly Hasidic lady finds the priest familiar; but can't be.

We drop back several years and meet the Paisans, a teenage "club" of the Fabulous Fifties, a group of high school guys who like to be "doin' shit, havin' a little fun." Turns out they are amateur burglars, a clear fact to which they are oblivious, if you will. Watch out for them-there bullets.

Then there's the gun, "*Una Baretta, senza numero,*" in spite of the Paisans' Iron-Clad Rule: NO GUNS.

Big caper. Huge trouble. Y'call it murder, or what? Enter Father Michael.

Along comes Barbara with her life-long influence. It's warm and touching; it's poignant. The storyline might have been quite different from here if only it were not happening in those staid '50s.

Wrestling in high school leads to a college scholarship where a joke leads to haircutting. Then total shock hits with the impossible-to-imagine move to Hollywood.

After barber school, beauty school is a beaut, alright. Oh wow, is that Ritchie Valens? Enjoy the hairstyles and music of the early '60s.

Enjoy the saga of Cosmo's.

Love and marriage go together with a little coughing that escalates to a major problem, to understate the fact. With Jewish doctors all over the place, Joe and Father Mike crank up mental and spiritual activity. A baptism in the operating room? By a Jewish doctor?

The crisis peaks. OMG, not an x-ray! Quick, somebody call the cops! Holy pandemonium!

And then a funny thing happens on the way to ever-after. What did Father Michael say?

We crank it up about 14 years. Meet the kids. What happened? Was he or wasn't he? What statue, where? Who else saw him? Does anybody know for sure? Holy twist, it's a mystery! Sounds more like fiction, many would say, but they'd be wrong. Kimberley had it right, without a doubt.

O. Henry lives!

Love Letters from the Mark Twain Hotel
Synopsis

On January 2, 1934, a "Happy Birthday and Hooray-For-Hollywood" party was celebrated in the Little Italy section of Cleveland, Ohio. The honoree was 18-year-old Paul J. Micale. Paul already had his ticket on the 8 a.m. train to Hollywood the next morning. Alas, Paul never even saw the train, for his parents, wouldyabelieve, drove him instead to Moehler's Barber College in downtown Cleveland, where they enrolled the shocked young man.

For the next several years, Paul worked as a barber, then later as a real estate salesman, while continuing his love affair with acting by appearing on many of Cleveland's theatrical stages.

Sliding the Time bar to springtime, 1959, we see Paul appearing in the lead of a play called *Wayside* at the Cleveland Playhouse. Columbia Pictures bought the script, the Columbia exec promised Paul, now 43 years old, the lead in the movie, if only he lived in Hollywood.

It's Labor Day, 1959. Paul starts for Hollywood and his Date with Destiny by driving fabled Route 66. His wife Pat, along with their high school sophomore daughter and college sophomore son, stay behind to complete the sale of the family home.

Paul told his family he "sang all the way," and never tired, but slept each night "like a log." Once in Hollywood, Paul at first took a room at the Padre Hotel before transferring to the actor-wannabe-favorite Mark Twain Hotel on Wilcox Avenue, catty-corner across from the Hollywood Post Office. Feeling the greatest excitement of his life and fighting the loneliness caused by missing his family, Paul launched his assault on Hollywood.

From September of '59, we are blessed with 11 letters Paul that wrote home. He vividly describes his daily adventures in detail, naming people he met, reviewing conversations and most interestingly, sharing his most intimate thoughts and life philosophies with his wife and kids.

From October, 39 letters survived the ravages of Time. In one he wrote, "Sorry for the short letter of yesterday...." Yesterday's letter was 12 pages.

November contributes 24 letters, really great stuff; many will choke a cynic. December, only three letters survived to see the twenty-first century. More than 70 letters total. Lucky us!

All the letters are presented with little edit and even include Paul's capitalization, underlining and commentary marks so readers can experience the complete, robust flavor. Readers truly have a ringside seat experiencing how this actor stutter-started his career. The side commentary throughout is provided by Paul's writer-son, Joe, who also fills in some blanks so readers get the whole story.

Sure you know Paul Micale. A second page would be needed to list his 30-plus-year history of the many movie & TV credits, (presented in epilogue) but the movies that help identify him best are **Rocky II, III** and **V**. Paul portrayed Father Carmine, Rocky Balboa's favorite priest.

Paul and Pat spent their final days at the Motion Picture and Television Home in Woodland Hills, California. Pat departed on Friday, January 15, 1999 and Paul followed on Saturday, January 16, 1999.

"It was a beautiful, appropriate exit," says son Joe. "I couldn't have scripted it better."

We'd like to hear from you!

Little Joe would like to know which of the two books you might like to read next.

Please let him know — along with any other comments — by emailing him at: joe@bfpublishers.com

Thanx for your input!

LaVergne, TN USA
17 June 2010
186476LV00005B/57/P

9 781450 536554